THE CAMBRIDGE COMPANION TO
FRENCH LITERATURE

In this authoritative and accessible account of French literature, sixteen essays by leading specialists offer provocative insights into French literary culture: its genres, movements, themes, and historic turning points, including the cultural and linguistic challenges of today's multi-ethnic France. The French have, over the centuries, invented and reinvented writing, from the Arthurian romances of Chrétien de Troyes to Montaigne's *Essais*, which gave the world a new literary form and a new standard for writing about personal thought and experience; from the highly polished tragedies of French classicism to the satirical novels of the Enlightenment; from Proust's explorations of social and sexual mores to the 'new novel' of the late twentieth century; and from Baudelaire's urban poetry to today's poetic experiments with sound and typography. The broad scope of this *Companion*, which goes beyond individual authors and periods, enables a deeper appreciation for the distinctive literature of France.

John D. Lyons is Commonwealth Professor of French at the University of Virginia, and Chevalier de la Légion d'Honneur. He is the author of eight books on French literature, including *French Literature: A Very Short Introduction* (2010), and *The Phantom of Chance: From Fortune to Randomness in Seventeenth-Century French Literature* (2011).

A complete list of books in the series is at the back of this book

GW00566876

THE CAMBRIDGE
COMPANION TO
FRENCH LITERATURE

EDITED BY
JOHN D. LYONS

CAMBRIDGE
UNIVERSITY PRESS

CAMBRIDGE
UNIVERSITY PRESS

University Printing House, Cambridge CB2 8BS, United Kingdom

Cambridge University Press is part of the University of Cambridge.

It furthers the University's mission by disseminating knowledge in the pursuit of education, learning and research at the highest international levels of excellence.

www.cambridge.org
Information on this title: www.cambridge.org/9781107665224

© Cambridge University Press 2016

First published 2016

Printed in the United Kingdom by TJ International Ltd. Padstow Cornwall

A catalogue record for this publication is available from the British Library

Library of Congress Cataloguing in Publication data
The Cambridge companion to French literature / edited by John D. Lyons.
pages cm. – (Cambridge companions to literature)
ISBN 978-1-107-03604-8 (hardback)
1. French literature – History and criticism. 2. French literature – French-speaking countries – History and criticism. I. Lyons, John D., 1946– editor.
PQ103.L95 2015
840.9–dc23
2015022170

ISBN 978-1-107-03604-8 Hardback
ISBN 978-1-107-66522-4 Paperback

CONTENTS

List of illustrations   *page* vii
Notes on contributors   viii
Chronology   xi

Introduction   1
JOHN D. LYONS

1   Romance, *roman*, and novel   3
    KAREN SULLIVAN

2   Joan of Arc and the literary imagination   18
    DEBORAH MCGRADY

3   Poetry and modernity   34
    MARC BIZER

4   The graphic imagination and the printed page   52
    TOM CONLEY

5   Tragedy and fear   70
    JOHN D. LYONS

6   *Galant* culture   85
    ELIZABETH C. GOLDSMITH

7   Varieties of doubt in early modern writing   102
    MICHAEL MORIARTY

8   Nature and Enlightenment   118
    CAROLINE WARMAN

CONTENTS

9 Nostalgia and the creation of the past   135
   ROSEMARY LLOYD

10 Exoticism and colonialism   151
    JENNIFER YEE

11 Poetic experimentation   168
    CARRIE NOLAND

12 The renewal of narrative in the wake of Proust   187
    EDWARD J. HUGHES

13 French literature as world literature   204
    CHARLES FORSDICK

14 Literature and sex   222
    ELISABETH LADENSON

15 The literary-philosophical essay   241
    IAN JAMES

16 The novel in the new millennium   258
    WARREN MOTTE

    Guide to further reading   273
    Index   281

LIST OF ILLUSTRATIONS

4.1 Title page of François Rabelais, *Pantagrueline prognostication* (Lyon: François Juste, *c.* 1532). FC5.R1125.532 pa, Houghton Library, Harvard University. *page* 55

4.2 Reverse title page of François Rabelais, *Pantagrueline prognostication* (Lyon: François Juste, *c.* 1532). FC5.R1125.532 pa, Houghton Library, Harvard University. 57

4.3 Pierre de Ronsard, *Amours de Pierre de Ronsard* (Paris: Veuve M. de La Porte, 1562), (a) frontispiece verso (Ronsard), and (b) frontispiece recto (Cassandre). FC5.R6697.552a, Houghton Library, Harvard University. 60

11.1 Page from Stéphane Mallarmé, *Un Coup de dés jamais n'abolira le hasard* (Paris: Nouvelle Revue Française, 1914). FC8.M2957.914c, Houghton Library, Harvard University. 183

NOTES ON CONTRIBUTORS

MARC BIZER is Professor of French at the University of Texas at Austin. He is the author of *La Poésie au miroir: Imitation et conscience de soi dans la poésie latine de la Pléiade* (1995), *Les Lettres romaines de Du Bellay* (2001), and *Homer and the Politics of Authority in Renaissance France* (2011).

TOM CONLEY is Abbott Lawrence Lowell Professor of Romance Languages and Literatures and of Visual and Environmental Studies at Harvard University. His books include *Film Hieroglyphs* (1991), *The Graphic Unconscious in Early Modern Writing* (1992), *The Self-Made Map: Cartographic Writing in Early Modern France* (1996), *Cartographic Cinema* (2007), *An Errant Eye: Topography and Poetry in Early Modern France* (2011), and *À fleur de page: Voir et lire le texte de la Renaissance* (2014). In 2014 appeared *Illustrations conscientes: Mélanges en honneur de Tom Conley*, edited by his former students.

CHARLES FORSDICK is James Barrow Professor of French at the University of Liverpool and Arts and Humanities Research Council Theme Leadership Fellow for 'Translating Cultures'. His research interests cover travel writing, colonial history, postcolonial literature, and the Francophone Caribbean (especially Haiti). His publications include *Victor Segalen and the Aesthetics of Diversity* (2000), *Travel in Twentieth-Century French and Francophone Cultures* (2005), and *Ella Maillart, 'Oasis interdites'* (2008). He was, from 2012 to 2014, President of the Society for French Studies.

ELIZABETH C. GOLDSMITH is Professor Emerita of French at Boston University. She has published on conversation, letter writing, memoirs, and literary culture in the early modern period, focusing on women writers. Her most recent book is a biography of the sisters Hortense and Marie Mancini. Current projects include an anthology of seventeenth-century travel writing and a study of the letters of John Singer Sargent to Auguste Rodin and other artists in late nineteenth-century Paris.

EDWARD J. HUGHES is Professor of French at Queen Mary, University of London. Among his books are *Marcel Proust: A Study in the Quality of Awareness* (Cambridge 1983; paperback reprint, 2010), *Writing Marginality in Modern French Literature: from Loti to Genet* (Cambridge 2001; 2nd edn, 2006), and

Proust, Class, and Nation (2011). He is the editor of *The Cambridge Companion to Camus* (Cambridge 2007).

IAN JAMES is a Reader in Modern French Literature and Thought in the Department of French at the University of Cambridge. He is the author of *Pierre Klossowski: The Persistence of a Name* (2000), *The Fragmentary Demand: An Introduction to the Philosophy of Jean-Luc Nancy* (2006), *Paul Virilio* (2007), and *The New French Philosophy* (2012).

ELISABETH LADENSON is Professor of French and Comparative Literature at Columbia University and General Editor of *Romanic Review*. She was formerly director of the Comparative Literature programme at the University of Virginia. Her books include *Proust's Lesbianism* (1999) and *Dirt for Art's Sake: Books on Trial from Lolita to Madame Bovary* (2007). She is currently writing a book about Colette.

ROSEMARY LLOYD is Rudy Professor Emerita, Indiana University Bloomington; Fellow Emerita Murray Edwards College, University of Cambridge; and Adjunct Professor, University of Adelaide. Her publications include studies of Baudelaire, Flaubert, and Mallarmé, as well as books on jealousy, still life, and childhood in French literature. She has also published translations of prose and poetry from the nineteenth to the twenty-first century.

JOHN D. LYONS, Commonwealth Professor of French at the University of Virginia and Chevalier de la Légion d'Honneur, is the author, most recently, of *The Phantom of Chance: From Fortune to Randomness in Seventeenth-Century French Literature* (2012). He is currently writing a book about the concept of the tragic.

DEBORAH MCGRADY, Associate Professor of French at the University of Virginia, is the author of *Controlling Readers: Guillaume de Machaut and His Late Medieval Audience* (2006) and co-editor with Jennifer Bain of *A Companion to Guillaume de Machaut* (2012). She is currently completing a book manuscript on 'The Writer's Gift: Revisiting the Patronage Paradigm in Late Medieval French Literature'.

MICHAEL MORIARTY is Drapers Professor of French at the University of Cambridge, and a Fellow of Peterhouse. He was Professor of French Literature and Thought at Queen Mary, University of London, from 1995 to 2011. His most recent book is *Disguised Vices: Theories of Virtue in Early Modern French Thought* (2011). He is a Fellow of the British Academy and Chevalier dans l'Ordre des Palmes Académiques.

WARREN MOTTE is Professor of French and Comparative Literature at the University of Colorado. He specializes in contemporary writing, with particular focus upon experimentalist works that put accepted notions of literary form into question. His most recent books include *Fables of the Novel: French Fiction since*

1990 (2003), *Fiction Now: The French Novel in the Twenty-First Century* (2008), and *Mirror Gazing* (2014).

CARRIE NOLAND is the author of *Poetry at Stake: Lyric Aesthetics and the Challenge of Technology* (1999), *Agency and Embodiment: Performing Gestures/ Producing Culture* (2009), and *Negritude Voices in Modernist Print: Aesthetic Subjectivity, Diaspora, and the Lyric Regime* (2015). Collaborative interdisciplinary projects include *Diasporic Avant-Gardes*, co-edited with the language poet Barrett Watten, and *Migrations of Gesture*, co-edited with anthropologist Sally Ann Ness. At present, she is working on a book project on the choreographer Merce Cunningham. She teaches French and Comparative Literature at the University of California, Irvine.

KAREN SULLIVAN is the Irma Brandeis Professor of Romance Culture and Literature at Bard College. She is the author of *The Inner Lives of Medieval Inquisitors* (2013), *Truth and the Heretic: Crises of Knowledge in Medieval French Literature* (2005), and *The Interrogation of Joan of Arc* (1999). She is currently working on the perceived danger of reading romance.

CAROLINE WARMAN is Associate Professor of French at the University of Oxford and a Fellow of Jesus College. She is the author of *Sade: From Materialism to Pornography* (2002) and has written widely on eighteenth- and nineteenth-century literature and intellectual history. She has translated Isabelle de Charrière's *The Nobleman and Other Romances* (2012) and co-translated (with Kate E. Tunstall) Denis Diderot's *Rameau's Nephew* (2014). She is currently working on Diderot's *Éléments de physiologie*.

JENNIFER YEE is Associate Professor of French at the University of Oxford, and a Tutor and Fellow of Christ Church. She is the author of *Clichés de la femme exotique: Un regard sur la littérature coloniale française entre 1871 et 1914* (2000) and *Exotic Subversions in Nineteenth-Century French Fiction* (2008), as well as numerous articles on colonial literature, Indochina, and gender studies. She is currently working on a volume called *The Colonial Comedy: Imperialism in the French Realist Novel*.

CHRONOLOGY

842	Oaths of Strasbourg
c. 1040–1115	*La Chanson de Roland* [*The Song of Roland*]
c. 1160–75	Marie de France, *Lais*
c. 1177	Chrétien de Troyes, *Lancelot, le chevalier de la charrette* [*Lancelot, the Knight of the Cart*]
c. 1230–75	Guillaume de Lorris and Jean de Meun, *Le Roman de la rose* [*The Romance of the Rose*]
c. 1362–5	Guillaume de Machaut, *Le Voir dit* [*The True Story*]
1405	Christine de Pizan, *Le Livre de la cité des dames* [*The Book of the City of Ladies*]
1532	François Rabelais, *Pantagruel*
1539	François Ier, Edict of Villers-Cotterêts
1549	Joachim Du Bellay, *Défense et illustration de la langue française* [*Defence and Enrichment of the French Language*]
1552	Pierre de Ronsard, *Les Amours de Cassandre* [*The Loves of Cassandra*]
1558–9	Marguerite de Navarre, *L'Heptaméron* [*The Heptameron*]
1580–95	Michel de Montaigne, *Les Essais*
1607–27	Honoré d'Urfé, *L'Astrée* [*Astrea*]
1637	René Descartes, *Les Discours de la méthode* [*Discourse on Method*]
	Pierre Corneille, *Le Cid*
1649–53	Madeleine de Scudéry, *Artamène, ou, Le grand Cyrus* [*Artamene, or The Great Cyrus*]
1666	Molière, *Le Misanthrope*
1670	Blaise Pascal, *Pensées* [*Thoughts*]
1677	Jean Racine, *Phèdre*

1678   Marie-Madeleine Pioche de La Vergne, Comtesse de
            Lafayette, *La Princesse de Clèves*
1704–17   Antoine Galland, *Les Mille et une nuits* [*One Thousand and
            One Nights*]
1721   Charles-Louis de Secondat, Baron de La Brède et de
            Montesquieu, *Les Lettres persanes* [*Persian Letters*]
1759   Voltaire, *Candide, ou l'Optimisme*
1772   Denis Diderot, *Supplément au Voyage de Bougainville*
1782   Pierre Choderlos de Laclos, *Les Liaisons dangereuses*
            Jean-Jacques Rousseau, *Les Confessions*
1791   Donatien Alphonse François, Marquis de Sade, *Justine, ou,
            Les malheurs de la vertu* [*The Misfortunes of Virtue*]
1802   François-René, Vicomte de Chateaubriand, *Le Génie du
            christianisme* [*The Genius of Christianity*]
1831   Victor Hugo, *Notre-Dame de Paris* [*The Hunchback of
            Notre Dame*]
1837–43   Honoré de Balzac, *Les Illusions perdues* [*Lost Illusions*]
1857   Gustave Flaubert, *Madame Bovary*
1857–68   Charles Baudelaire, *Les Fleurs du mal* [*The Flowers of Evil*]
1871–93   Émile Zola, *Les Rougon-Macquart*
1873   Arthur Rimbaud, *Une saison en enfer* [*A Season in Hell*]
1896   Henri Bergson, *Matière et mémoire* [*Matter and Memory*]
1897   Stéphane Mallarmé, *Un coup de dés jamais n'abolira le
            hasard* [*A Throw of the Dice Will Never Abolish Chance*]
1900   Colette, *Claudine à l'école* [*Claudine at School*]
1913   Guillaume Apollinaire, *Alcools*
1913–27   Marcel Proust, *À la recherche du temps perdu* [*In Search of
            Lost Time*]
1924   André Breton, first *Manifeste du surréalisme* [*Manifesto of
            Surrealism*]
1925   André Gide, *Les Faux-Monnayeurs* [*The Counterfeiters*]
1933   André Malraux, *La Condition humaine* [*Man's Fate*]
1936   Georges Bernanos, *Le Journal d'un curé de campagne* [*The
            Diary of a Country Priest*]
1938   Jean-Paul Sartre, *La Nausée* [*Nausea*]
1939   Nathalie Sarraute, *Tropismes* [*Tropisms*]
            Aimé Césaire, *Cahier d'un retour au pays natal* [*Notebook
            of a Return to the Native Land*]
1942   Albert Camus, *L'Étranger* [*The Outsider*]
            Francis Ponge, *Le Parti pris des choses* [*The Voice of
            Things*]

1943	Georges Bataille, *L'Expérience intérieure* [*Inner Experience*]
1949	Simone de Beauvoir, *Le Deuxième Sexe* [*The Second Sex*]
1951	Marguerite Yourcenar, *Les Mémoires d'Hadrien* [*Memoirs of Hadrian*]
1952	Samuel Beckett, *Waiting for Godot / En attendant Godot*
1955	Maurice Blanchot, *L'Espace littéraire* [*The Space of Literature*]
1957	Alain Robbe-Grillet, *La Jalousie* [*Jealousy*]
1958	Marguerite Duras, *Moderato Cantabile*
1960	Claude Simon, *La Route des Flandres* [*The Flanders Road*]
1961	Franz Fanon, *Les Damnés de la Terre* [*The Wretched of the Earth*]
1975	Hélène Cixous, *Le Rire de la méduse* [*The Laugh of the Medusa*]
	Marie Cardinal, *Les Mots pour le dire* [*The Words to Say It*]
1977	Roland Barthes, *Fragments d'un discours amoureux* [*A Lover's Discourse: Fragments*]
1980	J.-M. G. Le Clézio, *Désert*
	Jacques Derrida, *La Carte postale* [*The Postcard*]
1992	Emmanuel Hocquard, *La Théorie des tables* [*Theory of Tables*]
1995	Andreï Makine, *Le Testament français* [*The French Testament*]
2007	*Pour une 'littérature-monde' en français* [*Manifesto for a World Literature in French*]
2009	Marie NDiaye, *Trois Femmes puissantes* [*Three Powerful Women*]

JOHN D. LYONS

Introduction

Literature could be defined as the repertory of those texts that survive long after the moment of their composition. Of course, there are many other ways to say what literature is. Aristotle said that poetry is distinguished from history by its fictional quality, and on this view poetry is what tells of those things that could have happened rather than what actually did happen. Thus, even if history were written in verse, it still would not be poetic. The linguist Roman Jakobson, on the other hand, described the 'poetic function' by reference to the formal features of a text, independently of judgments about reality and fiction, and late twentieth- and early twenty-first-century literary experimentation – including novels written for Twitter and texts that arbitrarily omit a certain letter of the alphabet – lends weight to this view. However, readers are probably not deeply concerned with such boundary disputes. And in the academic study of literature, particularly of French literature, fiction and non-fiction, prose and verse, manifestoes and slogans, aphorisms and editorials, pamphlets, emblem books, and treatises – all have found their place.

The broad and pragmatic view – the view that what successive generations have chosen to save, reread, adapt, and perform constitutes literature – is especially appropriate in the context of French culture, which has over the centuries and through various means created an extensive canon of readings that educated people recognize, at least by name, as landmarks (*points de repère*) and signposts of French culture. In the course of centuries, French has spread around the globe, and publications in French have increased exponentially. Precisely because so much today is written in French, this *Companion* focuses intensely on writing in France itself, making the necessary distinction between 'French literature' and 'literature in French'. This choice is not evaluative but simply practical: it would be impossible in a volume of this size to provide an in-depth and comprehensive introduction to all the literature that has been written in French in more than a millennium. Yet, as several chapters will show, what is written in France – the traditional

'Métropole' or figurative 'Hexagon' of the French map – reflects activity of writers across the globe.

It may be useful to think of each of the following chapters as windows onto French literature over the ages. The view from some windows overlaps with the view from one or more other windows, but in each case the viewpoint onto the outside landscape will be different. All contributors are deeply knowledgeable scholars/critics invited to provide not a standard survey with the goal of coverage but rather personal and perhaps even controversial insights into this living and evolving literary tradition. William Faulkner wrote once, 'The past is never dead. It's not even past' (in *Requiem for a Nun*) and this is an idea worth keeping in mind for this *Companion*. Despite the hallowed and quite reasonable practice of organizing our knowledge of texts according to the centuries and decades in which they were written, with a bit of reflection it is easy to realize that a book from the fourteenth century may belong just as much, and in some ways even more, to the nineteenth or twentieth centuries than to the Middle Ages. How can this be? This can happen not only because more recent readers may have psychological, linguistic, historical, and even medical insights that confer a new and different significance on the book, but also because, quite simply, the book is available to more readers now than it was then. Unread manuscripts can turn up in archives and be printed, erupting into the literary marketplace centuries after the death of their authors. We can take as an example the works of the notorious Marquis de Sade, whose works were not widely available during his lifetime but all of which are now available in excellent editions. Should we consider Sade a writer of the eighteenth century, the century when he lived and wrote? Or should we consider Sade a writer of the twentieth century, the century in which his writings first reached a wide public?

The combination of timeliness and timelessness that literature offers can be perceived in the web of essays that constitute this *Companion*. This book is intended as a 'companion' in the old and simple sense that it is available to accompany you in your explorations of French literature, wherever they begin. Just as there is no 'right' and no 'wrong' place to start reading French books, no logical inaugural text, there is also no necessity to read the chapters of this *Companion* in any particular order. The chapters of this book are interlaced just as the French literary tradition itself consists of connections, often unexpected, from period to period, author to author, book to book.

I

KAREN SULLIVAN

Romance, *roman*, and novel

According to a certain linear, progressivist view of literary history, the romance was superseded by the novel because it failed to represent reality as it actually is.[1] In eighteenth-century England, writers such as Henry Fielding, Daniel Defoe, and Samuel Richardson composed the first novels just as a new middle-class reading public was emerging, eager to consume their works. Influenced, directly or indirectly, by Enlightenment philosophy, it is said, this public conceived of truth as something attained through observation, rather than imagination, and as a result appreciated the real, empirical world depicted in novels over the ideal, fantastical world of romances. Whereas romance forefronted types, such as valiant knights, beautiful princesses, and crafty sorcerers, the novel featured individuals, such as Tom Jones, Emma Woodhouse, or Oliver Twist. As types, the characters of romance were either extremely good or wicked; while, as individuals, those of the novel presented more complicated combinations of virtues and vices. Whereas romance recounted marvellous adventures, such as the slaying of dragons or the casting of magic spells, the novel related everyday occurrences, such as the finding of a new job or the meeting of a new love interest. Finally, whereas romance was set in some unspecified time and place of the distant past, the novel was set in a named village or city of the present or near-present day. The improbable and therefore incredible characters, plots, and settings of romance, it seems, naturally gave way to the probable and therefore credible characters, plots, and settings of the novel. Although this shift from romance to the novel occurred over 250 years ago, the novel remains the privileged literary genre today, it has been argued, because it was perceived, and continues to be perceived, as representing life 'as it really is'.

According to an alternative anti-linear, anti-progressivist view of literary history, however, romance was never really superseded by the novel because the earlier genre had never, in fact, failed to represent reality.[2] In England, the triumph of the novel over romance is less clear than it may seem. While critics of the eighteenth century often contrasted the novel and the romance, through the middle of that century they also used these two terms synonymously. By the end of that century, the novel had definitively displaced romance in the literary marketplace; but romance had infiltrated the novel, making its characters, once more, very good or very evil, its plots twisted and supernatural, and its settings dark and exotic. The Gothic novel advertised its affiliation with romance in its titles: Ann Radcliffe published *A Sicilian Romance* (1790) and *The Mysteries of Udolpho: A Romance* (1794), and M. G. Lewis produced *A Monk: A Romance* (1796). Meanwhile, in France, the victory of the novel over romance is even less evident. While French literary histories distinguish the 'romance' (*roman*) of the Middle Ages, the psychological 'novel' (*roman*) of the seventeenth and eighteenth centuries, and the realist 'novel' (*roman*) of the nineteenth century, with its modernist and postmodernist successors, the fact that the French language (like all major European languages, except English and Spanish) uses the same word for romance and the novel prevents the contrast between these two genres from becoming absolute. If novels appear to differ markedly from romances, it may be, not so much because they represent reality in a way in which romances fail to do, but, rather, because they employ conventions, such as the journey of self-discovery or the marriage plot, which are sufficiently familiar to us to have blinded us to their own artificiality. Even if one were to accept that the commonplaces of the novel are closer to reality than those of romance, it is still questionable whether such closeness is actually what audiences seek. Although the ordinary characters, plots, and settings with which the novel is historically identified remain privileged today in elite, literary fiction, the extraordinary characters, plots, and settings with which romance is associated continue to flourish in popular genre fiction, including fantasy, science fiction, and children's literature.

Instead of postulating the alleged anti-realism of romance, as a way in which to highlight the alleged realism of the novel, it may be helpful to attempt to understand what 'realism' would have meant in the Middle Ages, at the time when the first romances were being composed. Like modern novelists, medieval thinkers recognized the desirability of texts that represented life 'as it really is', but they tended to conceive of such texts, not simply in and of themselves, but in terms of the effects they would produce upon their readers. Scripture, the most truthful of all texts, was thought to function as a mirror, reflecting the reality outside it. Augustine refers to Scripture as 'a faithful mirror ... which indicates, not only the beauties of the people drawn toward it, but also what are deformities and vices'.[3] Gregory the Great, echoing Augustine, writes, 'Holy Scripture opposes to the mind's eye a kind of mirror, so that our inner face can be seen in it'.[4] Bernard of

4

Clairvaux affirms similarly, 'The testimonies of the Scriptures . . . are mirrors. In them, the souls of the just consider themselves, as in a mirror.'[5] Literally speaking, of course, Scripture represents Abraham and Isaac, Jesus Christ and the Virgin Mary, and St Peter and St Paul, not the reader who is studying its pages. Nevertheless, in representing these holy figures, Scripture also, in some sense, represents the reader, who naturally compares him- or herself to these models and finds him- or herself to fall short of them. Because Scripture is a mirror, Augustine advises, 'See if you are what it says. If you are not this, shudder that you may be it.'[6] Because Scripture is a mirror, Gregory counsels, 'It relates the deeds of the saints and provokes the hearts of the weak to imitate them.'[7] Because Scripture is a mirror, Bernard urges, 'Consider all that is shining in the mirror. If you apprehend in yourself something crooked, correct it; something right, hold onto it; something deformed, reform it.'[8] Not only Scripture, but any truthful text, even a romance, can function like a mirror in which we see certain characters but also, by way of contrast, ourselves: it inspires us to imitate or warns us to spurn these models. Romance is true, for its authors, in the same way in which an example is true: it is the concrete illustration that makes an abstract argument become comprehensible and, therefore, persuasive.

History

According to one tendency in medieval literature, a romance is a 'history' (*estoire*) rendered 'in a romance language' (*en romanz*), as opposed to Latin. Over the course of the twelfth and thirteenth centuries, works appeared in Old French about the history of Greece, Rome, and France, but those about the history of Britain would have the longest-lasting effect. These writings were inspired by Geoffrey of Monmouth, a cleric from Oxford, who recounts in his *Historia regum Britanniae* (1130s) how King Arthur beat back the Saxon invaders from Britain, conquered thirty kingdoms, and established a glorious if short-lived court. Wace, a Norman-French poet from the island of Jersey, translated Geoffrey's book from Latin prose into French verse in his *Livre de Brut* (1150–5) and thus enabled the Arthurian material to make the transition from Latin 'history' (*historia*) to French 'romance' (*roman*). The context of Arthur and his Round Table provided the backdrop for the verse romances of Chrétien de Troyes, especially the *Chevalier de la charrette* (*The Knight of the Cart*, c. 1170–82), which introduced the character of Lancelot of the Lake, the lover of Arthur's queen, Guinevere; and the *Conte du Graal* (*The Story of the Grail*, 1181–90), which brought in Perceval and the Quest of the Holy Grail. So intriguing was the unfinished *Conte du Graal* to audiences of the time that a series of continuators added 54,000 verses to the work's original 9,000 lines and so finally brought it to a conclusion. As the years went by, more authors took advantage of this rich material. At the turn of the twelfth and thirteenth centuries, Robert de Boron composed a verse *Joseph d'Arimathie* and *Merlin*, and either wrote or inspired prose versions of these works, as well as the prose *Didot-Perceval*. Between the 1210s and the 1240s, the anonymous authors of the prose Vulgate and Post-Vulgate Cycles provided a continuous narrative of the Arthurian saga from the first appearance of the Holy Grail at Jesus Christ's Passion; to the translation of that vessel to Britain; to the rise of Arthur as the destined monarch of Britain; to the love between Lancelot and Guinevere; to the quest of the Holy Grail; to the final wars between Arthur and Lancelot and, then, Arthur and Mordred. A century later, the author of the lengthy *Perceforest* (1330–44) contributed a pre-history to Arthur's Britain. While these Arthurian texts refer to themselves as 'romances' (*romans*), they also refer to themselves as 'histories' (*estoires*). Romance thinks of itself as true because it records what actually happened in the past, yet it also thinks of itself as true because it furnishes exemplary characters – mirrors, if one will – whose precedent one should follow.

Medieval authors believed that history could be understood to be true since it relied on eyewitness testimony or trustworthy sources. For Isidore of Seville, the sixth- and seventh-century compiler of the *Etymologiae*, 'Histories consist of true deeds that have happened.'[9] Deeds can be known to have happened, first, if one has seen them oneself; Isidore writes: 'Among the ancients, no one would write history unless he had been present and had seen those things which were to be written down.'[10] John of Salisbury, the twelfth-century historian, affirms similarly in his *Historia pontificalis*: 'In what I am going to relate, I shall, by the help of God, write nothing except what I myself know to be true, through sight or through hearing.'[11] Because medieval authors so valued eyewitness testimony, they privileged *De excidio Trojae historia* – the account of the Trojan War attributed (falsely) to Dares Phrygius, a Trojan priest who was said to have seen this conflict – over the *Iliad* attributed to Homer, who was said to have lived many centuries after the war. In his *Roman de Troie*, Benoît de Sainte-Maure writes of Dares: 'Each day, he wrote down that which he saw with his eyes ... We should believe him and hold his history to be true more than he who was born five hundred years or more afterwards and who ... knew nothing of the facts, except through hearsay.'[12] Second, deeds can also be known to have happened, it was believed, if one has consulted well-informed and trustworthy sources. In addition to what he has seen and heard about the popes, John of Salisbury asserts that he will write in his history 'what is supported by the writings and the authority of credible men'.[13] With their insistence upon believing only what they have seen or what they have found in a trustworthy source, medieval authors assumed a critical stance towards the history they recounted.

Like history, a romance about Arthur and his knights can be considered to be true, according to its authors, if it fulfils these criteria. Early Latin records had provided only brief, scattered references to Arthur, but Geoffrey of Monmouth was able to furnish a full account of this king's life and career, he claims, because he had consulted 'a very old book in the British language' (presumably Welsh) given to him by Walter, an archdeacon at Oxford.[14] Wace does not identify Geoffrey's *Historia* as his source, as it must have been, but he too claims that his account of these kings is a translation of an earlier text: 'Master Wace, who recounts the truth about it, has translated it.'[15] Like Geoffrey and Wace, Chrétien de Troyes cites written sources for some of his romances. In his romance *Cligés* (1176), he writes: 'We find this history [*histoire*], which I wish to recount and retrace to you, written in one of the books of the treasury of [the cathedral of] my lord St Peter at Beauvais. The story was drawn from there, which testifies that the history [*estoire*] is true.'[16] At times, such as in the Second[17] and Third Continuations[18] of Chrétien's *Conte du Graal*, the *estoire* on which authors base their works seems to be not so much a written 'history' as an oral 'story' that preserves the authentic tradition of what happened. At other times, such as in Gerbert de Montreuil's Continuation, the *estoire* remains a written, if unnamed, text.[19] While neither Chrétien nor his Continuators identify the author of the 'history' or 'story' (*estoire*) upon which they depend, Robert de Boron attributes his Arthurian tales to Merlin, who, he states, dictated these events to the cleric Blaise, who in turn wrote down what he heard. The Vulgate Cycle attributes its accounts to the Knights of the Round Table, who were said to recount their adventures whenever they returned to court; to four clerics who supposedly transcribed in Latin the testimony of these knights; and to Walter Map, a chaplain of Henry II of England, who allegedly found these clerics' records in the treasury in Salisbury and had them translated into French. By presenting their texts as translations of earlier texts, medieval authors located their authority in the 'translation' or 'transferral of learning' (*translatio studii*) from ancient Greece and Rome to modern Britain and France or in a similar translation or transferral of learning from older vernacular sources to their own works, even as they transformed or invented that which they were allegedly transmitting. The tendency of the authors of Arthurian romance to insist that they are writing 'according to the history' or 'according to the story' provided by such sources establishes that they, like medieval historians in general, will report only what they know to be true.

While history was understood to be true in that it relied upon eyewitness testimony or trustworthy sources, it was also understood to be true in that it promoted exemplary characters from whom one could learn a lesson. Bede, who completed his *Historia ecclesiastica gentis Anglorum* in 731, writes: 'If history records the good deeds of good men, the solicitous hearer is instigated to imitate what is good. If it commemorates the evil deeds of wicked men, the devout, pious listener or reader is aroused to avoid all that is harmful and perverse.'[20] As Bede sees it, when the historian writes down what happens, he necessarily gives form to the inchoate matter of these events; he distinguishes between good and evil acts; and he records the former so that they may be imitated and the latter so that they may be spurned. Twelfth-century historians similarly saw themselves as exposing the workings of God in the world and the moral lessons that could be obtained from such interventions. Henry of Huntingdon, who composed his *Historia Anglorum* in five editions between 1129 and 1154, represents himself as revealing how God ensures that good men are rewarded and evil men are punished. As a result, he states: 'In this work the diligent reader will find that which is to be followed and that which is to be fled. If, with the cooperation of God, he is improved through the imitation and the avoidance of these things, this would bring to me the most desirable satisfaction.'[21] John of Salisbury writes of all chroniclers: 'Their intention has been the same, that is, to relate worthy matters so that, by those things which are done, the invisible hand of God will be made manifest and so that, by the examples set forth of reward or punishment, men will be rendered more careful in fear of the Lord and in the cultivation of justice.'[22] History is valuable, these historians agree, not just because it provides us with particular facts about this or that ruler's fate, but because it provides us with universal truths one can see reflected in that fate and that one can use to guide one's own behaviour.

Like history, Arthurian romance can be considered to be true, according to its authors, if it promotes exemplary characters whose lives might prove instructive. In *Yvain* (1170s), Chrétien de Troyes speaks of 'Arthur, the good king of Britain, whose prowess teaches us that we, too, should be valiant and courteous'.[23] Not only Arthur, but Arthur's knights should inspire us to emulate their virtues. According to the Vulgate Cycle's prose *Lancelot*, of all these knights, none is more worthy of imitation than Lancelot. He is the 'the best knight in the world',[24] 'the best knight presently alive' (vol. 8, pp. 74 and 207), and 'the best ... knight who ever lived' (vol. 4, pp. 187 and 209; vol. 8, pp. 58–9). What distinguishes Lancelot from other knights is, not the absolute difference of the 'ideal' and the 'real' – the word 'ideal' did not exist in Old French – but the relative difference of the best and the good. Although he stands on the highest step of the ladder of excellence, all noble men can be found perched on one of its rungs. The best of knights, Lancelot is also the 'mirror' of knights. In the prose *Lancelot*, King Bademagu attests: 'Never did God make him except to be a mirror for other knights' (vol. 4, p. 187). With Lancelot a 'mirror for other knights', the prose *Lancelot* functions as a 'mirror for knighthood'. It represents Lancelot in a series of complex circumstances, where it is difficult, at first, to determine how the best knight should act. How should a lover respond when, having rescued his lady from her abductor, he is rejected with no explanation? How should he act when, through his fidelity towards his lady, he risks bringing about the death of a damsel who languishes because he does not return her love? What should he do when his lady and his closest friend both seek his company? The interest in all of these episodes lies in seeing how the best knight (i.e. Lancelot) will apply abstract principles to concrete situations and, hence, in learning how lesser knights – such as ourselves – should behave in such circumstances as well. Arthur has Lancelot's adventures written down, the texts make clear, only so that there may be some record of their excellence for posterity. The prose *Lancelot* relates that he did so 'in order that the descendants who came after him might know the marvels Lancelot had accomplished during his life' (vol. 6, pp. 53–4). Romance enables the many mediocre people of the present to remember the few exemplary people of the past, and it stirs them to try to imitate their behaviour.

If romance is history, then, it may not be literally true; but it is figuratively true. Lancelot, it must be recalled, never existed. He was a fictional character dreamed up by Chrétien or by an oral tradition with which Chrétien was familiar. Not only did Lancelot never exist, but a knight as excellent as he is said to have been could never have existed. No man could have fought other knights throughout his entire adult life and never have suffered defeat, as he is said to have done. No man could have loved one woman throughout all that time and never have been unfaithful to her in deed or in thought, as he is said to have been. Because Lancelot never existed and could never have existed, the account of his adventures that Lancelot supposedly provided at court, that the clerics supposedly transcribed, and that Map supposedly translated is all a lie. Yet the romance itself might respond to that critic by arguing that it *is* history, because it is real, but it is real in the sense that it is true. According to the prose *Lancelot*, as a youth Lancelot is being instructed in the ways of chivalry by the Lady of the Lake, and he is overwhelmed by the number of extraordinary qualities she says that a knight should possess. He asks his tutor: 'Since knighthood began, has there ever been a knight who had all these virtues in himself?' (vol. 7, p. 255). He wonders if such a perfect knight could exist, not just as an idea in one's mind, but as a reality in the world. The Lady of the Lake replies that, before Jesus Christ, John the Hyrcanian and Judas Maccabeus possessed all the virtues she lists and that, after the Passion, Joseph of Arimathea, King Pelles of Listenois, and Helain the Fat achieved a similar feat. In the past, there have existed knights who exemplified chivalry, the lady affirms, and, in the future, there will exist knights who do so again – including, she clearly hopes, her own pupil. If there are good and better knights, as we know that there are, there must be, logically speaking, a best knight, and that knight is the one we know as Lancelot. Like the Lady of the Lake's examples of great knights of the past, the prose *Lancelot*, and romance in general, is a rhetorical device used to illustrate that truth.

Romance as poetry

According to a second tendency in medieval literature, a romance is not 'history' (*estoire*) but 'poetry' (*vers*). The influence of contemporary troubadour (or Old Provençal) and trouvère (or Old French) lyric upon romances guaranteed that they addressed love affairs far more than their source texts had done. While Virgil's *Aeneid* depicts the union of Aeneas and Lavinia, the daughter of the king of Latium, as the product of political expediency, the romance of *Enéas* portrays it as the result of amorous passion. While Geoffrey's *Historia regum Brittaniae* focuses upon Arthur, the great military leader, Chrétien's *Chevalier de la charrette* and subsequent romances concentrate, instead, upon Lancelot and Guinevere, the great lovers. While these allegedly historical romances, in prose as well as poetry, were accentuating amorous themes, a series of non-historical verse romances were devoting themselves wholeheartedly to love. The anonymous *Floire et Blancheflor* (1150-2), Thomas of England's *Tristan* (1155-60), Béroul's *Roman de Tristran* (1170-90s), Jakemés's *Le Roman du Chastelain de Couci et de la Dame de Fayel* (late 1200s), and, most famous of all, the *Roman de la rose*, begun by Guillaume de Lorris (*c.* 1225-30) and completed by Jean de Meun (*c.* 1275), are just some of the better-known love stories of this era. At the core of these romances' claim to truth lies their assertion, not that their lovers really existed and really acted as they depict them as doing, but that their author understands love from his own personal experience and is therefore able to represent this sensation, faithfully and accurately, in this text. As the author of the *Roman de la poire* (mid-1200s) puts it: 'He greatly wastes his work and his pains who makes effort to rhyme about love if he neither feels nor has felt that sickness.'[25] Romance thinks of itself as poetry and, therefore, as true because it records what the poet actually felt, even when it transposes this emotion onto his character.

A lyric poem can be understood to be true, medieval authors believed, in that its poet sincerely expressed his or her feelings. To take the troubadour Arnaut Daniel as an example, the poet is inspired to sing because of the love he bears for his lady. 'Love for me at once smoothes down and gilds my singing,'[26] Arnaut announces. Elsewhere, he writes: 'Since Love commands me, I shall make a song ... for she has trained me nobly in the arts of her school.'[27] Love, Arnaut claims, not only inspires him to compose poetry, but teaches him how to do so, refining his verses. Bernart de Ventadorn, the most celebrated love poet among the troubadours, similarly connects his emotional experiences and his literary productions. He declares in one song: 'There is no use in singing if the song does not spring from the heart; and the song cannot spring from the heart if there is no heart-felt love there.'[28] Bernart's experience as a lyric poet derives, he claims, not from his impersonal knowledge of some history or story, but from his personal experience of love. For these lyric poets love, and compose songs to express that love.

A romance such as the *Roman de la rose* can be considered to be true, medieval authors also contend, because its author, like an author of a lyric poem, sincerely expresses his or her own feelings. Lorris and Meun both seem to identify with the Lover, the first-person protagonist of their poem. One day, while walking in the Garden of Delight, Lorris recounts, the Lover espies a rosebush, and on it, one perfect rose, which becomes the object of his desire. He appeals to Fair Welcoming, who personifies the maiden's positive response to his attentions, telling him: 'Know, fair sir, that Love torments me harshly ... The pain will never cease if you do not give me the rosebud that is better shaped than the others.'[29] The Lover has succumbed to love, which makes him yearn to possess the Rose, and he openly acknowledges this desire to one who stands to satisfy it. When he sees how alarmed Fair Welcoming becomes at his brazen demand for the Rose, however, he shifts his tack, saying: 'I repented for having ever said what I thought' (ll. 2953–4). Instead of asking to possess the Rose, he asks merely to be allowed to love her. 'I ask no other thing' (l. 3180), he avers – although he never ceases to plot to pluck this flower. Even as he becomes insincere towards Fair Welcoming, he remains sincere towards the reader, openly informing us of his deceit of others. In the course of his quest for the Rose, the Lover receives advice from a series of characters, including the Jealous Man, Genius, and Nature, who teach him that women do nothing but deceive men. In the context of this characterization of women, Reason counsels the Lover to deceive members of this sex instead. She advises: 'There are some of such a kind who ... promise [their ladies] their hearts and souls, and they swear lies and tell fables to those they find deceivable, until they have taken their pleasure with them ... It is always better, fair master, to deceive than to be deceived' (ll. 4389–4400). Part of the shock and, for many, the delight of the *Roman de la rose* lies in its exposure, not only of the Lover's ardour for his beloved, but of the deceits he is ready to employ in order to gain his way with her. In a letter she wrote criticizing the *Roman de la rose* (1401), Christine de Pizan, the prolific woman of letters, assumes that, when Meun (to whom she takes particular exception) was speaking through the mouth of the Lover and his other characters, he was expressing his own feelings, based upon his own experiences. Because Meun represented all women as wicked in his work, she hypothesizes, he must have frequented only wicked women. Because he urged lovers to deceive women 'until they have taken their pleasure with them', she speculates, he must have been consumed with lust. 'I suppose that the great carnality, perhaps, with which he was filled, made him give himself over to these desires more than to profitable ones',[30] she remarks. Meun's especially misogynistic contribution to the work becomes, as she sees it, evidence of his own bad mores. For Lorris and Meun and for Christine, the authors of romance, like the authors of lyric poetry, love, honestly or dishonestly, and they compose their romances to express that love.

Yet, while a lyric poem can be considered to be true in that the poet sincerely expresses his or her feelings, it can also be considered to be true in that he or she uses irony to distance himself from the amorous speaker and so deters readers from following this speaker's example.[31] It is not at all clear that Arnaut was inspired to sing because of the love he bore a lady. In a 'reason' or 'cause' (*razo*) appended to the love song 'I never had her, but she had me' ['Anc ieu non l'aic, mas ella m'a'], Arnaut is said to have entered into a contest with another jongleur at the court of Richard the Lionheart to see who could compose in more difficult rhymes. Because Arnaut was unable to compose his song by the deadline Richard had imposed, he memorized the one he heard the other jongleur practising all night, and he recited it as his own before the king the following day. When the truth came out, the king, amused by the deception, rewarded both men and gave them both gifts. The *razo* notes: 'And the song was given to Arnaut that says, "I never had her, but she had me."'[32] According to the anecdote, Arnaut strives to compose a love song, not in order to prove that he loves a lady – for no lady is mentioned here – but in order to prove that he can come up with more complex rhymes than the other jongleur. Although the 'I' (*ieu*) who 'never had her' in the jongleur's song could not possibly refer to Arnaut, the fact that he receives the right to this song all the same indicates that the speaker in such works was not always identified with the poet.[33] Likewise, it is not at all clear that Bernart always embraces the experience of love, which, he says, lies behind his verse. In relating how his lady rejected him in his most famous love song, he states, 'I despair of women. No more shall I trust them ... I fear and distrust all of them, for I know very well that they are all alike.'[34] By showing how he moved from disappointment with one lady to the condemnation of all women, from his personal unhappiness in love to an impersonal misogyny, Bernart illustrates the psychology of a man in love, but that of a man who has succumbed to confusion and despair. He acknowledges that, like Narcissus, he has been lost ever since he looked into his lady's eyes, 'that mirror which pleased me greatly'.[35] For these lyric poets, they may (or may not) love, but the songs they compose to express that love can, at times, criticize their behaviour as lovers.

The *Roman de la rose* can be regarded to be true, not only in that its authors sincerely expressed their feelings, but also in that they used irony to distance themselves from their Lover and thus discouraged readers from taking him as their model. In the course of his perambulations through the Garden of Delight, Lorris relates, the Lover finds the Fountain of Narcissus. Gazing into this pool, he beholds on its bottom two marvellous crystals, with which, when the sun shines upon them, one can see the entire garden. He explains: 'Just as the mirror shows things that are in front of it, without cover, in their true colours and shapes, so, I tell you truly, do the crystals reveal the whole condition of the garden, without deception, to those who gaze into the water' (ll. 1555–62). The Lover fails to realize that the two crystals he has examined in the fountain are his own eyes, because, like Narcissus, he has mistaken his own reflection for something else. Denying outright that the crystals can deceive, he affirms instead that, like a mirror, they represent reality exactly as it is. By doing so, Lorris suggests, the Lover fails to realize that that mirrors can indeed mislead, as they are shown to do later in the poem. In a speech on optics, Meun cites Nature as explaining how mirrors can make large objects seem small and small objects seem large; distant objects seem near and near objects seem distant; and phantoms appear, so that people think they see devils. Because of such mirrors, Nature warns, 'Many things are judged to be other than they are' (ll. 18245–6). However beguiled the Lover may be by the Fountain of Narcissus, Lorris and Meun use dramatic irony to establish that, as a result of looking in the mirror, he has judged love to be other than it is. In a response to Christine's letter criticizing the *Roman de la rose*, Pierre Col, a secretary in the Royal Chancellery, argues that, while Meun had once been a foolish lover, like the Lover in this poem, he had long since repented of his folly, and he was using his knowledge of foolish love to dissuade readers from pursing it. Far from speaking through the mouths of characters who speak ill of women, Col asserts, 'Master Jean de Meun introduced characters in this book, and he has each character speak according to what is appropriate to him, that is, the Jealous Husband as a jealous person, . . . and so on with the others.'[36] For Lorris and Meun and for Col, the authors of romance may have loved in their youth, but they may also use their romance to urge their readers not to follow in their path.

As the authors who conceive of romance as poetry see it, romance may provide examples of characters from whom one could learn a lesson, but it is not always clear what that lesson should be. Does Meun express sincerely his feelings when he cites characters who condemn mirrors in general, and the Fountain of Narcissus in particular, as deceptive, as Col contends? Or does he express his feelings sincerely when he cites the God of Love, who praises mirrors, and the *Roman de la rose* as a mirror, as revealing the truth, as Christine alleges? The God of Love declares of this romance: 'All those alive should call this book the *Mirror of Lovers* [*Miroër as amoreus*], so many benefits will they see there for themselves' (ll. 10649–52). Throughout the poem, Meun reinforces the God of Love's view that, by representing, faithfully and accurately, the Lover's experience of plucking the Rose, this book will teach its readers how to pluck roses of their own choosing. Addressing these readers as 'amorous lords' (l. 15159) and 'loyal lovers' (l. 15135), Meun assures them, '[y]ou will hear about the deed and the manner, youthful lords, so that, when the sweet season arrives, if the need comes upon you to go gather rosebuds, whether open or closed, you will act so wisely that you will not fail to gather them' (ll. 21675–82). While Col reads the *Roman de la rose* as ironic in its celebration of the Lover's attainment of the Rose, based upon certain passages in the poem, Christine reads it as sincere, based upon other passages. While Col claims that Meun has the Jealous Husband condemn women in order to illustrate how irrationally jealous husbands act, Christine writes: 'I tell you that almost all the characters are unable to stop vituperating against women.'[37] While Col maintains (with justice) that Meun should not be identified with his characters, Christine asserts (also with justice) that these characters all speak in an identical voice and thus reveal that they and their author are one and the same. Indeed, as Meun encouraged his followers to deceive women, she sees Col as attempting to deceive her by advancing his disingenuous interpretation of the text. 'You speak otherwise than how you think, with all due respect',[38] she warns. Because he does not dare to promote the deception of women openly, she surmises, he denies that Meun is himself promoting the deception of women, and therefore he attempts to deceive a woman himself. The same instability of language that allows a poet – or any writer – to express sincerity in love or in debate is what allows him to *seem* to express sincerity and, thus, not to express sincerity at all. As the archetypal lover shifts from the Vulgate's Lancelot to the *Roman de la rose*'s Lover, romance ceases to function like a clear mirror, representing good examples to be followed and bad examples to be shunned, and begins to function instead like a trick mirror, whose images make one question what one is in fact seeing.

Like the modern novel, medieval romance always strove to represent reality in its pages, but it did so with an eye to how that reality might be received by its readers. Both historical and poetic romances saw themselves, not as recounting 'fictions' (*fables*), which signified only within the text, but as recounting truths, which referred, faithfully and accurately, to the world without. For the romance claiming to be history translated into the vernacular, these truths had to do with external events of the past, such as the rise of King Arthur's kingdom and the adventures of the Knights of the Round Table. For the romance claiming to be lyric transformed into narrative, these truths had to do with internal emotions of the present: namely, the joys and sufferings of love in the human heart. Yet both historical and poetic romances saw the truths they contained, not as existing statically, in and of themselves, but as engaging dynamically with their audience. By seeing himself mirrored in the portrait of Lancelot, the reader learns what he must to do become a better knight. By seeing himself mirrored in the portrait of the Lover, he learns what he must do to seduce a maiden. In the context of medieval literature, the fact that a locutionary text, which states what was or what is, can have a perlocutionary effect, in stating what should be, in no way diminishes its truth value.

NOTES

1. See Ian Watt, *The Rise of the Novel* (London: Chatto and Windus, 1957) for the most compelling and influential version of this thesis. Although Watt identifies the novel as a specifically British invention, the rejection of romance with which this genre is associated has its roots in Miguel de Cervantes' *Don Quixote* (1605–15).
2. See Michael McKeon, *The Origins of the English Novel, 1600–1740* (Princeton, NJ: Princeton University Press, 1987; 2nd edn, 2002).
3. Augustine, *Contra Faustum Manichaeum*, in *Patrologia Latina*, ed. Jacques-Paul Migne, 217 vols (Paris: Garnier Frères, 1844–65), vol. 42, Book XXII, Chapter 60, col. 613. Translations in this chapter are my own unless otherwise stated.
4. Gregory the Great, *Moralia in Job*, in *Patrologia Latina*, ed. Migne, vol. 74, Book 11, Chapter 1, col. 553.
5. Bernard of Clairvaux, *Instructio Sacerdotis*, in *Patrologia Latina*, ed. Migne, vol. 184, Book 1, Chapter 11, col. 788.
6. Augustine, *Enarrationes in Psalmos*, in *Patrologia Latina*, ed. Migne, vol. 36, Psalm 103, Chapter 4, col. 1614.
7. Gregory the Great, *Moralia in Job*, Book 11, Chapter 1, col. 553.
8. Bernard of Clairvaux, *Instructio Sacerdotis*, Book 1, Chapter 11, col. 788.
9. Isidore of Seville, *Etymologiae*, ed. W. M. Lindsay (Oxford: Oxford University Press, 1911), bk. 1, ch. 41.

10. Isidore of Seville, *Etymologiae*, bk. 1, ch. 41.

11. John of Salisbury, *Historia Pontificalis / Memoirs of the Papal Court*, ed. and trans. Marjorie Chibnall (London: Nelson, 1956), p. 4.

12. Benoît de Sainte-Maure, *Roman de Troie: Extraits du manuscrit Milan, Bibliothèque ambrosienne, D 55*, ed. Emmanuèle Baumgartner and Françoise Vielliard (Paris: Livre de Poche, 1998), ll. 105–6 and 123–8.

13. John of Salisbury, *Historia Pontificalis*, p. 4.

14. Geoffrey of Monmouth, *A History of the Kings of Britain: An Edition and Translation of 'De gestis Britonum'*, ed. Michael D. Reeve (Woodbridge: Boydell, 2009), p. 5.

15. Wace, *Roman de Brut, A History of the British, Text and Translation*, ed. and trans. Judith Weiss (Exeter: University of Exeter Press, 2002), ll. 7–8.

16. Chrétien de Troyes, *Cligés: Édition critique du manuscrit B.N. fr. 12560*, ed. Charles Méla and Olivier Collet (Paris: Livre de Poche, 1994), ll. 38–43.

17. *The Continuations of the Old French 'Perceval' of Chrétien de Troyes*, 5 vols, ed. William Roach (Philadelphia, PA: University of Pennsylvania Press, 1949–83), vol. 4, l. 22620.

18. *Continuations of the Old French 'Perceval'*, vol. 5, ll. 4266 and 42430.

19. *La Continuation de Perceval*, 3 vols, ed. Mary Williams (Paris: Champion, 1922–75), vol. 1, ll. 7001 and 7007.

20. *Bede's 'Ecclesiastical History of the English People'*, ed. Bertram Colgrave and R. A. B. Mynors (Oxford: Clarendon Press, 1969), p. 2.

21. Henry of Huntingdon, *Historia Anglorum: The History of the English People*, ed. and trans. Diana Greenway (Oxford: Oxford University Press, 1996), p. 4.

22. John of Salisbury, *Historia Pontificalis*, p. 2.

23. Chrétien de Troyes, *Yvain*, ed. Claude Buridant and Jean Trotin (Paris: Champion, 1980), ll. 1–3.

24. *Lancelot: Roman en prose du xiiie siècle*, ed. Alexandre Micha, 9 vols (Geneva: Droz, 1978–83), vol. 4, pp. 147, 162, 216, 231, and 391, and vol. 8, pp. 36, 121, and 462. Subsequent references by volume and page number in the text.

25. Thibaut de Blaison, *Le Roman de la poire*, ed. Christiane Marchelo-Nizia (Paris: Société des anciens textes français, 1984), ll. 352–5.

26. 'En cest sonet coind'e leri', in *The Poetry of Arnaut Daniel*, ed. and trans. James J. Wilhelm (New York: Garland, 1981), pp. 40–3, ll. 5–7.

27. 'Ains que cim reston de branchas', in *The Poetry of Arnaut Daniel*, pp. 66–7, ll. 3–5.

28. Bernart de Ventadorn, 'Chantars no pot gaire valer', in *The Songs of Bernart de Ventadorn*, ed. Stephen G. Nichols, Jr., John A. Galm, A. Bartlett Giamatti, Roger J. Porter, Seth L. Wolitz, and Claudette Charbonneau (Chapel Hill, NC: University of North Carolina Press, 1965), pp. 80–2, ll. 1–4.

29. Guillaume de Lorris and Jean de Meun, *Le Roman de la rose*, ed. Daniel Poirion (Paris: Garnier-Flammarion, 1974), ll. 2898–2904. Subsequent references by line number in the text.

30. Christine de Pizan, 'June/July, 1401: Christine's Reaction to Jean de Montreuil's Treatise on the Roman de la Rose', in *Debating the 'Roman de la rose': A Critical Anthology*, ed. and trans. Christine McWebb (New York: Routledge, 2007), pp. 118–33 (p. 130).

31. See Simon Gaunt, *Troubadours and Irony* (Cambridge: Cambridge University Press, 1989).

32. Jean Boutière and Alexander H. Schutz, *Biographies des troubadours* (Paris: Nizet, 1964), p. 63.

33. See Gregory B. Stone's reading of this *razo* in *The Death of the Troubadour: The Late Medieval Resistance to the Renaissance* (Philadelphia, PA: University of Pennsylvania Press, 1994), pp. 62–5.

34. Bernart de Ventadorn, 'Can vei la lauzeta mover', in *The Songs of Bernart de Ventadorn*, ed. Nichols, pp. 166–8, ll. 25–32.

35. Bernart de Ventadorn, 'Can vei la lauzeta mover', l. 20.

36. Pierre Col, 'End of Summer, 1402: Pierre Col's Reply to Christine de Pizan's and Jean Gerson's Treatises', in *Debating the 'Roman de la rose'*, pp. 306–43 (p. 325).

37. Pizan, 'October 2, 1402: Christine's Response to Pierre Col', in *Debating the 'Roman de la rose'*, pp. 140–97 (p. 165).

38. Pizan, 'October 2, 1402', p. 149.

2

DEBORAH MCGRADY

Joan of Arc and the literary imagination

When Joan of Arc entered history as a peasant girl divinely inspired to free Orléans and see the exiled and disinherited 'King of Bourges' crowned Charles VII, King of France, she did so as a fantastical creature; one that sparked the creative imagination of all who heard of her existence. In the brief time spanning her meeting with the king in March 1429 to her execution in May 1431, many wrote about Joan, but most did so having never met her.

A presumed Lombard cleric living in the Normandy region declared in July 1429 that Joan's extraordinary story was hampered by the silence surrounding her, which he complained was imposed by unnamed forces.[1] This silence did not deter him or his contemporaries from speaking about her. In his case, he addressed his questions directly to an imaginary Joan: 'If I might dare to ask, what was your state of mind, your feelings, your thoughts when you first heard the angelic voices?' (p. 11). Drawing on his own creative devices, he entertained her possible responses and shared with Joan his assumptions. What occupied her thoughts? 'Perhaps nothing less than heaven, nothing more than the responsibility ordered by a poor father to look over the herd, nothing other than thinking of yourself' (p. 11). How did she react to the voices? 'Suddenly, startled by a divine breath, you trembled' (p. 11). But what did the voices say and how did Joan respond? To these questions, our cleric exclaimed, 'if only you could tell me the things you heard!' (p. 12). This raw frustration speaks for generations of writers who have confronted the gaps in Joan's incomparable tale. As our Lombard cleric attempted to flesh out circulated rumours in an imaginary conversation with his subject, so too biographers, poets, and dramatists have ceaselessly negotiated historical record and human psyche in an effort to tell Joan's story.

At the origin of Joan's story, fact and fiction have always been intertwined and from this concoction has emerged a historical figure that repeatedly bends to the imagination of her many authors. Within the French tradition alone, there is a wide range of well-known novelists, poets, and playwrights, including Voltaire, whose scandalous *La Pucelle d'Orléans* (1752) simultaneously mocked the excessive lyricism of Jean Chaplain's recent poem to the heroine, railed against the staid social and religious structures in pre-Revolutionary France, and lodged a damning assessment of female speech and empowerment. Most Johannic writings, however, offer a powerful counterweight to Voltaire's cynical view. French poets ranging from Christine de Pizan to Alfred de Musset and Alphonse de Lamartine, playwrights from Charles Péguy to Paul Claudel to Jean Anouilh, and novelists from Alexandre Dumas to Joseph Delteil to Michel Tournier have repeatedly resurrected this unparalleled French heroine to propose creative alternatives to the plethora of historical accounts produced from 1429 to the present day. To appreciate the unique challenge of writing on Joan and the attraction that has enticed both established writers and novices, one must consider Joan's emergence as a historic *and* literary figure as early as the summer of 1429 when she amazed and perplexed her contemporaries.

We arguably know more about Joan of Arc than any other medieval figure. She was the subject of three trials: the reported Poitiers Trial of 1429, for which there is no extant copy, which prompted Charles' decision to give her an army; the Interrogation of 1431 that culminated in her execution by fire; and the 1455–6 Rehabilitation Trial that sought to re-establish her reputation. Through extant records, we can trace her genealogy: we have details concerning her upbringing, ranging from her religious training, the womanly skills she mastered, the village activities she enjoyed and those she avoided, and the opinions of family, neighbours, soldiers, and judges regarding her conduct. Owing to the trial records, we have many answers to the earlier questions our Lombard cleric longed to have answered: Joan's Interrogation reserved pride of place to her voices, her first meeting with the king, and details about her battle activity. And yet, with so much of her life part of the legal record, she still remains a mystery.

So diffuse and malleable was Joan's character at the time of her 1920 canonization that Maurice Barrès could claim that all parties were free to shape her narrative according to their beliefs:

> Are you a royalist? She is the heroine who made it possible for the son of Saint Louis to be consecrated according to the Gallican sacrament at Reims. Do you reject the supernatural? Never was anyone more realistic than this mystic; she was practical, indisciplined, and sly, as soldiers are in every period ... For republicans, she is a child of the people, more magnificent than any of the acknowledged great ... Finally, socialists cannot forget that she said: 'I have

been sent to console the poor and unfortunate.' Thus all parties can lay claim to Joan of Arc. But she transcends them all. No one can confiscate her. Around her banner the miracle of national reconciliation can be accomplished today, just as it was accomplished five centuries ago.[2]

Barrès brazenly exploited the creative impulse at the core of Johannic literature. He freely blended conflicting versions of her story, adopted flagrant anachronisms, and unabashedly attributed unspoken words to his heroine.

This manipulation of Joan by one of her most fervent admirers who had long lobbied for a national holiday in her honour demands that we take another look at Joan's reception history. Scholarly treatment of Joan of Arc's role as a political and religious icon has long shrouded her status as an unparalleled creative force. For writers such as Jules Michelet, who interrupted his multi-volume *History of France* to compose an impassioned biographical fiction of Joan of Arc, or Péguy, who was driven to theatre by his desire to document Joan's 'inner life',[3] Joan was not their creation but their creator. Rejecting the impulse to bend Joan to their desires as advocated by Barrès, many authors speak of a debt and a responsibility to Joan to correct the self-serving narrative promoted by religious and political institutions by calling on their creative imagination.

Joan's appearance on the political stage in 1429 was a literary event of surprising magnitude that seems never to have lost its aura of wonder. Joan of Arc took shape in and through contemporary texts, a reality, as we shall see, of which she appeared cognizant at the time of her 1431 Trial. Let us first consider two texts written in the summer of 1429: one believed to be authored by the theologian Jean Gerson; the other, by the well-known writer Christine de Pizan. These texts, along with the Lombard's letter, document the emerging narrative that would come to define Joan during her lifetime. The 1431 Interrogation can then be approached as more than the interrogation of Joan as a person, since it engaged heavily with her portrayal in these early texts. The Interrogation record suggests a hint of creative liberty insofar as the extant version witnessed in three manuscripts represents a revised account in Latin of the official trial minutes recorded in French. These minutes are available in two later manuscripts dating from the late fifteenth and early sixteenth centuries.[4] The closing section will focus on her twentieth-century reception. The nineteenth century prepared the way for a radically new encounter with Joan. Between 1841 and 1849, Jules Quicherat provided the first complete edition of her trial. His edition offered partial access to her voice and contemporary testimony. This documentation ultimately freed Joan from her secondary role in history. She quickly emerged as an iconic figure in French art and literature, as witnessed by Michelet's biographical fiction of her, published in 1853, and Ingre's 1854 *Joan of Arc at the Coronation of Charles VII*. But it is perhaps in drama that one sees the greatest impact of Quicherat's work. Access to the presumed voice of Joan registered in the trial transcripts inspired a cottage industry of dramatic works over the next century, of which plays by Péguy and Jean Anouilh are among the most memorable. Their works, written over the first half of the twentieth century, provide rich examples of how modern authors unwittingly followed in the Lombard cleric's footsteps. Where he expressed frustration before the unknown – 'if only you could tell me the things you heard!' – so they found her registered words in the trial documents to leave so many questions unanswered and in need of exploration.

Joan's unfolding story

The summer of 1429 was abuzz with word of Joan. Her entrance into the exiled king's confidences required explanation, as did her leadership in the French army's victory in Orléans on 8 May 1429. A great diversity of voices emerged to fill the narrative gap. Theological summations, official communiqués, personal letters, diaries, and lyric accounts provide a dizzying array of first 'readings' of the young woman who quickly came to be known as 'la Pucelle' [the Maid].

Many of these voices drew from an established corpus of scriptural and classical literature to make sense of Joan. Take the examples of two royalist intellectuals chased from the capital in 1418 by the Burgundians: Jean Gerson, former chancellor of the University of Paris, and Christine de Pizan, prolific writer closely linked to the Valois princes, both of whom suggest in their writings that they were compelled, in part, to write on Joan to address both her opponents as well as her cautious supporters, including the king. Both relied heavily on Scripture and classical models to make sense of Joan's behaviour and actions.

The widely circulated treatise 'About a Marvellous Victory' dates itself six days after Joan's first victory. It proclaims that the recent battlefield success overwrote the 'rumours' circulating about Joan and set the stage for a new narrative.[5] Gerson, the likely author, reminded readers of the many who met Joan and 'believe[d] in the word of the Maid', including the king's council, his soldiers, and the people.[6] Where our Lombard cleric turned to his imagination to give voice to Joan, the author of the 'Marvellous Victory' directed readers to established 'sacred and secular history' to flesh out the tale of this famed girl they had not yet met.[7] Readers were directed to study and sing well-known hymns that would provide the tools for structuring 'a devotion suitable to the present event'.[8] The author then provided the ingredients of an appropriate narrative for Joan by evoking the feats of biblical figures, including Deborah, Judith, and even Judas Maccabaeus, as well as saints (St Katherine and St Cecile) and mythological warrior women, from the virgin warrior Camilla in Virgil's *Aeneid* to the Amazonian female warriors. No longer subject to rumour, Joan was shown to have clear literary antecedents and, in effect, her story was already written.

Christine de Pizan's 'Tale of Joan of Arc', internally dated to the final days of July 1429, visited similar literary terrain, but she went further by making an explicit link between her story and Joan's. Joan not only liberated the people of Orléans, she also freed our poet. Christine announced at the outset of the poem that because of Joan, she broke an eleven-year silence, transforming her 'language from one of tears to one of song'.[9] The resulting poem recounts two extraordinary events: that of a young girl who performed uncommon heroic feats, past and future; and a silenced poet who resurfaced as an inspired prophet.[10]

Joan's actions beg for a poet to assure that her story be told. These events should be 'told everywhere, for it is worthy of being remembered, and may it be written down – ... in many a chronicle and history book' (stanza 7). Christine, however, left this history writing to others; she was more concerned with alerting the living to the extraordinary moment they were experiencing. In her estimation, there was no established narrative that could encapsulate this story. Here was a 'wonderful' thing (stanza 8), an 'extraordinary' occurrence (stanza 10), and 'a miracle' (stanza 11) that had been achieved not by the expected hero, but by a 'young virgin' (stanza 11). Christine rehearsed the list of expected biblical models only to reject these narratives as insufficient. Among Moses, Gideon, Joseph, Esther, Judith, and Deborah, there are 'none who can compare with her ... He has accomplished more through this Maid' (stanza 28). Nor do the stories of Hector or Achilles match the Maid, since she surpassed them in strength (stanza 36). With known narratives failing, Christine turned to an unexpected textual legacy authored by a triumvirate of illustrious prophets – Merlin, the Sibyl, and Bede – who 'foresaw her coming, entered her in their writings' (stanza 31). Distinct from the biblical and classical narratives, these prophecies announced Joan's 'coming', but they left no tale. It fell solely to Christine to author the yet-untold story.

It has been rightly pointed out that Christine's unprecedented authoritative voice in this work owed much to Joan as she became a sibyl to her heroine.[11] What has been ignored in this reading, however, is the extent to which Joan's exceptionality ruptured the poet's relationship to established narrative. Whereas many of her earlier writings detailed the heroic lives of past women – including those listed as inferior examples to Joan – Christine turned away from authoritative texts to claim for Joan an entirely new narrative that projected Joan into the future, where Christine predicted that she would conquer both Jerusalem (stanza 43) and Paris (stanzas 53–4). That Christine got the history wrong matters little. What this poem reveals is the extent to which Joan's story exposed past heroic accounts as conservative. Christine needed to shed this literary past and her status as learned poet to speak as a visionary, thereby joining her heroine in embarking on a new path. Little did either woman know that soon an organized effort would be made to suppress this emerging narrative.

A woman of her word

Joan's story did not follow the plot lines imagined by Christine. Captured outside Compiègne on 23 May 1430, Joan was to be subjected to a radical retelling of her story that took shape in the trial records produced after her execution on 30 May 1431. Qualifying the trial as a highly mediated document, scholars have described it both as 'a literary text of the highest merit' and a 'masterpiece of dramatic tension'.[12] To understand these claims, it is important to keep in mind that we lack a direct transcription of Joan's trial. Instead we have two main sources that come to us in the form of later copies produced of the now lost originals: the French minute, identified as such because the document was a summary in French that had been produced each evening of the daily proceedings; and the Latin account of the trial produced following Joan's execution, which was heavily dependent on the French minute.[13] The relationship between the two versions is complex, but a comparison of the two makes apparent that the authors of the official Latin version took a number of creative liberties. Most obvious was the selective use of direct discourse to register Joan's voice. To the extent, therefore, that we hear Joan speak, it is due to her interrogators' decision to cite selectively. Nonetheless, these legal documents strongly suggest that both Joan and her interrogators regarded the trial record as key to her legacy.

It was not only in producing the official version of the trial that we see Joan's interrogators concerned with shaping Joan's story to justify their final decision. This intention manifested itself from the very first days of the trial, where the judges strove to debunk the narrative fleshed out in the contemporary texts examined thus far. The judges made a public display of Joan from the outset when they decided to hold open court. On the first day, Joan entered the room 'bound in iron chains and fetters'[14] – what better way to override the heroic image of the victorious maiden? On the second day, the record informs us that the image of Joan as a shepherdess was based on a misconception since she informed her judges that she 'did not go to the fields with the sheep and other animals' (p. 53). On the following day, the interrogators strove to construe her claims of divine inspiration as evidence of heretical activity and thus she was long interrogated on village beliefs concerning fairies, local prophecies, and magical trees. On 28 March 1431, judges brought forward seventy accusations against Joan, which would eventually be whittled down to twelve. In its first iteration, the list repeatedly accused Joan of making heretical claims, telling lies and tall tales, boasting, and making prophecies (pp. 123–55). In short, she was accused of authoring a false account of her life.

The judges manipulated Joan's responses to author a new account of her story. For example, her first cited words in the trial record suggest a refusal to tell the truth; when asked to take an oath to tell all, Joan refused, explaining: 'I don't know what you wish to ask me. Perhaps you might ask me things I can't tell you' (p. 49). Direct citation often highlights Joan's refusal to speak, as well as providing powerful examples of her belligerence. On 27 February, when asked about her fasting practices, she retorted: 'What does this have to do with your trial?' (p. 64). On 3 March, Joan's words registered a determination to evade questioning: 'This doesn't concern your trial' (p. 78); 'You will get nothing more out of me now' (p. 79); and 'I'm not advised to answer you now' (p. 80). The line of questioning, the formal accusations, and even Joan's cited responses reveal an attentive engagement not simply with the young woman before them, but also the narrative constructed by Joan's supporters.

It is not only Joan's interrogators who were concerned with the dissemination of her story. In spite of her being illiterate, Joan made astonishing use of the written word in shaping her identity. Nowhere is this more obvious than when a letter addressed to the English and dated 22 March 1429 entered into evidence. This letter represents the earliest extant text on Joan, but is all the more distinctive because Joan 'authored' the text. On the heels of her first interrogation in Poitiers, she composed a letter that charged the English to 'surrender to the Maid sent by God, the King of Heaven, the keys of all the good towns you have taken and violated in France' (p. 134). The letter identified three divinely inspired intentions Joan intended to undertake: to chase the English from France; to return the land to Charles, 'the true heir' (p. 134); and to lead the French king into occupied Paris. Joan's bellicose words were justified by her close alliance with God: the letter registers on four occasions her status as God's messenger. Perhaps most striking is Joan's self-naming. In a letter of just over 600 words, Joan identified herself in the third person six times. Rather than use her common name, Joan adopted the evocative sobriquet, the Maid, a title that removed her from the everyday and placed her in a celestial realm where she loomed as a prophetic figure of the greatest purity. As we have seen, these very qualities would find an echo in the writings of her learned contemporaries, Gerson and Christine, composed that same summer.

The letter played a pivotal role early in the 1431 trial. During the fifth session of her Interrogation Trial (1 March 1431), the document was read out loud. Joan acknowledged her authorship of the letter, but qualified this by indicating that in three instances the letter they cited contained 'words [that] were not in the letter she sent' (p. 72). These three passages were critical in the case against Joan since they provided evidence of her inappropriate adoption of masculine behaviour and her support of violence over peaceful negotiations. Two of the contested phrases (where she identified herself as captain and as ready to kill) are also of interest because they represent a unique instance where the first-person voice of Joan replaced the third-person account: 'If you refuse this, I am a captain of war, and wherever I find your men in France, I will force them to leave, whether they wish to or not. If they refuse to obey, I will have them all killed. I am sent by God, the King of Heaven, to chase you one and all from France' (p. 134). In denying authorship of the very passage that asserted to be in her voice, Joan introduced the real possibility of deliberate manipulation of her words by others and signals a need to proceed cautiously in interpreting Joan's recorded words as truly her own.

The letter incident is only the first example of Joan confronting her textual self. As the Interrogation continued, she became increasingly aware of the many texts representing her. On 14 March 1431, when enduring her third day of interrogation in the closed quarters of her cell rather than the open courtroom, Joan referred to the scribes in the room recording her answers. Anticipating that she would be sent to Paris for further questioning, Joan requested that a copy of the transcript be made available for her future judges so they could read her past responses (p. 101). The following day, she responded to repetitive questioning by reminding them that she had already answered their questions and that they had access to her words in their 'book': 'You have my answer to this. Read your book very carefully and you will find it' (p. 107). On the same day, she proposed that she would consult with her voices and over the weekend, if a clerk returned, her answers would 'be put into writing' (p. 106). Months later when Joan lay near death, the interrogators arrived at her bedside to read the preliminary list of seventy accusations. Too sick to defend herself, Joan called on her judges to 'read [their] book', which the scribe of the Latin text explained in a marginal comment was a reference to 'the schedule the reverend archdeacon was holding' (p. 171). During the same confrontation, when questioned about her claims of prophecy, Joan declared that her previous statement on this matter stood as 'written in the book' (p. 177). These moments of textual self-awareness reveal Joan taking stock of her status as a textual being – as a subject constructed by these documents. This textual referencing assigned weight to her recorded words and claimed for them an enduring role in assuring that her story would remain alive in written form, but it also introduced a complex and problematic version of auto-citation. Joan's belief that this text was a faithful record of her words led her to understand 'their' book as really her own.

In her final days, Joan's relationship with text would become more circumspect. As is well known, Joan abjured only to recant, claiming that she did not recognize the oath she was said to have taken and signed (p. 196). It is an interesting twist to Joan's story that the oath is not on the official record, instead it references an unrecorded 'text of a certain schedule in French that was read to her, which she pronounced and signed with her own hand' (p. 192). Here we find her accusers quite literally putting words into her mouth that she would first repeat only to later deny as her own. In the end, the record suggestively equates Joan's refusal to accept authorship of this text to signing her death warrant.

If the carefully mediated account of the 1431 trial cannot be said to provide a transparent record of Joan's own words, it certainly testifies to her complex textual existence. The trial reveals that she was conscious of the important role text played in shaping her identity and increasingly aware that she would live on in texts. In recanting her abjuration, Joan's final act was as an author; granted, one who denied a text she had signed. In the brief intervening time before her execution, Joan's textual presence substantially diminished from the court record. In a rare moment in the trial record, Joan's final words before execution were partially recorded in French rather than Latin. She was first cited in French as hesitating over her voices: 'whether good, whether bad spirits, they came to me' (p. 206). But as the bishop continued to interrogate her, Joan would be recorded in Latin as having repeated thrice that she knew herself to have been deceived by her voices. Joan's final words, in the official trial record, show her wavering over the veracity of the voices that had dictated her story from the beginning. In spite of this self-denouncement, this self-erasure, Joan would have many more chances as a literary subject to retell the tale.

Giving voice to Joan

Joan as a textual being whose words shaped her existence – whether declared in letters, linked with prophecies, or recorded in the trial – emerged as a lasting theme over the centuries. Interest in Joan's story never waned, but post-Revolutionary France, where politicians, clerics, and artists struggled to reconstruct a new narrative for the nation, emerged as particularly fertile ground for Johannic literature. Some of the most memorable portrayals of the Maid in modern French literature echo Christine's attraction to a story perceived as not yet told. But what distinguishes this tradition in particular is the fascination with Joan's voice, an interest undoubtedly influenced by Quicherat's edition of the trial. Following the edition, Johannic literature increasingly favoured dialogue over narrative, and we see an important shift towards theatre as a favoured genre for telling Joan's tale.

Charles Péguy looms large in Johannic studies but rarely for the literary experimentation manifest in his haunting portrait of Joan. It is not an exaggeration to claim that Joan converted Péguy first to literature and then to Catholicism. While attending France's prestigious École normale supérieure, the institution that forms future lycée and university teachers, Péguy announced a planned leave of absence so that he could dedicate his full energies to writing the story of his hometown heroine after having read Quicherat's 1849 five-volume work on the trial and most likely Michelet's influential biography of the heroine.[15] Initially intending to write a historical study, Péguy changed course, explaining in a letter to a friend that history writing was not equipped to address Joan's 'inner life'.[16] Experimenting with theatre and poetry, he composed a three-part drama on Joan published in 1897. The play has never been performed in its entirety, in large part because of length (the first edition consisted of 752 pages), but also because of the work's experimental nature. In a rare moment of self-mockery, Péguy wrote a fictional dialogue entitled *Entre deux trains* [*Between Two Trains*] in 1900, in which he imagined two school friends summarizing his first attempt to tell Joan's story. They describe it as 'a drama in three parts that includes an incalculable number of bizarre acts, with ridiculous cues, requiring, all things considered, six or eight hours of performance, a performance that will never happen'.[17] This description only begins to account for this play's experimentation. The 1897 work is an ambitious hybrid theatrical production that mixes prose and alexandrine verse, voice and staged silences, to create a distinctive work that not only registers one of the most sensitive and spiritual accounts of Joan in her own voice, but that breaks with dramatic conventions to question the ability of voice and performance to narrate a life. Georges Bernanos evocatively described Péguy's play as 'Joan of Arc overheard by Péguy'.[18]

Jeanne d'Arc, drame en trois pièces [*Joan of Arc, a Drama in Three Plays*] attempts to tell Joan's full story. Each play shifts to a new town: first Domrémy, where Joan answers her voices; Orléans, the site of her first victory (entitled 'Les Batailles'); and finally Rouen, where she is interrogated.

Careful to recite the key moments in Joan's biography, Péguy's theatre nonetheless favours the heroine's thought process over her action. For example, 'À Domrémy' privileges Joan's internal discussions with God and her voices as well as debates on spiritual matters with the fictional character Mme Gervaise, who represents a spiritual alternative to the church. These reflective moments regularly erupt into alexandrine verse. In fact, by Act III of the 'À Domrémy' play, Joan's inner lyric voice takes centre stage and her poetic meditations will be the text registered in the final two acts (Acts IV and V).

Lyric is further enhanced by repetition and marked silences, a technique Gilles Deleuze interpreted as serving to cultivate interiority and intimacy.[19] In the 1897 play, measured silences, as indicated in the stage directions, enhance the function of repetition in Péguy's writing. Here stage directions regularly interrupt dialogue to introduce moments of silence that are sometimes prescribed as 'brief', 'long', or 'pretty long' (see, for example, 'À Domrémy', Act II, scene iii) or timed pauses between scenes and acts that range from fifteen seconds to twenty minutes.

If Péguy's signature usage of lyric, repetition, and silence serve in the production to bring us closer to Joan through intimate interaction with her thought processes, these techniques eventually signal an impenetrable divide separating Joan from her audience. In ' À Rouen' these same techniques track Joan's progressive fading from view. ' À Rouen' consists of two Parts. Part I, Act I opens with Joan's interrogators discussing her at length before she appears on stage. When she finally enters the courtroom, Joan's silence, prominently indicated in the script by ellipses, dominates the 'dialogue' of Part I, Act I. When she finally begins to speak, Péguy draws her interventions directly from the 1431 trial transcripts. These highly scripted responses introduce a marked degree of repetition; as was the case with the trial, Péguy's Joan is prone to remind repeatedly her judges that some issues 'are not of their concern' ('À Rouen', Part I, Act I). These rote responses join with the signalled silences to create a very different Joan from that witnessed in 'À Domrémy' and 'Les Batailles'. Through repetition of known citations, Joan becomes increasingly distant and the silences emphasize the growing void between the audience and Joan, who is disempowered by the interrogation process. Part I, Acts II to V afford only rare speaking moments to Joan. In this final play, verse rarely appears and when it does, it is Joan's interrogators who control poetic expression. In Part I, Act II, a lyric sermon is delivered in which Joan's eternal damnation is vividly detailed, as are Joan's imagined cries for help in Hell. Master Evrard concludes his threats by informing Joan that her cries will be 'drowned in silence on Waves of Suffering'.[20] It is only after this sermon that Joan's lyric voice re-emerges, but only to register her extended meditation on Evrard's threats; midway through her lament, her guards demand her silence, thereby confirming Evrard's final threat and announcing the end of Part I, Act II. 'À Rouen', Part I, Acts IV and V take place in Joan's prison cell, but she remains silent, uttering only the final line in which she expresses disbelief at her sentence of life imprisonment. When Part II (which is made up of a single act) begins, much has transpired in the interim. This final act concludes with Joan praying before she heads off stage to face her execution. The curtain falls, leaving the audience to contemplate the discrepancies between the scripted account of Joan's life and death, and the intensely intimate scene we have just witnessed. In Péguy's theatrical world, Joan's execution is supplanted by a lasting silence that invites the audience to imagine the appropriate endpoint of her tale.

Writing in the 1950s, Jean Anouilh envisioned a dramatically different theatrical affiliation for Joan in *L'Alouette* [*The Lark*]. In the thirty years following Joan's canonization in 1920, the theatre world experienced a Johannic renaissance: George Bernard Shaw's *St Joan* premiered in 1923; Bertolt Brecht's *Die Heilige Johanna der Schlachthöfe* [*Saint Joan of the Stockyards*] was broadcast in 1932; and Paul Claudel's *Jeanne d'Arc au bûcher* [*Joan of Arc at the Stake*] premiered in 1938. Nonetheless, Anouilh took pains to profess his indifference to this theatrical legacy in a later essay entitled 'An Inexplicable Joy', in which he tells of a village priest who advised him to write about Joan, a summer spent in a country house buttressed against a church, and an attic study where he closed himself off entirely from the world to write his Joan play 'without a plan, without dates, without documents, with my boyhood memories, without anything but an "inexplicable joy"'.[21]

Where Péguy staged her growing silence and the receding trace of her story as a collection of historical events, Anouilh casts Joan as the stage director of her own lived performance. In the process, Anouilh draws our attention to Joan as a literary construction reinvented over time by her public, whether her judges, her comrades in arms, or herself. He casts her in a tragic framework that foregrounds the shared awareness of playwright and audience of her imminent demise. Anouilh's longstanding preoccupation with what he termed the artificial theatre – theatre that is self-consciously aware of its imitation of reality – takes on greater vigour with Joan's performance as both character and director of her life story.

L'Alouette opens with the cast appearing on a stage cluttered with the necessary props to tell Joan's entire story – benches for the trial, a throne for the coronation, and even wood bundled for the execution scene. The inquisitors, the king, fellow soldiers, and family members crowd the stage, ready to intervene in what will become Joan's narration of events, either as performers or as potential directors of events. Warwick, as the representative of the English crown, takes charge from the outset. He confirms the presence of all participants and, like a director, calls for the 'trial' to begin so that they can get to the point of the gathering: 'the faster she is judged and burned, the better it will be'.²² Cauchon, the leading inquisitor, calls for patience, reminding Warwick that 'there is the whole story to play' (p. 9) and 'her whole life to play' (p. 10). To Warwick's complaint that performing all of the battles would take too long, Cauchon pacifies him: 'Put your mind at rest, my Lord, we are too few to play the battles' (p. 11). Cauchon then designates Joan as the principal storyteller and invites her to begin the story as she sees fit. Joan chooses to go further back in time than even Warwick imagined: 'The beginning it is. That is always what is most beautiful: beginnings. At the house of my father, when I was still young. In the field where I looked after the sheep, the first time I heard the Voices' (p. 10). In the absence of available scenery, Joan verbally sets the scene: 'it is after the evening Angelus. I am very young. I still have my braids' (p. 11). When someone from that cast asks 'who is going to be the voice?' (p. 12), Joan assumes the role herself. Following a ventriloquized command from the Archangel that she leave her village (delivered by her in a 'deep voice', p. 13), Joan falls to the ground sobbing before the imaginary Archangel: 'Have pity on me sir! I am just a little girl' (p. 13). But, just as suddenly, Joan breaks character to acknowledge the failure of her performance. Did she sway the Archangel? 'Yeah, right! No pity for me. He was already gone and I had all of France on my back' (p. 14). Taking time to comment on her past performance, Joan entertains the playwright's preoccupation with the artificiality of the theatre experience – a hallmark of Anouilh's drama. But in Joan's own case, this meta-reflective moment brings attention to the enduring struggle in the telling of Joan's story. Where writers have traditionally portrayed Joan as a victim, a puppet of her persecutors, Anouilh created a self-conscious Joan, adept at playing her role, aware of her performance, and, as we shall see, keen on directing events.

In a masterfully staged scene recalling her early encounter with Baudricourt who would eventually lead her to the king's court, Joan casts herself as director and leads the dull-witted squire of Vaucouleurs to assume a new character and to obey her directions. In retelling this key moment in her story, Joan jumps directly to the moment of her private conversation with the squire. When Baudricourt casts about for a fitting narrative to explain Joan, she interrupts his efforts and informs him that he has 'an idea' (p. 41). But such a concept is outside his character and Joan will need to provide the script. 'I have an idea?' he asks (p. 41). Joan assumes his role and informs him of what he is thinking. 'You say to yourself', she begins (p. 42). Having persuaded Baudricourt to play the role she assigns him, she heads off to the king, where she must also direct his performance. When the king enacts the prescribed role she has detailed, Joan breaks out in applause over his performance before his stunned audience (p. 76).

Given the freedom at the outset of the play to tell her own tale, Joan takes full advantage to give the performance of her life. But her stage audience regularly questions her account. The promoter and the inquisitor from the trial regularly point out incriminating remarks. Warwick never tires of calling attention to the time passing: 'If we continue at this speed, we will never arrive at the trial. We will never burn her. Let her play her little story since it seems necessary, but quickly!' (p. 21). Characters also comment on her staging of events. As for the 'scene' with Baudricourt, Cauchon finds it 'a bit crude' while Warwick finds it immensely entertaining (pp. 44–5). And following the encounter with the king, Warwick bursts into laughter, adding 'evidently, in reality, things didn't really happen like that' (p. 77).

Regardless of Joan's efforts to alter or embellish the story, all players as well as the audience know that history cannot be rewritten. Joan thus endures the interrogation to arrive at the scene of her execution – the scene all have been expecting. As the fire is about to be lit, Baudricourt runs to the centre of the stage to call for a stay of execution. He criticizes the absence of the coronation scene in this account, arguing that 'Joan has a right to perform the coronation, it is in her story!' (p. 129). A now silent Joan is guided to her position beside the king while the king is dressed for the coronation. Reproducing the scene made famous in Jean Auguste Dominique Ingres's 1854 portrait of Joan at the coronation, Anouilh's play stalls history, thwarts the tragic conclusion. It is on this scene, 'as in a prize book' (p. 131) offered to schoolchildren, that the final curtain falls.

As with the other writers studied here, Anouilh draws our attention to the deep affinity that writers have had not simply with Joan as a heroine or a muse, but as someone who shared with writers the struggle of telling one's own story, who experienced the risk of narration, and who was forced to accept that her version would not be registered. These writers recognized Joan as a textual being, one created through the writings of others and one often shaped by the words assigned to her. Each writer sought to recreate her silenced story rather than retell the sanctioned account. That these retellings often end with a silenced Joan marks both the promise and limits of the literary imagination: giving voice to Joan opens us to new versions, renews – even if temporarily – hope, calls attention to the invention of history; but what these texts also reveal is how struggling with these issues inevitably leads writers self-consciously to negotiate history and imagination, to make sense not only of her story but of the literary enterprise.

Perhaps Joseph Delteil best summed up the power of Joan when confessing that in envisioning the scene of her execution, she came to inhabit him fully and her story became his own: 'Your eyes stare into the depths of my soul. Your lips are silent, yet my ears are ringing with the sound of your voice ... you live in me, and I in you, and the pages of this book shall preserve us both eternally in one ink and one body!'[23] Joan clearly paved the way for this degree of creative intimacy given her own early awareness of her textual existence. Commanding in the last days of her trial that her interrogators consult 'the book' to find answers to questions already asked, Joan seems to have invited generations of authors to write the book that she believed to exist but whose grand narrative she rejected in her final moments. From a medieval Lombard cleric to Delteil, authors who have tackled the story of Joan may be better understood if we appreciate the abiding need to breathe life into a tale shrouded in secrecy, and silenced from the outset.

NOTES

1. Patrick Gilli, 'L'épopée de Jeanne d'Arc d'après un document italien contemporain: Édition et traduction de la lettre du pseudo-Barbaro (1429)', *Bulletin de l'Association des amis du Centre Jeanne d'Arc*, 20 (1996), 4–26 (p. 18). My translation. Subsequent references to Latin text indicated by page number in the text.

2. Qtd in Michel Winock, 'Joan of Arc', in *Realms of Memory: The Construction of the French Past*, ed. Pierre Nora and trans. Arthur Goldhammer (New York: Columbia University Press, 1998), pp. 433–82 (pp. 467–8).

3. From Péguy's letter to Camille Bidault dated 1895. Qtd in Bernard Guyon, *Péguy devant Dieu* (Paris: Desclée de Brouwer, 1974), p. 45. My translation.

4. On the textual witnesses, see Daniel Hobbins, ed. and trans., *The Trial of Joan of Arc* (Cambridge, MA: Harvard University Press, 2005), pp. 9–13.

5. Deborah A. Fraoli, *Joan of Arc: The Early Debate* (Woodbridge: Boydell, 2000), p. 209.

6. Fraoli, *Joan of Arc*, p. 209.

7. Fraoli, *Joan of Arc*, pp. 211–12.

8. Fraoli, *Joan of Arc*, p. 210.

9. Christine de Pizan, *Ditié de Jehanne d'Arc*, ed. Angus J. Kennedy and Kenneth Varty (Oxford: Society for the Study of Medieval Languages and Literature, 1977), stanza 2. Stanza numbers are henceforth given in parentheses in the text.

10. On Christine's use of Joan to establish her own prophetic voice, see Anne D. Lutku and Julia M. Walker, 'PR pas PC: Christine de Pizan's Pro-Joan Propaganda', in *Fresh Verdicts on Joan of Arc*, ed. Bonnie Wheeler and Charles T. Wood (New York: Garland, 1999), pp. 145–60.

11. Kevin Brownlee, 'Structures of Authority in Christine de Pizan's *Ditié de Jehanne d'Arc*', in *The Selected Writings of Christine de Pizan*, ed. and trans. Renate

Blumenfeld-Kosinski and Kevin Brownlee (New York: Norton, 1997), pp. 371–90.

12. Citations are, respectively, from Jelle Koopmans, 'Jeanne d'Arc auteur de sa propre légende', in *Jeanne d'Arc entre les nations*, ed. Ton Hoenselaars and Jelle Koopmans (Amsterdam: Rodopi, 1998), pp. 5–15 (p. 8), and Jean-Pierre Barricelli, 'Transcript, Legend, and Art: The Thematology of Joan of Arc', *Canadian Review of Comparative Literature* 88 (1988), 176–200 (p. 179). See also Barbara A. Hanawalt and Susan Noakes, 'Trial Transcript, Romance, Propaganda: Joan of Arc and the French Body Politic', *Modern Language Quarterly* 57.4 (1996), 605–31 (pp. 613–14).

13. See Daniel Hobbins, *The Trial of Joan of Arc* (Cambridge, MA: Harvard University Press, 2005). For a discussion of the various extant trial versions, see pp. 7–13.

14. Hobbins, *The Trial of Joan of Arc*, p. 51. Hobbins' translation referenced hereafter in the text by page number.

15. See Albert Béguin, 'Jeanne d'Arc écoutée par Péguy', in *Mémorial du ve centenaire de la réhabilitation de Jeanne d'Arc, 1456–1956* (Paris: Forêt, 1958), pp. 47–58.

16. Guyon, *Péguy*, p. 45.

17. Charles Péguy, *Entre deux trains*, in *Œuvres en prose complètes*, vol. 1, ed. Robert Burac (Paris: Gallimard, 1987), pp. 495–526 (p. 509). My translation.

18. Albert Béguin, 'Jeanne d'Arc écoutée par Péguy', p. 47. My translation.

19. Gilles Deleuze, *Différence et répétition* (Paris: Presses Universitaires de France, 1993), pp. 34 and 373.

20. Charles Péguy, *Œuvres poétiques complètes*, ed. Marcel Péguy (Paris: Gallimard, 1957, rpt. 1975), 'À Rouen', Part 1, Act 11, p. 302. My translation.

21. Pol Vandromme, *Un auteur et ses personnages: Essai suivi d'un recueil de textes critiques de Jean Anouilh* (Paris: Table Ronde, 1965), p. 221. My translation.

22. Jean Anouilh, *L'Alouette*, in *Pièces costumées* (Paris: Table Ronde, 2008), pp. 7–131 (p. 9). Subsequent references to original are indicated by page number in the text. Translations are my own.

23. Joseph Delteil, *Joan of Arc*, trans. Malcolm Cowley (London: Allen & Unwin, 1926), p. 259.

3

MARC BIZER

Poetry and modernity

In *Dead Poets Society*, Peter Weir's 1989 film, John Keating, a private-school English teacher intent on awakening his pupils from their bourgeois slumber and inspiring in them a love of poetry, asks one class, 'Language was developed for one endeavour, and that is?' The first student questioned draws a blank, and the second answers, unimaginatively, 'to communicate', to which Keating replies, 'No! To woo women.' In another scene, apparently set in the school chapel, he has his pupils recite a poem by Robert Herrick, 'To the Virgins to Make Much of Time', which Keating uses to give his students a portentous lesson about living their lives wisely.

Such a reference to popular American film is not as incongruous as it might seem. The first question it raises is one of accessibility. Keating's students initially bemoan the fact that they will have to read William Shakespeare; first mimicking an overly austere British acting tradition, their teacher then quickly captivates them with renditions of Macbeth by Marlon Brando and John Wayne, actors whom the students admire. More importantly, writers from the Renaissance (albeit the English one) figure prominently in the film: Shakespeare of course appears front and centre here, but so too does John Milton's contemporary Herrick – whose poem 'To the Virgins to Make Much of Time' strikingly echoes the ode 'Mignonne, allons voir si la rose' ['Darling Let Us See If the Rose'] by an illustrious sixteenth-century French predecessor, Pierre de Ronsard. The English and French Renaissances were hardly separate phenomena, and French influences frequently carried over into the English Renaissance which came later. Finally, like a great deal of Renaissance literature, but perhaps a little less self-consciously, the film peddles clichés. First Keating tries to transform the theme of *carpe diem*, which appears in the Roman poet Horace and returns in Herrick's and Ronsard's poems, from a poetic commonplace into a heavy message for his pupils, whom he is trying to keep from becoming carbon copies of their parents. Then, even more boldly, he teaches them that poetry can be an instrument of seduction.

Thus, the film asks questions pertinent to this essay. How can French Renaissance poetry be made accessible to a general, literate public today? What are its typical subjects? This last question, not usually asked of modern writers, hints at a chasm between early modern and post-Romantic literature. Like Keating's pupils, today the eyes of general readers tend to glaze over at the mention of poetry in general – let alone Renaissance verse – because it seems so hopelessly arcane, difficult, removed from everyday speech and thought. Indeed, to a certain extent that is true, and the situation is aggravated precisely because poetry was as prominent in the Renaissance as it is marginalized today. The practice of poetry was deemed essential to most fields of knowledge, and most thinkers, scholars, and political figures of the period wrote poetry and saw themselves as poets.[1] Poetry was not merely associated with private reading but also with public spaces: celebrating noble births, commemorating royal entries into towns and cities, lampooning public figures during the Wars of Religion. But we are less familiar, less intimate with poetry not only because it is removed from our daily experience, but also because the creative processes underlying it have changed. Far from seeking to be original (the concept of originality was not applicable to literature until the eighteenth century), Renaissance poets generally took the road more travelled, as it provided security and authority and an audience. That meant borrowing both topics and phrasing from others, most often predecessors (especially the Ancients or the Italians). In addition, as in earlier times, poets tended to adopt masks – malleable, interchangeable ones, to be sure (the word *persona* derives from a Latin word meaning to give forth sound through a mask) – and often played with roles. While, for us, choosing a well-trodden path in terms of subject, expression, and tradition itself would not seem to leave much margin for writerly freedom, for Renaissance poets and writers in general, it meant having access to a toolbox well stocked with conventions, themes, and turns of phrase; for them, mastery of poetry implied proficiency in the art of variation, and a poet's virtuosity could be measured in terms of how skilfully he or she accommodated the constraints and how deftly he or she handled the tools available. In writing verse, then, French Renaissance poets established three types of connections: with their addressees, with earlier writers and sources, and also with contemporary poets, the community of writers who shared the toolbox and with whom they were often competing.

It is commonly thought that the Renaissance was hastened in France as a result of exposure to Italy's earlier (and mature) Renaissance during the invasion of Italy by Charles VIII's armies in the mid 1490s. However, it is François Ier, crowned in 1515, who was celebrated by poets and writers as having restored literature and culture, in part by establishing royal lectureships in Greek, Hebrew, and Latin, which upset the monopoly of the University of Paris, a faculty of theology. Much of the period was, however, deeply marked and brought to a close by the devastating Wars of Religion between Catholics and Protestants, which Henri IV ended with the Edict of Nantes (1589). Between these dates, verse evolved greatly, as did the manner in which poets saw and presented their work. In addition, our evaluation of the respective worth of these different poets has also changed over time in accordance with differing critical ideologies. For example, the Grands Rhétoriqueurs – a series of poets who wrote at the Burgundian and Flemish courts, and who displayed considerable technical virtuosity through word-play but also through acrostics and the physical disposition of their verse (by having lines pictorially resemble the subjects) – were later denigrated as mere scribes lacking imagination. They were rehabilitated in the 1970s when literary criticism took a more linguistically, structurally oriented turn. From within the Rhétoriqueurs emerged the first significant vernacular figure of the French Renaissance, the Protestant poet Clément Marot (son of the Grand Rhétoriqueur Jean Marot), who was involved in such typical huma-nist activities as translation and literary imitation of classical and Italian models. The later Pléiade poets sought to hide their debt to Marot, perhaps in part because he was a transitional figure who wrote poems that did not fit into their new canon of approved ancient genres. Marot himself was con-scious of the winds of change, and thus he rebaptized some of his poems, first published as *Chansons* [*Songs*], a genre associated with the Middle Ages, as epigrams, a typically prestigious poetic form carrying an ancient cachet that was now a sign of fashionable modernity. Marot was an extremely versatile poet whose translations of the Psalms brought him lasting fame, but he is also known for his witty epistles. For example, he wrote verse letters to the king requesting help while making light of the serious difficulties he faced during the nascent religious conflict, such as being sent to prison for eating meat during Lent. This 1527 epistle ends with a conceit typical of epigrams:

> Treshumblement requerant vostre grâce,
> De pardonner à ma trop grand audace
> D'avoir empris ce sot Escript vous faire:
> Et m'excusez, si pour le mien affaire
> Je ne suis point vers vous allé parler:
> Je n'ay pas eu le loysir d'y aller.

> [Very humbly requesting help from Your Grace
> Though it really wasn't my place
> To have undertaken this silly ditty;
> Yet I beg you to take pity,

For to visit you I haven't had the pleasure
Because life hasn't given me the leisure.][2]

This epistle highlights how effective poetry could be – for in an age when letters were the primary means of communication, witty verse could liberate a person from incarceration. Letter writing experienced a rebirth in the Renaissance, and, accordingly, verse letters or epistles were an exceedingly popular and important poetic form to which Marot contributed a great deal. His most lasting legacy may have been the greater presence of the poet in his or her work as a result of the Protestant emphasis on the believing individual and her or his individual faith.

A vulgarizer in the best sense of the term, Marot translated some of the love sonnets of Petrarch, the renowned fourteenth-century Italian humanist who had rediscovered Cicero's letters, and who so felt the aching loss of the Ancients that he wrote fictive letters to (among others) Cicero, Virgil, Horace, and Homer. Petrarch had bet his future on his Latin writings, which included an incomplete epic; posterity instead fell in love with his vernacular lyric poetry written in Italian, the sonnets of the *Canzoniere*, which are devoted to his unrequited love for a woman, Laura, whom he may have glimpsed in an Avignon church in April 1327. While Petrarch continues the lineage of love poets lamenting a beautiful and unyielding lady, what is new is Petrarch's extraordinarily careful assemblage of 366 poems, which he called 'scattered rhymes' ('rime sparse'), that transform a threatening female absence into a coherent, stable, presence. The first poem of the *Canzoniere* is a preface encapsulating the love experience as a 'youthful error', evoking the antithetical experience of both 'vain hopes' and 'vain sorrow'. The myth of Apollo's pursuit of the mortal Daphne and her transformation into a laurel bush takes on an iconic status to describe the inaccessibility and fugacity of the beloved. While this clever repurposing of an often-represented mythological scene implied Petrarch's own striving for poetic glory (since Apollo was the patron of poets), what really caught the attention of future poets was the stylistic convention of the antithesis, the use of the oxymoron to suggest the contradictory torments felt by the poet in love. Sonnet 134 deserves to be cited in its entirety:

> Peace I find not, nor must I wage war;
> and I fear, and hope, and burn, and freeze;
> and fly over heaven and lie on the earth;
> grasp nothing, and yet embrace the world.
>
> Prisoner of one who neither opens nor locks me,
> neither claims nor releases me;
> Love does not slay me yet does not loose me,
> does not wish me live nor frees me from the net.

I see without eyes, and shout without a tongue;
and long to die yet call for help;
and hate myself and love another.

I eat pain, laugh while weeping;
both death and life offend me.
I am in this state, Lady, for you.[3]

It is difficult for us to imagine the impact of Petrarch's model, but for centuries thereafter, fledgling poets across Europe would imitatively complain of their heartless, mute beloved while using similar oxymora.

When the Lyonnais poet Maurice Scève claimed in 1533 to have uncovered Laura's tombstone, it set off a sensation in France. The location and time could not have been better chosen. Ever since the Italian wars, Italy had loomed large in the conscience of French writers and poets, and its culture – and literature in particular – elicited great envy. The Renaissance had quickly arrived in Lyon: on a major route from Italy towards the north, the city had received the technological revolution of the printing press earlier than the rest of France, and its poets were eager to shine. In 1544, Scève published his *Délie* (1544), adopting for this collection of ten-line poems what has been called a Petrarchan 'idiom' to describe his love for a woman who may have been another Lyonnais poet, Pernette Du Guillet.[4] However, she remains as obscure and unapproachable as Petrarch's Laura, and, indeed, Scève elevates her to another level by calling her 'Délie', an anagram of 'l'idée'. This form of idealization draws upon another crucial Renaissance poetic tradition, that of Neo-Platonism, which sought to reconcile terrestrial love, seen as idolatrous, with yearning for the Creator. At the outset of his *Délie*, Scève links his work to Petrarch's by playing on the word 'error', which now means less an experience to be ashamed of than a youthful vulnerability on the one hand,[5] and, on the other, the reflection of a sort of aspiration to a polished, diamond-like quality accompanied by an expression of poetic modesty in the prefatory poem to *Délie*.[6] Scève's extremely 'hard', hermetic epigrams work within the conventions of the Petrarchan idiom, yet his language and images are combined in ways uniquely his own, as evidenced by these lines in poem 129 about the beloved's departure:

Car dès le poinct, que partie tu fus,
Comme le Lieure accroppy en son giste,
Ie tendz l'oreille, oyant vn bruyt confus,
Tout esperdu aux tenebres d'Egypte.[7]

[For the moment you left,
Like the Hare crouched in its seat,

I strain my ear, hearing muffled steps,
Stunned by the darkness over Egypt.][8]

Finally, Scève's work is influenced by the Renaissance tradition of the emblem-book: pictorial illustrations accompanied by a saying or proverb. There are emblems to introduce a prominent theme of each of the forty-nine groups of nine ten-line poems (making up a total of 449). Scève thus indulged the Renaissance readers' love for images and text, an adult pleasure that has today largely been relegated to the graphic novel.

The third poet from Lyon writing in the Petrarchan vein, Louise Labé, who published her own collection of Petrarchan poetry in 1555, has been controversial both in the sixteenth century and in our own time: then, because as a bourgeois woman writing about feminine desire, she came across as licentious, although her preface exhorts 'vertueuses Dames d'eslever un peu leurs esprits par-dessus leur quenoilles et fuseaus'[9] [virtuous women to lift their heads a little above their spinning wheels] and set themselves to writing now that men no longer deny women access to knowledge and learning; now, because in 2006, Mireille Huchon, a scholar of the French Renaissance from the Sorbonne, wrote a book denying that the historical figure Labé had written the poetry attributed to her: her persona was, according to Huchon, a 'paper creature', the invention of a group of male poets including Scève himself. Thus, in a twist, the distant, obscure beloved woman of male Petrarchan poetry, who in a thrilling reversal had become a poetess desiring a mute, unresponsive man, was, in a sense, suddenly unmasked as a man by a female scholarly critic. Labé's authorial status may never be definitively proven, but what remains fascinating in the writings attributed to her is the overturning of the Petrarchan idiom, in a similar vein to, but more boldly than Pernette Du Guillet. Thus, in Labé's sonnet 8, it is the poetess who burns of fire and ice, incarnating a new Daphne: she declares 'je sèche et je verdoie' (l. 8) [I wither and I become verdant]. Sonnet 7 develops a Neo-Platonic conceit where Labé calls her beloved her 'soul' without which she (the body) will soon die unless the male beloved reacts more favourably towards her. Lastly, sonnet 10 subverts the playful objectification of women as mere body parts. Labé here responds to a male-authored collection of poetry, *Les Blasons anatomiques du corps féminin* [*The Anatomical Blazons of the Feminine Body*] (1536). In witty verse, physical attractiveness and even musical talent are dismissed as irrelevant in the face of omnipotent love. While attempts to define 'feminine writing' can often involve hopelessly circular reasoning, in this instance, the strongly gendered conventions of Petrarchan love poetry – indeed of love poetry in general – allowed any poet to readily assume 'male' and 'female' roles. However, it also meant that any love poetry inescapably reacted to and even rendered homage to the conventions and idioms created by men.

Pierre de Ronsard was the sixteenth century's most famous and prolific poet. Born in the Vendôme area in France, he was blessed with good connections in addition to nobility. He served as a page to François Ier, and then went to Paris where he studied under the famous scholar of Greek Jean Dorat with Jean-Antoine de Baïf and Joachim Du Bellay, who would become key members of the Pléiade group of poets. By the mid 1550s, Ronsard had published five books of odes and several books of sonnets (he would go on to master ancient genres such as the eclogue, the hymn, and the elegy). Ronsard adopted, as did Scève in *Délie*, the long-standing Latin tradition of love poetry devoted to one lady – with the difference that over the course of his career, there were three beloveds: Cassandra, Marie, and Helen. Rather than signifying fickleness, the three women represented, more than anything, different styles. The first lady, the Cassandra of *Les Amours de Cassandre* [*The Loves of Cassandra*], harkened back to the priestess Cassandra of the Trojan War, and in accordance with the latter's prophetic speech is associated with more erudite, obscure verse. Even within this first style, the love sonnets, numbering in the hundreds, are remarkable examples of variation, drawing from Greek, Latin, and Italian models, incorporating Neo-Platonic and Petrarchan themes, yet they eschew the reserve usually associated with such topics. Indeed, the first edition of the *Amours* from 1552 is placed under the sign of amorous passion, since it depicts on its frontispiece both Ronsard and Cassandra glancing at each other on facing pages with inscriptions in Greek and Latin respectively, stating 'When I saw her, I lost my mind' and 'She both caught and was caught.' More often than not, Ronsard dives fully into a sensual verve, imagining himself here as Jupiter gaining access to Danaë:

> Je vouldroy bien richement jaunissant
> En pluye d'or goute à goute descendre
> Dans le beau sein de ma belle Cassandre,
> Lors qu'en ses yeulx le somme va glissant.[10]

> [I'd like to turn the deepest of yellows
> Falling, drop by drop, in a golden shower,
> Into the beautiful bosom of my lovely Cassandra,
> As sleep is stealing over her brow.]

Subsequent stanzas compare the poet to Jupiter transformed into a bull in order to seduce Europe, and, as Narcissus plunging into Cassandra, imagined as a fountain. As this sonnet 20 suggests, Ronsard also had a streak of cruelty (not to mention misogyny). Indeed, in one of his most famous odes illustrating the cliché of *carpe diem* – the poem that doubtless inspired the John Herrick piece recited in *Dead Poets Society* – Ronsard constructs a syllogism proving to Cassandra that she should yield to the poet before she withers like the rose whose fading he invites her to consider:

> Mignonne, allon voir si la rose
> Qui se matin avait declose
> Sa robe de pourpre, au soleil,
> A point perdu, cette vesprée,
> Les plis de sa robe pourprée
> Et son teint au vostre pareil.[11]

> [Darling, let us see if the rose
> that this morning had opened
> its scarlet dress in the sun,
> has lost, at vespers,
> the folds of its scarlet dress,
> and its colour, to yours identical.]

This poem has found its way into the popular, even commercial imagination: in a modern reversal, an enterprising French underwear company decorated Parisian bus stops with posters of a young woman wearing rose-printed underwear, inviting men with a bold 'Mignon, allons voir si la rose. . .'.

As already mentioned, Ronsard was a member of the Pléiade, a group of poets claiming to introduce a new kind of verse largely based on classical models that would bring glory to the king and to France. The wealth of mythological imagery in the sonnet 'Je voudrais bien richement iaunissant' ['I'd like to turn the deepest of yellows'] and Ronsard's use of the genre of the ode were consistent with the Pléiade's vision of the poet as both divinely inspired and deeply erudite. Accordingly, Ronsard's early work was met with a kind of consecration formerly reserved only for classical poets writing in Greek and Latin: the humanist Marc-Antoine de Muret undertook to make the learnedness of *Les Amours de Cassandre* more accessible to Ronsard's readership by publishing a commentary which not only explained, for example, the mythological name 'Cassandre' as 'daughter of Priam, king of the Trojans', but also highlighted – adding to the cachet of Ronsard's verse – the borrowings from others such as Petrarch and Anacreon. Soon afterwards, the Pléiade poet Rémy Belleau also wrote a commentary on Ronsard's *Amours* (the second book), sympathetically explaining in great detail the poet's motives and emotions.

It is noteworthy that just as Ronsard offered to make Cassandra (and later, Helen) famous through his poetry, he also claimed to have done the same for the landscapes of his native region (particularly the Gâtine forest), a place of refuge from the difficulties of contemporary life. Yet he was very much engaged in the politics of his time, siding with the Catholics during the Wars of Religion by writing the long poems known as the 'Discours sur les misères de ce temps' ['Discourses on the Miseries of Our Time']. He is also known for the *Franciad*, an epic that he never finished. The Pléiade had made the writing of the 'long French poem' or epic one of the mainstays of its programme, and after he was named the official royal poet, Ronsard struggled in his epic to retell the Trojan origins of the French monarchy, just as Virgil had done with Augustus. He only wrote four books out of the projected twenty-four, complaining that the king insisted he include all sixty-three royal predecessors. The *Franciad* was published in 1572, a month after the St Bartholomew's Day massacre of French Protestants that ushered in the worst years of the Wars of Religion; and thus it is an ironic twist that the epic, designed to help unify French Protestants and Catholics by celebrating their common origins, remained incomplete.

Joachim Du Bellay, born in Liré near Angers in the Loire Valley, was another important Pléiade poet, distinguished as the author of the *Défense et illustration de la langue française* [*Defence and Enrichment of the French Language*] (1549), the manifesto setting forth the group's raison d'être and founding principles. The *Défense* was a testament to a French cultural inferiority complex with respect to Italy: Du Bellay explains that France had fallen behind because the French had preferred great deeds to great works. The *Défense* also manifests the Pléiade's arrogance (in the chapter 'Des Poëtes Françoys' ['On French Poets'], he states that only the Greeks and Romans are worthy of imitation[12]). It seems somewhat hastily composed and rather derivative, having been cobbled together from passages translated almost word for word from Quintilian, Horace, Cicero, and the author of a similar treatise written for Italian literature, Sperone Speroni. But it made a name for Du Bellay, drew attention to the group that identified itself mainly as the 'Brigade' and later became known as the 'Pléiade' (after the constellation and a celebrated group of Alexandrian poets in antiquity), and provoked the ire of contemporaries, particularly those favouring the poetry of Marot, whose advocate Thomas Sébillet had published an *Art poétique* championing rather different principles only a year earlier. Du Bellay's own poetry first appeared that same year and the next: his *Olive*, a collection of 'love' sonnets devoted to a protectress, Marguerite de Valois, daughter of Henri II, was of Neo-Platonic and Petrarchan inspiration, typical of a new poet earning his stripes. But aside from some other minor poetry and a translation of the fourth book of Virgil's *Aeneid*, what is most notable in Du Bellay's early work is that in 1552 he published a satirical poem 'Contre les Petrarquistes'

['Against the Petrarchists'] that foreswore Petrarchan poetry, denouncing it as false, feigned, and fictitious. The poem is at the same time a hilarious send-up of the themes and language of Petrarchan poetry (and a sonnet of his own *Olive*, in the final stanza), as if Du Bellay wanted to display his mastery of the genre before repudiating it.

At this time the poet had the opportunity to be a Secretary as part of the diplomatic mission of a distant cousin, Cardinal Jean Du Bellay, with whom Joachim left in 1553 to go to Rome. His decision was doubtless motivated both by ambition and longing. On the one hand, Du Bellay was part of a new generation of aristocrats who sought a career in the service of the French monarchy. On the other, the voyage to Rome, a 'return' to the city and civilization representing the humanists' cultural and historical legacy, was itself almost a commonplace of humanist literature. Upon arrival, Du Bellay professed disappointment on at least two counts: his disenchantment at finding only the ruins of Rome is the subject of the thirty-two sonnets of the *Antiquitez de Rome* [*Roman Antiquities*]; his dismay with Roman and papal life forms the basis for the 191 sonnets of the *Regrets*. More significant is what both collections represent in terms of the evolution of lyric poetry in the period. While the *Antiquitez* is a compilation in French of lugubrious lamentations commonly found in Renaissance Latin verse on the causes of the fall of Rome and the chasm between the grandeur of ancient Rome and Rome's present state, an important study has shown that Du Bellay continued to use the language of Petrarchan love poetry and treated Rome as an 'imperial mistress' in composing the collection.[13] The *Regrets*, which provide snapshots of both contemporary Roman life and the poet's state of mind, are astounding because of the multi-layered contradictions and contrasts on which they are based. While Ronsard had sought the high ground in his poetry, Du Bellay staked out the middle and low – indeed, the prosaic – in verse described self-deprecatingly as 'journals' and 'ledgers'; yet Du Bellay dares to compare his travails to those of Odysseus and Jason, the latter having been lucky to return home, 'plein d'usage & raison, / Vivre entre ses parents le reste de son aage' [full of experience and wisdom, / spending with his kin the rest of his life].[14] However, it took Odysseus twenty years, and Du Bellay only four.

Du Bellay's explicit forerunner in the *Regrets* is the Roman poet Ovid, who wrote exile poetry from the Black Sea (some in the language of the natives, the Geti), yet Du Bellay paradoxically dares to liken his stay in the Eternal City to 'exile' – and when he returns to France and re-experiences court culture, he declares to his former teacher Jean Dorat that he wishes to go back to Rome. In an especially plaintive sonnet, he claims to have been abandoned by 'France mere des arts, des armes, & des loix' [France, mother of arts, war, and laws[15]] (sonnet 9, l. 1), leaving him like a sheep left in a windy, cold field subject to the threat of wolves, an injustice because, as he concludes, 'si ne suis-je pourtant le pire du troppeau' [yet I am not, of all your flock, the worst] (l.14).[16] Du Bellay consistently underscores how his cares and his mundane responsibilities sap his inspiration and make it impossible for him to write poetry; yet the stay corresponds to the most fertile period in Du Bellay's life.

In addition to the *Antiquitez* and the *Regrets*, he composed the *Poemata* (Latin verse) and the *Divers Jeux rustiques*. The sonnet, traditionally a vehicle for amorous sentiment, is used by Du Bellay for wide variety of purposes: lamentations (elegy), satire (the most vehement of which were published on a special insert included with the first edition of the *Regrets* in 1558, yet not again before the nineteenth century), currying favour with patrons, and addressing contemporaries. Indeed, while the love sonnet always had epistolary functions, under Du Bellay's plume the sonnet becomes a formidable instrument for building community, addressing fellow poets and secretaries, and in general maintaining relationships with like-minded men. Building on Marot's use of the epistle, the sonnets of Du Bellay's *Regrets* are in effect verse letters to which other poets sometimes respond in their own works. Thus one of Du Bellay's most frequent addressees – none other than Ronsard himself – emerges as a friendly rival, one portrayed as benefiting from the patronage of the king and important figures at court, but more wittily (and critically) as a poet 'stuck' in the genre of love poetry ('Jamais ne voira-on, que Ronsard amoureux?' [Will one see Ronsard as anything but a love poet?], sonnet 23) and unable to move forward with his *Franciad*, for his Francus (the eponymous hero of the epic) 'est encore pourtant sur le Troien ravage, / Aussi crois-je (Ronsard) quil n'en partit jamais' [is still on the Trojan banks, and I think, then, Ronsard, that he'll never leave].

Sonnet 31, in which Du Bellay claims to surpass Odysseus (and Jason) in the misfortune of exile, is one of the most famous French poems of all time, learned by most French schoolchildren with the aim of instilling national pride. Its second stanza goes:

> Quand revoiray-je, helas, de mon petit village
> Fumer la cheminee, & en quelle saison,
> Revoiray-je le clos de ma pauvre maison,
> Qui m'est une province, & beaucoup d'avantage?   (l. 5–8)

> [When will I see, alas, of my little village
> The chimney smoking, and in what season,
> Will I see the enclosed field of my poor house,
> Which to me is a province, and a great deal more?][17]

The next two stanzas establish the poet's paradoxical preference for the simple slate roofs of his native Anjou over the marble palaces of Rome:

> Plus me plaist le sejour qu'ont basty mes ayeux,
> Que des palais Romains le front audacieux,
> Plus que le marbre dur me plaist l'ardoise fine:
> Plus mon Loyre Gaulois, que le Tybre Latin,
> Plus mon petit Lyré, que le mont Palatin,
> Et plus que l'air marin la douceur angevine.   (ll. 9–14)

> [More pleasing to me is the house that my ancestors built,
> Than of the Roman palaces the imposing façade,
> More than hard marble pleases me fine slate:
> More my Gallic Loire, than the Latin Tiber,
> More my little Liré, than the Palatine hill,
> And more than the sea air the sweetness of Anjou.]

Yet rather than being formative of a French national identity as intended by the modern French ministry of education, Du Bellay's sonnet trumpets a *regional* identity, a homesickness for the village where he was born. It is all the more surprising, then, that in 2007, a French singer going by the name of Ridan (the anagram of his real first name, 'Nadir') recorded an album entitled 'L'Ange de mon démon' which included a rendition of this very poem entitled 'Ulysse', to which he adds some lines of his own creation that confuse, perhaps intentionally, the Sirens of Homer's *Odyssey* with the sirens of French police cars. The irony of a singer of North African origin, a *beur*, appropriating a sonnet by a French aristocrat should not be lost, let alone his use of Du Bellay's theme of alienation when Ridan may be ambivalent about calling France 'home'. Perhaps his homage to and affinity for Du Bellay consists of maintaining the same sorts of paradoxes.

One of Du Bellay's exchanges with Ronsard included lively banter about Du Bellay changing languages. The fact that we tend to forget – that Du Bellay's poetic production in Rome included two volumes of Latin poetry – should alert us to the stakes of literary history, particularly as it is written in modern universities, which tend to separate modern and classical languages into different departments. Vernacular and Latin literacy were very much complementary and parallel in the French Renaissance, with Latin being the lingua franca, the language understood by all learned people throughout Europe. It is true that many poets opted for either Latin or for French. An early sixteenth-century poet by the name of Salmon Macrin wrote almost exclusively in Latin, as in the case of his erotic poetry to his wife Gelonis, and other poets, notably Ronsard, composed almost exclusively in French, although the latter certainly had the ability to write Latin verse. Despite the remarkable progress of the vernacular in all areas (in 1539, the Edict of Villers-Cotterêts had made French the sole administrative language of the entire kingdom at the expense of regional languages and Latin), Latin retained a certain cachet: the Pléiade poet Rémy Belleau actually translated some of Ronsard's sonnets into Latin in order to honour him, and the perception that the language conferred immortality on all that was written in it explains why Belleau would eventually translate his own French poetry into Latin, signifying a new-found confidence in his identity as a writer. In his *Défense*, Du Bellay had condemned those poets who eschewed French in favour of Latin, the more prestigious of the two, as being 'whitewashers', always at a disadvantage with respect to their models, but Du Bellay was unabashedly a bilingual poet who often wrote poems on similar topics in both French and Latin. Accordingly, in Latin he wrote a long poem entitled 'Desiderium patriae' ['Longing for One's Country'] that encapsulates many prominent themes from the *Antiquitez* and the *Regrets*. In addition, the Latin poems are mostly addressed to the same people as Du Bellay's French sonnets: Ronsard, Jean de Morel, other Pléiade poets, or people close to the Pléiade, such as Dorat. Yet one did not pass between Latin and French with impunity. It was more challenging to distinguish oneself in a language such as Latin whose literary conventions and traditions were even better defined than those of French – and even bilingual writers recognized that their mastery of Latin was impeded by the fact that they had not, as they put it, sucked the language with their mother's milk. In writing the *Poemata*, Du Bellay was nevertheless aware of being personally in contradiction with his defence of vernacular poetry. The first time, he explains, somewhat laboriously and obliquely in Latin, that in Rome and far from France, Latin makes sense. The second time, in a witty epigram introducing a section of his *Poemata*, Du Bellay compares his French muse to a wife and the Latin muse to a mistress: the former, with whom he has produced bountiful offspring, is associated with duty, but the latter with pleasure. This poem introduces a cycle of love poems about and to a certain Faustina, but the real subject of his poetry is the conventions of Latin love poetry (elegy) itself. Du Bellay's Latin poetry doesn't have the same ease as his best French verse, seems more heavily indebted to sources (perhaps in part because they are more easily identifiable without a change of language), and for the same reason tends to highlight the processes that produced it. In Latin, Du Bellay was, in a sense, in love with writing love poetry, but in French he borrowed its conventions, language, and even its preferred vernacular form, the sonnet, in order to evoke his relationship with places: Liré, France, Rome. In these peregrinations between French and Latin, France and Rome, home and not-home, lyric and satire, praise and blame; in giving voice to a richly conflicted identity in his Roman poetry; Du Bellay demonstrates one of the quintessential characteristics of the Renaissance writer: namely, the versatility of the self. At the same time, his conscious development of a poetic voice across two languages, his awareness of self-contradiction and his practice of self-parody constitute an example of fluid personal identity that is strikingly modern.

We have spoken of the longing to write an epic to anchor France (and its king) in an ancient, mythical past and of Ronsard's *Franciad* which not only could not be completed, but was a failed attempt to unify France on the basis of that past. France's most successful epic would come from the protestant Agrippa d'Aubigné, whose *Tragiques*, published anonymously in 1616, depict the persecution of French Protestants in biblical terms. Aubigné, too, began his poetic career by writing Petrarchan love verse (dedicated to the niece of Ronsard's Cassandra) that already relied on unusually violent metaphors:

> J'ouvre mon estommac, une tumbe sanglante
> De maux enseveliz: pour Dieu, tourne tes yeux,
> Diane, et voy au fond mon cueur party en deux
> Et mes poumons gravez d'une ardeur viollente.[18]

> [I open up my bosom, a bloody tomb
> of hidden troubles; in God's name, turn your gaze,
> Diana, et look in the depths at my heart split in two
> And my lungs marked by violent passion.]

It is significant that Aubigné frames the beginning of the first of seven books of the *Tragiques*, 'Miseries', as a turning away from his earlier love poetry; another sort of fury inspires him – indignation – and thus Ronsard's crystal fountains are replaced by streams 'rouges de noz morts' [red with our dead].[19] At the same time, his long epic draws in part on the already transformed love lyric of his predecessors: his description of France as 'une mere affligee', an afflicted mother unable to nurse her Esau (the Catholics) and Jacob (the Protestants) with anything but blood surely owes a great deal to Du Bellay's sonnet beginning 'France mere des arts, des armes, & des loix'.[20] The female body is no longer playfully divided into parts by male poets, but rather torn asunder by the king's warring subjects.

Ronsard may never have transcended the genre of love poetry to the extent that Du Bellay did, but he clearly (and cruelly) emphasized in the Petrarchan and Neo-Platonic worldviews the presence of the ephemeral in the eternal. This preoccupation with the contingent was key to the notion of modernity as defined by the nineteenth-century symbolist poet Charles Baudelaire, who, in his essay 'Le Peintre de la vie moderne' ['The Painter of Modern Life'], observed of the painter Constantin Guys: 'Il a cherché partout la beauté passagère, fugace, de la vie présente, le caractère de ce que le lecteur nous a permis d'appeler la *modernité*'[21] ['He has everywhere sought after the fugitive, fleeting beauty of present-day life, the distinguishing character of that quality which, with the reader's kind permission, we have called "modernity".'[22]] The modernity of Baudelaire's poem 'Une charogne' [A Carcass] from *Les Fleurs du mal* [*The Flowers of Evil*] (1857) comes from closely following Ronsard's ode 'Mignonne, allons voir si la rose' and infusing it with a romantic aesthetic of the ugly and vile:

> Rappelez-vous l'objet que nous vîmes, mon âme,
>   Ce beau matin d'été si doux:
> Au détour d'un sentier une charogne infâme
>   Sur un lit semé de cailloux,
> Les jambes en l'air, comme une femme lubrique,
>   Brûlante et suant les poisons,
> Ouvrait de façon nonchalante et cynique
>   Son ventre plein d'exhalaisons.   (ll. 1–8)[23]

> [Remember the object that we saw, my soul,
>   This beautiful, sweet summer morning:
> At the bend in a path a vile carcass
>   On a bed strewn with pebbles,
> Legs in the air, like a lecherous woman,
>   Burning and sweating poisons,
> Was showing in a manner nonchalant and cynical
>   Her belly full of emanations.]

Baudelaire begins in the same way with a verb in the imperative: as a putative demonstration to the beloved, inviting her to consider the fate of a living thing, the carcass replacing the rose. Baudelaire's poem, of course, eschews the preciousness of Ronsard's ode, for instead of the rose's petals dropping, we see an animal likened to a harlot, legs in the air. Baudelaire's aesthetic consists of juxtaposing the themes and language of love poetry with the unspeakably ugly and repulsive, combining attraction and revulsion. Whereas Ronsard concludes his 'Ode à Cassandre' by exhorting Cassandra,

> Cueillés, cueillés vôtre jeunesse
> Comme à cette fleur, la vieillesse
> Fera ternir vôtre beauté.   (ll. 16–18)

[Gather, gather your youth,
Just like the flower, old age
Will tarnish your beauty.]

Baudelaire assails his beloved by establishing an equivalence between her and the 'filth', all the while addressing her using commonplaces of traditional love poetry:

— Et pourtant vous serez semblable à cette ordure,
  A cette horrible infection,
Étoile de mes yeux, soleil de ma nature,
  Vous, mon ange et ma passion!   (ll. 37–40)

[— And yet you will be similar to this filth,
  To this horrible infection,
Star of my eyes, sun of my nature,
  You, my angel and my passion!]

In a sonnet to an unyielding Helen published much later than his ode to Cassandra, Ronsard had threatened that she would be filled with regret at having rejected such a famous poet:

Je seray sous la terre et fantôme sans os
Par les ombres myrteux je prendray mon repos:
Vous serez au fouyer une vielle accroupie,
Regrettant mon amour et vostre fier desdain.²⁴

[I will be under earth and, a spirit without bones,
By the shadows of myrtle I will have my rest,
You will be an old hag at the hearth,
Mourning my love and your proud disdain.]

Baudelaire takes this further: positing his beloved's body being 'kissed' by vermin, in a wink to Neo-Platonic poetry he posits oxymoronically that his own immortality will come from 'the form and divine essence' of his rotting lady:

Alors, ô ma beauté! dites à la vermine
  Qui vous mangera de baisers,
Que j'ai gardé la forme et l'essence divine
  De mes amours décomposés!   (ll. 45–8)

[So, O my beauty! Tell the vermin
  That will eat you with kisses,
That I have kept the form and the divine essence
  Of my decomposed loves!]

The teacher John Keating's pupils had laughed when he told them that language, and presumably poetic language in particular, had been invented

49

to 'woo women', but we have seen that, taken figuratively, this is true: French Renaissance poets drew upon the rich traditions, conventions, and idioms of love poetry to profess their love for patrons, friends, landscapes, country, and their own practice of poetry inspired those like Baudelaire who sought to define what it was to be modern. Indeed, this 'dead poets society', whose individual members produced very different works, collectively helped to give birth to contemporary notions of identity.

NOTES

1. See François Rigolot, *Poésie et Renaissance* (Paris: Seuil, 2002), p. 11.
2. Clément Marot, 'Marot Prisonnier escript au Roy, pour sa delivrance', in *Œuvres poétiques*, ed. Gérard Defaux, 2 vols (Paris: Classiques Garnier, 1990), vol. 2, p. 317, ll. 63–8. All translations are my own unless otherwise indicated.
3. Translation by John Lyons.
4. I. D. McFarlane, *Renaissance France 1470–1589: A Literary History of France*, ed. P. E. Charvert, 6 vols, vol. 2 (New York: Barnes and Noble, 1974), p. 48.
5. 'L'Œil trop ardent en mes jeunes erreurs / Girouettait, mal caut, à l'impourvue' [The eye too fervent in my youthful errors spun like a weathercock, careless, idly] (poem 1, l. 1); Maurice Scève, *Délie: objet de plus haute vertu*, ed. Françoise Charpentier (Paris: Gallimard, 1984), p. 51. Translation by Richard Sieburth: Maurice Scève, *Emblems of Desire: Selections from the 'Délie'*, trans. Richard Sieburth (Philadelphia, PA: University of Pennsylvania Press, 2003), p. 5.
6. 'Je sais assez que tu y pourras lire / Mainte erreur, même en si dures Épigrammes' ['I know all too well that you can read / Many errors, even in such hard epigrams'] ('À sa Délie' / 'To His Delia', p. 49, ll. 5–6).
7. *Délie*, ed. Charpentier, p. 123, ll. 7–10.
8. Scève, *Emblems of Desire*, trans. Sieburth, p. 47. I have slightly modified this translation.
9. Dedicatory Epistle to Clémence de Bourges, Louise Labé, *Œuvres complètes*, ed. François Rigolot (Paris: Garnier-Flammarion, 1986), p. 42.
10. Pierre de Ronsard, *Œuvres complètes*, ed. Paul Laumonier, vol. 4 (Paris: Didier, 1957), sonnet 20, pp. 23–4.
11. Pierre de Ronsard, *Œuvres complètes*, ed. Paul Laumonier, vol. 5 (Paris: Didier, 1957), 'Ode à Cassandre', p. 196.
12. Joachim Du Bellay, *La Deffence, et Illustration de la Langue Françoyse (1549)*, ed. Jean-Charles Monferran (Geneva: Droz, 2001), Part I, Chapter 2, p. 127.
13. Wayne A. Rebhorn, 'Du Bellay's Imperial Mistress: *Les Antiquitez de Rome* as Petrarchist Sonnet Sequence', *Renaissance Quarterly*, 33.4 (1980), 609–22.
14. Joachim Du Bellay, *Les Regrets et autres œuvres poétiques*, ed. M. A. Screech and J. Jolliffe, 3rd edn (Geneva: Droz, 1979), sonnet 31, ll. 3–4.
15. Norman R. Shapiro, trans., *Lyrics of the French Renaissance: Marot, Du Bellay, Ronsard* (New Haven, CT: Yale University Press, 2002), p. 207. Translation slightly modified.
16. Slight modification of Shapiro's translation.
17. My translation, but non-Francophone readers should consult the Helgerson translation of Joachim Du Bellay, *The Regrets; with, the Antiquities of Rome*,

Three Latin Elegies, and The Defense and Enrichment of the French Language, trans. Richard Helgerson (Philadelphia, PA: University of Pennsylvania Press, 2006).

18. Agrippa d'Aubigné, *Le Printemps*, stance 6, ll. 1–4, cited by Keith Cameron, *Agrippa d'Aubigné* (Boston, MA: Twayne, 1977), p. 34.

19. Agrippa d'Aubigné, *Les Tragiques*, ed. Jean-Raymond Fanlo (Paris: Champion, 1995), p. 58, l. 63.

20. 'I have nothing left but blood to feed you' ['Je n'ay plus que du sang pour vostre nourriture'], p. 63, l. 130.

21. Charles Baudelaire, *Œuvres complètes*, ed. Claude Pichois, 2 vols (Paris: Gallimard, 1975), vol. 2, p. 724.

22. Charles Baudelaire, *The Painter of Modern Life and Other Essays*, trans. and ed. Jonathan Mayne, 2nd edn (London: Phaidon, 1964), p. 40.

23. Baudelaire, *Œuvres complètes*, vol. 1, XXIX, p. 31.

24. Pierre de Ronsard, *Œuvres complètes*, ed. Jean Céard, Daniel Ménager, and Michel Simonin, 2 vols (Paris: Gallimard, 1993), vol. 1, sonnet 43, p. 400.

4

TOM CONLEY

The graphic imagination and the printed page

In what might be called the 'adolescence' of print-culture, the two decades of innovation between 1530 and 1550 saw the printed page celebrate sound through graphic form. These two decades bore witness to invention owing to the force of analogy and to the autonomy of print in relation to what it conveys: endowed with a life of their own, in a variety of fonts, printed characters become a new language of the gods, virtual hieroglyphs capable of releasing arcane or concealed meanings before the eyes of those who know how to read them. The same moment saw several important developments: the birth of lexicography-inspired grammar books in which language becomes visualized; the advent of the emblem – a composite creation in which language and image correlate; and, finally, book designs in which daring combinations of woodcut images and typography were to display aesthetic prowess beyond the requirements of pragmatic communication. In this respect the legacy of the great authors of the Renaissance is tied to the graphic form of their writings, their printers' studio becoming a laboratory where aesthetic experiment is tantamount to new science. Their works implicitly ask their readers – in ways that anticipate the interactivity of the internet – to become their co-creators. We might do well to imagine Renaissance books as virtual installations or sites where performing readers turn the graphic matter of meaning, the form of content, into events that take place on the surface of the printed page. Let us look at three canonical authors, Rabelais, Ronsard, and Montaigne, located in the first, the middle, and the last of the sixteenth century: each of them stands as a point of reference, respectively, for humanism (1525–50), for the literary turn towards Italy in the age of Henri II (1552–62), and finally for the late and bloody years of the Wars of Religion (1580–95).

Content and graphic form

We begin by reflecting on the way in which the greatest works of French literature find indelible signature in the force of their form. Harnessed to *fond* (or content), *forme* has long been a tenet of stylistics, a field of enquiry vital to the study of literature. The distinction between form and content, especially given that the two French words bear a convenient resemblance to each other, has held firm in the pedagogical tradition of the *explication de textes*, a systematic examination of literary fragments that aims to tease out of a piece of writing its commanding themes or the forces of contradiction informing its expression. Close analysis of this kind has been a vital means to discern ideas, messages, philosophical, or even ethical reflections under the mantle of 'style', a term a philosopher might call 'a manner of thinking'.[1] In the mode of Montaigne, who asserted that 'nous sommes sur la manière, non sur la matière du dire' (p. 928) [we are dealing with the manner and not the matter of discourse],[2] the stylist or specialist of the manner of writing accounts for the ties linking the 'tenor' or implied content of a work to its 'vehicle'; in other words, the modes of transport or metaphors that convey its impressions to the reader. Given that content is usually purported to be of an order higher than that of the material support, it has gone almost without saying that the form conveying an idea disappears when a successful delivery is made.

To contextualize study of the graphic imagination in the Renaissance within the French culture of today we must recall how theorists of the last seventy years complicated or even erased the distinction between form and content. In his epochal *Qu'est-ce que la littérature?* [*What Is Literature?*] (1947), Jean-Paul Sartre bid adieu to belles-lettres, or at least to poetry. Prose, he wrote, the best of all vehicles of content, conveys messages. Its function entirely pragmatic; it reflects ideology and makes clear a commitment to changing the world. Sartre implored the reader of prose to look *through* the printed words in order to grasp their meaning and hence to engage an existential relation with the human condition. By contrast poetry, he asserted, draws attention to the medium. Its form becomes a function of its content. As a result, its messages are perforce occulted, complicated, even wilfully confused and obscured, often with the effect of leaving readers if not mired in its matter, at least in a state of heuristic perplexity. Though himself an admirer and keen reader of poetry, Sartre embraces prose in order to engage, in the wake of the devastation of the Second World War, what he would call the creation of unforeseen existential territories.

Reacting against Sartre's plea for a politics of content, both structuralists (Claude Lévi-Strauss) and poststructuralists (Jacques Derrida, Roland Barthes, Gilles Deleuze) called attention to writing as inscription, as evidence of force, or more broadly in the context of the history of colonial development, a manifestation of power and control. In *Les Mots et les choses* [*The Order of Things*] (1966) Michel Foucault distinguished between the Renaissance, which belonged to an age of 'analogy', in which language and matter are mixed and the form of a thing is taken to resemble what it means; and an age of representation, in which words stand in place of the qualities of 'things' (*choses*). In this new era, which began with the scientific turn of the seventeenth century, signs become isolated from their referents. Foucault noted that twentieth-century literature in fact seeks to retrieve the complexities of sixteenth-century writing, in which little distinction is made between marks and words, indeed where the near-identity of words and things attests to 'cet être brut' [this brute being], this the living matter of language that the modern age seeks to recover from the sixteenth century.[3] In this spirit he brought to the early modern canon a new and compelling appreciation.

François Rabelais, *Pantagruel* and *Gargantua*

François Rabelais began an extensive collaboration with three printers in Lyon in the early 1530s – Sebastian Gryphe, François Juste, and Claude Nourry – and it was around this time that he composed a pamphlet whose graphic form embodies what was to become the great force of his later writing (see Figure 4.1).

This *Pantagrueline prognostication certaine veritable & infallible pour lan mil. D.xxxiii* (probably Lyon: François Juste, *c.* 1532) was inspired by numerous almanacs of similar ilk in the tradition of the shepherd's calendar. It exploits the form of the page to juxtapose alternative ways of reading and seeing. On four folios are printed, first, its title above a woodcut illustration lifted from a recent edition of Sebastian Brant's *Nef des fous* (Lyon: possibly François Juste, 1530), followed on the verso and upper recto portion of the following page a dedicatory note to the 'liseur benevole' [friendly reader].[4] On the remaining pages the implied author, a soothsayer who predicts, tongue-in-cheek, what will become of the world in the year ahead. The disposition of the title page sets the reader in a mood of ludic gravity. The title indicates that it is 'nouvelement compose au profit & advisement de gens estourdis et musars de nature par maistre Alcofribas architriclin dudict Pantagruel' [newly composed for the profit and counsel of fools and nitwits by Master Alcofribas, steward of the stated Pantagruel]; but the woodcut image, severely cropped along the lower border, ostensibly in order to allow space in which a textual legend is placed, displays a tall fool (identified by his cap whose skull and ears are adorned with bells), his right hand raised towards the heavens and to the bright sun in the upper left corner of the frame. The fool addresses his shorter companion, a scholar (dressed in an ample tunic), the index finger of his right hand pointing towards the horizon. The scholar seems to be listening to his foolish partner's counsel. Below the

Figure 4.1 Title page of François Rabelais, *Pantagrueline prognostication* (Lyon: François Juste, *c.* 1532). FC5.R1125.532 pa, Houghton Library, Harvard University.

image is printed 'De nombre dor non dicitur / ie nen trouue point ceste annee quelque calculation que ien aye faict, passons oultre, den asi sen deface en moy, qui nen a sy en cherche. Verte folium' [Of the golden number nothing can be said, I find none despite whatever calculation I've made this year, may others not be upset with me, I who have looked into the matter closely. Turn the page].

The floating aspect of the five lines of the title that in the lexicon of emblems would be a superscription (*superscriptio*) is matched by the words below, in subscription (*subscriptio*), to the image itself, in an inscription (*inscriptio*). As he would appear in a virtual comic book, one of the inter-locutors – possibly the fool whose hand gestures towards the words of the title – could be uttering the words of the title to his wise companion, thus identifying himself as the *architriclin* or steward of the absent author, named at the end, placed at the keystone of the printed utterance. Either he or the sage could also be stating what is printed below. The arrangement of the material on the page makes the reader wonder who indeed is speaking. Despite the macaronic style in which words of different languages are mingled ('de nombre dor non dicitur') it is impossible to tell who is the wise man and who might be the fool. Yet, on the recto, the two voices are seen and heard together. When, following the order, 'verte folium', to turn the page we wonder if, with these two refugees from the ship of fools, two idioms are conflated in the imperative. 'Verte folium': do we see Erasmian folly in the printed writing (in *lettre bâtarde*, or 'bastarda', a form of gothic script used in the fourteenth and fifteenth centuries), or do we defer judgment until, both literally and figuratively, in the context of folly, we have 'turned' a new 'folium' or better, a new 'leaf'?

The text on the verso that would resolve the issue prompts further doubt (see Figure 4.2).

Crowning the passage below, the pious invocation wishing to confer upon the reader the good fortune of peace in Jesus Christ appears to contradict the ludic aspect of the words and image printed on the other side of the folio. The incipit begins with a 'serious' disclaimer of the fallacious character of recent prognostications written 'a lombre dung verre de vin' [under the shadow (or influence) of a glass of wine]. The ludic tone returns no sooner than reference is made to the fifth Psalm: 'You will destroy all those who utter lies.' In what follows the author praises attentive souls who accept alterity when, meeting travellers hailing from foreign lands, they eagerly listen to the travellers' words and, in doing so, seek to obtain from them a sense of a veracity. Things comic and things of import may be of the same order, just like the relation of the title page to the dedication that follows.

Y 79-63

⸿Au fiseur beniuose Salut
et paix en Jesucḡzift.

Onſiderât infiniz abus eſtre perpetrez a cauſe dung
tas de Prognoſticatione de Loain faictes a ſombze
dung verre de vin/ Je vous en ay pzeſentement cal⸱
cule vne ſa pſus ſceure et veritabſe que fut oncques veue/ cō
me ſexperience vous ſe demonſtrera. Car ſans doubte veu q̄
dit ſe.ppḡete Royaſ.ps. v. a Dieu. Tu deſtruiras tous ceuſp
qui diſent menſonges/ ce neſt par ſegier pecḡe de mêtir ainſi
a ſon eſcient/ et enſembſe abuſer ſe poure monde qui eſt cu⸱
rieuſp de ſcauoir choſes nouueſſes. Cōme de tout temps ont
eſte ſinguſieremêt ſes Francops/ ainſp que eſcript Ceſar en
ſes commêtaires et Jeḡã de grauot on mpṫoſogies Gaſ⸱
ſicques ce que nous voyons encozes de iour en iour par Frã⸱
ce ou ſe pzemier pzopos quon tient a gens fraiſchement ar⸱
riuez ſôt. Queſſes nouueſſes? ſcauez vous rien de nouueau?
Qup dit? qui bzuit par ſe monde? Et tant p ſont attentifz q̄
ſouuêt ſe courrouſſent côtre ceuſp qui vienent de paps eſtrã
ges ſans apozter pſeines bougettes de nouueſſes. ſes appeſ
ſant veaup et idiotz. Si doncques cōme ifz ſont pzomptz a
demander des nouueſſes. autant ſont ifz faciſes a cropze ce q̄
ſeur eſt annôce/ debuzoit on pas mettre gens dignes de ſop
a gaiges a ſentree du Royauſme/qui ne ſeruiroient dauſtre
choſe ſp non de epaminer ſes nouueſſes quon p apozte/ a ſca
uoir ſp eſſes ſôt veritabſes? Qup certes. Et ainſi a faict mõ
bon maiſtre Pâtagrueſ par tout ſe paps de Dtopie q Dipſo
die. Auſſp fup en eſt iſ ſi bien pzins q tât pzoſpere ſô territop
re/quifz ne peuuent de pzeſent ananger a Bopze et ſeur con
uiendza eſpandze ſe vin en terre/ſp daiſſeurs ne ſeur vièt rê⸱
fozt de beuueurs q bons raiſſars. Douſât doncques ſatiſſai⸱
re a ſa curioſite de tous bons compaignons iap reuoſue tou⸱
tes ſes pâtarches des cieuſp caſcuſe ſes quadratz de ſa Lûe.
crocḡete tout ce que iamais penſerent tous ſes Aſtrophiſes/
Hppernepḡeſiſtes/Anemophiſaces/Dzanopetes/q Ombzo
pḡozes/et confere du tout auecques Empedocſes/ ſequeſ ſe

Figure 4.2 Reverse title page of François Rabelais, *Pantagrueline prognostication* (Lyon: François Juste, *c.* 1532). FC5.R1125.532 pa, Houghton Library, Harvard University.

At least two voices are seen speaking the same words within printed discourse that lacks any graphic mark (a parenthetical statement or a deictic, that is, a sign pointing to the context) that would distinguish the one from the other. Reflecting on the utility of gatekeepers assigned to listen to newcomers from afar, the speaker splits into two characters: one who is active and the other passive; one who is wise and the other, ironic or given to folly, who calls the words into question: 'devroit on pas metre gens dignes de foy a gaiges a lentree du Royaume/qui ne serviroient daultre chose sy non de examiner quon y aporte/a scavoir si elles sont veritables? Ouy certes. Et ainsi a faict mon bon maistre Pantagruel par tout le pays de Utopie et Dipsodie' [Ought we not set trustworthy souls at the entry of the kingdom who would serve only to examine the reports that are brought forth, that is, is they are true. Yes surely. And thus did my good master Pantagruel through the countries of Utopia and Dipsodia.] Given that, unlike modern transcriptions, the original edition does not divide the text into paragraphs, because the two figures on the recto can be seen across the print in immediate view, he who utters 'Yes surely' ('ouy certes') could be calling his interlocutor into question. The borrowed image, the disposition of the typography and its compressed formatting convey a mix of doubt and affirmation no less than the *mise en scène*, the performance, of the dialogue.

In the Chapter 8 of *Pantagruel*, Rabelais's vernacular work that follows the *Prognostication*, the eponymous hero receives a letter from his father, Gargantua, who describes how the new medium of print brings the dark or 'gothic' age of his past into new and unforeseen radiance: 'Le temps estoit encores tenebreux et sentant l'infelicité et calamite des Gothz, qui avoient mis a destruction toute bonne literature' [The time was tenebrous and smacked of the infelicity and calamity of the Goths, who had put to destruction all good literature].[5] With the advent of print Gargantua sees a page being turned not only in technology but in the whole way of knowing the world. Like the passage from night to day and back again, one world moves within and emerges from the other. The title pages of the last editions of *Pantagruel* and *Gargantua*, in 1542 revised by Rabelais and printed by François Juste, attest to the presence of the one in the other. In a funnel-like design in the style of a *cul-de-lampe* (an ornamental image) that endows the frame of page with a sense of visual perspective, each element of the title is printed in roman characters (the first line of appreciably greater point-size than those that follow) that converge upon gothic characters below. *Pantagruel* displays a date that is set in roman numerals while the name of the publisher and his address are in the gothic *lettre bâtarde*. Likewise, in *Gargantua* the text is poised over 'Livre plein de Pantagruelisme' [book full of Pantagruelism] and the same name and place in the older typeface. A newer typeface announces what will follow in the older typeface, and at the same time the title notes that just as the title page of *Pantagruel* announces that it has been written 'par feu M. Alcofribas, abstracteur de quinte essence' [by the late M. Alcofribas, abstractor of quintessence], has restored and composed the book of his hero's deeds, so also the 'vie tres horrificque du grand Gargantua, pere de Pantagruel' [very horrific life of the great Gargantua, father of Pantagruel] has *since* been assembled by the steward of the same name. The comic chronicler of times past is about to be reborn in the name of a more sagacious alter ego, 'F(rançois) Rabelais', soon to be known as a medical doctor. This rebirth occurs four years later, in the *Tiers Livre* (1546), in which roman type and elegant cursive entirely replace the gothic counterpart in the two works of 1542. The evolution of the graphic form of Rabelais's works signals that of its content and, in turn, the ways that the material is conveyed and understood.

Pierre de Ronsard and love's landscape

Contradiction is less apparent in the elegant presentation of the sonnets comprising much of Pierre de Ronsard's *Amours* in the first edition of 1552, where perhaps the poet intervened less directly than Rabelais in shaping his work. Building on the co-presence of portraits of Petrarch and Laura in recent editions set in a heart-shaped frame, the title page presents woodcut images of Ronsard on the left and Cassandre on the right, each isolated in an oval surround. They stare at each other across the spine that binds the folios on which their portraits are printed together yet alone, separated from one another in their frames and isolated in the space of each of the pages. Facing each other as they do, they anticipate the isolation of the material assemblages, the sonnets themselves, set in paratactic relation with each other – that is, in a co-ordinated rather than in a subordinated relation (simply placed one after the other) – as they are displayed in Figures 4.3a and b.

In contrast to what modern readers know of the collection, the sonnets are *not* topped with roman numerals as they will be in later editions, nor does the layout break the architectural frame (ten beats on the horizontal axis and fourteen lines the measure of the vertical vector), initial quatrains or tercets on one page giving way to their remainder on the top of the next. The sonnets form a quadrangle: two on one page and two on the next.

Set in italic, the first lines of the quatrains and tercets establish the vertical axis of the margin on the left. The new italic font causes the poem to appear to be bending forward under an unspoken – or mute – force of inspiration that drives them ahead. In what appears to be Ronsard's visual wit, each sonnet can be read both as a meaningful content and as a mass of

Figure 4.3 Pierre de Ronsard, *Amours de Pierre de Ronsard* (Paris: Veuve M. de La Porte, 1562), (a) frontispiece verso (Ronsard), and (b) frontispiece recto (Cassandre). FC5. R6697.552a, Houghton Library, Harvard University.

fragmentary iterations visible, much as in an abstract painting, across and about, even *all over* the printed page. From its outset the sixty-sixth sonnet invites readers to see it as a landscape that the arrangement of the printing sets in motion, an effect turning a Petrarchan formula into visual virtuosity.

The elements depicting the rolling hills of the poet's Val-de-Loire in the first two quatrains return in the last tercet that sums up the scene in a rapid-fire enumeration. The twelve attributes depicted in the space above return below, in the final three lines, before the poet sets himself, 'moy', at the cornerstone of a work where movement ends in an impression of an architectural form:

> Ciel, air, & vents, plains, & montz descouuers,
> Tertres fourchuz, & forestz verdoyantes,
> Riuages tortz, & sources ondoyantes,
> Tailliz razez, & vous bocages verds,
> Antres moussus a demyfront ouuers,
> Prez, boutons, fleurs, & herbes rousoyantes,

Coustaux vineux, & plages blondoyantes,
　　Gastine, Loyr, & vous mes tristes vers:
Puis qu'au partir, rongé de soing & d'ire,
　　A ce bel oeil, l'Adieu ie n'ai sceu dire,
　　Qui pres & loin me detient en esmoy:
Ie vous supply, Ciel, air, ventz, montz, & plaines,
　　Tailliz, forestz, riuages & fontaines,
　　Antres, prez, fleurs, dictes le luy pour moy.[6]

[Sky, air, & winds, plains and uncovered hills,
　　Forked ridges, & verdant forests,
　　Sinuous shores, & swelling springs,
　　Logged plantings, & green thickets,
Mossy grottoes half-open,
Meadows, buds, flowers, & reddening grasses,
　　Viney hillsides, & blond beaches,
　　Gâtine, Loire, & you my sad verses:
For on leaving, wracked with care & anger,
　　To that beautiful eye, I knew not how to say farewell,
　　Which near & far move me still.
I beg you, sky, air, winds, mountains & plains,
　　Plantings, forests, shores, & fountains,
　　Grottoes, meadows, flowers, speak for me.]

Unlike its ostensible Italian model by Astemio Bevilacqua, the landscape of the poem thrusts forward with an impression of velocity. It seems to fuse the beloved female's body with a landscape – an impression strengthened by the contemporary vogue of poetic descriptions of women's bodies (the 'blasons du corps féminin') by poets such as Clément Marot – and the text emphasizes the zones that a libidinal gaze would find erogenous: 'uncovered hills', '[f]orked ridges', 'verdant forests', and, remarkably, '[m]ossy grottoes half-open'. A phantasm of the physical beauty of the absent beloved melds with the verbal landscape. Upon cursory glance – not to be dismissed in favour of closer and slower reading – the letters of the poem convey a throttled force of ocular attraction. Yet, because the poem stages the scene of the poet gazing at his lady's eye at the moment she vanishes from view ('To that beautiful eye, I knew not how to say farewell') recalling the woodcut images of the frontispiece, it also invites its readers to look at the work from afar, as if from a hillock or any of the 'uncovered hills' announced in the incipit – that is, the first words of the text. An uncommon and enthusing play of form emerges from the graphic matter: a profusion, first, of twelve ampersands that tend to split the poem in half where they fall at the half-line point (the hemistich) of the ten-syllable verse (the decasyllable) in the first, second, third, fourth, sixth, seventh, and eighth lines before the syntax seems to gather itself in the two tercets. A device based on economy, related to the adage to 'make haste slowly', in this poem the ampersand translates the rush of inspiration while emphasizing the spatiality of the graphic form. A literally curious piece of stenography, the ampersand seems to ask us to think about itself, and about what it later becomes in its relation to a poetics of continuous addition and amplification. In 'Ciel, air, & vents' the mark figures in an enumeration and is invariably preceded by a comma, which (given that the latter is known to be a *point queue* – a point with a tail – a period endowed with a male member) nestles in the erotic landscape of the poem.[7] We recall that in the Renaissance language of cartography, rows of ampersands were drawn in laboured fields to designate carefully tilled vineyards.[8] In the strangely alluring *Cousteaux vineux* (viney hillsides), in which hillsides (*côteaux*) planted with grapes in Ronsard's *terroir* are punningly meshed with the shears (*couteaux*) that prune the vines, the ampersand appears as an integral element in the visual landscape of words. Notable, too, is how the printer chooses the letter *z*, whose foot or *queue* (literally, 'tail') extends beyond its square as if almost to touch the commas contiguous to it: 'Sinuous shores, & swelling springs', etc. The italic font, a fairly new and still uncommon typeface, encourages graphic fantasy to eroticize (in other words, to energize) a poem that in the tempo of its form stages modulations of desire.

When the sonnet is seen as part of the four-part presentation of the poems (if we see the book open with two facing pages), adjacent to the three pieces above or to its left, the eye seizes upon iterative formulas that virtually cut across the containing mass in which they are first discerned. The 'uncovered hills' of the first line, whose very spacing allows two readings and two perspectives, as both 'uncovered hills' and as concealed or 'covered worlds' ('mondes couverts'), finds a visual echo in the poem in the upper left corner of the opposite page, in 'Les montz d'Epire' (The hills of Epirus), engaging thus a diagonal itinerary. 'Et ton bel œil' (And your beautiful eye, l. 3) in the sonnet below finds its counterpart in 'A ce bel œil' (To this beautiful eye, l. 10), which in the poem just above is in the incipit as 'L'œil qui rendroit le plus barbare apris' (The eye that would make the most barbarian learned, l. 1), which transmutes into 'Son bel œil' (Her beautiful eye, l. 11), just as in the same poem to the left, 'ma rime si basse' (my lowly rhyme, l. 7) finds a complement to the immediate right in 'mes tristes vers' (my sad verses, l. 8). In short, in simply calling the formulas 'Petrarchan' or relegating them to a lexicon of clichés that are at the author's behest the creatively spatial mobility of the poems is diminished: they are best studied in their original form in which reading becomes interactive and in fact, in the itineraries it draws, of an interpretive geography.

It could be said that, like the poems he tweaks in each successive edition of the verse, so also Ronsard causes his printing to undergo alteration. Of uncommonly strong visual presentation that changes according to aesthetic and political vagaries of the time when they are printed, the poems demand to be understood in terms of their successive strata, their historic layers, almost like geological sediments: first, in 1552; then, in 1553, when Marc-Antoine Muret presents an edition of the *Amours* with gloss and commentary translating for uninitiated readers the Greek and Latin mythography informing the poet's invention; later, when the landscapes of the poems turn into miniature hieroglyphs, in 1560, in four compact volumes comprising the first edition of the *Complete Works*, where much of the spelling of the earlier material returns, albeit in the context of a new distribution and arrangement conceived to address the author's friends and admirers. When a great folio edition of the works appears in 1584 (in which poems have undergone further emendation), once again graphic design imparts a sense of the moment when they are published. A funerary monument appearing at the height of the Wars of Religion, completed when the poet's health was rapidly declining, the book becomes a great chronicle of a career that changes as it advances and declines, from the beginnings of the reign of Henri II to insidious conflict that marked the decline and fall of the Valois dynasty.

Montaigne's *Essais*

In a similar sense the evolving form of the content of Montaigne's *Essais* merits extended study. As he says in 'De l'institution des enfans' [Of the education of children] (Book 1, Chapter 26), '[l]e vray miroir de nos discours est le cours de nos vies' (p. 138) [the true mirror of our writings is the course of our lives]. Changing in accordance with the context in which it was written, the book would seem to be an undulating surface of the world on which both the author and his readers would find distorted reflections. Much as the complete works of Rabelais and Ronsard, in flux and change, remain open-ended and unfinished – albeit at a time when the formatting of printed books begins to settle – so also the *Essais* bear traces of shift and alteration. In their sum the essays can be studied geologically, as a sedimentary landscape of writing in which the mass of printed characters, viewed from afar, amounts to historical layering in a landscape. In order to show how the work changes, translators and editors of modern editions take care to distinguish three major layers or strata. They dot the text with marks (sometimes slashes, elsewhere minuscule letters in superscription) designating which material is published in the first edition of two volumes, published by Simon Millanges in Bordeaux in 1580; what is emended or added in the quarto edition in Paris by Abel Angelier in

1588; what follows in the posthumous text of 1595, also issued by Angelier, which includes the material Montaigne had added or sometimes adjusted in autograph in the margins of his personal copy of the 1588 edition (the Exemplaire de Bordeaux). Following the indisputable hypothesis that early in the twentieth century editor Pierre Villey formulated in a study in consort with his own carefully stratified edition of the *Essais* (in which passages are marked as belonging to A, B, or C layers), readers daring to proceed from the beginning to the end, starting with '[p]ar divers moyens on arrive à pareille fin' [by diverse means we arrive at the same end] (Book 1, Chapter 1) and after more than a thousand pages, finishing the itinerary at the end of 'De l'expérience' [Of experience] (Book III, Chapter 13), we discover how the author's sources change and how, in turn, the essays themselves evolve from the author's embrace of a stoic ethos (following a crisis of faith at a central point in the work) to an Epicurean and wryly Socratic worldview. Because the essays witness revision and rewriting over more than twenty years from their beginning to the posthumous edition, what Villey called the sources and evolution of the *Essais* belongs to a geology of form. And because its printed pages are a virtual palimpsest replete with rewriting, occasional erasure, and correction, the essays invite the eye to visualize them as at once in the depth of field of their composition, *à même la page*, on the very surface of the printed page.

In their original form, lacking indentations or division into paragraphs that would designate how and where reflections begin and end, the essays implicitly ask readers to account for how the reflections make sense of the form. The essays demand that readers visualize how the meaning they obtain from the printed characters is related to vagaries of perception, often of a give-and-take of intra-missive and extra-missive vision by which readers can 'look at' the text as it also gazes upon them. In this way the printed page is akin to Freud's famous *Wunderblock* or 'mystic writing pad' that analyses as it is being analysed.[9] To a large degree what seems to be the strongly motivated psychoanalytical dimension of the *Essais* is due to the way the graphic matter relates to the autobiographical 'body' that Montaigne portrays in printed form. First, and from the very outset as seen in the title page of the 1588 edition and the annotated dedication to the reader of the Exemplaire de Bordeaux, two visual strategies are key: one architectural and the other anatomical.

What he announces to be a book 'of good faith' is conceived spatially, as a home whose entry or portal leads into domestic area where the author states beguilingly that he cares little about the readers whom he invites to enter. No sooner than noting that the volume is destined for his kin or members of his 'maison' (house), he insists that he wants to be *seen* in his 'façon simple, naturelle, et ordinaire' [simple, and ordinary, fashion]. He is depicting or 'painting' himself with printed characters. Seen first in the attention he draws to his 'conditions et humeurs' [conditions and humours], an anatomical turn leads to a comparison of the form of the essays to the painted and tattooed bodies of the denizens, no doubt the Tupinamba of the recently discovered New World. Were I one of them, he writes, 'Je t'assure que je m'y fusse tres-volontiers peint tout entier, & tout nud. Ainsy lecteur, je suis moy-mesmes la matiere de mon livre' [I assure you that I would have painted myself entirely, and entirely nude. Thus reader, I am myself the matter of my book]. Montaigne's celebrated remark suggests that, impressed as they are on the page that would be his epidermis, the inked characters are both the signs of who he is and the physical remains of who he was. The graphic material mediates on one level the present and past and on another the literal and figurative aspects of the self-portraiture to follow. If the annotations of the Exemplaire de Bordeaux are taken into account, lines of brown ink comprise an element integral to the verbal picture. A narrow swath is drawn across a piece of the 1588 material (ll. 9 and 10), and above it are added, also in the same colour, words of a seemingly terse and fitting reformulation. Below (l. 13), he cuts a trait through 'mes imperfections' [my imperfections] suggesting he does better to stick with 'ma forme naïfve' [my naïve form] than, although it may be fitting in a *captatio benevolentiae*, to overemphasize self-deprecation. And, in the last line, after the date of 12 June 1588, the day he launches the first edition in three volumes, he coyly backdates the writing as 1 March 1580. Adjacent to and both above and below the sentence stating that he would have painted himself in the fashion of those 'qu'on dict vivre encore sous la douce liberté des premieres loix de nature' [who are said to be living under the gentle liberty of the first laws of nature] (ll. 14–15) are five smudges in blue ink: given the bodily character of the work (even if they were blotches on the part of the librarian who inked onto the lower corner of the page the stamp of the Bibliothèque municipale de Bordeaux), the marks belong to the self-portrait. The page itself is painted, *peinte*, depicting the absent body of the man who is himself the matter of the *Essais*.

The preface signals that while the self-portrait, the ostensible project of the essays, is taken literally, or as the French say, at the foot of the letter (*au pied de la lettre*), the printed writing requires a haptic reading: a reading that requires the physical sensation of touch. What Montaigne calls his 'si frivole et si vain' [a so frivolous and so vain] subject becomes exceptionally graphic in 'De la vanité' [Of Vanity] (Book III, Chapter 9). In that essay Montaigne writes that the headings of his chapters, not necessarily summarizing the material that will follow, sometimes 'signify' what they might mean – that is, they simply point at what the essay is about, as with an index finger. The meaning will be shown allusively, in a poetic gait that goes 'à sauts et à gambades' [in jumps and gambols]. Such is the emblematic character of the beginning of the chapter. Conceived in the mode of an emblem (that is, a closely correlated image with a caption), the title and chapter heading figure within a spatial frame defined by the final sentence of the preceding essay. He writes, changing his words when penning revisions into the essay after 1588, 'Tous jugemens ~~universels~~ en gros sont laches et ~~dangereux~~ imparfaicts' [All ~~universal~~ judgments in gross are loose and ~~dangerous~~ imperfect'], and the first of what follows 'Il n'est est à l'avanture aucune plus expresse que d'en escrire si vainement' (p. 945) [There is perchance none more obvious than to write of it so vainly]. In the mode of an emblem, the words of the title 'De la vanité' resonate visually. In its spacing it can be at once 'de la vanité' (properly, of vanity) and 'de l'avan(t)ité' (the scansion implying an essay about times before, *avant*, versus those now, new, or novel). Rhyming with '*avan*ture' and '*vaine*ment' just below, the title corresponds with what had been stated in the ostensible frivolity of the preface – at the same time it proposes to move errantly and incontinently, in a manner that would be 'lache' (slack), much in the manner of what he decries just above, about universal judgments. Given that for as long as he has paper and ink he will go where he might, he implies that his thoughts, blowing where they might, will saddle the wind ('vent').

Seasoned readers of the essay take delight in the ironic tenor of the affected modesty that marks the sentences below.[10] 'Vaine', a sixteenth-century reader would have noted, plays on 'vesne', what Randle Cotgrave calls a 'fizzle', or Jean Nicot, 'une venne, *id est*, une vesse, *Flatus ventris*' [a fizzling fart, that is, a *vesse*, a wind from the lower belly].[11] Montaigne recalls having known a gentleman (himself, perhaps) for whom, upon arranging a week's dejections in a row of six or seven chamber pots, all other communication 'just stank'. Turning to himself, remarking 'ce sont icy un peu plus civilement, des exremens d'un vieil esprit, dur tantost, tantost lache' (p. 946) [here, a little more civilly, are the excrements of an old mind, sometimes hard, sometimes soft], he invites reader to gaze upon the congealed ink of the printed characters as both physical remainders of his mental and physical ablutions. Given the stress he places on a common and Latin inflection in *excre-mens*, he aligns vanity with an ageing writer's mental excretions.

In a nutshell, Montaigne's association of the printed matter of the *Essais* with bodily dejections or remainders is due to the intimacy of the relation the sixteenth-century writer holds with the mode of production of printed writing. In view of longstanding tradition of the manuscript and technologies of transmission of knowledge prior to what Walter Benjamin famously called 'the age of mechanical reproduction', he and others who exploit the medium in its youth turn the very matter of their writing into what the contemporary theorists noted above would call the force of their form. Historians agree that, following the age of the incunabulum (that is, the period in printing history before 1500), printing firms in the early years of the sixteenth century witness untold experiment with typography and illustration. As time passes the aspect of the book stabilizes to the point where, at the end of the century, it becomes more a means of communication (or, as Michel Foucault argued, of representation) than, in areas that include the emblem and the illustrated book, an end unto itself.

In the brief overview in the paragraphs above three great writers are shown making the most of their respective moments. Rabelais heralds the potential of print for the dissemination of knowledge everywhere and to everyone in the ambient world. Imbued with symbolic magic, his earliest work, a thin pamphlet, becomes a site where printed characters surrounding a borrowed woodcut indicate they belong to an ever-expanding world in which experiment and discovery attest to its sacred character. Juxtaposing gothic and italic typography to suggest that the printed book makes vitally present worlds both old and new, in a typological fashion he juxtaposes one world and another.

As Rabelais recedes from the horizon after the turn of the middle of the century, poets shaping the Pléiade in its first wave articulate poetry inspired by words and images in books of fables and emblems from ateliers in both Paris and Lyon. Its members turn collections of sonnets into mosaic landscapes of consubstantially mental and geographical facture. Now and again, notably in his early work, Ronsard's poems are conceived as pictures for which graphic forms can be at once letters as well as points and units of line. Endowed with perspective and, given that they figure in a genre defined by the limits of a frame, printed characters can be seen in a virtual depth of field. They become signs that turn words they compose into forms, even landscapes bearing uncanny visual tension. Upon cursory glance his *Amours* are a cavalcade of Petrarchan commonplaces, while close inspection reveals that the collection can be taken, much like that of François Ier at Fontainebleau, as an extensive gallery of pictures, or even an assemblage of amorous 'takes' (bearing comparison with photography) seen as they are read. When examined as such, whether in sum or in detail, the graphic matter releases untold force exceeding the commonplaces they convey.

Approaching their final shape at the time of Ronsard's death (1585), Montaigne's *Essais* appear to reflect the settling of typographic experiment that had marked the first half of the century. In each of the three major editions (1580, 1588, 1595) the text of the essays, in Roman type, is formatted without being divided into paragraphs. Often isolated in the midst of the textual mass, citations from Latin sources and other languages (generally Italian or Greek) punctuate (or even seem to 'aerate') the density of the surrounding matter. They become points of reference that draw attention to the meshing of the borders and edges of the essays, notably too in the quasi-emblematic configuration of the titles themselves. The texts that end one essay and begin another are often in intimate relation with the title and number of the chapter they seem to frame, thus turning the latter into an enigmatic picture or icon that is in dialogue with the essay over which it stands. There results a textual cartography in which a word or a figure – what in 'De la vanité' Montaigne calls an 'embleme supernumeraire' (p. 508) [supernumerary emblem] – draws attention both to the graphic disposition of the material and, in turn, to the effort of the reader to account for how he or she is perceiving and understanding the material as such. In doing so the reader plots a cognitive itinerary through the essay, or what one modern critic has famously called a mode of 'cognitive mapping'.[12] In the spirit of the ongoing and unfinished work of these three canonical writers – unfinished, because we are still discovering its potential – today, in an age where digital technology allows close examination of the shape and form of printed writing, we do well look afresh and more broadly at the generative force of the forms of French literature.

NOTES

1. Gilles Deleuze and Félix Guattari, *Qu'est-ce que la philosophie?* (Paris: Minuit, 1991), p. 51.
2. Michel de Montaigne, *Les Essais*, ed. Pierre Villey (Paris: Quadrige, 1965), p. 938. See also the Montaigne Project: <http://www.lib.uchicago.edu/efts/ARTFL/projects/montaigne> (accessed 26 June 2015).
3. Michel Foucault, *Les Mots et les choses* (Paris: Gallimard, 1966), pp. 58–9. Here and elsewhere all translations from the French are mine.
4. See the digital copy of the edition held in the Harvard University Houghton Library (FC5.R1125.532 pa). Mireille Huchon makes clear the presence of Brant's satires throughout the author's works and travels from Poitiers de Lyon, noting that they 'légitiment, aussi bien pour le contenu que pour la forme, l'appellation de *satire* à donner à l'œuvre de Rabelais' [justify in terms both of form and content the name *satire* that can be awarded to Rabelais's work]; Huchon, 'Rabelais et les satires de la *Nef des folz* de 1530', in *La Satire dans tous ses états*, ed. Bernd Renner (Geneva: Droz, 2009), pp. 77–92 (p. 92); see also her *Rabelais* (Paris: Gallimard, 2011), pp. 103–6.
5. François Rabelais, *Gargantua*, in *Œuvres complètes*, ed. Mireille Huchon (Paris: Gallimard, 1994), p. 243. See also the digital copy of the 1542 edition of *Gargantua* in the Douglas H. Gordon Collection of French Books, available at http://search.lib.virginia.edu/catalog/uva-lib:770688/view#openLayer/uva-lib:1022141/1243/880.5/1/1/0 (accessed 29 June 2015).

6. *Les Amours de P. de Ronsard vandomois: ensemble le cinquiesme de ses odes* (Paris: Chez la veuve de Maurice de La Porte, au clos Bruneau, à l'enseigne S. Claude, 1552), p. 33. (Harvard University Houghton Library *FC5.R6697.552a.)

7. On the comma, typographer Étienne Dolet notes that '[l]e premier poinct est appellé en Latin incisum: & en Francoys (principalement en L'imprimerie) on l'appelle vng poinct a queue, ou virgule: & se souloit marquer ainsi', in *La Maniere de bien traduire d'une langue en aultre. Davantage. De la punctuation de la langue Francoyse. Plus. Des accents d'ycelle. Le tout faict par Estienne Dolet natif d'Orleans* (Lyon: Dolet, 1540), f. bi.r.

8. François de Dainville, *Le Langage des géographes* (Paris: Picard, 2002), p. 210; Catherine Delano-Smith, 'Signs on Printed Topographical Maps, ca. 1470–1640', in *History of Cartography*, vol. 3: *The European Renaissance*, ed. David Woodward (Chicago, IL: University of Chicago Press, 2007), pp. 528–90 (p. 574).

9. Sigmund Freud, 'Notiz über den "Wunderblock"', *Internationale Zeitschrift für Psychoanalyse*, 11 (1925), 1–5; in English as 'A Note upon the Mystic Writing Pad', in *The Standard Edition of the Complete Psychological Works of Sigmund Freud*, ed. James Strachey, vol. 19 (London: Hogarth, 1986), pp. 227–32. In his *Fabulous Imagination: On Montaigne's 'Essays'* (New York: Columbia University Press, 2009), using similar material, Lawrence Kritzman develops an intensely psychoanalytical reading of the *Essais*.

10. On how Montaigne leaves the impression of moving about, at once carefully and aimlessly, see Mary McKinley, *Les Terrains vagues des 'Essais': Itinéraires et intertextes* (Paris: Champion, 1996).

11. Randle Cotgrave, *A Dictionairie of the French and English Tongues* (London: Adam Islip, 1611); Jean Nicot, *Le Thresor de la langue françoyse* (Paris: n.p., 1606). Or Étienne Tabourot, in a riddle appended to his *Escraignes dijonnoises* (Paris: Jean Richer, 1603): 'Qu'est-ce qui va par la chambre, & n'a ni pied ni membre? Response: C'est une vesse' [What goes about in a room and has neither foot nor body? Answer: It's a fizzling fart] (f. 58v).

12. Fredric Jameson, *The Geopolitical Aesthetic: Cinema and Space in the World System* (Bloomington, IN: Indiana University Press, 1992), pp. 188–9 *et passim*.

5

JOHN D. LYONS

Tragedy and fear

In November 1667, Jean Racine's *Andromaque* was performed at the Hôtel de Bourgogne, a theatre near today's Forum des Halles, in Paris, on the right bank of the Seine. *Andromaque* was the young playwright's breakthrough piece. It can serve as a starting point for thinking about French dramatic tragedy. In fact, this play, loosely based on a passage in Virgil's *Aeneid* and bearing the title of a tragedy by Euripides, displays Racine's approach to problems that are inherent in the conception and dramaturgy of tragedy in France. One of those problems is precisely the matter of how to begin.

The first scene of *Andromaque* opens as the protagonist Oreste is in the midst of a conversation with his friend Pylade, whom he finds unexpectedly after months of separation. Oreste has come to Epirus as emissary of the Greeks, charged with the mission of taking custody of, or slaying, the child Astyanax, son of the Trojan prince Hector and his wife Andromache. After Hector's death at Troy, his widow and son became slaves of Achilles' son Pyrrhus. The latter had promised to marry Menalaus' daughter Hermione, who loves Pyrrhus passionately, but he has fallen in love with his captive Andromache. Oreste's personal reason for accepting this mission to Epirus is, in fact, to take away with him his cousin Hermione, for whom he has had an unrequited love since their youth together.

This entanglement of lives and purposes is all set forth in the opening conversation, and the graceful way Racine deals with the awkward task of filling in the audience and the reader with the necessary background information is the first and most practical manifestation of the problem of getting started. Racine, rare in this respect if not unique among French tragic authors of his day, knew Greek well and had read Aristotle's *Poetics* in that language – we have his notes on the text. The first scene of *Andromaque* shows how seriously the playwright took the injunction to begin in the middle of things, a concept familiar to us in the Latin injunction to start *in medias res*. The very first word of the play is 'Oui', as Oreste seems to reply to something his friend has said. Thus, the beginning of the play is not the beginning of the conversation represented. There an unknown something that precedes, and in so strikingly starting with the omission of the first part of the characters' exchange, the author was no doubt cleverly signalling to his audience the importance of the burden of the past in this play. In fact tragedy is one of French culture's most conspicuous borrowings from Greco-Roman antiquity. As La Bruyère wrote twenty-one years after the first performance of Racine's play: 'Everything is already said, and I have come too late.'[1] At numerous points in *Andromaque* the characters struggle to establish their own identity and to come out from under the shadow of their heroic ancestors. Piqued by his cousin Hermione's comment that he lacks courage, Oreste sarcastically offers to re-enact the Trojan War, with Hermione playing the role of her mother Helen and Oreste the role of his father Agamemnon. Andromaque claims ecstatically that in her son Astyanax, her husband Hector has been resuscitated; at another moment, Pyrrhus is said to be both the son and the rival of Achilles. Racine and his fellow sixteenth- and seventeenth-century playwrights could say as much. They are both the heirs and the rivals of antiquity.

It is a truism that tragedy flourished in two epochs and places: in fifth-century BCE Athens, and in Western Europe from the 1580s to the 1680s. Writers of tragedies in that second period could only begin with an awareness of their indebtedness and even their subordination to their predecessors Aeschylus, Sophocles, Euripides, and Seneca. They also knew that tragedy came from somewhere else. While many genres had foreign origins, sometimes acknowledged in the name (such as romance, *roman*), they had had the time to be assimilated into French culture over hundreds of years. Tragedy, in contrast, was a recent arrival, and in 1549 the poet and theorist Joachim Du Bellay presented the restoration of the ancient Greco-Roman genre as a noble project worthy of a king.[2] Such dramatic works would replace farces, mysteries, and morality plays that had, in Du Bellay's opinion 'usurped' the place of ancient theatrical models. With terms such as 'restoration' and 'usurpation', the writing and discussion of French tragedies were intertwined with allusions to the fraught relationship between France as a nation with a national language at a time when a break from the recent past – what we now call the Middle Ages – gave the works of antiquity a paradoxically modern cachet. The situation of the characters in *Andromaque* gives an echo of the difficult situation of tragedy as a genre. It must follow and imitate antiquity and yet establish itself as new, not as a set of translations or direct imitations.

Just as in *Andromaque*, the story of tragedy in France was well under way before it reached a dramatic crisis. And just as the first few scenes of Corneille and Racine's tragedies typically include dialogue that is meant to fill in what happened before, we need to backtrack a bit to see what preceded the convergence of forces that propelled tragedy to a position of such public importance that the Académie française and the prime minister, the Cardinal Richelieu, gave the genre a quasi-official position in the kingdom.

French tragedy and its difference

Is French tragedy tragic? Many theatre-goers and readers, accustomed to Elizabethan or Greek tragedies, at first encounter with French plays called 'tragedy', are disconcerted by what they find or by what they do not find. The piles of corpses that litter the stage at the end of plays by Shakespeare or Thomas Kyd and the choruses bewailing the stark horrors of the House of Atreus are gone, and in their place we often find a king or emperor reconciling adversaries in the midst of optimistic prophecies of future prosperity. Many English-speaking critics flatly deny that French drama can be worthy of the adjective 'tragic' – if they even deign to notice French works. One writer asserts: '*Le Cid* is not tragic, while *Romeo and Juliet* is.'[3] Another writes: 'Twice only has tragedy flowered to full perfection, once in Periclean Athens and again in Elizabethan England. The great tragic artists of the world are four, and three of them are Greek.'[4] Terry Eagleton, a model of encyclopaedic literary and philosophical knowledge and probably the writer on tragedy who has been the most catholic in his scope, limits the examples of French tragedy considered in his *Sweet Violence* to three works: Corneille's *Le Cid* and *Cinna*, and Racine's *Phèdre*.[5]

Clearly theorists and critics can easily find grounds to exclude almost any dramatic work from the category of tragedy by applying the narrowest imaginable criteria. For example, one might rule out plays with 'happy endings' – this is the basis for eliminating plays such as Corneille's *Le Cid* (1637) in which the hero survives, becomes a glorious general, and is promised the hand of the woman he loves, and such as Racine's *Athalie* (1691) in which the parricidal queen of Israel is killed and the innocent young heir to the throne is crowned in her stead. But if we use this argument to exclude these French dramas we will need to disqualify much Greek tragedy as well. In addition to the tendency of English readers to judge all serious drama by comparison to Elizabethan theatre, an additional obstacle to appreciating French tragedy comes from the widespread (and not entirely undeserved) reputation of French culture as cerebral and elitist, and the impression that French tragedy is rationalist, formalist, analytical, and concerned principally with psychology. Although there is a grain of truth to this view, it is the basis of a reductive view of the plays that form our current canon of French tragedy. The historical basis of this limiting view consists of three overlapping historical trends: the pacification and modernization of French culture under the Bourbon monarchs at the end of the French civil-religious wars, a widespread turn towards the practice of introspection in both philosophical and religious life, and the rise of a highly literate group of women readers and authors.

First, an English-speaking person familiar with the works of Shakespeare, Marlowe, George Chapman and other Elizabethan and Jacobean dramatists might expect from French writers similar stagings of recent events from national history or events in neighbouring countries with an immediate impact on France. Indeed, at the transition of the sixteenth to the seventeenth centuries, numerous French tragedies portrayed incidents from the French religious wars (1562–98), events similar to those that appear in such English plays as Chapman's *Bussy d'Ambois* (1607). But during the reigns of Henri IV, Louis XIII, and Louis XIV (1589–1715) the French stage eschewed direct representation of recent political and religious, not as a result of royal edicts but through a tacit preference for indirection, what one critic has called 'l'art de l'éloignement' [the art of distancing].[6] Instead, efforts were made to produce dramas that made no direct reference to the conflicts of the civil wars nor to the present century. Tragedy could sometimes be understood, by contemporaries, to allude indirectly to current events, but such connections were almost never explicit. Moreover, with the arrival of the Bourbon monarchs after Henri IV's accession in 1589 there was a major cultural modernization of France, in part carrying out the literary programme of the Pléiade poets of enriching the French language and of making modern French literature equal to the literature of antiquity. In this sense, seventeenth-century French tragedy can be considered to parallel the urbanistic renewal of Paris.

Second, in the midst of the violence of the wars of the sixteenth century, philosophical common ground emerged among thoughtful writers on both Protestant and Catholic sides. Greco-Roman antiquity could be shared without the animosities over theological and scriptural differences. Among the ancient texts rediscovered were the works of Stoic and Epicurean philosophers (about which more later) who encouraged introspection and meditation. Much of French literature in the following century is imprinted with the careful parsing of feelings and thoughts and thus of motivations for action.

A third concurrent cultural influence on tragedy was the rise of women as an audience for and influence upon literature and manners. This influence is apparent already early in the century in the well-known salon of the Marquise de Rambouillet (from 1620 onwards) and later in the work of Madeleine de Scudéry and her circle. The phenomenon of learned women and their attempt to refine courtly manners and to change the way men and women related to one another emotionally and sexually is known sometimes as 'préciosité' and sometimes as 'culture galante'. This movement encouraged politeness, refinement of language, an emphasis on conversation, a reduction in physical violence, and careful attention to female–male emotional interaction with substantial attention to the feelings of women. It is also worth noting that, on the French stage, women's roles were played by women, not by boys, as was the case in Britain until the end of 1660.

Given these converging influences, it is not surprising that French tragedy should have a simplified and elegant format (just as the urban design of Paris became simpler, with a clear overall layout) with less emphasis on battles and murders and more on conversation and emotional and moral dilemmas. Each play, when considered in its printed version, is divided into five acts, and the acts are subdivided into scenes. The term 'scene' does not denote a change of place or décor but indicates simply a change in the characters on stage. So when three people are speaking and one leaves the stage the printed text will indicate a new scene. All speaking parts consist almost exclusively of rhymed twelve-syllable Alexandrine verse. Stage directions are minimal, sometimes entirely absent from the printed text, but the dialogue usually offers clues to the intended movements, postures, and gestures. There are usually between seven and twelve characters, and in seventeenth-century tragedies there are almost never choruses, with the notable exception of Racine's two final works, the biblical tragedies *Esther* and *Athalie*.

The impact of *Le Cid*

With regard to the content of French tragedy during its major period of dominance (approximately from the late 1630s until the 1680s, when opera, *tragédie lyrique*, became a successful rival), one single play had a major and paradoxical impact. That play was not, as originally written and performed, a tragedy, but rather a tragi-comedy. This is Pierre Corneille's *Le Cid*, a huge popular success. 'Tragi-comedy' was a designation widespread in the dramatic production of the 1620s and 1630s. This was an untheorized genre (it had no ancient pedigree nor any philosophical warrant of the type the *Poetics* provided for tragedy) of which the single consistent characteristic was that the plot ended happily for the main characters. In *Le Cid*, two young Castilian nobles love each other intensely and are on the verge of being engaged to marry when a sudden quarrel between their fathers created an apparently insurmountable obstacle. Rodrigue is required by honour to kill the father of his beloved Chimène – this is, in a certain sense, the *Romeo and Juliet* of French culture. The play caused a sensation because of something that appeared to its critics as a moral and dramaturgic flaw of major proportions. Chimène not only continues to love Rodrigue after he kills her father in a duel, but loves him even more intensely. Although she makes every effort, in public, to see that Rodrigue is punished for killing her father, in private Chimène makes it clear to her lover that she admires him for his achievement and, indeed, that she would have been ashamed of him if he had failed to challenge her redoubtable father.

It is easy to discern the impact of the newly empowered female audience in making *Le Cid* a success. The love between Rodrigue and Chimène is placed on the same level of importance as Rodrigue's military prowess and courage. In other words, male-female relationships become as important as the exclusively male domain of military action. Moreover, Chimène's dilemma as a woman of maintaining what she perceives as her family honour (punishing Rodrigue for killing her father) is given actually more attention than Rodrigue's challenge of fighting to defend his family's honour. Physical violence – the grisly details of combat – are excluded from the stage in order to concentrate on the decision process and the feelings of the principal characters. The feelings of the principle characters, their struggles of conscience and their decisions made on the basis of their love, are the main focus of the drama. In *Le Cid* the introspective turn of literary culture and *galant* culture converge.

Corneille's rivals were savage in criticizing the play and its huge success. Richelieu charged the newly formed Académie française to review it and to write a report. This official document, 'Les Sentimens de l'Académie française sur la tragi-comédie du *Cid*' [Sentiments of the French Academy on the subject of the tragi-comedy *Le Cid*], along with various other pamphlets, poems, and so forth, is part of what is called the Querelle du *Cid* [Quarrel of *Le Cid*]. This controversy had the effect of promoting Corneille's play into a position of national concern and of making known to a wide public a set of poetic principles and terms, such as plausibility, character, and singleness of action. It is possible that the subsequent history of French tragedy would have been quite different had the critical world chosen to focus instead on Corneille's slightly earlier and less well-received tragedy, *Médée* (1635). As a tragi-comedy in its initial form (it was republished in 1648 in a slightly rewritten form and labelled a 'tragedy'), *Le Cid* did not draw on a subject from antiquity (unlike *Médée*, which was clearly modelled on Seneca's play of that name), but instead adapted a contemporaneous Spanish play by Guillén de Castro (1618) – in other words, a relatively modern subject – and packed a multitude of events into the five acts. Not only does Rodrigue fight two duels, but he also defeats a Moorish army (and thus receives the honorific title of 'le cid' from the defeated enemy).

The Académie's criticism of the play centred on its implausibility, perceived in two aspects. The first, less serious flaw was said to consist of the large number of events that are represented as transpiring in twenty-four hours. Rodrigue in that time fights two duels and leads the Spanish troops to victory in a major battle, but he also has time to meet twice in private with Chimène. The more serious fault concerned the feelings and conduct of Chimène. It was considered implausible that a young heiress of a good family would show the killer of her family that she loved him and would express the hope that he would survive her attempts (required, she felt, by her honour) to have him killed. Her apparent acceptance, in the last scene, to marry Rodrigue was the ultimate misconduct on her part. The Académie referred to her as 'denatured' and comparable to a 'prostitute'.

Le Cid offered a model for many subsequent tragedies, and Corneille's reaction to the combination of popular success and critical controversy led him to elaborate a detailed account of his poetic principles, *Les Trois Discours sur le poème dramatique* [*Three Discourses on the Dramatic Poem*] (1660). Here Corneille showed that he had taken the Académie's criticism to heart and had elaborated an approach to writing tragedy that countered these critiques. First of all, the fact that the historical events on which *Le Cid* was based included the ultimate marriage of Chimène and Rodrigue justified, in Corneille's mind, the otherwise implausible aspects of his work. Indeed, he went further, and claimed that the subject of any truly great tragedy must be implausible: 'the great subjects that stir the passions so that their impetuous demands run counter to duty or to the affections of kinship, must always go beyond plausibility'.[7] The playwright's task was to begin an implausible event and then recreate the psychological conditions in which people might credibly do such a thing. Closely related, in Corneille's mind, to the issue of implausibility was the importance of transgression within the tragic plot. Powerfully transgressive actions were the most conducive to strong emotion, both on the part of the characters and on the part of the audience of the play. This approach to structuring the tragic plot can be seen in such works as *Horace* (1640), in which the title character kills both his best friend and his sister and in *Rodogune* (1644), the play that Corneille apparently considered his favourite, in which a mother kills one of her adult sons and tries but fails to kill the second.

The emphasis on male–female love, what we would anachronistically call romantic love, persisted after *Le Cid* as a major feature of French tragedy. This is in sharp contrast to most tragedies of antiquity, with a small number of exceptions, such as Seneca's *Medea* and Euripides' *Hippolytus* (where male–female love simply does not work very well). In ancient tragedies the relations of men and women are important but usually within an established institutional framework as father–daughter, brother–sister, or husband–wife so that winning or losing the affection of a member of the opposite gender is not key to the plot. As we can see in *Andromaque*, on the other hand, courtship and the formation of a couple is at the core of many French tragedies. The difficulties of forbidden or unrequited love take many forms and occur within situations that raise other questions of a moral or institutional nature but the story of the couple is usually foregrounded. There are innumerable variations on this plot. In Alexandre Hardy's tragi-comedy *La Force du sang* (*c.* 1612), a young woman is raped in the dark by an unknown man at the beginning of the play and ends by bearing his child and then finally marrying him. In *Rodogune*, two brothers fall in love with the same woman, who offers to marry the brother who will kill his mother. In Racine's *Britannicus* (1669), a power struggle between the emperor Nero and his mother Agrippina is intertwined with the doomed love of the more legitimate claimant to the imperial power, Britannicus and his cousin Junie.

In these plays, as later in Racine's, there are usually deaths – though not always: no one dies in the course of *Cinna* (1642), although many deaths precede the opening scene. Instead, as Corneille himself explained it, what matters is the danger of death. If we compare *Horace*, for instance, to *Hamlet*, where Fortinbras orders that the bodies on the stage be carried away for burial, or to the many killings that occur in Middleton's *The Revenger's Tragedy* (1607), we can see how relatively few deaths occur in the course of a typical tragedy by Corneille. In Racine's tragedies there are still fewer: two in *Andromaque*, *Britannicus*, and *Phèdre*, and none in *Bérénice*. This does not mean that death is less important or less significant in French plays. The opposite may indeed be the case in that each individual death in these plays receives more attention and requires more time and deliberation. In *Le Cid*, with the exception of the unnamed victims of the off-stage battle that Rodrigue leads, only one person dies: Chimène's father. But that death occupies almost the entirety of the play if we consider not only the hero's hesitation to engage in the duel, his decision to do so, efforts by various parties to prevent the duel, and then the aftermath of the duel with much discussion of Rodrigue's possible death in revenge for his killing of Chimène's father. In Racine's *Andromaque*, there are only two deaths. They occur at the end of the last act. There is much discussion of people being killed, and much hesitation about carrying out these mortal threats. In short, human life is represented as a precious thing that cannot be taken lightly. For someone accustomed to French tragedy, it is easy to look on the frequent and almost casual murder of the English stage as a way of trivializing life. It is possible to become desensitized to murder in the English dramatic tradition.

Such an effect can be, from the point of view of an habitué of French theatre, reinforced by the admixture of humour.

Tragedy, fear, and grief

We can be so struck by the ways French tragedy is different from tragedy in other cultures – its limitation of incidents, its elegant diction and versification, its concentration in time and space – that we overlook the core elements that link the tragedies of the seventeenth century to the tragedies of antiquity and other early modern cultures. French tragedy, like all tragedy, represents incidents that are frightful and that provoke a network of emotions centred on death, mutilation, pain, and loss. This is the case since the earliest writings on tragedy in Plato's *Republic* and Aristotle's *Poetics*. Plato's example of an event represented in tragedy is the case of 'a good man who loses his son'.[8] The poet, according to Plato's Socrates, makes us feel sorry for such a man. Rather than repress grief and use reason, a man watching a tragedy gets carried away with his feelings and approves wailing and lamenting in a womanish way. Aristotle countered in the *Poetics* that tragedy represented the emotions of fear and compassion in order to cleanse the audience of such feelings. Although it is doubtful that any practicing playwright pondered seriously the obscure and much debated Aristotelian notion of emotional catharsis, everyone seems to have agreed that tragedy aims above all at serious emotional impact on the audience through feelings of fear, horror, sorrow, compassion, and so forth, all feelings occasioned by something frightful. The historical record shows that even in periods when tragedies were not being written, such as the Middle Ages, tragedy was conceived as a genre that concerned horrible loss, and Plato's example of 'a good man who loses his son' (usually with the additional complication that this is the good man's fault) would have been recognized from antiquity to the Renaissance as typical.

   If the emotions of fear and compassion (*phobos* and *eleos*) have such pertinence in discussions of tragedy, what is the relation between the two? The plays that occasion such emotions appear are almost always plays in which someone kills someone or comes close to doing so. Fear and grief imply a temporal perspective: fear precedes a deadly act and grief follows it. Plato emphasizes grief and lamentation. Aristotle promotes fear, saying that the best kind of tragedy is one in which a man, who is about to kill his child or friend recognizes that person just in time, and avoids this loss. In actual tragedies, as for these two philosophers, what remains central is death and the perspective of a kindred person about that death.

In the preface to Jean de Mairet's pastoral tragi-comedy, *La Silvanire* (1631), the writer defined tragedy for his readers (it is significant that he felt he should do so): 'Tragedy is nothing other than the representation of a heroic incident in misery.'[9] Later, Corneille defined tragedy as a play concerning important (aristocratic) characters, in which some important political issue hangs in the balance, and in which the protagonist risks death. Even if the other requirements are met (noble characters and important political issue), and even if someone other than the hero dies or risks death, it is the serious danger for one of the main characters that is the ultimate and indispensable requirement. Such a way of looking at things – that is, to require only that the hero *risk* death – is so radically different from the tradition across the English Channel that it is not surprising to hear members of an English-speaking public deny that *Cinna* or *Le Cid* is a tragedy, but it is also much closer to Aristotle's *Poetics* and to the practice of antiquity.

It happens that the cultural interest in fear in the late Renaissance was not limited to the theatre. While tragedies were once again being written and performed on the stage in France, there was a powerful revival of interest in philosophies that made the management of fear an important topic. Stoicism and Epicureanism became influential schools of thought. The work of Epictetus was published and translated in numerous editions from the mid fifteenth century, and the first French translation was in 1567.[10] Erasmus edited two editions of Seneca's works in the early sixteenth century.[11] Justus Lipsius widely propagated Stoic ideas in his *De constantia* [*On Constancy*] (1583), and Montaigne became known as the 'French Seneca'.[12] He was also heavily influenced by the Epicureanism of Lucretius, whose *De rerum naturae* [*On the Nature of Things*] was available in an important 1564 edition.[13] Montaigne discusses fear and the avoidance of fear, specifically fear of death, in his *Essais* in the chapter 'De la peur' [On Fear] but also in numerous other passages. The Christian apologist Blaise Pascal, who is reputed to have said that Epictetus and Montaigne were his two favourite authors, made a very different use of fear from other writers in this expansive group of writers concerned with fear, since Pascal wished to shake his non-religious interlocutor out of complacency with regard to death. Tragedy was, for Pascal, precisely the apt connection, something that would appear to his reader as a vivid and familiar representation of the horrifying and definitive end of life. He wrote, 'the last act is bloody, however beautiful the comedy may be in all the rest'.[14] The term 'comedy' should not mislead us here, since it was the inclusive French term for dramatic performance, and the genre that includes a bloody death is clearly tragedy.

The risk of violent and untimely death is the core of tragic drama, but it is not the fear of such a death that fills the thoughts and struggles of tragic characters. For French tragedy, the question about what occasions fear is very revealing. In Racine's *Britannicus*, there are two violent deaths that occur in the course of the play. These occur suddenly and take the victims by surprise, so neither one spends much time expressing fear of death. Britannicus, son of the emperor Claudius, dies instantly as he drinks wine poisoned on the instructions of Nero. He has not spent the preceding hours fearing death. Indeed, he dies at a moment of great happiness at the reconciliation that seems to have taken place with his stepbrother. Later, Nero's confidant and advisor Narcisse is torn to pieces by a mob enraged by Britannicus' death and by Nero's attempt to take Britannicus' lover Junie as his second wife. While the entire play is drenched in the memory and the threat of murders within the extended imperial family, its characters are not particularly concerned with their own deaths. They are not motivated by attempts to save their own lives. What is at stake, centrally, in the dramatic action is Junie's attempt to save the life of her lover Britannicus. This is one end – both logically and chronologically – of a chain of interconnected and particularized fear.

The plot of *Britannicus* can be seen as an indirect power struggle between Nero and his mother Agrippine in which Britannicus and Junie are pawns. Agrippine fears the loss of power, as she perceives her son, whom she has put on the throne through years of conspiracy, emancipating himself from her. Nero, for his part, fears being kept forever under his mother's thumb and also fears being perceived as her puppet. If he can divorce the wife forced upon him by Agrippine, Nero can assert his own political and sexual power. If Agrippine can prevent this shift in Nero's marital status, she can use the couple Junie–Britannicus as potential replacements on the throne, maintaining a balance of political power in which she would always be the broker. Racine's tragedy thus hinges on preserving or ending Britannicus's life, but the ultimate act of killing Britannicus – in today's idiom we might speak of 'the nuclear option' – provides the basis for a large number of other threats and manipulations that subtly occupy most of the five acts of the play.

The main characters in French dramatic tragedies are highly aware of the probability that they will die prematurely and violently. However, the situations represented in these plays are not simply those of warriors heading off to battle: this is the stuff of epic. Instead, we find members of the aristocracy off the battlefield in an urban or domestic setting dealing with inglorious or at least ethically questionable and sometimes even shameful killings. They experience fear for themselves, fear that they will be killed, but more often they fear the deaths of family members and loved ones. In many plays, even though their own death is a distinct possibility, it is not their own death that worries them but either the death of someone else or the loss of something that they hold dearer than life.

Let us consider, for example, Tristan L'Hermite's 1636 play, *La Marianne*. In the first scene, one of the two protagonists, Herod, recounts a frightening dream of being alone in a dark and horrifying forest. Hearing the name of his beloved but estranged wife Marianne called out loud in a plaintive and funereal voice, he rushes towards the source of the call, only to find himself standing on the bank of a pond that is red with blood. From the waters emerges the partly decomposed corpse of Marianne's brother, whom Herod killed. At some length the description insists on what is most terrifying and repellent in this vision. The corpse's mouth is dead and yet it speaks, and so forth. This first act sets the tone for the play as a whole. It is about death and about the way the dead are not sufficiently dead. They haunt the living and threaten them. What is at issue, however, is more complicated than Herod's fear of his own death as a result of the murders he himself committed in the past. What is frightening is something that appears in Greek and Roman tragedy as well as in French tragedy: the death of a loved one, particularly a death for which the protagonist himself or herself is responsible. In the course of *La Marianne*, Herod orders that his wife, whom he loves with an unusual passion, be killed. He is persuaded (by her enemies) that she is unfaithful to him and that she has plotted to kill him. Even so, he seems ready to forgive her, but she makes no concessions and seems even to welcome death, in large part because it is the way to inflict the greatest harm on Herod. This calculus turns out to be correct, and after Marianne's execution, Herod goes completely mad, imagining that he sees Marianne in the sky and that he can speak with her. As the play ends, Herod, before falling into a swoon (perhaps deathly) speaks to Marianne and says that his soul is following her into death.

In *La Marianne*, as in most French tragedies, the death of another significant person preoccupies the protagonists. Within the horizon of the unrelenting awareness of the imminence of death the principal question for the protagonist is: 'What is more important to me than the risk that I will die?' For Herod, that more important thing is Marianne. While he is outraged by the idea that she has plotted his death, it is not death itself that bothers him. He is, as Tristan writes in the preface, a 'clever and courageous tyrant'. He keeps hoping that Marianne will repent, beg his forgiveness, and live. Marianne knows this, and insists on dying, because she too values something more than her own life: vengeance for Herod's prior killing of her family. The tragedy becomes a cat-and-mouse game in which the intimate enemy dares the other to destroy himself. Or, as another analogy to the fundamental tragic mechanism in this period we may think of those legendary monkey traps consisting of a box through which the monkey can reach his hand to grasp some delicious food that cannot, however, be pulled out. The monkey stubbornly clings to the bait, the story goes, until the hunter comes to take the monkey away. It is true that the power of this trap is based on desire, rather than fear, but desire can be conceived as inverted fear. Clinging to the desired object equals fearing that that object could be taken away. In the geometry of tragic emotion, next to the pair fear–desire is the other pair fear–grief. Grief views the calamity in retrospect; fear views that same calamity prospectively.

The permutations on this formula are almost infinite. In *Phèdre*, the eponymous heroine fears first one thing and then another more than death. Initially, she dreads the shame of revealing that she loves and desires her stepson Hippolyte. Later, having admitted this passion, what she fears is that a younger woman, Aricie, will enjoy Hippolyte's love. Hippolyte begins with twin fears: on one hand the wrath of his father and on the other hand the fear of being unworthy of his father, having no heroic distinction of his own. Thésée, known for his fearless battle against monsters and marauders, does not fear death, but his angry condemnation of his son reveals the fear of being disgraced if he leaves an incestuous rapist son unpunished.

The indirection that we perceive in tragic fear, the way it afflicts the protagonists not in the head-on military combats but indirectly with regard to the death of other people or the loss of something that seems more important than life itself can be seen in *Le Cid*. Rodrigue shows no fear at all when faced with the challenge of leading a hastily organized group of Castilian nobles to fend off a surprise night-time attack by the Moorish adversary. He hesitates, as if in fear, at the prospect of a duel with the most terrifying warrior in the Spanish army: the great general who is the father of his beloved Chimène. But what troubles him is not the high probability of his own death in this one-on-one combat. Instead, his greatest worry is not that he will die but rather the contrary that he will kill his adversary. Corneille emphasizes the highly paradoxical nature of this fear, the fear of victory. Rodrigue realizes that if he defeats the Count and thus survives, he will incur the loss of Chimène, who will then become his enemy.

Another way of stating this situation is to say that tragedy, at least as it appears in early modern France, necessarily concerns fears surrounding the risk of death in non-military situations, and thus non-heroic situations. The main characters of such plays derive their sense of identity from battle, but in tragedy they face challenges in which physical strength and strategic cunning are of no avail. Success in combat may lead directly to disaster at home. Consider Corneille's *Horace*, in which the title character has secured a Roman victory over Alba by killing the three Alban champions. As soon as he returns to the city, he slays his sister in a fit of rage because she curses his victory (one of the slain was her betrothed). Horace makes the clearest statement of the strange and unhappy relationship between the heroic state of the fighter in war and the unheroic situation of the survivors of victory. He says: 'For my honour, I have already lived too much' (l. 1582). He has 'overlived', something that many protagonists of tragedy have in common.[15] They often do not wish to live, fearing the corrosive effect of time itself on their heroic status. Thus Polyeucte, a principal figure in the martyr tragedy of the same name, rushes impatiently to his death, for fear that he will live past his moment of heroic, grace-filled resolve and purity. Or they outlive their success and face inglorious death, the kind that negates their standing as heroes. They may be killed by a wife, a friend, or an ally. Rather than die in a fair fight they may be stabbed in ambush or poisoned. They may survive such a conspiracy against them, as the emperor Auguste does in *Cinna*, but henceforth they know that anything is possible, that they can trust almost no one.

Tragedy is therefore overwhelmingly a civil or domestic and post-heroic genre, and, as we have already said, concerns not so much the hero's fear for his own safety but his fear or grief on account of the death of someone near and dear. Jason, in Corneille's *Médée*, is the hero of the adventure of the Argo, but after this adventure he finds himself unable to prevent his wife from killing his two young sons and the woman he now loves, who burns to death from contact with a poisoned dress. The Thésée of *Phèdre* returns home with a lifetime of heroic achievement behind him, and only moments after returning knows that he will never outlive the shame or sorrow of having caused the death of his innocent son. In Corneille's *Rodogune*, Prince Antiochus survives, but what a life he has ahead of him knowing that his mother has killed his twin brother and came within seconds of poisoning him. The play concludes as he watches her writhe in agony, having swallowed the lethal potion, and hears her curse him and his offspring.

Playwrights continued to write tragedies in France in the early decades of the eighteenth century. Voltaire's *Œdipe* (1718) and *Zaïre* (1732) were great popular successes, but new dramatic forms displaced tragedy as the characteristic theatrical form. The *comédie larmoyante* [tearful comedy] such as Nivelle de La Chaussée's *Mélanide* (1741) and the *drame bourgeois* [bourgeois drama] such as Diderot's *Fils naturel, ou, Les épreuves de la vertu* (1747) became the vehicle for Enlightenment social criticism with stories set in contemporary France. No longer centred on violent death and its horror, the genres that succeeded tragedy shift the emotional register from fear to resentment, an emotion well suited to a time in which audiences leave the theatre indignant at the sight of injustice and resolved to demand real social change.

NOTES

I wish to thank Rosemary Lloyd and Marc Bizer for their careful and helpful readings of an early version of this chapter.

1. Jean de La Bruyère, *Les Caractères, ou, Les mœurs de ce siècle* (Paris: Gallimard, 1975), section 1, 'Des ouvrages de l'esprit', p. 65. My translation, here and elsewhere in the chapter.
2. Joachim Du Bellay, *La Deffence, et illustration de la langue françoyse (1549)*, trans. Jean-Charles Monferran (Geneva: Droz, 2001), Book 11, Chapter 4.
3. D. D. Raphael, *The Paradox of Tragedy: The Mahlon Powell Lectures* (Bloomington, IN: Indiana University Press, 1960), p. 29.
4. William Macneile Dixon, *Tragedy* (London: Arnold, 1924), p. 23.
5. Terry Eagleton, *Sweet Violence: The Idea of the Tragic* (Oxford: Blackwell, 2003).
6. Thomas G. Pavel, *L'Art de L'éloignement: essai sur l'imagination classique* (Paris: Gallimard, 1996).
7. Pierre Corneille, *Trois Discours sur le poème dramatique*, ed. Bénédicte Louvat and Marc Escola (Paris: Flammarion, 1999), p. 64.
8. Plato, *The Republic* (London: Penguin, 1987), Book x, p. 381.
9. Jean de Mairet, in Jacques Scherer, ed., *Théâtre du XVIIe siècle* (Paris: Gallimard, 1975), vol. 1, p. 482.
10. *La Traduction française du manuel d'Épictète*, ed. Léontine Zanta, trans. André de Rivaudeau (Paris: Champion, 1914).
11. See John Sellars, *Stoicism* (Berkeley, CA: University of California Press, 2006), p. 141.
12. See Donald Murdoch Frame, *Montaigne: A Biography* (New York: Harcourt, Brace & World, 1965), p. 310.
13. Montaigne used this edition by Denis Lambin; Michel de Montaigne, *Les Essais* (Paris: Gallimard, 2007).
14. Blaise Pascal, *Les Provinciales: Pensées, et opuscules divers*, ed. Gérard Ferreyrolles and Philippe Sellier (Paris: Livre de Poche, 2004), fragment 197, p. 929.
15. Emily R. Wilson, *Mocked with Death: Tragic Overliving from Sophocles to Milton* (Baltimore, MD: Johns Hopkins University Press, 2004).

6

ELIZABETH C. GOLDSMITH

Galant culture

In the seventeenth century, the growing sophistication of court life, along with an expansion of the urbanized, reading public cantered in Paris, led to the emergence of new literary forms along with changing tastes in literature and art. The seventeenth century was also a period when European nobilities were generally transitioning from being primarily a warrior-magnate caste to a class that justified and expressed its privilege through superior education, focused on literature, philosophy, and the arts. A new kind of novel, hearkening back to the chivalric romances of the Middle Ages and drawing on Renaissance Italian epic romances and courtly dialogues, evoked idyllic worlds whose inhabitants strove to cultivate refinement, pursue ideal love, and invent a code of behaviour that came to be known as 'la galanterie'.

Honoré d'Urfé

The novel that became almost a guidebook to new modes of noble behaviour was *L'Astrée* [*Astrea*], by Honoré d'Urfé. Urfé himself was a member of the old nobility who had fought in some of the bloodiest battles of the religious wars, had been imprisoned, and served as a diplomat. Turning to writing in the wake of the Wars of Religion, in 1607 Urfé published the first part of his multi-volume work. It tells the story of a group of elegant shepherds and shepherdesses who inhabit a vast landscape protected from the outside world, where they are free to search for a better life inspired by art. The work blended the epic tale of the fall of the Roman Empire and the birth of France with the love story of Astrée and her gallant suitor Céladon, set in a pastoral world. The novel enjoyed an international success.[1] The shepherds and shepherdesses who spent their time talking about love also held tremendous appeal to readers of the day who were all too familiar with the violence and enmity that had so damaged the social fabric of France during a prolonged period of civil wars. The characters in *L'Astrée* are rural shepherds who talk and act like a new, purified version of noble sociability. Urfé situated his novel in his own ancestral province of Forez, near Lyon. It is imagined as a place of refuge from a violent world where a group of noble women and men have chosen to live as shepherds, apart from the tensions of court and city.

The love story framing this 5,000-page novel follows a generic convention of romance since antiquity. It is the tale of Céladon's love for Astrée, her refusal of this love, and the adventures of both characters during their long separation. Céladon throws himself into the Lignon river in a failed suicide attempt, and then wanders through the valleys and forests of southern France. A female ruler named Amasis presides over a court that is periodically visited by different characters. For at least a century after the book was first published, readers treated the novel as a cult object; a lens through which they could view their own lives and find ways to imitate the type of romance that the novel described. Women and men moved easily from talking about the characters and situations in the novel to comparing real experiences to the ones their favourite fictional characters had lived. Marie de Rabutin-Chantal, Marquise de Sévigné, describing her outings to the country in letters to her daughter written in 1676, found that the best way to capture her experience was to compare it to the readings they both knew so well: 'I am so sorry that you cannot see these local dances . . . in these fields and woodlands, it is a joy to watch the descendants of the shepherds and shepherdesses of Lignon, dancing.'[2]

Many painted portraits of the day portrayed members of the nobility dressed as Céladon, Astrée, or other famous characters from Urfé's novel. Even musical compositions were influenced by the story. Music written for the *musette*, an instrument modified from the bagpipe and featured in descriptions of the social gatherings of the novel's characters, was introduced into orchestral works written for performances in royal gardens. The instrument would later make a regular appearance in paintings of fashionable *galant* gatherings by Antoine Watteau.

The publication of Urfé's novel, which appeared in four parts between 1607 and 1627, coincided with a proliferation of manuals of etiquette and advice books on how to succeed in society. This literature on courtesy aimed at creating a modern definition of noble identity, based not only on birth and military valour but on personal cultivation, education, and model conversation. The new ideal model of social education and formation was one based on sociability in the company of women. Women, in fact, were not only expected to be present and participate in social gatherings; they were viewed as possessing a superior understanding of what good conversation meant. Traversing all of the literature on politeness and courtesy was the principle of mixed company, the importance, for men, of seeking out the conversation of women if they wished to acquire the attributes of *courtoisie, civilité, politesse, galanterie*. Women were expected to recognize their own natural 'inner politeness' and learn how best to cultivate it.

The early modern space for cultivating sociable skills and talking about popular novels such as *L'Astrée* is one that since the nineteenth century has come to be called the salon. In the seventeenth century salon gatherings were called 'ruelles' (alcoves), referring more precisely to the spot in a room where visitors would gather around the bed of their hostess to converse. In the case of one of the most famous of Parisian salon hostesses, Scudéry, the social gatherings were given the name of the day of the week in which they took place. The intimacy of the salon marked it off from the court, and allowed it to function as an alternative space for the cultivation of courtly behaviour, or the style of social interaction deemed most suitable for the circles surrounding royalty. It was in the conversational culture of the salon that new and elusive concepts such as *galanterie* and *honnêteté* (noble politeness or worthiness) were defined, practised, and exemplified. Salon society attempted to model a social behaviour that was lofty but not hierarchical, and this aversion to hierarchy extended most notably to a revision of traditional gender relations.

Madeleine de Scudéry

One of the most influential and popular novelists of the seventeenth century, Madeleine de Scudéry received a better education than that of most girls of her social background and time. She and her brother Georges were both writers. Starting in the 1630s, they frequented the literary salons of the fashionable Marais district in Paris, where many noble families had their city residences. The two siblings collaborated on works of fiction that enjoyed immediate success. In 1641 Madeleine published her first novel, *Ibrahim, ou, L'illustre Bassa* [*Ibrahim or The Illustrious Bassa*], under her brother's name. This practice of using the name of her brother as her pseudonymous signature was one that she continued for most of her prolific career as a writer, despite the fact that her own authorship was openly acknowledged in the gazettes, memoirs, and letters of the day. Although the precise nature of his contributions is uncertain, Georges did clearly collaborate to some extent with his sister in the writing of her novels, and he wrote the prefaces to several of her books.

Artamène, ou, Le grand Cyrus [*Artamène, or The Great Cyrus*], Scudéry's second novel, published in ten volumes between 1649 and 1653, assured her celebrity both in France and abroad. The French civil wars known as the Fronde were coming to a close during this same period, and Scudéry dedicated the novel to the duchess of Longueville, who had been a leader in the uprisings against the throne. Although its characters were drawn from historical sources and the setting was the Persian empire of Cyrus the Great, *Artamène, ou, Le grand Cyrus* was a roman à clef, in which most of the major characters could be identified with real people among Scudéry's contemporaries. The worldly society that Scudéry portrayed in *Artamène* and her other novels was shaped by and imitative of romance, with the action related to a central love story filled with obstacles to its consummation. But the social world of the characters also evoked the kinds of conversations held in salon society. Dialogues incorporated into the plots organize themselves around philosophical, social, and psychological topics that the speakers name and try to define, such as 'friendship', 'invention', 'magnanimity', 'anger', 'self-knowledge', and 'lying'. Scudéry included in the novel a character sketch of herself as the poet Sappho, expounding with her friends on platonic love and the life of the intellect. Inaugurated in 1653, Scudéry's salon gatherings continued for five years and regularly received notable writers and cultural figures including Jean Chapelain, François, Duc de La Rochefoucauld, Marie-Madeleine Pioche de La Vergne, Comtesse de Lafayette, Sévigné, and Charles Perrault. Readers viewed the novel's character portraits and conversations as exemplary models of gallantry and civility. And in the long story of Sappho published in the tenth and final volume of her novel, Scudéry describes a female utopia, the mythical land of the Amazons. In seventeenth-century France, 'amazon' was a term used to refer to intellectual women. In Scudéry's utopian vision, women govern according to the laws of love and constancy and writing and the life of the intellect are their most desirable vocations. Ideal masculinity is 'imagined as predicated on a rapprochement with women and femininity, and further, on the notion that men needed to become more like women than the reverse', as Lewis Seifert has observed.[3] Sappho is the ideal intellectual woman writer, as distinct from the negative stereotype of the 'learned lady', also explored in the character of Damophile who serves as a ridiculous double to Sappho. Damophile is unable to make light of her own learning. Sappho's musings on the role of the writer point to the tricky negotiation that a woman writer of the time had to make, in order to pursue learning and also thrive in a social environment intolerant of its display. Seventeenth-century debates concerning the education of women focused as much on the question of how education should be displayed as on its substance, as Linda Timmermans has detailed.[4] Clitandre's speech in

Molière's play *Les Femmes savantes* [*The Learned Women*] would sum up the prevailing attitude:

> I like a woman who, though she may know
> The answers, does not always let it show;
> Who keeps her studies secret and, in fine,
> Though she's enlightened, feels no need to shine.[5]

In her later works Scudéry focused increasingly on the discussions of salon society addressing psychology and behaviour. The most famous episode in Scudéry's third novel *Clélie*, published between 1654 and 1660, concerns an allegorical map of the human heart, called the 'Carte du pays de Tendre' [map of the land of tenderness]. Three types of tender friendship, based on esteem, gratitude, or inclination, are placed on the map, along with itineraries that aspiring friends must follow to reach the three destinations. As a basis for friendship or romance, esteem stemmed from the rational capacity to judge a person's intrinsic worth, while inclination was closer to attraction not based on reason. A friendship stemming from gratitude would be based on a personal obligation or appreciation of another person's generosity. The map and the commentary it generates in the novel's conversations added explicit psychological analysis to many of the conventional devices of romance, and reflected topics that were being discussed in *galant* culture. Among the most influential topics of discussion generated by Scudéry's map was a theory of love valuing reason over passion and explicitly discouraging marriage. Erotic love is not banished from Scudéry's utopian vision of amical and amorous relationships. But it is based on a level of compatibility that she seems to recognize is unachievable, or rarely sustainable, in the real world. Scudéry's novels were attacked and labelled as subversive by some, including the poet and critic Nicolas Boileau, who published a harsh satire on novels in which *Clélie* and the 'Carte du pays de Tendre' were targeted as fostering waywardness among women and the decline of marriage as a social institution.

In the 1660s Scudéry moved away from the lengthy heroic novel genre and turned to shorter narrative forms, publishing three novellas: *Célinte* (1661), *Mathilde d'Aguilar*(1667), and *La Promenade de Versailles* [*The Versailles Promenade*] (1669). These works are more realistic than her novels in that they are situated in modern times with the action taking place in locations that would have been familiar to her readers. Scudéry continued to portray characters – and address readers – who themselves were captivated by epic novels and their grand and complicated plots. In the first part of *Mathilde d'Aguilar* the company retreats to the country in order to cut themselves off from the rest of society, where they select pseudonymous identities taken from *Clélie* and *Artamène, ou, Le grand Cyrus*. In *La Promenade de Versailles* the friends tell each other stories, drawing on contemporary events in the news, in which the conduct of the characters is explicitly contrasted with the manner in which heroes from an epic novel would have behaved. The last phase of Scudéry's career as a writer was devoted to ten more volumes of collected conversations, many of them excerpted from her novels. These were regarded by her contemporaries as representing the best of her writing and, unlike her earlier works, they were published under her own name. They reflect the collective efforts of Scudéry's milieu to cultivate the art of talk and develop a new aesthetic and practice of conversation. Translated almost immediately into English, the conversations contributed to a body of literature describing new 'French' styles of living that by the end of the century had been widely imitated by elite circles in England, Germany, Italy, and Spain.

The English poet, dramatist, and translator Katherine Philips held social gatherings for literary discussions in the style of Scudéry's *samedis*. The members, beginning with Philips, who was known as 'the matchless Orinda', took coterie names drawn from literature and legend. Philips's translation of Corneille's play *La Mort de Pompée* grew out of the collective activity of her salon gatherings.

Scudéry's Sappho hates marriage, just as she hates tyranny, and every discussion of marriage turns to the possibility that a husband may become a tyrant and a wife his slave. Personal freedom for women could only come through reading and conversation with educated and people who were willing to debate received wisdom and tradition. The strong stance against marriage by Scudéry and her circle was inevitably mocked and satirized, but Sappho herself dismisses such attacks as coming predominantly from 'young men, merry and rash, who bragged that they could not read, they prided themselves on the sort of militant ignorance that gave them the audacity to censure what they knew nothing about'.[6]

Not surprisingly, and despite or perhaps because of her enormous popularity, Scudéry's works and the notion of ideal gender relations that they promoted came under attack. The new ideology of politeness was clearly in conflict with more traditional definitions of noble superiority based on inherited status and military prowess. Louis de Rouvroy, Duc de Saint-Simon would complain in his historical memoirs that the instruction received by Louis XIV in the salons of his mistresses came at the expense of a more serious education in the family history of the old nobility.[7] The moralist Jean de La Bruyère critiqued modern sociability as emasculating. He describes the men of the court who achieve success because of their excessive flattery of women, and views the polished politeness of mean as not only hypocritical but excessively effeminate.[8] Already in 1663, in his play *Les Précieuses ridicules* [*The Affected Ladies*], Molière had lampooned the fascination of young society women with the world of Scudéry's novels, and he returned to the satire of intellectual women in his 1672 *Les Femmes savantes*. Beyond the question of gender relations as imagined in *galant* culture, critics pointed out the real-life impossibility of achieving the kind of social equality, even within a carefully circumscribed elite, that was so carefully cultivated in ideal conversation and promoted in seventeenth-century guides to interaction.[9] The rigorous self-effacement required of perfect sociability was a discipline that was judged to be impossible in the real world. Authentic verbal interaction would gradually come to be regarded as something to be found only in intimacy, and based on a new ideal of sincerity, a precious and rare capacity of speech that could not thrive in an inevitably competitive social world driven by vanity and ambition.

The commitment to respect and reciprocity that underlies *galant* culture as it was cultivated in the seventeenth century makes it a forerunner of modern definitions of politeness and manners. But the meaning of the word *galanterie* itself underwent a transformation by the end of the century. The utopian gender relations envisioned in bestselling novels by Urfé and Scudéry was no longer sustainable as a model for *galant* culture. The word *galanterie* itself took on a negative connotation, and was increasing used to suggest scandalous, not polite, behaviour. Love had been considered an emotion not necessary in a marriage, but as William Reddy argues in his study of the history of emotions, 'by 1700 . . . love within marriage takes on the status of an ideal, in which friendship and sexuality are linked, and familial affection becomes the natural model of love'.[10] This was due in part to changing attitudes towards marriage and the rise of a new cultural doctrine of sentimentalism, ultimately most vigorously championed in the works of Jean-Jacques Rousseau.

In the school for girls that Louis XIV and Françoise d'Aubigné, Marquise de Maintenon established in 1684, Scudéry's collected *Conversations* were at first part of the core curriculum. But Maintenon became dismayed when she saw what kind of discussion this reading list was generating among her pupils, who were taking strong positions against domesticity and the boredom of married life. So she replaced some of Scudéry's texts with dialogues that she wrote herself, emphasizing the virtues of piety, self-discipline, marital fidelity, and the cultivation of intimacy within marriage.[11]

But salon gatherings were not only concerned with the collective project of refining manners and reforming the nobility. Worldly society, particularly in what Faith Beasley has called the 'second wave' of salons, such as Marguerite de La Sablière's, flourishing in the 1670s and 1680s, increasingly emphasized literary creation and the invention of new literary genres.[12] Marie-Catherine

Desjardins, Madame de Villedieu stands out as a unique figure in the effort to give a new twist to the *galant* tradition. The only woman author of her time who earned her living from writing, Villedieu introduced a type of narrative in which the intrigues, closely drawn from contemporary events and social scandals, seem to critique the utopian aspirations of earlier heroic novels such as those by Scudéry. She had an astute understanding of how to capture the interest of a new public of worldly readers and worked closely with her publisher Claude Barbin to market her works effectively. With her collection of narratives called the *Annales galantes* [*Gallant Histories*], published in 1670, Villedieu inaugurated a type of behind-the-scenes history that critiqued official accounts of past events and foregrounded the role of women in political history. With her pseudo-autobiographical *Mémoires de la vie de Henriette de Molière* [*Memoirs of the Life of Henriette de Molière*], published in 1672, she introduced a new mixed genre of fictional memoirs, blending real contemporary events and episodes from her own life with an invented tale of an adventurous woman determined to build her own life.

Villedieu's experiments in autobiographical publication were viewed with some scepticism by other women writers who found that the new attention to the 'naturally' superior qualities of women's speech and writing carried with it certain dangers. In one of her published conversations 'On Writing Letters', Scudéry warned women against freely expressing their feelings in letters, for such letters too easily escape the writer's control. In 1668 Villedieu had not been able to prevent the printing of a collection of her own *galant* love letters, which was circulated under the title *Lettres et billets galants* [*Gallant Letters and Notes*]. The unauthorized sale of these letters to the printer Claude Barbin, known for his astute marketing of popular novels, was just one example of a new public fascination with a certain kind of women's writing: the expression of the abandoned woman in love. In 1669 Barbin published what was to be a runaway bestseller and one of the first epistolary novels – *Lettres portugaises*, the letters of a nun seduced and abandoned by a French soldier.

From its beginnings, salon culture helped to popularize literary works mixing different forms of writing – poetry, letters, fiction. Writing that was characterized as *galant* encompassed a wide array of genres, from verse to novels, letters, maps, memoirs, and prefaces. Delphine Denis has described what she calls the 'figurations' of *galanterie* as a kind of staging of sociability in all of its forms, including conversation, games, and other ephemeral creative projects.[13] Scudéry's published conversation on 'l'air galant' calls for more writing that blends different genres. The conversational format of a literary work also lent itself to an open-endedness that some authors considered an important feature of the literature termed *galant*. Readers could think of themselves as participating in the social world that produced the works they were reading. Villedieu, for example, would regularly promise sequels that she never produced, leaving the field open to other authors and storytellers to take up the task.[14] Jean de La Fontaine, most famous as an author of fables, in 1669 published *Les Amours de Psyché et de Cupidon* [*The Loves of Psyche and Cupid*], a fairy tale in verse and prose that seemed to exemplify this new aesthetic. Dedicating the piece to his patron Marie Anne Mancini, Duchesse de Bouillon, La Fontaine frames the story of the mythical Psyche with a leisurely conversation between four friends on an outing to Versailles. The friends vow to banish anything academic from their conversational style. They read the story of Psyche aloud to each other and comment on it, discussing different ways to tell the story and all the while admiring the latest improvements in the gardens being built under the new young king. The four friends are suggestive of a new image of creativity and writing in a social world in which relaxed dialogue and cultivated sociability can produce the best kind of artistic inspiration. The myth that they narrate and discuss is the story of a young woman who is ordered to take a husband she has been told is a monster. The frightening tale seems on the one hand suggestive of a modern horror story, like the fairy tale Bluebeard, featuring a young woman whose curiosity leads her to open forbidden doors and confront the monstrous unknown. At the same time the drama of a woman's betrothal to a 'monstrous', unknowable husband was all too familiar to readers for whom arranged and proxy marriages were the norm. The sister of the Duchesse de Bouillon, Marie Mancini, had been shipped off to Rome a few years earlier to marry a man who was a stranger to her and who had a reputation for violence. In La Fontaine's narrative, the four male friends are touched by Psyche's decision to disobey her new husband. They meditate together on the limitations of the traditional idea of a 'happy ending' in fiction and in life.

The Psyche story poses questions about the relationship between knowledge and love, questions that would be central in the works of Madame de Lafayette, the novelist of the period who is probably the best known today.

Marie-Madeleine Pioche de La Vergne, Comtesse de Lafayette

Born in 1634 to a family with close ties to the court of Louis XIII, Lafayette was accustomed to court culture from an early age, having served as a lady-in-waiting from the age of fifteen to Anne of Austria, the French queen. She was a close friend of Scudéry and other major literary and political figures including La Rochefoucauld, Jean-François-Paul de Gondi, Cardinal de Retz, and the writer Gilles Ménage, who was one of her tutors. Married to a provincial nobleman, she moved with him to his property in the Auvergne but returned to Paris after only three years, establishing an independent residence there, where she remained for the rest of her life. It was in Paris that she turned to writing fiction. In 1662 she published, anonymously, a short historical novella, *La Princesse de Montpensier*. The little book created a sensation, in part because it placed a real historical figure, the ancestor of one of Madame de Lafayette's friends, into a fictionalized love story with a dubious moral message, and in part because of the original ways in which the story set out to blend well-known historical facts with fiction and romance.

Lafayette situated her stories in modern European history, using mostly real figures as her characters, whose family names were familiar to her contemporary readers. She drew attention to the fact that she intended her fictions to be read as historically plausible, initially entitling her first book *Histoire de la Princesse de Montpensier*. It was situated in France during the Wars of Religion. Despite its economy of style, the narrative includes specific references to real battles, military manoeuvres, and political events. The story takes place in two different spheres of action, one public and one private, both violent and potentially lethal in very different ways. Against the historical backdrop of the most murderous and treacherously provoked mob violence of the religious wars – the massacre of Huguenots that began on St Bartholomew's Day, 24 August 1572 – she weaves a story of marriage and illicit passion, taking place in a country estate far from the court and fields of battle.

As in all of Lafayette's fiction, a distinguishing mark of each character is their relative skill in negotiating each sphere and moving between them. The two worlds are separate, but intimately dependent on each other. To survive in each, the most important skill one can have seems to be the ability to keep secrets. Communication is difficult, but it is almost impossible to get off on one's own and find solitude. Characters must learn to manipulate the plausible overlay of public and private motivations. Lafayette shows us real public events inevitably being used by the historical figures as covers or disguises for private ambitions. Everyone must always be concerned with their public persona, with how they appear to others and how their actions reflect the identity of their family name. In the hyper-public world of Lafayette's novels, where public behaviour always serves as a veneer for private passions, the central figure of the novel is particularly vulnerable. In *La Princesse de Montpensier*, it is a girl married off by her family at the age of fourteen, who moves to her husband's isolated property and is left there with no female friend in whom she can safely confide her private thoughts.

But the urge to uncover other people's secrets, as strong as it is in Lafayette's fiction, is never as strong as the need to deceive oneself.

Lafayette shows herself to be a master of psychological analysis, always both understated and intensely powerful. In her most famous novel, *La Princesse de Clèves*, published anonymously in 1678, the central character is a young noblewoman maturing in the oppressive atmosphere of court intrigue. As in *La Princesse de Montpensier*, the plot is drawn from events at the French court of the sixteenth century. Into a group of characters including Catherine de Médicis, the Duke of Guise, and the young Mary Stuart, she placed a central figure of her own invention, a young woman trapped by the dynastic marriage market who must face the dangerously few choices offered to her that might lead to a happy ending for the plot of her own life.

Lafayette's first readers recognized in her novel a reflection of their own time more than that of history. The book precipitated a major literary quarrel, conducted in print via a popular gazette of the day, *Le Mercure galant*. Readers sent letters to the gazette, arguing over whether or not the novel's heroine should have confessed to her husband that she was falling in love with another man. They argued about the novel's realism and the moral implications of her story. The controversy extended to Lafayette's readers in England, where each of her novels was published in translation within a year of their appearance in France.

Themes central to *La Princesse de Clèves* are examined in all of Lafayette's fiction: the difficulty of sincere communication; the fugitive quality of love; the tensions between ethical principles and worldly demands; the constraints of marriage. In her writing, as in many seventeenth-century romance novels, a frequent plot device is the stealing of a woman's private writing. Committing one's thoughts to writing is frequently described as a dangerous undertaking – it can be misinterpreted, misunderstood, lost, or otherwise fall from the writer's control. One of Scudéry's conversations had debated the question of whether women should write intimate letters at all, because they were so likely to go astray or be misinterpreted by unintended readers. In *La Princesse de Clèves* any kind of verbal self-exposure – spoken or written – is shown to be dangerous and particularly if it borders on confession. Retreat from the world and from conversation is a solution that holds a strong appeal for her female characters. But the difficulty of decisions such as these, and their slow maturation in the minds of the protagonists, is what most fascinates Lafayette. Exemplary behaviour is achieved at a great cost. In the darkest of Lafayette's scenarios, as in the posthumously published *La Comtesse de Tende* (1724), the heroine's urge for escape is suicidal. In *La Princesse de Clèves*, retreat is a solution that is closer to a form of religious devotion.

Lafayette's vision includes a profound critique of marriage, continuing the debate that Scudéry had pursued in her novels. But in Scudéry, *galant* culture consists of a refusal of passion and its replacement by tender friendship, while in Lafayette, such friendship is almost non-existent. Lafayette also seems to cast a dubious eye on contemporary discussions of marriage as an evolving institution, challenging the efficacy of legal practices and even evoking the possibility of divorce, as Joan DeJean has argued.[15] The 1670s were the years in which the French state asserted control over marriage as a legal contract, rendering the religious sacrament a secondary step. Numerous published treatises appeared in this period in an attempt to redefine what constituted a valid marriage in the eyes of the law, and what conditions might lead to the dissolution of the marriage contract.

Lafayette's use of the word *galanterie*, in one of her famous characterizations of court society ('ambition and gallantry were the sole occupation of the court'), already points to a darker side of polite society than anything envisioned in the romance novels of Scudéry and Urfé.[16] As time went on, the term 'galant' would take on this negative connotation to the exclusion of any other, and come to mean only transgression, infidelity, or transitory amorous escapades undertaken out of personal ambition.

Lafayette died in 1693, having in the last years of her life withdrawn from Parisian society. But she continued to engage in social life through letter correspondence, as did many of her contemporaries who found themselves separated from the social vortex of Louis XIV's court. Writing letters, in fact enabled a number of individuals of the period to gain fame as authors. The most famous of these was Lafayette's close friend, the Marquise de Sévigné.

Marie de Rabutin-Chantal, Marquise de Sévigné

Madame de Sévigné occupies a special position in the history of French literature. She is one of the best-known writers in the language, but she never wrote anything intended for publication. Her fame derives exclusively from her correspondence, made up of thousands of letters that were first published after her death. Widowed at a young age, Sévigné lived most of her life independently in her home in the Marais district in Paris, where she had spent her youth, and where she was quickly assimilated into the elite social circles of court and city. Sévigné had considerable freedom in the conduct of her life. Her commentary on social events and court politics, conducted through conversation and letter writing, was highly valued for its wit, style, and acuity in a social world where gossip and political action were never very far apart.

The writing of familiar letters, cultivated as an art form as well as a means of disseminating news and information, was a practice that could easily lead to a certain kind of fame. Letters were widely distributed to be copied and imitated. In this society where conversation was also considered an art, letters were theorized about, liberally included in novels and memoirs, and analysed for their intrinsic 'naturalness', a trait that could only be achieved, it was thought, by imitating the oral quality of conversation. Early in the seventeenth century the introduction of a central postal system, established by royal authority, provided a material condition which favoured the new attention to letter writing. By 1627 regular courier routes had been set in place across the country and after the rebellions of the Fronde, the French Queen Anne of Austria and her prime minister, Cardinal Mazarin, established a special postal service within Paris, to facilitate quick letter communication between neighbourhoods.

The increasing concentration of political and economic power in the person of the monarch also made it more expedient, in the last three decades of the century, for members of the nobility to maintain constant contact with events at court. Whether travelling in the provinces or exiled indefinitely from Paris, anyone who hoped to gain favour with the king had to be informed of the most recent news from the capital. Printed pamphlets such as the *Gazette de Hollande* and the *Muse historique* also appeared during this period, but they were distributed no faster than private letters. A reliable correspondent could provide at least as much information to aristocrats absent from court as a printed newsletter.

Some of Sévigné's correspondents over her lifetime were people who had been exiled, such as her cousin Roger de Rabutin, Comte de Bussy, who had been imprisoned and then banished to his country estate after writing a satiric narrative of court life. There he was to remain for the rest of his days, but there he also managed to keep himself at the centre of the social world he had lost by sustaining letter communication with over 150 correspondents. In their letter exchanges Sévigné and Bussy-Rabutin kept up a constant discussion of political, cultural, and personal events – written discussions that were frequently circulated to a wider public.

Sévigné's principal correspondent was to be her daughter Françoise-Marguerite, who in 1671 moved to Provence with her new husband the Comte de Grignan. Three-quarters of the letters of Madame de Sévigné that we know today were written from mother to daughter. They reveal an intense, often contradictory relationship. Madame de Grignan's move to the provinces precipitated a profound sense of isolation in her mother, an experience that was new to this woman known by all to be a paragon of sociability. In the process of building her correspondence with her daughter Sévigné discovered new sources of inspiration for her vocation as a writer. Her letters written from Paris are rich and personal chronicles of behind-the-scenes events in an extremely volatile social milieu. Her letters written from her family property in Brittany evoke more intimate memories that she can share with her daughter. She fills her descriptions of the woods and the familiar property with allusions to their shared taste for pastoral romance, and invites her correspondent to imagine herself with her in the same stable company of their favourite landscapes and books.

The literary fairy tale

One of the short narrative forms that emerged out of the conversational culture of the salons at the end of the seventeenth century was a new type of fairy tale, drawing on folk tradition but also on forms of elite entertainment that were both escapist and contestatory. Running counter to a religious tone at the royal court that was increasingly pietistic, under the influence of an ageing king and his devout consort Madame de Maintenon, literary fairy tales seemed to defend the values and practices of a more secular, *galant* culture. The most famous of the fairy-tale collections from this period is Charles Perrault's *Contes de ma mère l'Oye* [*Tales of Mother Goose*], published in 1697; it includes such familiar favourites as Sleeping Beauty, Little Red Riding Hood, and Cinderella. But most of the authors of literary fairy tales written at the end of the century were women, the most prominent among them being Marie-Catherine d'Aulnoy, Henriette-Julie de Murat, Marie-Jeanne L'Héritier, and Catherine Bernard. While drawing on Greek and Roman mythology as well as topoi from medieval romance (for example, the maiden in the tower) or contemporary fable (as in the practice of dividing a story into narrative and moral), the female authors of fairy tales distinguished their work from the folk-tale tradition and referred to themselves as 'modern fairies'. They also drew inspiration from the pastoral and heroic romances of the early seventeenth century, in their leisurely insistence on character traits defining the perfection of their heroes and heroines, in their fondness for extraordinary coincidences within plots and in the use of long conversations and interpolated tales. Their stories are longer than the short tales we have come to think of as typical fairy tales. Like early novels, they often include lengthy digressions from the main plot and detailed descriptions of place. Their leisurely focus on description, their detailed attention to elaborate architectural spaces, material objects, social gatherings, and the inevitable importance of powerful female fairy characters for advancing the action, all marked their departure from folk tradition.[17] And while the plots of the literary fairy tales usually make their way to a conventional happy ending, marriage is examined with a critical eye. Arranged marriages are viewed with special harshness. Love has its own elaborately examined magical force, following the code of *galanterie* as elaborated by Scudéry in her novels, with intelligence or *esprit* being the highest form of inspiration that love can produce and sustain in a woman.

While the places described in the literary fairy tale are always designated as far-away and imaginary, contemporary readers could easily recognize familiar landscapes and elite residences, especially the gardens of Versailles, which are transformed in the tales of Aulnoy and Murat into spaces of escape, inhabited by aristocrats who live as equals, thus 'refashioning the monarch's monopoly over court spectacle', as Alison Stedman has remarked.[18] The fairy tales of Madame d'Aulnoy seem to engage particularly strongly with a defence of salon culture and worldly society against hostile critics. She draws on the newly invented – and popular – genre of opera, incorporating into her narrative choruses commenting on events, sung verse, and supernatural movement suggestive of the stage machinery used in opera that was so pleasing to contemporary audiences. Anne Duggan has studied the peculiar blend of material culture and myth in Aulnoy's tales, showing how she transforms some of the standard loci of opera into utopian spaces evocative of salon conversations.[19]

The popularity of the novels of Scudéry, Urfé, Lafayette, Villedieu, and other French writers in seventeenth-century Europe contributed in no small part to the spread of French language and elite culture during this period.[20] Seventeenth-century London was home to a salon culture that intentionally echoed the communities both imagined and enacted by Scudéry and her circle. Aphra Behn and Katherine Philips were two English writers who drew inspiration from their contemporary French women novelists. Literary discussions such as the one over *La Princesse de Clèves*, conducted via letters to the *Mercure galant* and other gazettes of the day, helped extend the real population of so-called exclusive salon circles to much more distant communities of readers. The expansion of the book trade in the seventeenth century, along with the development of the periodical press, made it possible for many more people to participate, to some degree, in the supposedly elite and exclusive literary circles of Paris and the court. The works of Urfé, Villedieu, Aulnoy, and many others were translated immediately into many languages. In England, *Artamène, ou, Le grand Cyrus* was disseminated within weeks of its publication in France, even in the midst of the disruptions in trade caused by the civil uprisings of the Fronde.

The influence of French style and sociability as manifested in fiction and social practice was felt strongly in England, where French ideas about conversation and gallantry were studied as philosophical doctrines in opposition to the theory of egoism found in writers such as Thomas Hobbes.[21] But as in France, by the eighteenth century there was also a strong critical reaction abroad to the cultural artefacts of *galanterie*, along with a change in the meaning of the word as it was used to describe behaviour and relations between men and women. When France was at war with England after 1688, the notion of French gallantry and sociability became highly politicized and associated with a moral and cultural subversion of English authority and moral fibre. However, as Daniel Gordon and Dena Goodman have argued, the French concepts of *galanterie*, conversation, and equality in social relations between men and women would be central to the formation of the Enlightenment notion of sociability and a modern society's capacity for egalitarian discourse.[22]

NOTES

1. Translations were produced as each of the parts appeared in French, for example *The History of Astrea* (London: N. Okes for John Pyper, 1620), and *Von der Lieb: Astrae und Celadonis* (Mumpelgart: Jacob Foillet, 1619).
2. Marquise de Sévigné, *Correspondance*, ed. Roger Duchêne, 3 vols (Paris: Gallimard, 1972–8), vol. 2, p. 313. My translation.
3. Lewis C. Seifert, *Manning the Margins: Masculinity and Writing in Seventeenth-Century France* (Ann Arbor, MI: University of Michigan Press, 2009), p. 146.
4. Linda Timmermans, *L'Accès des femmes à la culture (1598–1715)* (Paris: Champion, 1993), pp. 319–86.
5. Molière, *The Learned Ladies*, trans. Richard Wilbur (New York: Dramatists Play Service, 1977), p. 10.
6. Madeleine de Scudéry, *The Story of Sapho*, ed. and trans. Karen Newman (Chicago, IL: University of Chicago Press, 2003), p. 21.
7. Duc de Saint-Simon, *Mémoires*, ed. Delphine de Garidel (Paris: Flammarion, 2001), p. 235.
8. See David Harrison, 'The Politics of Politesse', in *Teaching Seventeenth and Eighteenth-Century French Women Writers*, ed. Faith Beasley (New York: Modern Language Association, 2011), pp. 303–9 (p. 308).
9. For a summary of this literature, see Elizabeth C. Goldsmith, *Exclusive Conversations: The Art of Interaction in Seventeenth-Century France* (Philadelphia, PA: University of Pennsylvania Press, 1988), pp. 17–40.
10. William Reddy, *The Navigation of Feeling: A Framework for the History of Emotions* (Cambridge: Cambridge University Press, 2001), p. 158.
11. Madame de Maintenon, *Dialogues and Addresses*, ed. and trans. John J. Conley (Chicago, IL: University of Chicago Press, 2004).
12. Faith Beasley, 'Salons and Innovation', in *Teaching Seventeenth and Eighteenth-Century French Women Writers*, ed. Faith Beasley (New York: Modern Language Association of America, 2011), pp. 64–75.
13. Delphine Denis, *Le Parnasse galant* (Paris: Champion, 2001), p. 127.
14. See Rudolf Harneit, 'Quelques aspects de la réception de Madame de Villedieu et Jean de Préchac en Europe', in *Madame de Villedieu, ou, Les audaces du roman*, ed. Nathalie Grande and Edwige Keller-Rahbé (Lyon: Littératures classiques, 2007), pp. 223–37.

15. Joan DeJean, *Tender Geographies: Women and the Origins of the Novel in France* (New York: Columbia University Press, 1991), pp. 94–114.
16. Lafayette, *The Princess of Clèves*, ed. and trans. John D. Lyons (New York: Norton, 1994), p. 10.
17. See the Introduction to *Enchanted Eloquence: Fairy Tales by Seventeenth-Century Women Writers*, ed. Lewis C. Seifert and Domna C. Stanton (Toronto: Centre for Reformation and Renaissance Studies, 2010), pp. 18–23.
18. Alison Stedman, Introduction to Murat, *A Trip to the Country*, ed. and trans. Perry Gethner and Alison Stedman (Detroit, MI: Wayne State University Press, 2011), pp. 1–20 (p. 16).
19. Anne E. Duggan, *Salonnières, Furies, and Fairies: The Politics of Gender and Cultural Change in Absolutist France* (Newark, DE: University of Delaware Press, 2005).
20. See Karen Newman, 'The French Disease', *Comparative Literature*, 64.1 (2012), 33–48.
21. See Lawrence E. Klein, 'The Figure of France: The Politics of Sociability in England, 1660–1715', *Yale French Studies*, 92 (1997), 30–45.
22. Daniel Gordon, *Citizens without Sovereignty: Equality and Sociability in French Thought, 1670–1789* (Princeton, NJ: Princeton University Press, 1994); Dena Goodman, *The Republic of Letters: A Cultural History of the French Enlightenment* (Ithaca, NY: Cornell University Press, 1994).

7

MICHAEL MORIARTY

Varieties of doubt in early modern writing

Contrary to a widespread prejudice, medieval intellectual culture was focused on debate. The formal disputation was an essential part of a university education, and many scholastic writings adopted the disputation format, giving arguments on both sides of a question before resolving the issue. In St Thomas Aquinas's *Summa theologiae* the treatment of each point begins by setting out objections to the view the author maintains, which are answered after the exposition and proof of that view. Thus, before arguing for the existence of God, he cites arguments against it.[1] The rational basis for established beliefs could thus be challenged: one could argue, say, like William of Ockham, that God's existence is known only through faith. This is an entirely different matter, however, from rejecting the beliefs themselves; moreover, debates of this kind were officially confined to churchmen.

The twin developments of printing and the Reformation changed all this. From around the 1530s, a French layman or laywoman might decide, on the basis of argument, reading, or personal experience, to withdraw from the institution that until then had informed, or aspired to inform, every aspect of his or her existence, literally from cradle to grave. Those who withdrew were not withdrawing from religion, but adhering to the new institutions of the Reformed religion. Even though they were, in the end, a minority in France as a whole, their change of allegiance affected those who did not follow them, turning mere acquiescence in the status quo into a decision to adhere to it; a decision for which those who stayed Catholic had to find some grounds akin to those that, for others, motivated secession.

It is hard not to see some connection between this crisis of religious allegiance and the rise of philosophical scepticism in the early modern period. The humanist salvage of ancient philosophy brought to light the sceptical theories of the New Academy and, more importantly, the more radical scepticism of Pyrrho.[2] In a powerfully original study of 1960, the historian Richard Popkin argued for a strong connection between the revival of Pyrrhonism and the Reformation controversies.[3] He pointed out, first, that theological arguments between Protestant and Catholic turned on the identification of a reliable 'rule of faith' to settle disputes. Protestants swore by Scripture alone, while Catholics urged that scriptural interpretation itself needed to be validated by the traditions of the church. This helped, he argued, to prepare the ground for the reception of Pyrrhonist discourse, which emphasizes the necessity (and the unavailability) of a criterion of truth. Second, he pointed to the use by various Catholic writers of sceptical arguments: there are mysteries of faith that human reason cannot resolve; it is therefore safer and wiser to accept the traditional wisdom of the church. The use of sceptical arguments, therefore, by no means implied scepticism in the modern sense of disbelief in religion.

Popkin's interpretations of the relationship between sceptical argument and religious alignments have been questioned by scholars. But it is hard to deny his claim that the appearance in 1562 (the year the Wars of Religion between Catholics and Protestants broke out) of Henri Estienne's Latin translation of Sextus Empiricus' Pyrrhonist *Hypotyposes* was a milestone in the history of scepticism. It was certainly heavily exploited by Montaigne in the longest and most complex of all his essays, the 'Apologie de Raymond Sebond'.[4] Raymond Sebond was a fifteenth-century theologian, whose *Natural Theology* [*Theologia naturalis*] Montaigne had translated at his father's behest. Sebond had argued that Christian belief could and should be supported by reason. Montaigne begins by defending this general approach; but when it comes to objections against Sebond's particular arguments, he does not trouble to refute these in detail. Instead, he argues that those who find fault with Sebond in the name of reason are not entitled to do so: for the human reason they are operating with is desperately fallible. In order to show this, Montaigne brackets out the religious perspective altogether, proposing to consider man deprived of all divine grace and enlightenment.

The attack on reason takes the form, initially, of an attack on anthropocentrism, to use an anachronistic term; human pride, to use Montaigne's own. Not only are the heavenly bodies manifestly superior to us in the influence they exert on our lives; our belief in our superiority to animals is without foundation. They show patent signs of intelligence and reasoning; they have language; they have something like moral virtue, and are capable of strong emotional attachments. Behind the wealth of anecdotes (fascinating, entertaining, sometimes incredible) that go to make his case lies the central claim that humanity and the animals belong to and are circumscribed by a single order of nature: 'We are neither above them nor below them.

"Everything under the Sky", said the Wise Man, "runs according to like laws and fortune"' (p. 513).[5]

Suppose, though, we concede, for argument's sake, that when all is said and done we humans have exclusive possession of reason; that we are the only species capable of philosophy (in the general sense of the pursuit of knowledge or wisdom). The question then arises whether philosophy has actually benefited us at all. Has it made us happier, wiser, more virtuous? Apparently not: 'I have seen in my time hundreds of craftsmen and plough-men wiser and happier than University Rectors – and whom I would rather be like' (p. 542). Has it, above all, succeeded in discovering the truth? In the first place, not all philosophy professes to discover the truth in the first place. Montaigne distinguishes three main categories of philosopher. Those of the first type (the so-called 'dogmatists': Aristotelians, Stoics, Epicureans) think they have knowledge; the second, the Academic sceptics, think it impossible to find. The Pyrrhonists, thirdly, are still looking, but in the meantime, as Montaigne shows at some length, they cast doubt on any truth-claims they encounter: their aim is the tranquillity that comes from perfect suspension of judgment. Even the 'dogmatists', he suggests, are far more tentative and exploratory than might be supposed. So it may be a mistake to take philo-sophy's truth claims seriously. But if we do, we shall certainly be disap-pointed. Montaigne argues the sceptical case from two directions: first, with respect to the supposed object of knowledge; second, with respect to the supposed knower. By listing incompatible views in quick succession, he casts doubt on the capacity of philosophy to arrive at any certainty about God or gods. As for astronomical theories, these are no more than elaborate fictions. But our knowledge of the human body is no more reliable. We have no idea how it interacts with the soul, assuming that we have one. But if we know neither soul nor body, we cannot know ourselves. In which case, how can we know anything else?

If the objects we aspire to know are unattainable, that is not surprising given the limitations of our knowledge-seeking capacities. Our powers of judgment are unstable: they are influenced by external causes, and also internal ones, such as the state of our bodies and the passions. If we could apprehend the truth, there would be some truths universally apprehended and agreed on. There are none: moral beliefs and the laws vary drastically from one society to another. Accepting, for argument's sake, the scholastic principle that all our intellectual concepts derive ultimately from sense-perception, Montaigne proceeds to show that our senses are untrustworthy. First, their number is limited: the world might appear very different if we had additional ones; second, they are fallible; third, they contradict one another. We can know what objects are only via our perceptions, therefore cannot measure our perceptions against the objects, therefore cannot be sure of the truth of our perceptions. We would need a criterion to validate our sense-perceptions: the senses themselves will not do, but nor can reason, since its deliverances also require validation. Finally, no knowledge is possible because both we and the world we seek to know are in constant flux. 'We have no communication with Being' (p. 680); only faith, the gift of divine grace, can enable us to transcend the limits of humanity.

The connection with the contemporary religious crisis is explicit, France still being locked in the Wars of Religion when the *Essais* first appeared in 1580. Arguing for the absence of an independent criterion of knowledge, Montaigne makes the analogy with the current religious controversies: only an impartial judge could be reliable, but any Christian must by definition have already taken a stance on the issues. The essay is dedicated to Marguerite, Queen of Navarre; as the Catholic wife of a then Protestant ruler (the future Henri IV of France, who eventually converted to Catholicism to secure his succession to the throne) she was a pivotal figure in the politics of the time. When Montaigne praises Pyrrhonism for its practical consequences (teaching the distrust of human reason, it encourages submission to established religion and law), he is implicitly but clearly presenting it as an antidote to the subversive dogmatism – as he would see it – of the Protestants.

The 'Apology' is a treasury not just of arguments but of metaphors, and both would be drawn on by later writers. Knowledge is constantly compared to a building requiring a foundation (pp. 606, 678); its need for verification is conveyed by references to a 'touchstone' (p. 608), 'compasses', 'set-square', 'ruler' (p. 678), 'instrument of judgement' (p. 679). This latter set of metaphors is clearly inspired by the Pyrrhonist concept of the criterion. But the Pyrrhonist inspiration goes well beyond this. The critique of sense-experience can be found in Sextus Empiricus: so can the technique of listing a host of contrary views on a particular question, so as to cast doubt on our ability to resolve it. This last technique frequently sustains a relativist position: when pointing to the variety of moral values, Montaigne observes that '[a]ny object can be seen in various lights and from various points of view: it is chiefly that which gives birth to variety of opinions: one nation sees one facet and stops there; another sees another' (p. 655). As for religious beliefs, 'We are Christians by the same title that we are Périgordians or Germans' (p. 497). Yet Pyrrhonism is also a dangerous weapon: after all, if Montaigne's critique of human reason has disarmed Sebond's opponents, it has also demolished Sebond's own reasoning. Montaigne therefore urges Marguerite to stick to the conventional arguments of Sebond, and to resort to Pyrrhonist arguments only in extreme circumstances, as an antidote to pestilential Protestant discourse. Nor, indeed, is his argumentation exclusively Pyrrhonist: at times he seems to come closer to the Academic school of sceptics. We have seen that they too thought certain knowledge unattainable, but they held that some views were more probable than other. Thus Montaigne argues that belief in an incomprehensible power, a perfect and good God behind the universe is the most probable view, just as the most probable view is that we have one soul, residing in the brain, and operating through the different organs of the body. Elsewhere, though, Montaigne cites the Pyrrhonist critique of probability (what is probable is what seems truest – but if you don't know the truth itself, how do you know what seems most like it?) – concluding, however, that this makes Pyrrhonism more probable than Academicism. The paradoxes are irreducible. But to commit himself to one or other school would be foreign to Montaigne's exploratory purpose: he quotes with approval the words of an ancient Greek sage, Pherecides: 'I make no claim to know what truth is or to have attained truth. Rather than lay subjects bare, I lay them open' (p. 558).

A more problematic appearance of inconsistency arises with reference to authority. All disciplines, Montaigne argues, are based on authoritative texts, like those of Galen or Aristotle, whose basic principles we are in effect forbidden to question; this is a form of intellectual tyranny. But Montaigne frequently asserts the need for submission: it is not for us to prescribe ourselves our moral duties. Religious faith is not something we have gained from our own efforts; it comes from an external authority. Once you invite, like Luther, the common people to question some established beliefs, you jeopardize all established beliefs; what law and tradition have imposed is rejected as a tyrannical yoke, and the end result is 'loathsome atheism' (p. 490). Human reason flounders in the sea of opinion, once it has left the path traced by the church. Our mind needs the restraint of religion, law, custom, punishment, and rewards; it needs blinkers to stop it from straying. Montaigne is no liberal individualist. One could argue that there is no inconsistency here: philosophy claims to give a rational account of everything, and therefore has no right to appeal to authority, whereas it is precisely because God transcends human capacities that we cannot expect to achieve knowledge of him by rational means; the humble acceptance of revelation is the appropriate response. Internally, this is consistent; but in the future it could be, and was, argued that the critique of authority in philosophy could be extended to the religious domain itself.

In refusing to submit to authority in philosophy Montaigne emancipates his own search for truth. He describes himself as doing philosophy by accident: in looking to develop his own ideas, he is surprised to find himself in agreement with philosophical discourse. But if philosophy cannot disclose what lies beyond experience, this is all the more reason to examine our own experiences of thinking, feeling, judging: 'I study myself more than any other subject. That is my metaphysics; that is my physics.'[6] This 'radical reflexivity', to use an expression of Charles Taylor's,[7] does not always yield certainty: rather, self-exploration reveals how our experience of ourselves, as of everything else, is radically relative and perspectival; rather than an abiding self, what at first appears is a flux of contradictory states: 'Anyone who turns his prime attention on to himself will hardly ever find himself in the same state twice . . . Every sort of contradiction can be found in me.'[8] And yet, 'provided that he listen to himself', a person can discover a core of selfhood, a 'master-form' underlying the shifts of passion.[9] Some kind of certainty, therefore, can be accessed in the self's own experience of itself.

But the reality accessed is morally complex, resistant to being analysed in Aristotelian fashion as settled dispositions towards virtue or vice:

> When I scrupulously make my confession to myself I find that the best of the goodness in me has some vicious stain. And I am afraid that Plato, even in his most flourishing virtue – (and I say this who am the most genuine and loyal admirer of it, as of all virtues of similar stamp) if he had put his ear close to it (and he did put his ear close to it) – he would have heard in it some sinister sound of a human alloy, even though it were a muffled sound which only he could detect. Man, totally and throughout, is but patches and many-coloured oddments.[10]

Montaigne's legacy of doubt is complex. Sceptical arguments of the type he used were exploited by later writers, sometimes with the explicitly religious agenda of which Popkin speaks, sometimes in such a way as to imply, rather, detachment from or rejection of faith. The most creative appropriations of his epistemological legacy were, however, those, very different, of René Descartes and Blaise Pascal.

To Descartes, Montaigne bequeathed both philosophical and rhetorical equipment: in the first category, an arsenal of arguments against the reliability of sense-perception, including the crucial insight that through the senses we access objects not as they are but as the senses represent them; in the second, a model of acceptable dissent from established forms of knowledge and a set of metaphors to motivate that dissent. More generally, he suggested that truth was to be found by turning one's back on established knowledge and searching within oneself. Images of building and urban development are freely used in Descartes's *Discours de la méthode* [*Discourse on Method*] of 1637, where their function is complex: they serve not only, as in Montaigne, to suggest that existing knowledge lacks solid foundations, but to establish an ideal of certainty. They are also used as a measure of prudence, to justify Descartes's project of rebuilding knowledge as a mere redevelopment of his own property, rather than a wholesale challenge to the existing fabric of knowledge.[11]

But doubt is an essential part of Descartes's reconstructive enterprise. Part IV of the *Discours* exhibits how Descartes negotiates the transition from doubt to certainty, but the possibility of doubt is most fully explored in the *Meditationes de prima philosophia* [*Meditations on First Philosophy*] of 1641.[12] The text reconstructs the experience of a Meditator (to be distinguished from the author Descartes) determined to eliminate his false beliefs, and, to this end, digging up their foundations. Since he thinks that all his knowledge is founded on sense-perception (in accordance with the scholastic consensus, as endorsed by Montaigne) he is troubled by the thought that the senses are unreliable. Attempts to distinguish circumstances in which they are reliable from those in which they are not founder on the fact that our sense-experience in dreams is as vivid as in so-called real life. But surely, he asks himself, basic mathematical truths are valid whether we are dreaming or awake? Suppose, however, that God has so created him that he can be deceived even about these. Or if there is no God and his existence is the result of chance, how does he know that he not so imperfect as to be condemned to continual error? If that is so all his beliefs are open to doubt. To prevent him simply lapsing back into them through force of habit, he imagines that not God but an all-powerful evil spirit is systematically deceiving him. At least this will prevent his assenting to anything that is not true. But it seems equally to make it impossible for him to discover any truth that is not open to doubt.

The famous exception is of course the Cogito: if I am deceived, I must exist; indeed, while I am thinking, I must exist (the actual formula 'I am thinking, therefore I am' occurs in the *Discours de la méthode*, Part IV, but not in the *Meditations*). Here, then, is a first truth, and one derived not, after all, from sensation but from the experience of thinking. Interrogating that experience further, the Meditator realizes that he apprehends himself as a thinking thing, distinct from his body; but he cannot be sure that this distinction corresponds to reality until he has been able to exorcize the evil spirit by the realization that his idea of God as the supremely perfect being implies that God must actually exist (which leaves no room for an all-powerful malevolent entity). Moreover, since his cognitive faculties, like his very existence, are a gift of God, they cannot be radically defective, for God is all-perfect. They must, then, be reliable if properly used; in other words, if he assents only to what he clearly and distinctly perceives, he cannot err. Clear and distinct perception, then, validated by God, is the criterion the sceptics thought impossible to find; and since he clearly and distinctly perceives that his idea of himself as a substance that thinks is entirely different from his idea of a body, as a substance extended in space, his mind or soul is distinct from his body.

The criterion of clear and distinct perception is taken up in two important works of philosophy from later in the century: Antoine Arnauld and Pierre Nicole's *La Logique, ou, L'art de penser* [*The Art of Thinking*] (1662) and Nicolas Malebranche's *De la recherche de la vérité* [*The Search for Truth*] (1674). The *Logique* attempts to revive the art of thinking by reducing it to basic mental acts (conception, judgment, reasoning, and arrangement).[13] It insists on the distinction between clear and confused ideas. Ideas arising from sensation are confused: when I feel pain in my injured hand, the pain is vivid enough, but I feel it in the hand itself, whereas the feeling belongs to the soul. But we have clear ideas of ourselves as thinking things, of matter as extended (occupying three-dimensional space), of basic categories such as existence, duration, number, and even, to some extent, of God, inasmuch as we know he must have certain attributes.[14] The fundamental rule of reasoning is: 'Everything contained in the clear and distinct idea of a thing can be truthfully affirmed of that thing.'[15] Malebranche provides his own version of this criterion, but he too founds certainty on the experience of a mental act (though introducing an affective dimension to it): 'We should never give complete consent except to propositions which seem so evidently true that we cannot refuse it of them without feeling an inward pain and the secret reproaches of reason.'[16]

Yet Malebranche differs radically from both Descartes and Arnauld and Nicole as to the scope of our clear ideas. We have no idea of our soul itself, let alone a clear idea of its nature: we know of it only what we feel taking place in us, and for all we know this consciousness of ourselves reveals only the tip of the iceberg.[17] Here Malebranche's thought converges with a pervasive concern in seventeenth-century religious and moral writing with the limitations and delusions of self-knowledge – of which more shortly. In any case, there was disagreement not only as to the scope of the criterion of clarity and distinctness: the criterion itself had been challenged by objectors to Descartes. Thus the Epicurean philosopher Pierre Gassendi appealed, as Montaigne had done, to the proliferation of different opinions as implying the absence of a universal criterion of truth; everyone, he remarks, thinks he clearly and distinctly perceives the view he defends.[18]

Arnauld, Nicole, and Malebranche all reflect in different ways a revival of the influence of St Augustine that profoundly marked seventeenth-century French culture. Until the late thirteenth century, when the Christianized Aristotelianism of St Thomas Aquinas established itself in the universities, Augustine had been the dominant intellectual presence in Latin Christianity. The Reformers' appeal to him in support of their views on grace, free will, and predestination brought his works back into the limelight, an effect perhaps reinforced by the sceptical critique of Aristotelian scholasticism. Certainly, his explorations of inner experience, his investigation of his own personality and motivations, his practice of thinking as self-communing rather than the application of logical protocols was congenial to readers formed by Montaigne or Descartes or both.

The most zealous 'disciples of St Augustine', as they styled themselves, were to be found in the communities of Port-Royal. Port-Royal was originally a female monastery in the countryside near Paris, which was reformed by an energetic abbess, Mère Angélique, Antoine Arnauld's elder sister. The community moved to a new house in Paris, but in 1638 a group of pious laymen, the so-called Solitaires, moved into the old monastery premises, devoting themselves to a life of strict piety, without taking formal religious vows. They also set up an excellent and innovative school (where Racine was educated). The two groups, the nuns and the laymen, were strongly influenced by the spiritual teachings of Jean Duvergier de Hauranne, Abbé de Saint-Cyran, and by the hardline neo-Augustinian theology of his friend the Flemish theologian Jansenius, whose *Augustinus* was published in 1640. Jansenius stressed the corruption of human nature by the Fall, the weakness of the human will, and the necessity for salvation of a gift of divine grace vouchsafed not to all but only to the predestined: although he was firm in his allegiance to Rome, those theories struck suspicious readers as uncomfortably close to Calvinism. Pascal's family came into contact with the Port-Royal milieu, leading to his first conversion to a life of piety. This did not divert him from his scientific and mathematical activity, but his 'second conversion', after a mystical experience in November 1654, led him to concentrate exclusively on religious issues. He campaigned on behalf of the 'Jansenists' in the brilliant polemic of the *Provincial Letters* (1656–7), not only attacking the theology of grace propounded by their Jesuit opponents, but accusing the Jesuits' moral teaching of corrupting Christian ethics.[19]

Pascal's intense religious faith co-existed with a knowledge of its own contingency. That is, he profoundly believed that faith was a gift of God, which is not given to all, and he was acutely aware of its absence in other people. In particular, he had encountered unbelief in his own society, a defiant aristocratic shaking-off of the religious yoke, a typically modern insistence on being unaccountable for one's conduct to anyone but oneself.[20] The habit of doubt could foster this attitude; but, properly managed, doubt could dissolve it. As in Descartes, doubt could be its own antidote.

'Doubt' here is also another name for Montaigne. Pascal's attitude to his precursor is consciously ambivalent. He thoroughly values Montaigne's demolition of human reason, which puts paid, as he sees it, to the rationalism of Protestants and atheists, as well as to those who pride themselves on virtue unconnected with religion (Pascal's account of Montaignian scepticism in fact incorporates some distinctively Cartesian motifs, like that of the all-powerful deceiver: he is more interested in patterns of thought than in philological accuracy). But he regards Montaigne's existential response to his doubts as pernicious; he sees it as a complacent acquiescence inimical to moral effort. In this respect, Montaigne's essentially pagan ethic (as Pascal sees it) is inferior to the pagan ethic of the Stoics. The Stoic Epictetus held that all our efforts should be devoted to recognizing God's will and acting accordingly. But he possessed a confidence in the power of human reason to achieve this end that could only appear as wildly optimistic to a reader of Montaigne. His moral ideal is lofty, but it founders on an inflated sense of human capacities. Montaigne has a proper sense of the limits of human capacities, but lacks a worthy moral ideal. These opposing viewpoints share a common failing: they fail to recognize that man's present state is not that in which he was created; that we are a fallen species.[21] On account of Adam and Eve's transgression, the human intellect has become confused and darkened and above all our will has become corrupted. No longer 'indifferent' (equally balanced) between good and evil, it is positively attracted towards evil; away, that is, from God and towards whatever can gratify our utterly self-centred self-love. Only divine grace, a heavenly influence that overpowers the attraction of created things by a superior pleasure in obedience to God, can enable us to do good.[22]

The doctrine of the Fall, central to Augustine's presentation of Christianity, is likewise key to Pascal's attempt to counter unbelief, an attempt which occupied most of his intellectual efforts in the last few years of his short life. His projected Apology, or defence of the Christian religion, was never completed and the surviving textual evidence does not allow us to reconstruct his argumentative sequence with certainty. The following exposition is thus only one possible reconstruction.

Pascal argues that human reason is radically incapable of delivering certainty. It is not just that we cannot achieve knowledge of ultimate metaphysical truths (although as a matter of fact we can't), we can't ground our most critical existential decisions (like the choice of an occupation) in conceptual reason. Instead of tracing rational connections from one idea to another, we connect ideas on the basis of vague and sometimes irrational affinities detected by the imagination alone. If we could base our social order on reason and justice, universal values, our laws, societies, and values would not differ as extremely as they do from country to country. We have in fact no access to such values. Our apprehension of reality depends on our point of view; the words of our language lump together irreducibly plural and diverse realities. And yet we persist in acting as if our actions could be rationally justified (S 47–111). These arguments are broadly Pyrrhonist in inspiration, and the debt to Montaigne is obvious. We are supposedly rational creatures: but our de facto irrationality seems to imply that our condition is little better than that of the animals. This is what Pascal means by speaking of the 'wretchedness' ('misère') of the human condition.

But if we were mere animals how could we form ideals of reason and justice transcending our experience? And why would we cling to belief in those ideals, despite the bitter lessons of experience? Why do we feel dissatisfaction with our condition, if, like the animals, we are simply part and parcel of the natural world? Moreover, there are certain basic intuitions (for instance, that space, time, movement, numbers exist) that we cannot prove but which Pyrrhonism cannot dispel. All this is brought together under the category of human 'greatness' ('grandeur'). The two categories of wretchedness and greatness both refute and confirm each other: our wretchedness is a fact, but in our consciousness of it we transcend it (S 137–64).

Pascal argues that the Christian doctrine of the Fall (that we were created in greatness, but that, as a penalty for Adam and Eve's sin, we have fallen into wretchedness) serves to explain this contradiction (S 164, 182). This does not make Christianity true; but, since its account of human nature is verified in experience, it is worthy of intellectual respect. But it also promises an escape from our manifest unhappiness. It is therefore irrational not to investigate its truth-claims. 'Rational' here is not defined in terms of conceptual reason, which we know to be unreliable in the human sphere, but in terms of the often implicit practical rationality that governs our decision-making. Indeed, in one of his most complex and controversial passages, Pascal suggests that a rational assessment of the pros and cons of belief, in which we weigh the attractions of earthly happiness against the eternal happiness promised by Christianity, must necessarily lead us to wager in favour of belief, or, if belief is psychologically impossible, to perform the self-conditioning actions (rituals, for instance) that will remove the psychological obstacles (S 680). As for Christianity's truth-claims, these are to be found in the evidence of history, properly interpreted (S 256–380); but we should never have troubled to examine that evidence if we had not learned that Christianity makes sense as a vision of human nature. (Enlightenment thinkers such as Diderot and Voltaire countered by extending scepticism to the historical record itself.)

Doubt, therefore, is strategically mobilized by Pascal to weaken confidence in the power of human reason to govern our lives, whether at the individual or the social level. At the same time, to prevent its issuing in a state of indifference to the truth and consequent renunciation of moral effort (the state he diagnoses in Montaigne), he reminds his reader that there are bed-rock certainties incapable of proof but immune to doubt; and that, despite our inability to measure possible courses of action against absolute categories of reason or justice, we can still use our practical reason to take advantageous decisions. No decision could be more advantageous than to opt for Christianity.

Beyond theological circles and controversies, Augustinian theology had a much wider cultural influence (some have used it as the key to Racine's tragedies: he was indeed educated at a Jansenist school; but the relevance of Jansenism to his plays is far from certain). It converged with the turn towards inwardness already referred to in connection with Montaigne and Descartes. But it also converged, in a more surprising way, with political developments and struggles. The late sixteenth-century Wars of Religion had been driven not only by religious passions, but by rivalries between aristocratic factions, the leaders of which had close connections with the gentry of their respective provinces, from whom they could draw military support in their conflicts. Through a combination of intimidation and inducements, the main thrust of royal policy, first under Cardinal Richelieu, the powerful minister of Louis XIII (1610–43), and then under Louis XIV (1643–1715) was to keep the great nobles at the court, competing non-violently for the royal favour. A ruthless observer of courtly behaviour, the moralist La Bruyère (in *Les Caractères*, 1688–96), stresses the elaborate strategic thinking and manoeuvring involved in this competition: the courtier's behaviour is powered entirely by self-interest, but he must conceal his objectives to avoid the shame of failure.[23] The historian Norbert Elias in 1975 compared the seventeenth-century court to a stock exchange, where what is at stake is not commercial value but one's reputation in the eyes of others.[24]

But there was an interruption in this process. Richelieu died in 1642, Louis XIII in 1643, and the new king Louis XIV was a child. His mother Anne of Austria became regent. During the years before he reached his majority France was torn by a series of civil wars known as the Fronde (1648–53). The magistrates of the higher courts (the *parlements*) and a fraction of the high aristocracy made, for a time, common cause against the regent's unpopular minister, the Italian Cardinal Mazarin. Not without bloodshed, the rebellion petered out as the alliance between *parlementaires* and magnates foundered on account of ideological differences, and the solidarity among the rebels gradually dissolved, largely on account of personal rivalries and conflicts, aggravated by the skilful interventions of Mazarin. Duplicity, scheming, betrayal, the pursuit of self-interest screened by proclamations of zeal for the public good, were the order of the day: in these respects, the aristocratic rebels against the court behaved exactly like the courtiers later analysed by La Bruyère.

It was in the years after this upheaval that one of the former *frondeur* magnates, the Duc de La Rochefoucauld, set about analysing the hidden mainsprings of human behaviour. In this task he had been preceded of course by Montaigne. But there were antecedents also in religious discourse. One of the key claims of Jansenism, taken over from St Augustine, was that the moral character of supposedly virtuous pagans (heroes or philosophers) was vitiated, because in professing to pursue virtue for its own sake, they were secretly gratifying their own pride (the theological point being that there is no true virtue without faith and grace). La Rochefoucauld's family had Jansenist connections, and when his *Maximes*, with their relentless unmasking of inauthentic appearances of virtue, were first published in 1665, the text was accompanied by a preface, not by La Rochefoucauld, associating the work with Augustine's attack on the virtues of the pagans (the preface, however, was jettisoned from subsequent editions).[25] Supposedly virtuous behaviour is traced to discreditable or morally indifferent goals:

> While laziness and timidity keep us to the path of duty, our virtue often gets all the honour.[26]
> We would often be ashamed of our finest deeds, if people could see all the motives that produced them. (409)

Self-interest in a major driver of our behaviour:

> Gratitude is like good faith in business. It keeps commerce going; we do not pay up because it is right for us to discharge our debt, but so that we can more easily find people who will lend to us. (223)

Alternatively, it is suggested that the behaviour results from factors over which we have no control, and we therefore deserve no credit for it:

> Strength and weakness of mind are ill-named; in reality they are only good or bad conditions of the body's organs. (44)

Yet, by a process of self-deception, we persist in crediting ourselves:

> When vices leave us, we flatter ourselves that we are the ones who are leaving them. (192)

Our sense of autonomous decision-making is illusory: we are unaware of the affective forces that propel us:

> Man often thinks he is the leader when he is being led; and while his mind is pointing him in one direction, his heart is imperceptibly drawing him in another. (43)

Everywhere self-love (*amour-propre*) prevails, a kind of second personality lodged within us, an appetite pursuing its own gratification, irrespective of our benefit. It vitiates all our relationships:

> What men have called friendship is simply fellowship, consideration for one another's interests, and exchange of favours; in fact, it is simply a transaction in which self-love always expects to gain something.   (83)

The genesis of the *Maximes* links the text to Augustinian thought, and it is certainly possible to read the text in keeping with an Augustinian religious agenda. But this is never made explicit within the text, and many maxims seem to reflect a very different set of interests and values (sexual love is pitilessly analysed as a zone of betrayal and self-betrayal, but there is no implication it should be eschewed on moral grounds). It is at least as plausible to see the book as a gentleman and courtier's vade mecum, a study in the complexity of human motives, an education in the arts of judgment and discernment, a warning against the troubles we bring on ourselves by our own self-deceptions, and a discreet endorsement of polite disinterested sociability. In this sense the inheritance of Montaigne is more crucial to La Rochefoucauld than that of Augustine.

Yet his concern with the complexities of motivation and the opacity of the psyche was shared with writers whose Augustinian connections are indisputable. Pierre Nicole, earlier encountered as the co-author of the Port-Royal *Logic*, was a moralist and psychologist whose acumen equalled La Rochefoucauld's. Accepting the Augustinian doctrine that charity (the love of God) is the only morally pure motivation, but that in the absence of divine grace, we are inevitably driven by self-love and cupidity (the love of created things for their own sake, also referred to as concupiscence), he stresses that the operations of grace are imperceptible. Hence our radical uncertainty as to our own motivations:

> We cannot distinguish whether it is from charity or from self-love that we act, whether it is God or ourselves that we seek.[27]
>
> Even though there is an infinite difference between self-love and the love of God, none the less the impulsions and actions that arise from these two very different principles are sometimes so similar, and we have so little light to pierce the darkness of the depths of our heart, that we do not clearly distinguish the principle behind our actions, whether it is cupidity or charity.[28]

And yet although self-love in principle sets human beings against one another, an enlightened self-love would prompt them to advance their own interests by behaving in ways compatible with others' self-interest.[29] Nicole has been claimed in this respect as a precursor of Enlightenment social thinking.[30] From another point of view he can be seen, along with La Rochefoucauld, as the supreme exponent of an early modern tradition of introspective moral and psychological analysis that feeds into the fiction of his own day (Lafayette's *La Princesse de Clèves*) and much later (it is still active in Proust). The introspective turn, the preoccupation with the self's response to the world, rather than with the world directly, was arguably prompted at least in part by the philosophical doubt promoted by Pyrrhonism. For Descartes and Pascal it offered ways of surmounting that doubt. For La Rochefoucauld and Nicole to investigate the self was to open up further abysses of uncertainty.

NOTES

1. St Thomas Aquinas, *Summa theologiae*, Ia, q. 2, a. 3.
2. On the influence of Academic scepticism, see Charles B. Schmitt, *Cicero scepticus: A Study of the Influence of the 'Academica' in the Renaissance* (The Hague: Nijhoff, 1972).
3. Richard Popkin, *The History of Scepticism from Savonarola to Bayle*, rev. edn (New York: Oxford University Press, 2003).
4. Montaigne, 'An Apology for Raymond Sebond', in *The Complete Essays*, ed. and trans. M. A. Screech (Harmondsworth: Penguin, 1993), Book II, Chapter 12. References to the 'Apology' will henceforth be given in parentheses in the main text.
5. The Wise Man's words are a loose rendering of Ecclesiastes 9.3.
6. Montaigne, Book III, Chapter 13, 'De l'expérience' ['On Experience'] (*Complete Essays*, p. 1217).
7. Charles Taylor, *Sources of the Self: the Making of the Modern Identity* (Cambridge: Cambridge University Press, 1989), p. 130.
8. Montaigne, Book II, Chapter 1, 'De l'inconstance de nos actions' ['On the Inconstancy of Our Actions'] (*Complete Essays*, p. 377).
9. Montaigne, Book III, Chapter 2, 'Du repentir' ['On Repenting'] (*Complete Essays*, p. 914).
10. Montaigne, Book II, Chapter 20, 'Nous ne goustons rien de pur' ['We Can Savour Nothing Pure'] (*Complete Essays*, p. 766).
11. Descartes, *A Discourse on the Method of Correctly Conducting One's Reason and Seeking Truth in the Sciences*, ed. and trans. Ian Maclean (Oxford: Oxford University Press, 2006). On the *Discourse* see also Ian James, 'The literary-philosophical essay', Chapter 15 in this volume.
12. Descartes, *Meditations on First Philosophy, with Selections from the Objections and Replies*, ed. and trans. Michael Moriarty (Oxford: Oxford University Press, 2008).
13. Antoine Arnauld and Pierre Nicole, *Logic or the Art of Thinking*, ed. and trans. Jill Vance Buroker (Cambridge: Cambridge University Press, 1996), pp. 23–4.
14. See Arnauld and Nicole, *Logic*, Part I, Chapter 9, pp. 48–53.
15. Arnauld and Nicole, *Logic*, Part IV, Chapter 6, p. 247; compare Book IV, Chapter 7, p. 250), first axiom.

16. Nicolas Malebranche, *The Search after Truth, Elucidations of the Search after Truth*, trans. Thomas M. Lennon and Paul J. Olscamp (Columbus, OH: Ohio State University Press, 1980), Book 1, Chapter 2, § 4, p. 10.

17. Malebranche, *The Search after Truth, Elucidations of the Search after Truth*, Book 111-11, Chapter 7, § 4, pp. 237–9; see also Elucidation x1, pp. 633–8.

18. Gassendi, Fifth Objections, III.1, in Descartes, *Meditations*, p. 170 (AT 7.278).

19. For a brief introduction to Jansenism, see Michael Moriarty, *Early Modern French Thought: The Age of Suspicion* (Oxford: Oxford University Press, 2003), pp. 18–49.

20. See the psychological sketch of unbelief in *Pensées*, fragment 681, in Blaise Pascal, *Pensées and Other Writings*, trans. Honor Levi, ed. Anthony Levi (Oxford: Oxford University Press, 2008). Future references to this text are by the number of the fragment (preceded by S, since the numbering used in this edition is that of Philippe Sellier).

21. See the conversation recorded in 'Discussion with Monsieur de Sacy', *Pensées and Other Writings*, pp. 182–92.

22. Pascal's fullest treatment of the effects of the Fall and of divine grace is in the unfinished *Écrits sur la grâce* [*Writings on Grace*]: see Pascal, *Œuvres complètes*, ed. Michel Le Guern, 2 vols (Paris: Gallimard, 1998–2000), vol. 2, pp. 209–316. Two of the most crucial sections are included in *Pensées and Other Writings*, pp. 205–26.

23. Jean de La Bruyère, *Characters*, trans. Jean Stewart (Harmondsworth: Penguin, 1970), 'Of the court', §§ 43, 64, 22, 42 (pp. 137, 143, 133, 136–7).

24. Norbert Elias, *The Court Society*, trans. Edmund Jephcott (Oxford: Blackwell, 1983), p. 91.

25. On the relevance of the controversy over pagan virtue to La Rochefoucauld, see Michael Moriarty, *Disguised Vices: Theories of Virtue in Early Modern French Thought* (Oxford: Oxford University Press, 2011).

26. La Rochefoucauld, *Maximes*, 169, in *Collected Maxims and Other Reflections*, ed. and trans. E. H. and A. M. Blackmore and Francine Giguère (Oxford: Oxford University Press, 2007). Future references are by the number of the maxim only.

27. Pierre Nicole, 'De la charité et de l'amour-propre', Chapter 12, in *Essais de morale*, 15 vols (Paris: Desprez, 1755–82), vol. 3, pp. 166–7. My translation.

28. Nicole, 'Des diverses manières dont on tente Dieu', Chapter 5, in *Essais de morale*, vol. 3, p. 204.

29. See Nicole, 'De la charité et de l'amour-propre', in *Essais de morale*, vol. 3, pp. 122–76.

30. See Pierre Force, *Self-Interest before Adam Smith: A Genealogy of Economic Science* (Cambridge: Cambridge University Press, 2003), pp. 76–8.

8

CAROLINE WARMAN

Nature and Enlightenment

Nature and its definitions and descriptions in all their contested variety trumpet throughout eighteenth-century French writing, gradually displacing discussions of the divine. Nature is the good origin, the state man abandoned as he fell into society and away from happiness or equilibrium, while the recognition that nature must be returned to, reinhabited, provides the simultaneous narrative that is the emergence from dark into light, or 'Enlightenment' as it will come to be known in English. This subsidiary term of 'Enlightenment', made famous by the German philosopher Kant and his essay 'What Is Enlightenment?' (1784), now commonly designates the entire century and study of it, whether in the French context or otherwise, though never without reference to it, owing in large part to its extraordinarily influential writers Montesquieu, Voltaire, Diderot, and Rousseau, all of whom strove to shed light on the mechanisms and abuses of society by setting them in the context of nature and what is natural. So nature is a term that always comes with baggage, generally in an implied or explicit moralized binary with society, and with an unstable relationship to religion: Is it an expression of the divine? Or does it replace it? Nature increasingly becomes the Whole into which everything else is fitted, and this means that we cannot talk about Nature exclusively through texts which describe it directly, but that we should also see it as the framework within which discussions of society or general human interaction take place.

Certain questions are asked again and again, not because eighteenth-century France had only one theme, but because the answers were felt to be so compellingly important: Why do we do what we do? Why do we behave as we do? Should we follow convention or our instincts? Can we change? Can society change? What would be the consequences of change? How can we become what we would rather be? The reader may notice this repeated 'we', and want to point out that the eighteenth-century thinker is unlikely to have many points in common with the modern student of these matters. This is true, but it is also true that Western society has inherited many of these questions, and appeals to them when it wants to talk about its values of democracy, equality, justice, and tolerance. It can be difficult to find the distance necessary for a critical perspective on eighteenth-century writers and thinkers because of this apparent match. Have we not already bought their narrative of the rejection of darkness when we assume that issues of nature, society, convention, justice, and so on, are indeed first explored in this century? Yet, having read the earlier chapters of this volume, we know that this is far from being the case. 'Enlightenment' questions and answers continue to play out Christian Europe's convulsive relationship with antiquity, in particular with Epicurus, the Greek philosopher whose theories of matter, the laws of the universe, and nature were best known through the Latin poet Lucretius's *De rerum natura* [*On the Nature of Things*] (first century BCE), theories to which the seventeenth-century philosopher Pierre Gassendi had given renewed credence, and which François Bernier disseminated in his *Abrégé de la philosophie de Gassendi* [*Summary of Gassendi's Philosophy*] (1684) to a reading public more willing to listen to them since Galileo's discoveries about the movement of planets, Harvey's work on the circulation of the blood, and a host of other discoveries which, despite contradicting biblical accounts, presented the workings of nature in provable detail. Perhaps we will go so far as to say that these questions are asked increasingly often, increasingly openly, increasingly urgently, and that the forms they take increasingly mirror the directness of the subject matter. They eschew conventions and conventional categorization, ranging across the myriad possibilities for direct expression, very often therefore in the first person. The forms they take therefore include the novel, memoir, dialogue, drama, letter, treatise, article, often within a single text, not excluding poetry, and in no way hampered by any anachronistic boundaries between what we now call fiction and non-fiction, or literature and science.

We find many of these aspects encapsulated in particularly intense form in Isabelle de Charrière's tragic novella of 1784, *Letters from Mistress Henley*, a text that will also serve to introduce the polemical and intertextual nature of eighteenth-century writing in French. The narrative consists of six letters written by a newly married woman to her friend. In them she relates how she met and chose her husband, and what her experience of living with him is. He is a rational and calm man who knows that the hubbub of society stirs up trouble and who keeps away from it, living in harmony with nature in the countryside. The problem is that his avoidance of society, although it accords with his own nature and with what is by the 1780s the received wisdom about the misery-inducing quality of town life, does not accord with her nature, and, furthermore, becomes an instrument of oppression restricting her freedom. Knowing she ought to admire the natural setting she lives in, she becomes conflicted:

> An old lime tree blocks a rather fine view from my window. I wanted it to be cut down; but when I looked at it up close, I saw with my own eyes what a great pity that would be. What makes me happiest in this brilliant season is to watch the leaves appear and unfurl, the blossom come out, a crowd of insects flying, walking and running in all directions. I know nothing about it, I learn nothing about it; but I contemplate and admire this full and animated universe. I get lost in this wholeness which is so astonishing and I won't say so wise as well, I am too ignorant: I do not know its ends, I do not know its means or its aim, I do not know why so many flies are given to this voracious spider to eat; but I watch, and hours pass without me thinking about myself or my childish griefs.[1]

She contemplates the spectacle of nature, and in so doing, situates herself among the many readers influenced by Abbé Noël Pluche's multi-volume work of the same name, the *Spectacle de la nature* (1732–50, 8 vols), and of which there were no fewer than nineteen editions in the course of the century. A survey of nature and the universe aiming to educate readers about the wonders of the natural world, it takes the form of a fictional dialogue, with four aristocratic characters courteously introducing nature to one other as part of a presentation of its subject and as the proof of God's existence via the manifold beauties of his creation. This was an important move on the part of theologians: it allowed the religious authorities to claim natural philosophy (what we now call science) as a pious undertaking instead of opposing or suppressing it as had been attempted the previous century, affecting such luminaries as Galileo, Descartes, and Bayle. The argument that the existence of God can be intuited by looking at the intricate beauties of creation was one which the fictionalized blind English mathematician Saunderson of Diderot's *Lettre sur les aveugles* [*Letter on the Blind*] would famously rebut in his death-bed speech, telling the priest who was attending him that 'that beautiful great spectacle ... was never made for me!'[2] And we can see that Mistress Henley also has some reservations about such an argument when she refuses to say that the universe is 'wise', has 'ends', 'means' or 'aim'. And yet she contemplates it, becomes absorbed by it, loses her emotions through simple perception, while the text skilfully pins down the different meanings of the word 'nature', be they human or universal, and which are not so much in conflict as occurring at different levels. Rousseau also resonates throughout this passage, via different texts: his last work, the *Rêveries du promeneur solitaire* [*Reveries of the Solitary Walker*] (composed in 1776–8, but published just prior to *Mistress Henley* in 1782), proposes just such calming and time-erasing contemplation for the desolate individual:

> As evening approached, I would come down from the heights of the island, and I liked then to go and sit on the shingle in some secluded spot by the edge of the lake; there, the noise of the waves and the movement of the water, taking hold of my senses and driving all other agitation from my soul, would plunge it into a delicious reverie in which night often stole upon me unawares.[3]

And yet the premises, which run throughout Rousseau's writings from beginning to end – that society removes our natural freedom, leads us to be in conflict with nature, and ourselves and that our only possible solution is to avoid society as much as possible – are contradicted by Mistress Henley's experience of misery, itself directly induced by her husband's adherence to these Rousseauian precepts. A further bitter nod to Rousseau's reach emerges when Mr Henley informs his pregnant wife, who is ill with distress, that she will probably not be permitted to breastfeed her child, despite it being her 'sacred duty' to do so, because of her 'temperamental fault[s]'.[4] In his treatise/novel about how to bring up a child in harmony with himself and with nature, *Émile, ou, de l'éducation* [*Émile, or On Education*] (1762), Rousseau had suggested that it was unnatural for high-born women not to breastfeed their children, and had started a sea-change in that direction. Despite some reservations about losing her autonomy, Mistress Henley had felt she ought to breastfeed her baby: her husband's judgment that she may not be fit to do so still removes her autonomy but also prevents her from bonding with her child. It pathologizes her.

Charrière's intimate but agonistic relationship with Rousseau's writings and her intense engagement with questions of nature, happiness, and power allow us to identify some of the different strands of this complex era. It can perhaps be most helpfully characterized as starting in 1715 with the death of Louis XIV, and moving into a new phase, not with the French Revolution, but with the rejection of the latter in the shape of Napoleon, and Chateaubriand's simultaneous pronouncement, in his 1801 preface to *Atala* (he wrote four!), that 'with this word nature, everything was lost'.[5] Some simple figures underpin this view: comparative catalogue searches of the seventeenth and eighteenth centuries for the total number of titles written in French containing the word 'nature' and derivations show a jump of between three and four times; in the nineteenth century the total number goes down by about 25 per cent from the eighteenth-century high.

Montesquieu's *Lettres persanes* [*Persian Letters*] (1721) and Voltaire's *Lettres philosophiques* [*Philosophical Letters*] (1734) are two influential texts which respond to many of the questions mentioned thus far, and which set the tone both in terms of form and content for much of what will follow. The *Lettres persanes* record the impressions of two Persian noblemen, Rica and Usbek, who have travelled to Paris and write letters home. As nothing is familiar to them, they see everything with fresh eyes, questioning much, and finding absurdity everywhere. Their reasonable surprise and judicious comments allow Montesquieu to inspect French customs and institutions and to take nothing for granted. Usbek is the more scrupulous observer and thinker; Rica is younger, wittier, and more likely to comment on such things as fashion. But it emerges that Usbek, lucid and wise as he is, is also a hypocrite. The remarks he makes about the tyrannical behaviour of Louis XIV command agreement, but Usbek cannot see that he is a tyrant himself, ferociously controlling through autocratic letters to his eunuchs the large harem he has left behind. He gives his wives no liberty and suppresses their natural instincts. His oppressive regime becomes intolerable: they rebel. One of his wives, Roxane, famously declares in the very last letter that 'I have rewritten your laws to conform to those of nature, and my mind has always kept its independence'.[6] Montesquieu shows us that empirical observation is not merely an intellectual exercise but that it comes with a moral responsibility to look in all directions: not just out but also in. He shows that while it is easy to see absurdity in unfamiliar things, it is very difficult to see oneself with the same clarity. He simultaneously employs a relativizing approach, showing that what is normal in one place is not only bizarre, but sometimes unacceptable or transgressive elsewhere, while also implying certain universal values to do with good fair government, the avoidance of power abuse, and the recognition that certain instincts and behaviours, such as falling in love, are natural and therefore right. The insights Montesquieu presents in fictionalized form in the *Lettres persanes* were ones he would continue to work on and elaborate: his magnum opus, *De l'esprit des lois* [*The Spirit of Laws*] (1748) is a global survey of the way in which people, history, and geography interact to produce different forms of government and different laws in different places at different times: it proposes that social systems are developmental and adaptive. It does not present European societies as the civilized standard from which other (primitive) cultures diverge, and, although it maintains a strictly neutral tone, it nonetheless makes it possible to evaluate tyrannies, monarchies, and republics as three models of government side by side.

Voltaire's *Lettres philosophiques* (1734) – which he initially had published in English (translated by a certain John Lockman) under the title *Letters concerning the English Nation* (1733) in order to secure a British audience, only thereafter extending and revising the French original that is now much better known – do not employ fictional tropes to the same extent as the

Lettres persanes. The letters are not addressed to anyone, nor are they signed, while the author and narrator seem to be one and the same. There is no framing narrative that turns the story back against its initial teller, such as Montesquieu had used; nor is Britain so far away or so exotic as Persia. There are no eunuchs. But it is nonetheless a descriptive account, delivered in bite-size chunks, of a foreign culture from the point of view of an outsider, and it extensively deploys the tools of observation and comparison, again to the detriment of France. Its positive depiction of Britain's religious tolerance, parliamentary system of government, and successfully mercantile society casts a shade over the intolerance, despotism, and bankruptcy of the author's own country. Voltaire here first uses the technique that would become his particular stylistic signature: the ability to present positions he advocates as common-sensical, while depicting everything else as perfectly ridiculous. His revulsion at intolerance and violence in the name of religion was well established, his epic poem about the French religious wars of the sixteenth century, the feisty *Henriade* (1728), already being famous. However, it was in the *Lettres philosophiques* that he first set out the bipartite style of clarity (the explicable, rational, and therefore true) versus obscurity (the inexplicable, irrational, and therefore false), which he would later use to such devastating effect in his famous novella, the wittily scathing *Candide* (1759), and in the tragically sober *Traité sur la tolérance* [*Treatise on Tolerance*] (1763), with its painful first chapter relating the race-hate trial and execution in 1762 of the Protestant Jean Calas (he had been falsely accused of murdering his son for having wanted to become Catholic).

The *Lettres philosophiques* are more optimistic than those later works (and indeed cheerily mock Pascal's pessimism about the human condition in his final Letter xxv). They ebulliently promote Locke and Newton, and were of capital importance in disseminating their work and thought in the Francophone world of letters, a task Voltaire would energetically pursue in tandem with his mistress, the mathematician Émilie Du Châtelet: she helped him compose his *Éléments de la philosophie de Newton* [*Elements of Newton's Philosophy*] (1737), and then went on to translate Newton's *Principia mathematica* (1687) into French (*Principes mathématiques de la philosophie naturelle*, completed in 1749; published in 1759). It was in the *Lettres philosophiques* that many readers first encountered the anecdote of Newton and the apple as an introduction to his theory of gravity (Letter xv; he had previously used it in his *Essai sur la poésie épique* [*Essay on Epic Poetry*] of 1727): he claims in the *Éléments* that he heard it from Newton's niece, Mrs Conduitt, and, in his hands, it became a means to transform a complex topic into a quirky human narrative about a great man's intellectual journey. The fact that it remains the most famous anecdote in circulation about Newton (although its genesis here is generally forgotten) is a measure of Voltaire's triumphant success in imprinting his version of Newton on the general public. And why is Newton so significant for Voltaire? Because he discovered that law of nature – gravity: 'the great Spring by which all Nature is mov'd'.[7] Voltaire wants to focus attention on how nature works, and on how best to see how it works, and he does this by talking about individuals who see clearly and who are committed to seeking the truth, specifically the truth in nature. And therefore Locke and Newton are inevitable heroes in the quest for truth. Furthermore, he uses the biographical approach to underscore not only the heroism of these figures but also the support their country provides them. This is again to the detriment of France. Of Descartes, he states baldly, 'he left France purely to go in search of Truth'.[8] This narrative of individual struggle and quest had already been perfectly explicit in Descartes. In his *Discours de la méthode* [*Discourse on Method*] (1637), which he presents as his intellectual biography, he writes: 'But like a man who walks alone, and in the dark, I resolved to go so slowly, and to use such caution in all things that, even if I went forward only a very little, I would at least avoid falling.'[9] This slow hobble through existential darkness strongly recalls such canonical texts of the dark night of the soul as we find in Augustine's *Confessions*, in the Psalms, or in the celebrated opening lines of the medieval Italian poet Dante's *Divine Comedy*:

> At one point midway on our path in life,
> I came around and found myself now searching
> through a dark wood, the right way blurred and lost.[10]

It should not be forgotten that early modern European metaphors of light and enlightenment do derive from this deeply Christian context and are not obviously secular in any easy way. Yet neither are they orthodox, and the anxiety and 'caution' that are so manifest in Descartes's account are likely to relate to his sense of diverging from a received view, which is not only the received and authorized one but also a *collective* view to which the pious are required to adhere. But Descartes had the blazing example of Montaigne's *Essais* to sustain his individual approach, and he gropes forward until he feels able to prove his existence because of and uniquely in relation to the fact that he himself can think: 'I think therefore I am': 'I judged that I could take it to be a general rule that the things we conceive very clearly and very distinctly are all true, but that there is nevertheless some difficulty in being able to recognize for certain which are the things we see distinctly.'[11] His reliance on observation and an individually elaborated series of propositions was foundational for those that came after him, or so Voltaire would claim: 'the path he struck out is since become boundless',[12] but Descartes's mistrust of sensory perception ('there is some difficulty [in recognizing] which are the things we see distinctly') would be confidently brushed aside by the English philosopher John Locke and those who would subsequently associate themselves with Locke's brightly explained empirical method. This confidence in nature and perception is new, and attests to a great shift away from the Christian account whereby nature is generally qualified as base nature, as something which leads to temptation, and is in any case a condition to which humans have been relegated following their banishment from the Garden of Eden. It was just such an understanding of human nature that had underpinned Pascal's *Pensées*, as the reader of earlier chapters may recall. This is not to suggest that the Christian Fall narrative no longer resonated, or that every philosopher henceforth trusted information that derived from the senses. This is far from being the case. But it is true that Locke gave French thinkers a way of reinforcing the authority of empiricism (observation-based methods of investigation) by removing any mistrust of the senses doing the observation in the first place. In this passage, Locke contemplates the mind of a child:

> Let us suppose the Mind to be, as we say, white Paper, void of all Characters, without any *Ideas*; How comes it to be furnished? Whence comes it by that vast store, which the busy and boundless Fancy of Man has painted on it, with an almost endless variety? Whence has it all the materials of Reason and Knowledge? To this I answer, in one word, From *Experience*: In that, all our Knowledge is founded; and from that it ultimately derives it self. Our Observation employ'd either about *external, sensible Objects; or about the internal Operations of our Minds, perceived and reflected on by our selves, is that, which supplies our Understandings with all the materials of thinking.* These two are the Fountains of Knowledge, from whence all the Ideas we have, or can naturally have, do spring.[13]

In sum, we have sensations, we observe things, we reflect on them, we compare them: they constitute our experience and thence our knowledge. Knowledge is not based on erudition but on individual experience. Every observant individual with experience is therefore authorized as an expert about the world in which they live. No wonder the first-person perspective became so ubiquitous, and a tool for understanding the world across so many genres: it was an authorized philosophical position. We should note moreover the way the mind is described: it is blank paper, which experience covers with writing. Everyone has a book inside them, literally: the mind is a book. The stage is set for a proliferation of writing about personal experience, and for it to be supposed that experience is *naturally* imprinted in words. That experience and language might be separate is not a notion which is present here; although it will later worry Rousseau deeply, and he will set about elaborating a style and a theory to bring them together (see, for example, his *Essai sur l'origine des langues* [*Essay on the Origin of Languages*] (*c.* 1755). Locke, however, ensures that the *natural* aspect of this cognitive process is duly emphasized when he evokes 'all the Ideas we have, or can naturally have': we see that careful, crucial shift: natural ideas originate here. And natural, in this context, means real.

Montesquieu's *Lettres persanes* and Voltaire's *Lettres philosophiques* are situated squarely within this philosophical tradition which places the highest value on the perception of the individual, and which sees perception as having a natural extension in the written word. Pierre Carlet de Chamblain de Marivaux's multi-instalment memoir novels, *La Vie de Marianne* [*The Life of Marianne*] (1731–42) and *Le Paysan parvenu* [*The Fortunate Peasant*] (1734–5) provide further examples of this new authorization of individual experience: their respective heroes Marianne and Jacob are not noble and they undergo all sorts of extraordinary experiences, not excluding exchanging sex for favours. They tell their stories from the vantage point of old age and the security that their life-long mental agility has won for them. Their identity is about the quality of their observation and reflection, and about their cumulative experience and individual struggles. It does not derive from social rank. This is a fascinating shift on Marivaux's part: his earlier plays had displayed an awareness of the artificial and arbitrary character of social rank, without showing any way to get free of it. His *Île des esclaves* [*Isle of the Slaves*] (1725) forces masters and servants to swap places for a while, but only so that the former can learn to be better masters; while his sparkling *Jeu de l'amour et du hasard* [*Game of Love and Chance*] (1730) is a rapid-fire comedy in which the rich daughter of the household swaps places with her maid so she can find out what her suitor is really like, while the suitor does the identical thing, for the same reasons. Socially suitably, the high-ranking pair then fall in love with one another, as do the servant pair, although they all do so (falsely) supposing that they are about to cross the social divide, and (falsely) believing that they're willing to make that jump. The darkness of the comedy plays out at the level of those delusions, because, as Marivaux presents the situation, what each lover actually falls in love with is a certain style of language and manner, and therefore with an inculcated social identity, not with any real underlying nature. This sort of opposition will be familiar to us through the terms of nature and nurture, although here it is not really education that is at issue, but social rank: the lovers appear to lack any nature independent of their social identity.

Running through these various texts, there is a further strand that we now need to lift out for inspection. The *Lettres persanes* present the most explicit case of it thus far, but it is implicit everywhere: observing the world also needs to involve observing oneself. Why should this be the case if world and self are distinct? The answer is that the terms of world and self are misleading, and that the same word should be used for both: nature. Nature outside, and nature inside. These need to be in alignment: when they aren't, it is because society has denatured them. How do we know that they have been denatured? Because our feelings tell us so. We have to learn to listen to and follow our feelings. Many of these texts use that most compelling of emotions, love, to play the lesson out. The *Lettres persanes* is just one example. But the lesson is not necessarily an unam-biguously high-minded one: stories of love following its natural course often end up involving physical pleasure, while written accounts of physi-cal pleasure often involve readerly pleasure, and then we find ourselves unavoidably in the realm of what a practised writer of this sort of litera-ture at the end of the eighteenth century, Restif de La Bretonne, will invent a name for, although that is not what he meant it to mean. The term is, of course, pornography: Restif intended it to designate treatises on prostitu-tion. The chronologically accurate term for the sort of literature that presents and describes scenes of pleasure, and that makes its relationship with the reader problematically complicit, is libertine literature.

In fact, 'libertin' (libertine in English) was a seventeenth-century term used to describe free thinkers, those who were not orthodox in their religious views, preferring to work out their positions in 'liberty'. By the eighteenth century, owing largely to their opponents' deployment of it as an insult designating loose morals, it comes to mean debauchery in various different forms, describing people who are debauched and immoral, as well as texts which depict debauchery or justify immorality. Although the term 'libertine' became an insult, it is also true that many writers of the eight-eenth century did indeed use desire ('debauchery') as a means of exploring natural instinct and the suppression thereof. These range from the veiled and allusive to the eye-wateringly explicit. An interestingly acceptable case, and one which opened up an extremely rich seam for the rest of the century, can be found in the fabulously popular *Mille et une nuits*, or *Thousand and One Nights*. These are still so current in anglophone culture in the form of the endless retellings of Aladdin, Ali Baba, and so on, that we may have lost sight of the fact that their first appearance in Europe was through a French version by the diplomat and orientalist Antoine Galland (1704–16, 12 vols). And it may well be that they tell us more about the French culture of the time than they do about any Arabic 'original'. Galland's role as a translator may have gone a little too unquestioned: he created a seamless whole, working partly from original manuscripts and partly from sources, and may also have supplemented them with stories of his own invention (Aladdin may be one such): his opportunistic publisher certainly did, to Galland's rage.

The framing story of the *Mille et une nuits* is familiar: the King of Persia, embittered by the fact that his first wife had taken lovers, exacts his revenge on all women by marrying someone new every evening and executing them at sunrise. Finally, his latest wife, Scheherezade, defers her execution by leaving the story she has spent the night telling him on a cliffhanger. He agrees not to kill her until he has heard how it ends, and this goes on for one thousand and one nights until he finally lifts the execution order, swearing his eternal love for her and her inventive stories. His first wife's illicit desire and his own retributive power provide the catalyst for the stories, and the themes of sexuality and power pervade the entire collection, much more than our familiarity with the edulcorated versions of our childhood might lead us to suspect.

Galland's tales offer a combination of ingredients that later writers will want to use again and again: the liberty that comes with being nothing but the translator, the foreign setting and point of view, the erotic context, the light touch, the seeming simplicity, the formal freedom which allows for tales within tales and for numerous digressions. Its very looseness and frivolity, its foreign craziness, its general entertainment value, mean that any threat it may have contained simply by being in print was neutralized in the eyes of the censoring authorities. Its pervasive eroticism was simply no problem at all because it emanated from the 'Orient' where 'they' are all heathens anyway. Edward Said's seminal work *Orientalism* (1978) will angrily point out that the 'Western' view of the 'Orient' is nothing but a self-serving construct. From an Enlightenment or more accurately a free-thinking point of view it is a construct of the utmost importance, because it allows writers a space in which to represent behaviour and modes of thought which otherwise cannot be expressed. Many seized on it with alacrity.

It will immediately be clear what texts such as the *Lettres persanes* owe to Galland's example, and they re-use moreover the distancing trope of translation which at once relieves the 'translator' of responsibility for its content while positioning the text as a documentary evidence. Many other authors will choose to do the same: variations on this theme include finding or being given a bundle of letters or other sorts of original manuscript. We find Voltaire, Françoise de Graffigny, Diderot, Rousseau, Pierre Choderlos de Laclos, and many others drawing on these techniques as they debate utopia and dystopia in polemical narrations of discovery, rejection, and conflict.

The genre of the frivolous tale or love story with its titillating aspects and exotic framing provides writers and thinkers of this period with a way of exploring ideas of nature and natural behaviour which test and some-times diverge from orthodox views. These texts hold on to their reader not only through interest or curiosity but through eroticism. Explicitly erotic libertine literature implicates the reader directly in its tales of freely followed instinct in the form of sexual desire. The philosophical novella attributed to Jean-Baptiste de Boyer, better known as the Marquis d'Argens, *Thérèse philosophe* [*Thérèse the Philosopher*] (1748), teaches a young woman to follow and value her erotic sensations, and also to justify them: the text alternates between sexual scenarios and philosophi-cal disquisitions on the importance of obeying the laws of nature. Its provocative binary model is one which Donatien Alphonse François, Marquis de Sade will later use as the primary structuring device of his startlingly sexualized novels *Justine, ou, Les malheurs de la vertu* [*Justine or the Misfortunes of Virtue*] (1791), *La Nouvelle Justine* [*The New Justine*] (1797), *L'Histoire de Juliette* [*The Story of Juliette*] (1797), in his dialogue *La Philosophie dans le boudoir* [*Philosophy in the Boudoir*] (1795), and also in his more veiled epistolary novel, *Aline et Valcour* (1795). They all replicate the same message, that is, that we must obey the laws of nature by allowing every instinct free rein.

The narrative of the young woman being awoken to the nature of desire and to nature in general, learning to follow it, and then learning to interpret the world in relation to it, is not limited to these bluntly sexualized texts: it has a classical heritage in Longus's Greek romance *Daphnis and Chloe* (second and third century CE) and it is very widely spread in eighteenth-century French literature. Rousseau's eponymous heroine in *Julie, ou, La nouvelle Héloïse* [*Julie or the New Héloïse*] (1761) offers one example, as does Jacques-Henri Bernardin de Saint-Pierre's *Paul et Virginie* (1788). A further case is provided in Étienne-Gabriel Morelly's strange and now little-known novel, the *Naufrage des isles flottantes, ou, Basiliade du célèbre Pilpaï* [*Shipwreck of the Floating Isles, or Basiliade of the celebrated Pilpay*] (1753), which advertises itself as a 'heroic poem translated from the Indian' (Morelly is alluding to Galland's translation, *Les Fables indiennes de Bidpaï* of 1724). The *Basiliade* is a picaresque story in which a young man fits himself for kingship by learning to follow the laws of nature: in the first chapter, two lovers are mystified by their sensations, but follow their impulses through to sexual fulfilment while being watched by their delighted parents who are hiding behind a tree. What is perhaps most extraordinary about this episode is that it is presented as morally uplifting: the lovers, in transports of delight, thank their parents and discuss the lesson they have learnt: 'until now we knew of no pleasures beyond breathing and enjoying the light: the first instants of our life will be counted from this moment'.[14]

Morelly's influential *Code de la nature* [*The Code of Nature*] (1755) presents itself as nothing more or less than a commentary on the earlier *Basiliade*, formalizing the message that had been presented in the earlier text in fictional form: its 'aim is to show that the real hero is man himself as formed by the lessons of nature' and to display the 'ravishing organization of the universe'.[15] It goes on to discuss nature and man's place in it in detail, and to present model legislation 'in conformity with the intentions of Nature'.[16]

All these cases present narrative scenarios in which the natural instinct of the young lovers pushes them in the direction of sexual union, and in each case the natural setting in which they find themselves – in *Daphnis and Chloe* it is a glade, in the *Basiliade* it is again a glade, in *Paul et Virginie* it is the ebullient flora of tropical Mauritius – shows the characters themselves, and beyond them, the readers, that their nature, and nature in general, are or should be in seamless harmony. Paying attention to nature can even become the narrative: in Rousseau's 'Fifth Promenade' he describes the joy of botanizing and of observing the reproduction of plants, and relates a festive outing to populate an island with rabbits;[17] Bernardin devotes detailed pages to his twelve-year-old hero Paul's skilful planting, and Paul's prowess as a farmer establishes his status as hero of nature.[18] For these writers and for many that followed them, describing the way characters interacted with the natural world around them was tantamount to describing character in general: passages evoking nature in its various manifestations and at different points of the year's cycle became, moreover, part of the literary repertoire.

Diderot gave Morelly both protection and visibility when he allowed the *Code de la nature* to be published under his name in his own *Œuvres* of 1772, yet problematized the way it turned nature into a set of potentially restrictive laws in his *Supplément au Voyage de Bougainville* [*Supplement to Bougainville's Voyage*], which appeared the same year in the *Correspondance littéraire*, the manuscript journal edited by Friedrich Melchior, Baron von Grimm and circulated to a restricted audience of the crowned heads of Europe, including Catherine the Great and the sister of Frederick the Great.

Nature, its depiction, its laws, and how human society conforms or diverges from it, are the triggers and the endpoints of most of these texts and the set of endlessly relaying conversations they have with each other. Buffon's massive, immensely successful, and royally authorized publishing enterprise, his survey of natural history, the *Histoire naturelle générale et particulière* [*Natural History, General and Particular*] (1749–88, 36 vols), with its elevating opening paragraphs and cautious disclaimers, supplies us with one position in this conversation. His definition of nature, neatly deferred until volume 12, courteously dismisses both the Pluche camp mentioned earlier and also atheists. He writes that:

> Nature is the system of laws established by the Creator for the existence of things and the succession of beings. Nature is not a thing, for that thing would be God; but it may be considered as a power which is alive and immense, which includes and animates everything, and which, subordinate to the power of the first Being, only started to act when he gave the order, and still only acts with his support or consent.[19]

Diderot and D'Alembert's extraordinary attempt to bring together all existing knowledge, practical and intellectual, in one place, their polyphonic *Encyclopédie, ou, Dictionnaire raisonné des sciences, des arts et des métiers* [*Encyclopaedia, or Universal Dictionary of Arts, Sciences, Trades and Manufactures*] (1751–72, 28 vols), provides another series of positions, depending on which article you read. There are fourteen separate articles on 'nature' and 'natural', not including the many other entries that include it in the headword in one way or another (which brings the total to 103 entries: ARTFL's online edition allows us to see that the word 'nature' and derivations appear 21,267 times in the *Encyclopédie* as a whole).[20] Nature applies to the study of the natural world in its botanical, geological, and geographical manifestations, to the sciences of what D'Alembert calls 'movement', that is, mechanics, physics, and astronomy more widely, to theories of natural justice, to aesthetics, theology, morality, and philosophy. The *Encyclopédie*'s polyphony is real: there are no fewer than 134 known contributors, and they occupy the full range of eighteenth-century positions, from the orthodox to the polemical and reformist. The latter will generally call on nature for support. Thus, we find instructions about how to run a successful sugar plantation in one piece ('Sucrerie'), as well as an impassioned diatribe against the unnatural inhumanity of slavery in another ('Nègres [commerce]'). The *Encyclopédie* had a much harder ride than Buffon's *Histoire naturelle*, and, having started out with royal approval, was finished in secret under the guidance of Diderot alone, partly excised of its more radical passages. Raynal's *Histoire des deux Indes* [*History of the East and West Indies*] (1770, 6 vols) – hiding its multiple authorship, and surveying the empires and markets of the world – provides a further series of positions, its moment in the conversation coming later, and being correspondingly more strident. In a passage discussing the wars of early modern Europe, and which we now know to be Diderot's, it passionately asks: 'Is it surprising that in the midst of these tumults, nature should awaken and cry from the bottom of our hearts, *Man is born free?*'[21] This passage serves as an example to prove the point made at the beginning of the paragraph: that this century of writing is always in conversation. Here, Diderot quotes one of Rousseau's most famous lines, from the opening paragraph of the *Contrat social* [*Social Contract*] (1762): 'Man is born free, and everywhere he is in chains.'

This is only one of the many points of contact between Diderot and Rousseau: wherever we look in one of their works, we are bound to find the other. Rousseau famously wrote that his prize-winning *Discours sur les sciences et les arts* [*Discourse on the Sciences and Arts*] (1750) came to him on his way to visit Diderot, then imprisoned at Vincennes to the consternation of the publishers backing the *Encyclopédie*, who feared to see their costly enterprise fail. There are shades of Rousseau in the endlessly problematic hero of Diderot's dialogue, *Le Neveu de Rameau* [*Rameau's Nephew*], while Rousseau's quarrel with his erstwhile friend is pored over in his *Confessions* and again in his *Rêveries*. Both are writers whose texts endlessly reward readers, and who dramatize the urgent questions of this period in striking, unexpected, and extraordinary ways, and who ceaselessly explore the meanings of nature. Diderot's *Rêve de D'Alembert* [*D'Alembert's Dream*] (1769) depicts an unpredictable material world of dynamic change, and presents it to us through the physiological excitement it provokes in his dreamer, the fictionalized D'Alembert, as the different levels of his consciousness work through the implications of being nothing more or less than a tiny part of an immense whole, all operating according to the same laws. Here Diderot considers what individuality can subsist in the wake of such visions: as Buffon had unworriedly declared, 'an individual, to whichever species he may belong, is nothing to the Universe'.[22] Rousseau's *Rêveries* similarly depict an individual (an autobiographical version of himself) coming to terms with the world, but the enthusiastic dynamism of Diderot's treatment is absent here: the immensity of nature reminds 'Rousseau' of how insignificant he and his troubles are, and envelops him in its soothing rhythms. We quoted just such a passage in the opening pages of the chapter, and the voice Rousseau gave to a certain sort of melancholic rejection of society that simultaneously expressed a form of depressed impotence with respect to nature's sublimity resonated widely and was much adopted. We saw an example of this in Charrière, and it will of course be of seminal importance to romanticism.

It is almost impossible to draw this survey to a close: every discussion of every text plunges us back into a resonating world of references to which there is no beginning and no end. Perhaps we'll simply end with the century, and with texts that are full of what has gone before them. If Marivaux's witty farces brought their lovers together but failed to find a chink in the armour of society, Pierre Caron de Beaumarchais's similarly witty plays do something a bit more, depicting individuals who reject the ways society treats them, and who succeed nonetheless. Figaro is the main character: in *Le Barbier de Séville* [*The Barber of Seville*] (1775) he was the nimble-minded valet who helps his master thwart the plans of an old man to marry a young woman; in *Le Mariage de Figaro* [*The Marriage of Figaro*] (1784), he is preventing that same master exercise a feudal abuse of power, and discoursing in a famous monologue (Act v, scene iii) about how his natural talents are thwarted by unfair society. And in *La Mère coupable* [*The Guilty Mother*] (1792), a play much influenced by the view Diderot expressed in his *Entretiens sur le fils naturel* [*Conversations about 'The Natural Son'*] (1757) that the dramatic conventions of comedy and tragedy were artificial and needed updating to reflect the real dilemmas of the modern family, Figaro is unquestionably the man in control, helping shore up a once powerful now vulnerable family from outside threats, and providing the moral leadership that is otherwise lacking. How writers and dramatists think about society and nature, how they represent them, and how they entertain their audiences, is clearly shifting fast.

What a writer tells his reader has changed. If, in the first part of the century, many writers will present nature in opposition to society, as the Chevalier in Pluche's *Spectacle de la nature* had done, stating that nature 'is a thousand times more beautiful than Paris with its pomp and gilding',[23] Louis-Sébastien Mercier will not reject Paris but simply set it in its natural context, assuming that this is the first thing his reader will want to know: 'Do you want to judge Paris physically?' he asks. The answer is that: 'It is built of chalk, and ... it stands on chalk.'[24]

NOTES

1. Isabelle de Charrière, *Letters from Mistress Henley*, in *The Nobleman and Other Romances*, trans. Caroline Warman (New York: Penguin, 2012), pp. 75–101 (p. 96).
2. Denis Diderot, *Letter on the Blind* (1749), in Kate E. Tunstall, *Blindness and Enlightenment: An Essay, with a New Translation of Diderot's 'Letter on the Blind' and La Mothe Le Vayer's 'Of a Man Born Blind'* (New York: Continuum, 2011), pp. 163–238 (p. 199).
3. Jean-Jacques Rousseau, *Reveries of the Solitary Walker*, trans. Peter France (London: Penguin, 1979), p. 86 (fifth walk; translation slightly amended).
4. Charrière, *Mistress Henley*, p. 97.
5. François-René, Vicomte de de Chateaubriand, *Atala, René*, ed. Pierre Reboul (Paris: Garnier-Flammarion, 1964), p. 42. My translation.
6. Charles Louis de Secondat, Baron de Montesquieu, *Persian Letters*, trans. Margaret Mauldon, ed. Andrew Kahn (Oxford: Oxford University Press, 2008), p. 213 (translation slightly amended).

7. Voltaire [François-Marie Arouet], *Letters concerning the English Nation*, trans. John Lockman, ed. Nicholas Cronk (Oxford: Oxford University Press, 2005), p. 73 (Letter xv).

8. Voltaire, *Letters concerning the English Nation*, p. 63 (Letter xiv).

9. René Descartes, *Discourse on Method*, trans. F. E. Sutcliffe (London: Penguin, 1968), p. 39 (Chapter 2, § 17).

10. Dante Alighieri, *Inferno*, trans. Robin Kirkpatrick (London: Penguin, 2006), p. 3 (Canto 1, ll. 1–3).

11. Descartes, *Discourse on Method*, p. 54 (Chapter 4).

12. Voltaire, *Letters concerning the English Nation*, p. 66 (Letter xv).

13. John Locke, *An Essay concerning Human Understanding* (1689), ed. Peter H. Nidditch (Oxford: Clarendon Press, 1975), p. 104 (Book ii, Chapter 1, § 2; original capitalization, punctuation, spelling, and emphasis).

14. Étienne-Gabriel Morelly, *Naufrage des isles flottantes* ('Messine' [Paris]: Compagnie des libraires, 1753), p. 21. My translation.

15. Morelly, *Code de la nature*, in *Œuvres philosophiques*, ed. Jean Pierre Jackson (Paris: Coda, 2004), p. 281. My translation.

16. Morelly, *Code de la nature*, p. 352. My translation.

17. Rousseau, *Reveries of the Solitary Walker*, pp. 84, 86.

18. Bernardin de Saint-Pierre, *Paul and Virginia*, trans. John Donovan (London: Owen, 1982), pp. 58–60.

19. Georges-Louis Leclerc, Comte de Buffon, 'De la nature. Première vue' [On Nature. First view], in *Œuvres*, ed. Stéphane Schmitt and Cédric Crémière (Paris: Gallimard, 2007), p. 985.

20. *Encyclopédie, ou, Dictionnaire raisonné des sciences, des arts et des métiers*, ed. Denis Diderot and Jean Le Rond D'Alembert. University of Chicago: ARTFL Encyclopédie Project (Spring 2013 Edition), ed. Robert Morrissey and Glenn Roe, available at http://encyclopedie.uchicago.edu, accessed 2 July 2015.

21. Guillaume Thomas François, Abbé Raynal, *Histoire philosophique et politique des établissements et du commerce des Européens dans les deux Indes*, ed. Anthony Strugnell, Andrew Brown, Cecil Patrick Courtney, et al. (Ferney-Voltaire: Centre international d'étude du dix-huitième siècle, 2010), vol. 1, p. 88. Original emphasis; my translation.

22. Buffon, 'De la nature. Seconde vue' [On Nature. Second View], in *Œuvres*, p. 994. My translation.

23. Noël-Antoine, Abbé Pluche, *Spectacle de la nature, ou, Entretiens sur les particularités de l'histoire naturelle*, 8 vols (Paris: chez la veuve Estienne, 1732–50), vol. 1, p. 2. My translation.

24. Louis-Sébastien Mercier, *Tableau de Paris* (1781–89), ed. Michel Delon, in *Paris le jour, Paris la nuit* (Paris: Bouquins Robert Laffont, 1990), pp. 1–588 (p. 34). My translation.

9

ROSEMARY LLOYD

Nostalgia and the creation of the past

That the French poet, Charles Baudelaire, chose to open the first great work of modernism, his poem 'Le Cygne' ['The Swan'], with a reference to antiquity is both significant and typical of his time. When the French Revolution of 1789 swept aside centuries of monarchical rule and attempted to replace it with a republic, the French turned to the past to find new forms of government and fresh ways of identifying themselves as French men and women. Moreover, the rapid changes in living conditions and the great movement of people from the country to the city that came about with that other upheaval, the Industrial Revolution, transformed in the space of a single lifetime both the physical surroundings and the social frameworks that had seemed so permanent to previous generations. Hardly surprising, then, that Baudelaire should seek an anchoring point in the shared experience of antiquity. His generation – at least the males of that generation – had been educated in a programme dominated by classical literature and languages; their imaginations were shaped by classical myths; and yet both the anxiety and excitement of the new and the awareness of rapid changes taking place were also central to their everyday experience.

When Baudelaire, walking through a city in the process of rapid transformation, social as well as physical, comes across a swan that has broken free from its cage and wanders aimlessly in an alien environment seeking its 'beau lac natal', the beautiful lake in which it was born, it reminds him of a rich series of other wanderers and exiles, from Andromaque, a victim of the Trojan War, through Robinson Crusoe, the seventeenth-century sailor marooned on an island, to an African woman now living in the Paris of the poet's own time. All of history, both official and personal, seems to be legible in the streets and monuments, the parks and cafés, the restaurants and cemeteries of Baudelaire's Paris, and his modernism depends in large measure on his transformation of that diverse material into the gold of poetry. For many writers of his time, indeed, history would be a vital lens for understanding and representing the contemporary world.

While the two revolutions were perhaps the most obvious instigations for this interest in the past, other events reinforced and sharpened a growing curiosity about the life of former ages. Napoleon's desire to mould his own empire on that of ancient Rome might have added to the turn to classical antiquity, but his campaign in Egypt brought with it the revelation of a yet more ancient civilization. This awareness was further intensified when a Frenchman, Jean-François Champollion, succeeded in deciphering the Egyptian hieroglyphics on the Rosetta stone. Deciphering the past, interpreting the secrets of the past, became common elements of nineteenth-century literature, both for their intrinsic interest and for the light they could shed on present problems.

The power of nostalgia, however, was not drawn merely from what lay outside France: the awareness that much that was seen as quintessentially local was under imminent threat of permanent disappearance also acted as a strong stimulus to writers, artists, musicians, and, with the invention of the daguerreotype in the late 1830s, to photographers too. This was the century which sought to collect folk tales and folk songs, which set out to make a permanent record, verbal or visual, of ways of life and forms of occupation that were rapidly dying out, and which realized that as those modern cathedrals, the railway stations, were rising from the ruins of buildings demolished to make way for them, so not only gothic cathedrals but small churches and civic monuments all across France were crumbling away.

Freed from the perception that the monarchy and the aristocracy alone must be shown as determining the country's destiny, it also became an age of great historians, whose writings helped mould new ways in which the French conceived of their past. In 1805, for instance, Louis-Pierre Anquetil, writing at a time when monarchical rule seemed abolished forever, published his fourteen volumes of French history from the Gauls to the end of the monarchy. In 1811 Joseph-François Michaud's *Histoire des croisades* [*History of the Crusades*] contributed to the growing vogue for the Middle Ages. The Swiss economist, political theorist, and historian Jean-Charles-Léonard de Sismondi started working on his massive *Histoire des Français* in 1818 and devoted the remaining twenty-three years of his life to completing it.

Perhaps the two historians who most influenced creative writers of the time were Augustin Thierry, whose *Lettres sur l'histoire de France* [*Letters on the History of France*] of 1820 have been described as more influential for the development of French romanticism than Alphonse de Lamartine's collection of poems, *Les Méditations*, published later the same year, and Jules Michelet, who produced his monumental study of French history, *Histoire de France*, in nineteen volumes, between 1833 and 1867. In *Les Lettres*, Thierry set out to show, as part of his patriotic duty, as he puts it, that the freedoms and rights desired and demanded by his contemporaries were not of recent date, but instead could be traced back to the Middle Ages, and to the conflicts and courage of past generations. Thierry's 1825 study, *Histoire de la conquête de l'Angleterre par les Normands* [*History of the Conquest of England by the Normans*], was also a powerful force in shaping contemporary thinking about the ways in which the medieval period formed the modern era. In terms of historiography, the work is also vital both for Thierry's insistence on the need for the historian to set aside contemporary patterns of thought and become immersed in the thinking of the period under discussion, and for the emphasis he placed on history as narrative. By telling the story rather than interspersing commentary in the midst of narration, he argued, he could confer 'a kind of historical life on the masses as well as on individuals, and as a result the political destiny of nations would offer something of that human interest that we cannot help feeling on reading the simple details of the adventures and the changes in fortune of a single individual'.[1]

Infused with a Romantic belief in the role both of the individual and of fate in the course of events, Michelet, for his part, set out to recreate the past in all its diversity, blending the political with the economic, the social with the artistic, the public with the private. At its best, his writing is powerful and pithy, highly imaginative, and deeply lyrical. Take for instance the following affirmation, built as much on alliteration as on reason: 'France has made France, and the fatal element of race strikes me as secondary. She is the daughter of her freedom. In human progress, the essential part belongs to the living force that is called humanity. Humanity is its own Prometheus.'[2] Or this lyrical assertion of the need for both tolerance and variety: 'Wherever Christians appear, the desert appears; wherever the Arabs are, water and life burst forth everywhere, streams run, the land grows green and becomes a garden of flowers. And the field of intelligence also flowers. Barbarians: where would be without them?'[3] Hardly surprising then, that such writing should exert such an influence on readers and writers alike.

Nor was it just historians who inspired creative writers to draw on the past. Stendhal, for example, writing his Romantic manifesto of 1823, *Racine et Shakespeare*, insisted on the public's need for representations of the conflicts that took place in the reigns of Charles VI, Charles VII, and François Ier in order to contemplate and resolve the problems of their own times. Indeed, the Romantics' image of the Middle Ages as a dynamic period of class conflict, leading slowly but unavoidably to the French Revolution, is a central tenet of their artistic as well as social credo. Victor Hugo, in the influential preface to his play *Cromwell*, began by tracing what he saw as the history of literature, from the lyricism of the primitive ages, through the epic that dominated the classical period, to the drama of the Christian era. In defining what he presented as the modern literature of Romanticism, he emphasized the way in which the union of the grotesque and sublime created the complexity and variety of contemporary literature, taking an obvious delight in tracing the historical progress of the grotesque from its timid beginnings in classical antiquity through the creativity of the Middle Ages (the many grotesque statues on cathedrals for example) to the complexity of Shakespeare. He went on to insist on the need for a new form of theatre, one that abandoned the classical unities and drew instead on a form of realism based on precise historical knowledge, local colour, and truth to human reality.

Among the first great creative works to show this influence of history was Francois-René de Chateaubriand's polemical and highly influential prose work *Le Génie du christianisme* [*The Genius of Christianity*] (1802). Searching for the causes of the French Revolution, which the aristocratic Chateaubriand saw as primarily destructive, he placed the blame squarely on the eighteenth century's rejection of the traditional Christian religion. In its glorification of gothic architecture and its praise of medieval literary epics as well as in the beauty of its language and the emphasis it placed on feeling rather than rationality, *Génie* played an immense part in shaping the Romantic movement in France. Here is Chateaubriand singing the glories of gothic architecture and relating it precisely to the nature of medieval France:

> The gothic order, for all its barbaric proportions, nevertheless has a beauty which is unique to it. Forests were the Divinity's first temples, and it was from forests that men took the first idea of architecture. This art must have varied according the climate. The Greeks turned the elegant Corinthian column with its capital embellished with leaves on the model of the palm tree. The enormous pillars of the old Egyptian style represent the sycamore, the oriental fig, the banana palm, and most of the gigantic trees of Africa and Asia. The forests of the Gauls in their turn passed into the temples of our fathers and our oak woods have also maintained their sacred origin. Those vaults carved into foliage, those jambs that support the walls and end abruptly like broken tree trunks, the coolness of the vaults, the darkness of the sanctuary, the shadowy wings, the secret passageways, everything retraces the labyrinths of the woods in the gothic church.[4]

It is this kind of blending of past and present, this sharp awareness of past ages which thus become, to the practised eye, legible in everything that surrounds us, that feeds into much of the nineteenth century's awareness of history, which was further aroused by the enthusiastic reception in France of the historical novels of the Scotsman, Walter Scott.

Of course the genre of the historical novel was well established in France long before the nineteenth century and the arrival of Scott. It had become highly popular in the course of the seventeenth century, when various women writers, notably Madeleine de Scudéry and Marie-Madeleine Pioche de La Vergne, Comtesse de Lafayette, used the historical past as a means of exploring such timeless matters as affairs of the heart and states of mind. Although the genre fell out of favour during the eighteenth century, by 1816, when Walter Scott's historical novels began to be translated into French, numerous women writers had already revived it through works which focused on history seen through the eyes of individuals, usually women, who were forced to decide between the grander world stage and their own personal lives.[5] Most notable among these are the highly prolific Stéphanie Félicité Du Crest de Saint-Aubin, Comtesse de Genlis, whose *La Duchesse de la Vallière* was published in 1804, while *Jeanne de France* came out in 1816; Sophie Cottin, whose immensely popular story set at the time of the crusades, *Mathilde*, was published in 1805; and the composer, playwright, and novelist Amélie Simons-Candeille, whose novel *Bathilde, reine des Francs* first appeared in 1814 while *Agnès de France, ou, Le douzième siècle*, came out in 1821. Studded with copious explanatory footnotes, these novels are to a large extent didactic in aim, in both historical and moral terms, for they not only set out to inform their reader about the times and societies in which the story takes place, but they present their heroines as models of goodness, courage, or self-denial. These women's novels, together with the translations of Scott's stories, were all part of a wider interest in the individual and the ways in which he or she influenced, and was influenced by, contemporary events.

This passionate quest for the roots of France led to a surge of interest in a period long neglected and even derided: the Middle Ages. This was when the repertory of French medieval literature was essentially rediscovered, and from this period, too, date the first great scholarly editions of medieval texts. The enticing lure of medieval architecture, whether in the form of the great gothic cathedrals, or in that of walled cities or private dwellings, can be found in such widely diverse romantic writers as Aloysius Bertrand, Théophile Gautier, and Victor Hugo, but it can also be seen much later in the century, when writers such as Émile Zola, in for instance his novel *Le Rêve* [*The Dream*], and Joris-Karl Huysmans, in *Là-bas* [*Down There*] and *La Cathédrale*, revised it for their own very different purposes.

Author and archaeologist Prosper Mérimée devoted an early play, *La Jacquerie* (1828), to exploring the peasant revolts of the fourteenth century, typifying Romanticism's vision of the medieval period, not as a stable monarchical age, but as a time of social conflict and class struggle. More importantly, in his role as Inspector-General of Historical Monuments, he set about cataloguing churches and other buildings in need of protection from decay and destruction.

In his *Gaspard de la nuit*, Aloysius Bertrand, best known perhaps for his influence on Baudelaire's prose poems, was drawing on the romantic power of the decay Mérimée lamented. A collection of short prose pieces based on the verse form of the *ballade, Gaspard* reveals a highly individual blend of images and vocabulary inspired by the Middle Ages. The prose poem 'Le Maçon' ['The Mason'] for example vividly brings alive for us, through the eyes of Abraham Knupfer, its mason, a medieval Flemish cathedral in a town engulfed by war:

> [The mason] sees the stone gargoyles vomiting water from the slates into the higgledy-piggledy abyss of galleries, windows, hangings, little steeples, turrets, roofs and scaffolding, stained with a grey dot by the indented and motionless wing of the falcon . . . And when evening comes, when the harmonious nave of the cathedral falls asleep lying with its arms stretched out like a cross, he catches sight from the ladder, on the horizon, of a village set alight by warriors, and flaming like a comet in the azure sky.[6]

Elsewhere, in sardonic mode, Bertrand laments the disappearance of chivalry in the France of his own day, together with the loss of interest in the legends and stories of the past. His poem entitled 'À un bibliophile', for instance, begins with an epigram pretending to quote a grandmother telling tales to her grandchildren: 'My children, the only knights are those you find in books.' The poem opens with the following question: 'Why restore the moth-eaten and dusty stories of the Middle Ages, when chivalry has disappeared forever, with the concerts of its minstrels, the enchantments of its fairies, and the glory of its noble men?' 'Every tradition of war and love is being forgotten', he laments at the end of the piece, 'and my fables will not even have the same fate as the complaint of Geneviève de Brabant, about which the seller of pictures no longer knows the beginning and never knew the end'.[7]

Yet not all writers felt that interest in the medieval period had disappeared. On the contrary, the poet, novelist, short-story writer, and critic, Théophile Gautier, lampoons what he saw as an over-enthusiastic passion for the Middle Ages in one of the stories he includes in his collection *Les Jeunes-France [The Young French]* (1833), 'Élias Wildmanstadius, ou L'homme médiéval' ['Elias Wildmanstadius, or the Medieval Man']. In a humorous survey of his contemporaries, the 'young French' of his book's title, he lists the Byronic, the artist, the passionate, and the bon viveur, but he argues that the most numerous grouping is, in fact, the medieval. His central character is depicted as having a fifteenth-century soul trapped in a nineteenth-century world. He lives in the oldest (and most uncomfortable) house he can find, surrounds himself with antique furniture and tapestries and dresses in clothes and shoes that recall the Middle Ages. Passionately moved by the music, literature, and architecture of the medieval period, he remains blind to the beauties of his own age. So enamoured is he of gothic architecture that when a lightning bolt hits the cathedral, he dies as if in sympathy with the building. Even more scathing was the attack Gautier launched in 1835, in the preface to his novel *Mademoiselle de Maupin*, in which he has a critic bemoan the cardboard medievalism that has become such a vogue: 'Oh you daubers who think you've produced local colour when you've plastered red on white, white on black, and green on yellow, what you've seen of the Middle Ages is merely the tree's bark, you've not guessed at its soul.'[8]

While such pseudo-medievalism might have been a popular, if brief-lived fad, a deeper concern with the relics of that period galvanized some of the most celebrated members of the Romantic movement. Notable among these were Mérimée, whose function as Inspector-General of Historical Monuments allowed him to commission architects to work on restoration projects, and Eugène Viollet-le-Duc, who became the foremost architect involved in restoring gothic monuments. An ardent theorist as well as practitioner, Viollet-le-Duc sought less to return a building to its former glory than to rebuild it according to his own notions of medieval perfection. His *Dictionnaire raisonné de l'architecture française du XIe au XVIe siècle*, first published in 1856, was highly influential not just in France but also in such countries as the United Kingdom and the United States.

There can be no doubt, however, that the most famous novel ostensibly inspired by the Middle Ages is Victor Hugo's *Notre-Dame de Paris* (1831), written not so much to explore a particular moment as to bring direct influence to bear on the present. From the opening chapter Hugo makes clear the interest and importance of the past for the present:

> If any of us, people of 1830, could be granted the possibility of mingling in our thoughts with those Parisians of the fifteenth century, and entering with them, rubbing shoulders with them, tripping over them, in that vast hall, so tightly packed that 6 January 1482, the spectacle would not be lacking in interest or charm, and we would be surrounded with things so old they would seem completely new.[9]

Hugo's main aim was to arouse popular interest in saving the great cathedral, which at the time the novel was published was at imminent risk of collapse brought about by decay, depredation, and neglect. In the note he added to his work in 1832, Hugo made clear that one of his main aims in writing it had been to inspire his nation with a love of its own architecture. The first chapter of the novel's third book opens with a biting attack on those who had allowed that great stone symphony – Paris's main cathedral, Notre-Dame de Paris – to fall into such a dilapidated state:

> Of course the cathedral of Notre-Dame is still today a majestic and sublime edifice, but, however beautifully she has preserved herself in growing old, it is hard not to sigh, not to be filled with indignation faced with the countless degradations and mutilations that man and time have simultaneously inflicted on the venerable monument, with no respect for Charlemagne who laid the first stone, or for Philippe Auguste who placed the last one.
>
> On the face of that old queen among our cathedrals, next to a wrinkle you can always find a scar. *Tempus edax, homo edacior*. Which I would like to translate as 'time is blind, man is stupid'.[10]

With its striking juxtaposition of the grotesque, represented physically by Quasimodo and morally by Frollo, and the sublime, manifested physically in Phoebus and spiritually in Esmerelda, and its consummate depictions of the power of the mob, Hugo's novel encapsulates many Romantic concerns, masterfully blending the past with the present, and above all using an imagined past to comment obliquely on an ever-suggested present.

While the Middle Ages may have exerted a particular charm for Romantic writers, it is probable that for many contemporary readers the seventeenth century was more immediately appealing, not merely because, being closer to their own period, the characters seemed more like themselves; but above all because it was an age dominated by that complex figure Cardinal Richelieu, who looms over some of the best-known historical novels of the nineteenth century as a figure of immense power and consummate skill in the handling of both the king and his underlings. Alfred de Vigny's beautifully crafted novel *Cinq-Mars* (1826), blends extensive research with a powerful imagination in its retelling of the story of the role played by Henri Coiffier de Ruzé, Marquis de Cinq-Mars in leading the most-nearly successful conspiracy against Richelieu. Its many evocative descriptions of battles, its portrayal of religious bigotry and the contagious fear of witchcraft, and its numerous depictions of other historical events, provide a vibrant context for Vigny's careful analysis of the young hero's largely misunderstood love for Marie de Gonzague, who is promised to the King of Poland. Yet while Vigny's historical imagination transformed his research into a lively evocation of the time and the places of his novel, his analysis of Cinq-Mars's emotions seems very much part of the nineteenth-century *vague des passions*, described by Chateaubriand: that sense of intense emotion combined with a feeling of emptiness and the conviction that all one's abilities would never find an outlet. The force of his analysis can be illustrated by a passage early in the novel, while Cinq-Mars is waiting for a siege to end, a fitting backdrop, as are many of Vigny's, for the hero's sense that his life is in abeyance:

> There are moments in life when we ardently long for violent shocks to take us out of our little sufferings; long stretches when the soul, like the lion in the fable, weary of the constant attacks of an insect, longs for a stronger enemy and summons up dangers with all the power of our desire. Cinq-Mars was in such a state of mind, which always stems from a sickly sensitivity of the organs and a perpetual agitation of the heart. Weary of constantly revolving in his mind the combination of events he longed for and those he feared; weary of applying to probabilities all the calculations his head was strong enough to muster, of calling to his aid all that his education had taught him of the life of famous men to compare them his own current situation; overwhelmed with regrets, dreams, predictions, nightmares, fears and all that imaginary world in which he had lived during his lonely journey, he breathed anew on finding himself hurled into a real world almost as noisy as the one he had dreamed up, and the sense of two real dangers restored the circulation to his blood and youth to all his being.[11]

Passages like this demonstrate the extent to which Vigny, like many other writers, used the framework of the past to explore contemporary predicaments.

An aspect that gives particular force to Vigny's writing is the relationship he creates between narrator and reader. As an example of Vigny's technique of making the reader a partner in the events, take the chapter entitled 'Le Cabinet' with its tone of intimate conversation between narrator and reader, and its precise depiction of a scene into which we are invited to enter: 'Look at the Mediterranean, which displays not far away its bluish water on the sandy shore. Penetrate into this city which is like Athens; but in order to find the man who rules it, follow this dark, uneven street, climb the steps to the old archbishop's palace, and let us enter into the first and largest of its rooms.'[12] Such a passage exemplifies one of Vigny's most frequent and powerful techniques, one he shared with Victor Hugo: that of making his reader an active observer of the events recounted. This is history not as mere backdrop or academic information, but as central to the existence not just of the characters but of the reader, too. While critics immediately after the novel's publication pedantically took apparent pleasure in noting small errors of detail, what strikes us now is the intensity and completeness of his historical imagination, fuelled by facts but able to shift and amalgamate those facts when the inner truth of the work demanded such transformations. Although it is history, in other words, that informs this novel, its force derives from the brilliance of its descriptive powers and the convincing nature of its psychological analysis.

With its depiction of the interrelationship of power and evil epitomized for Vigny by Richelieu, *Cinq-Mars* set in train a whole series of novels drawing on the historical events of this period. Three popular writers of the mid nineteenth century drew on this legacy to produce novels and plays that were far racier and far less subtle than *Cinq-Mars*, and that appealed to a broader public. These are works whose popularity stems less from the analytical and descriptive powers displayed by Vigny than from their rapidly unfolding plots and their memorable characters. The prolific novelist, play-wright, and journalist Alexandre Dumas produced numerous historical novels, among which the most loved are those featuring the three musketeers, Athos, Porthos, and Aramis, and their young Gascon friend, D'Artagnan. Here the brooding and sinister figure of Richelieu appears as a symbol of the arbitrary power of authority, to be equally feared and subverted, mocked and dreaded.

Frédéric Soulié is another example of this kind of exploitation of the nostalgia for the past, which is tightly embedded with the writer's appetite for popularity and profit. Turning his attention to the Languedoc region, primarily that area around Toulouse, Soulié drew on the area's picturesque traditions and local legends to produce highly popular sensationalist novels. His emphasis on the descriptive derives from Scott, whose novels, as Stendhal pithily wrote, were 'romantic tragedy, interspersed with lengthy descriptions'.[13] But Soulié's descriptions – laboured at best – at worst fall into the grotesque, as when the young count, returning home, comes across a horribly mutilated old man whose nose, upper lip, and ears have been cut off and whose face is a mass of suppurating wounds.[14] Soulié replaces the analysis of character and event that drives much of Vigny's novel by con-versation, letting his characters present themselves and their situations before the narrative voice provides a rapid summary of the historical moment.

Finally, Eugène Sue, whose *Mystères de Paris* was one of the century's bestselling works, also wrote popular historical novels, among them *Jean Cavalier, ou, Les fanatiques des Cévennes*, first published in 1840, in which he sets out to explore the persecution of the Huguenots between 1701 and 1708, an event he self-promotingly argues is without precedent in 'any century, any age, any world'.[15] A prolific writer, Sue blends melodramatic detail, historical exposition, and fast-paced adventure-telling to produce a presentation of the past imbued with the concerns and values of the present.

Other Romantic writers, too, made use of a historical framework to create novels whose primary interest is not, in fact, historical at all: rather, setting their works in the past liberated them to explore quite different concerns.

This is the case when Gautier ostensibly chooses the seventeenth century as the setting for his sparkling novel, *Mademoiselle de Maupin* (1835). While the protagonist is loosely based on the French opera singer, Julie d'Aubigny, known as Mademoiselle de Maupin, Gautier's interest lies less in any real historical facts than in creating what Baudelaire termed a hymn to beauty, set in an age removed from the rapidly growing ugliness and pragmatism of the Industrial Revolution.

While the court of Louis XIII and the formidable figure of Richelieu attracted several Romantic writers, other Romantics turned their attention to different ages and different countries. No doubt the finest historical play of the Romantic period is Alfred de Musset's *Lorenzaccio* (1834). Set in six-teenth-century Florence, this play – written to be read in an armchair, explains Musset, rather than to be seen on the stage – draws on the complex period that saw the Florentine Republic brought to an end and replaced by the rule of Alessandro de' Medici, whom Musset depicts as violent, corrupt, and depraved. Yet while the historical background is brought vividly to life in various short scenes interspersed throughout the play, Musset's main interest seems to lie in a series of moral dilemmas posed by the central character, Alessandro's cousin Lorenzo, known as Lorenzaccio, where the suffix indicates evil. Lorenzo seeks to gain the duke's trust by appearing even more corrupt than he is himself, and then to assassinate him in order to allow those in favour of a republic to gain control over the city-state. The questions Musset raises concern those of ends and means: Is the desire for freedom and for political renewal sufficient justification for murder? And those of the extent to which in simulating corruption we ourselves become irremediably corrupt: Is it possible to set aside a mask of evil once the reasons for donning that mask have been achieved? History here is above all a means of under-standing the present, and the study of historical figures a device for exploring the self. Nostalgia for the historical past, in other words, is also a longing to return to a personal past, before the loss of innocence.

Other writers who set their novels in a real or imagined past found inspiration in Napoleon's campaigns in Egypt, and in the increase in travel to the great Egyptian monuments that resulted from that campaign. Gustave Flaubert, for instance, first visited the region in 1849, with his friend, the writer and photographer, Maxime Du Camp, who a few years after his return published a book entitled *Le Nil: Égypte et Nubie* (1853). Ernest Feydeau, who was an archaeologist as well as a writer and journalist, published a detailed study of the funeral monuments and traditions of the people of antiquity, arguing that to adopt such a focus was almost to study their entire history. Gautier, whose debunking of the passion for things medieval has already been mentioned, brought a similar sense of humour to the time of the Pharoahs in his short story 'Le Pied de momie' ['The Mummy's Foot'] (1840), but approached it far more seriously in his *Roman de la momie* [*The Story of the Mummy*] (1857) where he combines an undoubted fascination with the deciphering of the hieroglyphs, in which he found a potent symbol for the deciphering of literary texts more generally, with the evocation of the massive architecture and statues of the Egyptians. It is to Feydeau that Gautier dedicates his novel, acknowledging the role his erudition and library played in allowing Gautier, as he puts it, to wander through the palaces, temples, and catacombs of ancient Thebes. In the prologue to his novel, moreover, Gautier shows the effect exerted on the mind by entering an Egyptian funeral chamber, where time stands still, as he, too, attempts to make it stand still in the novel: 'An invisible hand had overturned eternity's sand-clock and the centuries, fallen grain by grain like hours in the solitude and darkness once more began their fall. It was as if History had not taken place. Moses was still alive, Pharaoh reigned.'[16] It is a novel in which Gautier frequently loses sight of his readership to revel in the close, at times indeed exhaustive, description of buildings, clothes, musical instruments, and other objects to the detriment of plot and psychological plausibility.

The greatest work inspired by the region, however, is undoubtedly that of Flaubert, whose letters written to his mother during his travels in the Middle East reveal the extent to which he was both dazzled and moved by what he saw there. Whereas his more famous novels *Madame Bovary* and *L'Éducation sentimentale* [*A Sentimental Education*] focus on the middle decades of the nineteenth century, his novel *Salammbô* (1862) recounts a violent and passionate tale set in ancient Carthage. The historical period is that of the third century BCE, immediately before and during the Mercenary Revolt which took place shortly after the First Punic War (264–241 BCE). This allows Flaubert to set a timeless plot, that of lovers from different sides of a conflict, in a period of particular barbarity, exemplified by the sacrifice of children to the god Moloch, and in a place of harsh scenic beauty. He immersed himself in studies of the period, from the writings of the Greek historians Polybius, Appian, and Diodorus Siculus through Michelet's *Histoire romaine* [*Roman History*] (1839), but he was most interested in uniting a story of violence and cruelty with his own memories of travelling in the region, memories which were intensified when he visited Tunisia in 1858.

The more immediate past was also a potent source for writers. Making some kind of sense of the Revolution, its bloody aftermath, and the rise of Napoleon were of course alluring topics. With the fall of the Bourbon monarchy in 1830, and even more when Napoleon's ashes were returned to Paris in 1840, a disparate crop of playwrights and theatres rushed to put the emperor, his legend, his loves, and his victories on the stage. Stendhal devoted an early episode of his novel *La Chartreuse de Parme* [*The Charterhouse of Parma*] (1839) to an evocation of the Battle of Waterloo, seen through the astonished and uncomprehending eyes of the seventeen-year-old protagonist, whose dreams of chivalry collide with the chaotic and bloody reality of modern warfare. Honoré de Balzac, too, explores the legacy of the Napoleonic era in jaundiced terms in *La Cousine Bette* [*Cousin Betty*], where he presents the clash of ideals between the older generation, who served with Napoleon and who consider themselves entitled as a result to embezzle and forge what they cannot earn, and the younger generation, more pragmatic, more moralistic, and more dour.

Balzac's greatest contribution to the historical novel, however, is no doubt *Les Chouans*, first published in 1829, which offers his novelistic depiction of the uprising of Breton peasants, hoping to restore the Bourbon monarchy in the wake of the Revolution. While this early work owes much to Scott, particularly in its close depictions of people and scenery, it also points forward to Balzac's later, more characteristic works. There is, for example, the fascination with language, in this case with the particular vocabulary used by the guerrillas and with their picturesque nicknames (Marche-à-terre, Le Gars, Galope-Chopine, for example). And while he draws on Scott's techniques to create a fictional story set in a historical background and to make history come alive by avoiding the stereotypical hero or villain, Balzac goes beyond his mentor in the psychological reality of his analyses. His star-crossed lovers may represent historical types, but they remain real individuals, forced into heroism or betrayal by the situations in which they find themselves. The extensive description of scenery serves other purposes than the merely picturesque, just as later the description of the Vauquer pension, in *Le Père Goriot* [*Old Goriot*], for all its precision becomes allegorical. Thus, for instance, in the closing moments of *Les Chouans*, the fog that shrouds landscape and people throws into question, as Maurice Samuels convincingly argues, Scott's technique of inviting the reader to 'gaze on a vividly rendered past world' thus transforming description into 'an obstacle to historical truth rather than its pre-condition'.[17]

The most ambitious work inspired by history is, however, Hugo's massive poetic work, *La Légende des siècles* [*The Legend of the Centuries*], written between 1855 and 1877, in which he sets out to evoke the spirit of different ages, from the remote past to the future and even further into a period beyond time. His aim, as he puts it in the preface, is to 'express humanity in a kind of cyclical work, painting it successively and simultaneously in all its aspects, history, fable, philosophy, religion, science, all of them gathering together in a single and mighty upward movement towards the light'.[18] For him, history must always be, as he argues in characteristically pithy terms, something one listens to at the gates of legend, something the poet transforms into art. Unlike some of his contemporaries, who looked back to the past as a better time irretrievably lost, Hugo chose as the guiding thread of his collection a profoundly held belief in progress, an indelible image of humanity climbing up from darkness to the ideal. His collection opens, therefore, with evocations of chaos – 'Fog and reality, clouds and the globe!'[19] – before turning to a series of evocations of archetypal moments of the past. Drawing less on historical reality than on symbolic truth, Hugo focuses on figures, mainly from his own extraordinary imagination, that incarnate the particular moment in which they lived. The final poem, the stupendous 'Abîme' ['Abyss'], shows man triumphantly proclaiming his superiority for where nature merely produces a sketch, man concludes, to which the earth tersely responds: 'You are nothing but my vermin.'[20] The debate broadens to include the planets and constellations, closing with the infinite as it boasts that it holds the multiplicity of being in its sombre unity, and God asserting that with a single breath he could blow everything into darkness. History, then, for Hugo is a progression from darkness to light, a rope he can use to bind together an otherwise disparate collection of legends, myths, and stories, but at the same time something as fragile as a spider web that can be dispersed in an instant.

Baudelaire's image of a Paris in which everything evokes history is as rich as Hugo's, but rejects that guiding thread of progress: the image in his case is more one of layers that a chance encounter can unexpectedly unpeel. Other writers left different images of the role of history in everyday life. Mérimée offers perhaps one of the most striking in his short story 'La Vénus d'Ille' (1835), when a statue of classical antiquity is revealed as a result of drought. Her arm thrusts up through the dry soil, eager to grasp the present, as she will soon draw into a fatal embrace the man unwise enough to place a ring on her finger, as if to offer her marriage. It is an image that clearly reveals Mérimée's belief in the continuing power of the past to affect the present, despite all the conviction in progress that his contemporaries might hold. Equally powerful, though very different in nature, is the role revealed in the work of several novelists of the store selling antiques or curiosities from the past, a space where objects from disparate periods jostle together and where you are as likely to find a magic skin that promises to make your wishes come true at the cost of a few years of your life for each wish, as you are to find a mummy's foot that will transport you to the time of the Pharaohs. But while Balzac's *La Peau de chagrin* [*The Wild Ass's Skin*] and Gautier's 'Le Pied de momie' both unfold, as it were, from the cornucopia offered by Paris's shops, and do so in ways that show the mingling of historical periods that had come to dominate

French minds in the wake of the Revolution, I would argue that the work that most charmingly and most intricately reflects the intermingling of historical periods is Gérard de Nerval's *Sylvie*, which first appeared in serial form in 1853.

Nerval, who had realized from as early as 1842 that old songs, ballads, and customs that were once passed on from generation to generation were in danger of becoming lost, had set out to collect them, to save them from the ravages of time and the oblivion of a more commercially minded nation. While *Sylvie* is imbued with the melancholy caused by this sense of loss, it is also a work that reveals how the past can be read in everything that surrounds us, if only we know how to do so. Memory and dream, time as measured by a concierge's cuckoo clock and time as it is experienced by the individual mingle here, as the narrator travels from Paris to the Valois, the region that constitutes for him both geographically and historically the heart of France. Towns like Châalis offer memories of long-dead emperors, while the villagers perform dances whose origins go back to the mists of time. Ermenonville recalls Rousseau, while a flowering privet makes him think of the Latin poet Virgil. But Sylvie herself reveals the rapid changes that are transforming France, no longer singing the simply country tunes of her childhood but modulating operatic airs, and no longer making lace by hand but fashioning gloves using a mechanical device.

Baudelaire's call to writers and artists to reveal the heroism of modern life, a call he made in his account of the art salon of 1846, did not of course bring to an end the power of history to inspire literature, but it reflected a turn already made by many of his contemporaries, most notably Balzac, away from the past to concentrate on the modern. History may have lost some of its sway in the later years of the century, but for many it remained a vital way of attempting to come to terms with the many dilemmas posed by the traumatic changes of 1789 and by the coming of the Industrial Revolution; to make sense, in other words, of what was most distinctively modern.

NOTES

1. Augustin Thierry, *Histoire de la conquête de l'Angleterre par les Normands*, rev. edn (Paris: Eduard Blot, 1830), p. 6. This and all translations in the chapter are my own.
2. 'La France a fait la France, et l'élément fatal de race m'y semble secondaire. Elle est fille de sa liberté. Dans le progrès humain, la part essentielle est à la force vive, qu'on appelle homme. L'homme est son propre Prométhée'; Jules Michelet, *Œuvres complètes* (Paris: Flammarion, 1893–4), vol. 1, p. viii.
3. Jules Michelet, *Histoire de France au XVIe siècle* (Paris: Chamerot, 1857), vol. 7, p. 161.

4. François-René, Vicomte de Chateaubriand, *Génie du christianisme: extraits* (Paris: Larousse, 1962), p. 89. The complete work is available at http://roman tis.free.fr/chateaubriand/html/genduch.html, accessed 3 July 2015.

5. On this see Maurice Samuels, *The Spectacular Past* (Ithaca, NY: Cornell University Press, 2004), who also provides a very useful list of scholars studying women and the practice of writing history.

6. Aloysius Bertrand, *Gaspard de la nuit*, ed. Jean-Luc Steinmetz (Paris: Livre de Poche, 2002), pp. 71–2.

7. Bertrand, *Gaspard de la nuit*, p. 162.

8. Théophile Gautier, *Mademoiselle de Maupin* (Paris: Garnier-Flammarion, 1966), p. 36.

9. Victor Hugo, *Notre-Dame de Paris* (Paris: Garnier-Flammarion, 1967), pp. 39–40.

10. Hugo, *Notre-Dame de Paris*, p. 131. The Latin quotation literally means: 'Time devours, man devours even more so.'

11. Alfred de Vigny, *Cinq-Mars* (Paris: Folio, 1988) pp. 164–5.

12. Vigny, *Cinq-Mars*, p. 121.

13. Stendhal, *Racine et Shakespeare* (Paris: Garnier-Flammarion, 1970), p. 53.

14. Frédéric Soulié, *Le Comte de Toulouse*, new edn (Paris: Le Siècle, 1850), p. 4.

15. Eugène Sue, *Jean Cavalier, ou, Les fanatiques des Cévennes* (Paris: Le Siècle, 1864), p. 11.

16. Théophile Gautier, *Le Roman de la momie* (Paris: Garnier-Flammarion, 1966).

17. Samuels, *The Spectacular Past*, p. 208.

18. Victor Hugo, *La Légende des siècles* (Paris: Gallimard, 1950), p. 3.

19. Hugo, *La Légende*, p. 9.

20. Hugo, *La Légende*, p. 741.

10

JENNIFER YEE

Exoticism and colonialism

Stripped bare of all connotations, the exotic is simply that which comes from elsewhere. The word derives from the Greek *exotikos*, via the Latin *exoticus*, which have the near-neutrality of the English word 'foreign'. And yet in art and literature the term 'exoticism' carries pejorative connotations of Eurocentric, simplistic attitudes to non-Western cultures, suggesting stereotypes of palm trees and camels, or collectable knick-knacks. Worse still, if it is understood as a set of preconceived ideas about non-European lands and peoples, exoticism clearly lends itself to collusion with political imperialism. In French, the adjective dates back to the sixteenth century, and until the eighteenth century it was mainly used to refer to botanical specimens. By the time the noun 'exotisme' appears in 1845, however, it is far from neutral. Exoticism has sometimes been summed up as a valorization of other cultures over one's own, and the humanist critic Tzvetan Todorov has decried it as mere 'praise without knowledge', just as reductive as the racist nationalism that appears to be its exact opposite, since both deny the fundamental universalism of humanity.[1] This view, however, neglects the fact that the word 'exotisme' implies not only the attraction inherent in foreign things but also a knowing awareness of the hackneyed, preconceived nature of this attraction. In parallel with this connotation linked to the word itself, French literary exoticism moved from being a satirical device in the eighteenth century, to one that increasingly parodied its own presuppositions in the nineteenth. The early twentieth century then saw a notable attempt to reclaim exoticism from the stereotype by Victor Segalen, in his novels, poetry, and above all a series of notes towards an *Essai sur l'exotisme* (1904–18). Segalen's aim to construct an aesthetics of cultural diversity that would respect the complexities of difference is of immediate relevance to postcolonial literatures and the postcolonial world.

Part of Segalen's project was an attempt to use exoticism as a way of understanding the meeting of different cultures outside the forced relations of colonialism. He sought a response to diversity that would follow a dialectical movement between the self and the other, recognizing difference without attempting to overcome or mimic it. In a period when French colonial ideology was taking on new cultural centrality, his project was more aspirational than descriptive. More recently, and particularly since the publication of Edward Said's landmark study *Orientalism* in 1978, postcolonial theory has instead warned us of the dangers of ignoring colonialism, the second term of this chapter's title. Said showed us that proto-imperialist attitudes – a set of presuppositions about the place of non-European cultures in relation to Europe that prepared the way for political and economic expansion – are present within orientalist exoticism. Although the peak of France's modern imperial period was not to come until the 1880s–1930s, with a more sustained policy of conquest and the rise of the so-called *mission civilisatrice*, imperialist culture in the broader sense was apparent earlier in ways that varied from expansionist scientific and economic policies to a sense of mourning and frustrated ambition (notably in relation to the loss of France's seventeenth- and eighteenth-century colonies in India and the Americas). The short-lived Napoleonic Egyptian expedition of 1798–1801 can be seen as announcing a geopolitical vision in which France aimed to take a leading role in political expansion and the pursuit of universalizing scientific goals. Literary exoticism, too, was often implicitly imperialistic, sometimes long before active colonialism. And the first steps towards the conquest of Algeria, taken in 1830, correspond with the peak of the French Romantic period.

French and British literature of the nineteenth and early twentieth centuries was the terrain on which Said built his founding contribution to postcolonial theory in *Orientalism*. In recent decades critics have sought to nuance Said's polemical thesis by acknowledging the need to understand writing about extra-European lands and peoples not as one homogeneous whole, but as reflecting shifting attitudes and concerns as well as the gender, class, and political orientations of individual writers.[2] Others argue that literature, while part of a dominant discourse, is at the same time capable of criticizing that discourse.[3] Rather than seeing French literary exoticism as monolithic and immobile, the present chapter suggests some of the shifts it went through during the two centuries between Montesquieu's *Lettres persanes* [*Persian Letters*] in 1721 and Segalen's *René Leys* in 1922. It argues that we should understand exoticism in terms of a series of dialectical movements: between the implicit assertion of Western superiority and critique of France itself; or between a reification of the exotic and the ironic deprecation of such reification.

From a French perspective, England or Italy could be called exotic, but in the period that interests us here the word's connotations linked it mainly to extra-European locations. These include the Americas, which play a key role in the myth of the noble savage in the eighteenth century; the 'Orient', an extremely vague territory that by some accounts begins in Spain and Greece and continues all the way to China, but whose heartland is emphatically the Muslim Middle East; the 'Island', which the French imagination tends to situate either in the Pacific or in the West Indies; and, with increasing importance towards the end of our period, Sub-Saharan Africa.

Defamiliarization and Enlightenment critique

Although the word 'exotisme' had yet to be coined, the decorative arts of the seventeenth and eighteenth centuries were marked by the exotic modes of *turquerie* and *chinoiserie*, which imitated imported artefacts to create exotic-looking European objects. Literary exoticism flourished in the eighteenth century following the translation of the *Arabian Nights* by Antoine Galland (*Les Mille et une nuits*, 12 vols, 1704–17), which was to have a long-term influence on French and indeed world literature. Although they did not have a comparable impact on popular culture, other translations from oriental languages, notably Persian (such as the *Zend-Avesta, ouvrage de Zoroastre*, translated by Abrahim Hyacinthe Anquetil-Duperron, 1771) and Sanskrit (the *Bhagavad Gita*, translated by Charles Wilkins, 1785) were one of the contributing factors in the rise of Romanticism. Eighteenth-century exoticism also reflected the increasing popularity of travel narratives, particularly in the second half of the century in response to European naval exploration and economic expansion. Accounts of voyages, published by a new generation of highly cultivated ships' captains such as Cook and Bougainville, or philosophical travellers such as Volney, had a wide readership and long-lasting literary impact. In France, these different influences gave rise to the major genres adopted by literary exoticism in the Enlightenment: the exotic epistolary novel, the 'oriental' tale, and the pseudo-travel narrative.

Although it was not the first novel in letters, Montesquieu saw his *Lettres persanes* (1721) as launching the genre of the exotic epistolary novel. The epistolary form lent itself to the incorporation of mini-essays discussing philosophy, politics and morality. The adoption of an exotic perspective (in Montesquieu's novel most of the letters are written by Persians visiting Paris) provides a means of achieving defamiliarization, or 'estrangement'[4] from what might otherwise remain unquestioned within European society. The exotic epistolary novel thus offers a variant on the tradition of the 'holy fool' in which naïve questions are asked in an implicit Socratic dialogue. This 'pseudoethnography'[5] serves as a thought experiment in which universalism is challenged – or confirmed – by empirical experience. 'How can one be

Persian?' the French ask Rica, one of Montesquieu's Persian characters. And yet when he trades in his exotic clothing for local garments he blends in with the crowd and is ignored: the slight phonemic differences between *persan* and *parisien*, like the exterior difference of clothing, mask the fundamental universality of the human.[6]

Having foreign protagonists also made it possible for the *Lettres persanes* to approach sexuality with relative freedom, a dispensation which contributed to the fascination of the harem or Turkish seraglio. Orientalism thus facilitated a shift from the sentimental mode to an erotic or libertine attitude that, in turn, allowed a politicization of the *Lettres*.[7] The fictive harem clearly forms part of a sexual fantasy in which one man has access to many women, but it also functions as part of a political satire: the instability of the harem while its master, Usbek, is away in France stands as a warning against the dangers of absolutism.[8] Usbek is critical of tyranny in other societies, but strives to maintain it within his own harem. Montesquieu's success encouraged a spate of exotic epistolary novels, among them Françoise de Graffigny's *Lettres d'une Péruvienne* [*Letters of a Peruvian Woman*] (1747). The 'foreigner-in-France' narrative, in both its epistolary and non-epistolary forms (such as Voltaire's satirical novella *L'Ingénu*, 1767), tends to use the protagonist as a mere instrument allowing a fresh view of French culture and an 'outside' perspective from which to criticize it. While the attitude to the foreign culture may be reductive, the intention – within the culture of the writer – is oppositional: non-European peoples and cultures are a means of mounting a critique of Europe itself.

The *Mille et une nuits* and the *Lettres persanes* were also influential in the rise of the oriental tale. The beginning of the century had already seen a new interest in fairy tales, but the oriental tale proved more useful for the purposes of the *conte philosophique*. Voltaire, notably, used the genres of the oriental tale or the pseudo-travel narrative as the basis for satirical philosophical fables. Thus *Zadig, ou, La destinée: Histoire orientale* [*Zadig, or, the Book of Fate: an Oriental History*] (1747–8) is a picaresque adventure in which happiness is elusive since Zadig, despite his philosophical intelligence, is subject to the arbitrary traditions of the societies in which he lives. The freedom permitted by an exotic setting was again exploited by Voltaire in *Candide, ou, L'optimisme* [*Candide, or, Optimism*] (1759), *La Princesse de Babylone* (1768), and *Le Taureau blanc* [*The White Bull*] (1774). In *Candide* Voltaire uses the pseudo-travel narrative to stage a confrontation between Leibniz's optimistic rationalism and empiricism: in one key episode, Candide's encounter with a mutilated slave serves to undermine ideas of human benevolence and the doctrine that we live in the best of all possible worlds. Eighteenth-century Europe had a new sense of the world as a whole, and in these tales characters travel freely from one place to another at great speed. In effect, however, they remain within one country: the philosophical Elsewhere. Like Jonathan Swift's Lilliput (in *Gulliver's Travels*, 1726), this is a neutral land available for the purposes of thought experiments and political satire. Only a minimal grounding in perceived cultural mores attaches it to the Orient or the Americas.

The second half of the eighteenth century also saw the continued idealiza- tion of the 'noble savage', which drew on earlier sources, notably Montaigne and Las Casas. Here the defamiliarization of the everyday, so striking in the exotic epistolary novel, plays second fiddle to an idealization of nature or, at least, of cultures that seemed closer to nature than the court of Versailles. Rousseau's writings spurred on the cult of primitivism, but his idealism cannot be held entirely responsible for more simplistic conceptions of the 'noble savage', since he did not identify non-European societies with an original state of nature. Hayden White has convincingly argued that the 'noble savage' was in any case used primarily to undermine notions of nobility in Europe, rather then to revalorize the 'savage'.[9] The reference to nature in Enlightenment exoticism thus serves above all as a rebuke to the artificiality and tightly controlled norms of Western society.[10] Bougainville's account of his voyage to Tahiti in 1768 (*Le Voyage autour du monde* [*A Voyage around the World*], 1771) endowed the tradition of the noble savage with a new geographical focus: the South Sea island. It was to have a dramatic impact on the imagined exotic encounter not just in France, but across Europe. He presented the island as a new Cythera (the classical island of Venus) and saw it as an earthly paradise before the Fall, exempt from work, private property, and sexual taboos. Diderot's *Supplément au Voyage de Bougainville* (published 1792 but written in 1772) takes the form of a dialogue in which this primitivist valorization of Tahiti is held up for exam- ination. Diderot also wrote part of the Abbé Raynal's *Histoire des deux Indes* (1770; revised version 1774–80) which goes far beyond the trope of defami- liarization and actively denounces the effects of colonization in the Americas.

A significant shift in the idealization of nature appears in Bernardin de Saint-Pierre's *Paul et Virginie* (1788). Here the island exoticism of Mauritius (at the time called the Île de France) combines an idealist view of harmony between man and nature with a new pessimism that demonstrates the impos- sibility of reconciling a superior soul with the harsh realities of the world. The idyllic couple formed by two children raised far from the evils of civilization is destroyed when Virginie is sent to Paris for her education, and an opportune storm then thwarts their post-pubescent reunion. The sentimental and pastoral mode of *Paul et Virginie* seems a world away from the satire of Montesquieu or Voltaire, but it too arose in response to eighteenth-century travel writing (it began life as part of Bernardin de Saint-Pierre's *Voyage à l'île de France*) and philosophy (it was included in the third edition of his philosophical *Études de la Nature* [*Studies of Nature*] (first edition 1784). *Paul et Virginie* looks forward to Romanticism in its attention to the specific detail of tropical plants and scenery as a backdrop to the exploration of the Western self, but in some ways it simply repeats what was already a well-established idealization of exotic nature as a pre-lapsarian paradise (albeit one dependent on the 'natural' subservience of African slaves). Literary exoticism clearly risked becoming formulaic or self-perpetuating, a mere 'stock of fantasies that developed their own dynamics'.[11]

In the more satirical orientalist texts, too, an oppositional challenge to French absolutism easily slips into a proto-imperialism that sees the Orient as despotic, feminine, and immobile faced with a masculine and dynamic West. Meanwhile, in Africa and the Pacific contact with other peoples was almost always filtered through a rigid, hierarchical view of physiological difference that left little space for acceptance of cultural diversity. Eighteenth-century exoticism certainly tells us more about European self-representation in the context of increased 'global economic expansion and exchange'[12] than it does about the non-European countries and peoples it ostensibly takes as its setting or subject. Recent scholarship on the Enlightenment has however defended eighteenth-century exoticism, claiming that we should not read it with hindsight in the light of subsequent imperialism, but instead re-introduce the term 'cosmopolitanism' as a reminder of the Enlightenment commitment to cultural plurality.[13] Such revisionist approaches to the eighteenth century have sometimes sought to demonize the nineteenth century in comparison, holding it up as a period of imperialism and exotic clichés fit only for travel agents' brochures.[14] The next few sections of this chapter will try to reach a more nuanced view of the following period.

Romantic alienation and historicism

In Chateaubriand we find a transition between the Enlightenment use of the foreigner as 'holy fool', who asks revealing questions about what he sees, and the Romantic foreigner-as-alienated self. His early epic *Les Natchez* [*The Natchez: An Indian Tale*] (written 1791–9 but not published in full until 1826), named after the American Indian tribe, follows the adventures of Chactas, a late version of the naïve-foreigner-as-philosopher. A very different usage is however made of the protagonist in two short tales extracted from *Les Natchez* and published first separately and then as part of Chateaubriand's *Génie du christianisme* (1802). These tales, *Atala* (1801) and *René* (1802), dwell on the impossible situation of the individual faced with alienation in the Old World (where even Catholicism offers little comfort to a society torn by Revolution) and the decline of the New World (where doomed Indian tribes wander in exile). Chateaubriand, like Bernardin de Saint-Pierre, situated nobility of soul in exotic settings in response to alienation from contemporary French society. The anguished selfhood of the young Frenchman René, in the tale that bears his name, inaugurates the Romantic theme of the 'mal du siècle' against the backdrop of exotic exile.

At the same time, travel writing, too, accorded new centrality to subjective experience. Following its rise in the eighteenth century, the travel narrative gained a broader readership in the nineteenth, becoming a fully fledged literary genre marked in France by a subgenre known as the 'Voyage en Orient'.[15] Earlier travel narratives had often taken the form of a selection of letters or of ethnographic description; the Romantic travel narrative, following Chateaubriand's influential *Itinéraire de Paris à Jérusalem* (1811), instead offers impressions and emotions filtered through a single subjectivity over a broadly linear chronological period. Travel writing, and the Romantic alienated self set against an exotic backdrop, provided an impetus for literature throughout the century. The final poem of Baudelaire's revised *Fleurs du mal* (1861), 'Le Voyage', also situates the exotic impulse in the disjunction between the self and the world. And the theme is revisited in the novels of the late Romantic Pierre Loti, particularly *Aziyadé* (1879) and *Le Mariage de Loti* (1880).

It is tempting to dismiss Romantic exoticism as mere picturesque used as a backdrop for a focus on the self. It was however innovative in the importance it accorded to elements that were seen as 'typical' of the foreign culture or peoples. Whereas the Enlightenment oriental tale had tended to use exoticism as a means to make universal comments, the Romantics increasingly focused on *couleur locale*,[16] or exotic scenery, flora and fauna, as well as the details of exotic clothing, decor, and the physical particularities of different peoples. This was no mere descriptive fetishism, but a new focus on historical and cultural specificity in a rejection of the universalist Enlightenment view in which a Persian could become a Parisian through a mere slip of the tongue. The foreignness of language itself was also the subject of new attention. Enlightenment exoticism had tended to minimize the difficulties of communication arising from foreign contacts, so that a Huron arriving directly from his native America spoke fluent French. Similarly, whereas earlier exotic writing had tended to adopt a purely French style, there were new attempts at defamiliarizing the language of the exotic literary text itself in a 'making strange' of French from within to reflect foreign language forms.

Europe had come to define itself in terms of its modernity in a secular or historicist view of time that relegated non-European peoples to the past. Johannes Fabian has called this a 'denial of coevalness' between 'the West and the Rest'.[17] By the end of the nineteenth century the ideology of progress was explicitly invoked as a justification for colonialism, but long before that the geographical voyage away from Europe's capitals was experienced as a form of time travel. Indeed, the view of non-Western peoples as immobile and belonging to the past has been cited by Said as characteristic of the Western mode of thinking about the Orient that prepared the way for direct imperialism. The call for imperial intervention was also made explicitly by writers such as Lamartine who, in the 1830s, argued that a European conquest of Lebanon and Syria would be easy and desirable. France had of course had a (largely imaginary) model for imperialist intervention in the Eastern and Southern Mediterranean since Napoleon's abortive Egyptian expedition of 1798–1801. *Égyptomanie*, or the fashion for Ancient Egypt set off by this expedition, was initially most visible in the decorative arts, but was to have long-term consequences elsewhere too. Exotic literature, already understood in terms of a movement back in time, increasingly took the form of historical novels such as the *Roman de la momie* by Théophile Gautier (1857) or Flaubert's *Salammbô* (1862). Gautier's earlier novella 'Une nuit de Cléopâtre' ['One of Cleopatra's Nights'] (1838) shows us Cleopatra yearning for a conqueror who would be worthy of her, a giant for whom the colossal statues of her ancient land are waiting: for French readers this gap could only filled by Napoleon, who would arrive in Egypt some two millennia too late. And yet situating the exotic in the past cannot simply be reduced to a proto-imperialist ploy. Many Romantic and post-Romantic writers took an oppositional stance, rejecting what they saw as the homogenizing, dehumanizing effects of modernity. In this context, presenting other lands as 'pre-modern' is part of an 'anti-modern' strategy.[18]

The Romantic fascination with the exotic was derived in part from a feeling that intensity of sensation and the possibility of the marvellous were excluded from the rational West. The beginnings of industrialization, the rapid growth of Paris, and the reign of the bourgeoisie under the restored monarchy, seemed to define a newly drab world in the first half of the century. Enlightenment, and revolutionary secularism, had shaken the hold of Catholicism in France, and the sciences were beginning to take on official disciplinary forms, sanctified by academies and learned societies. The shift of mysticism away from Christianity is apparent in Romantic travel writing: for Chateaubriand, travelling in 1806, the voyage's logical endpoint was still the Holy Land; but it is Islam that fascinated later Romantic travellers such as Lamartine (1832–3 and 1835) and Nerval (1851). Exotic lands, and the

Orient in particular, were associated with an intact tradition of marvels and mysticism: fabulous wealth, extreme violence, enduring faith. So it was that literary exoticism played a part in filling what was experienced as a gap in religious experience.

A feeling that cultural difference was declining can be discerned in late Romantic travel writers' sense of their own belatedness. Such writing is ironically aware of the well-worn nature of the route taken: not only were there illustrious literary precursors such as Chateaubriand, but increasingly travellers were consulting the first practical travel guides (the famous Baedeker guides were published from the 1830s onwards). Travel itself became quicker, easier and less expensive thanks to steamships and rail links, and 1869 saw the opening of the Suez Canal which offered a much shorter maritime route to the East. Awareness of the repetitive nature of exotic tourism leads to Arthur Rimbaud's irony, in *Illuminations* (1873–5), at the expense of tourists who find 'the same bourgeois magic at every stop of the India-Mail!'; he also mocks the claims of imperialism:

> They are the conquerors of the world . . .
> On this boat they bring the education
> of races, classes and beasts.[19]

By the end of the nineteenth century the exotic was seen as being in irreversible retreat, and, when it was not ironic, exoticism operated in the mode of loss or nostalgia.[20] The naturalization of concepts of time, particularly in the late nineteenth century with the widening impact of Darwinian thought, reaffirmed the relegation of non-European cultures to the 'past'.[21] This came to be linked to the idea that certain peoples were biologically and historically doomed. Since exoticism was largely understood in terms of cultural immobility, signs of change in non-Western peoples tended to be seen as indications not that they, too, might have histories, but rather that they had fallen from their timeless exotic state into a second-rate imitation of modernity. This narrative of decline appears in an infantilizing rather than cynical mode in novels such as Loti's *Le Mariage de Loti*, which traces the decline of the Tahitian heroine Rarahu from untutored, childlike prettiness to corruption, illness, and death. Her contamination by contact with the outside world is a synecdoche for the contamination, and apparently inevitable decline, of her people, and thus the death of exoticism itself.

Pushing at the boundaries: exoticism and experimentation

Exotic literature is often seen as simply reiterating stereotypes and thus confirming the 'doxa' or ideological status quo. This view is not contradicted, but significantly nuanced, if we accept that exoticism has also facilitated certain forms of experimentation, most strikingly a questioning of gender identity. Exoticism, it has been argued, is part of an attempt 'to escape from the clutches of domestic accountability' by pursuing '[u]topian possibilities, whether sexual, gustatory, aesthetic, or experiential'; it is open 'to pleasure and even danger, but ideally without responsibility'.[22] Bougainville established a myth of the Polynesian island as an Edenic place of sexual permissiveness; earlier still, Galland's translation of *Les Mille et une nuits* had presented the Orient as offering sensual pleasure devoid of Christian guilt. Turkey and the Near East were associated with a particular form of sexual plenitude in the form of the fantasized harem, or better still the seraglio, in which one despotic male was in complete possession of numerous women. Ingres's paintings of odalisques, spanning the first six decades of the nineteenth century, drew on this myth of languorous, passive sexual availability, culminating in *Le Bain turc* [*The Turkish Bath*] of 1862. His rival Eugène Delacroix meanwhile showed the orientalist myth of feminine passivity tipping over into violence with *La Mort de Sardanapale* [*The Death of Sardanapalus*] (1827). Polynesian and oriental exoticism thus allowed the expression of two separate heterosexual fantasies. Following Said's *Orientalism*, we can see this as part of a binary opposition in which the West is masculine and active, in contrast to an Orient (or Tahiti) constructed as feminine and passive. There can be no doubt that this is in part what is going on.

And yet, as always with sexuality, there is more complex story to be told at the same time. Desire for the submissive odalisque is not always to be separated from identification with her, and Delacroix's reclining, silk-clad despot himself takes a passive pose. The ambivalence of identification and desire is also suggested by the significant role played by cultural cross-dressing in the European exotic tradition. Already in the eighteenth century there had been a vogue for portraits of aristocratic ladies in exotic clothing, usually Turkish. With the new drabness of men's clothing in the nineteenth century, cultural cross-dressing became a Romantic masculine fashion, and exotic lands seemed a refuge for colour and intensity of experience. Exotic disguise focuses the gaze on the surface, and the fantasized ease of cultural 'passing' trivializes any real difference, allowing the European alienated from his own society to 'become' the other. The model was George Gordon, Lord Byron, whose oriental travels, portrait in Albanian costume, and poetry celebrating renegade Europeans, set off an international cult (see Delacroix's painting *Combat du Giaour et de Hassan*, 1826, among others). Cultural ambivalence was closely associated with sexual ambivalence, as the orientalist cult of the bisexual Byron suggests, and cross-dressing was a disguise in more ways than one. The Orient was a space for sexual experimentation and (temporary) liberation from normative constraints. Exoticism thus accompanies a blurring of gender roles in Balzac's *La Fille aux yeux d'or* [*The Girl with the Golden Eyes*] (1835). There, as in Hugo's *Orientales* (1829), Flaubert's *Salammbô* (1862), and Octave Mirbeau's *Le Jardin des supplices* [*The Torture Garden*] (1899), the search for intensity, and the evacuation of moral responsibility, encourage a linking of the Orient with sado-masochism and fantasized violence.

The late nineteenth-century obsession with the *femme fatale* was also indissolubly linked to orientalism via the figure of Salomé, whose counterpart was the androgynous (because symbolically castrated) male. Loti's Turkish love story, *Aziyadé* (1879), includes dreamlike episodes in which a simple disguise allows an apparently effortless cultural and linguistic 'passing' so that the protagonist 'becomes' Turkish enough to explore the hidden side of Istanbul's nightlife in the company of effeminate young men. Much more explicitly, André Gide wrote of North Africa as a place of fulfilment for a homosexuality frustrated by his French Huguenot upbringing (*L'Immoraliste*, 1902). Sexual experimentation at a geographical distance is part of the Romantic-exotic promise of leaving the petit-bourgeois boundaries of identity behind. In reaction, from the 1880s onwards colonial literature warned of the dangers of overstepping psychological boundaries, through the theme of 'decivilization' in which the European colonist loses his (always his) identity to madness, generally in the arms of an exotic woman, in Africa or Indochina. More knowingly, and far more subversively, Rimbaud internalizes and identifies with the 'primitive' other in 'Mauvais sang' (*Une saison en enfer* [*A Season in Hell*], 1873).[23]

Literary exoticism also came to be associated with formal experimentation. Over the two centuries that concern us here it spanned different genres: in the eighteenth century it took the forms of the *conte oriental*, the epistolary novel, and the fictive travel narrative; in the nineteenth and early twentieth centuries it was to be found in poetry, the novel, and travel writing. The nineteenth century is generally seen as dominated by one literary genre, a monolithic 'domestic realist novel',[24] whose very definition appears to exclude exotic themes, displacing the shorter structure of the tale, which since Galland had been more readily associated with the fantastic and the oriental. So although the eighteenth-century oriental tale had successors in the gothic and fantastic modes, these were in turn marginalized by the resolutely materialist and historicist approach taken by the novel. The idea that this new novel was built on the exclusion of alien elements appears to be confirmed by Walter Scott's 1827 diatribe against the fantastic, that close cousin of exoticism. Scott's renewal of the historical novel was a key influence on Balzac's realist project to write the history of present-day France in his vast *Comédie humaine*.

Any idea of the nineteenth-century novel as a single, homogeneous, mono-logical form, however, runs counter to the notoriously supple nature of the novel, which is able to incorporate other genres within itself. Balzac and Flaubert included oriental elements *within* their most Parisian writings (*La Fille aux yeux d'or*, 1835; *L'Éducation sentimentale*, 1869). Both were also attracted by the genre of the oriental tale, which, like the pseudo-travel-narrative, provided a relief valve for writers of the domestic realist novel.[25] The short story or tale, inherited from the Enlightenment philosophical tale as well as the fantastic orientalism of the *Mille et une nuits*, lent itself to irony, parody, ellipsis, and other non-realist approaches (for example Gautier, 'Le Pied de momie', 1840; Flaubert, 'Hérodias', 1877; Jules Laforgue, 'Salomé', 1886). Nevertheless, the 1880s–1930s saw the rise of a French colonial literature that generally adhered to the conventions of the naturalist novel and can be seen as an attempt to apply 'domestic realism' to a non-domestic subject matter. It sought to distinguish itself from exotic literature, rejecting the latter's clichés, among them the Romantic filtering of all perception through the anguished European self. The end of the nineteenth century was however marked by a 'crisis' of the novel, when younger writers rejected the (more-or-less) omniscient, third-person narrator who had come to dominate literary practice. Exotic writing had long provided an alternative tradition. Loti's exotic novels, with their relentlessly subjective first-person narrator and elliptical style, took a deliberately impressionistic approach, as did earlier semi-fictional travel narratives by the orientalist painter and novelist Eugène Fromentin (*Un été dans le Sahara* [*A Summer in the Sahara*], 1857; *Une année dans le Sahel* [*Between Sea and Sahara: an Algerian Journal*], 1859). Some more or less 'colonial' writers also experimented by adopting a non-Western perspective. This is the case of novels set in Indochina by Albert de Pouvourville (*L'Annam sanglant* [*Blood-Soaked Annam*], 1898) and Émile Nolly (*Hiên le Maboul* [*Hiên the Crackpot*], 1909; *La Barque annamite* [*The Annamite Boat*], 1910), as well as Segalen's formally challenging modernist novel set in Tahiti (*Les Immémoriaux* [*A Lapse of Memory*], 1907).

In the visual arts, too, exoticism was used as a challenge to realism. The importation of Japanese woodblock prints, following the opening of Japan to Western trade after 1854, played a significant role in the transformation of French painting from the 1880s onwards. And in the early years of the twentieth century the influence of colonial imports – notably African art, particularly wooden masks – is to be seen in the modernist adoption of 'primitive' visual forms, such as Paul Gauguin's Tahitian paintings and sculptures, Henri Matisse's paintings, and certain works by Pablo Picasso. Both *japonisme* and *primitivisme* differ from orientalism, however, because they reflect a response to an artistic style and the importation of certain aesthetic modes, rather than a broader attitude to a largely fictive cultural ensemble. Literature offers a partial equivalent, with a new, Japanese-influenced emphasis on blank spaces and margins in poetry, for example, or Segalen's use in *Les Immémoriaux* of non-standard French to convey a fictive Tahitian perspective, including untranslated foreign words that disorient the French reader so that language acts as a metonym for the encounter with difference.

Critical exoticism and irony

A view of literary exoticism that sees it as simply rehashing a preconceived textual tradition risks neglecting not only the oppositional and experimental attitudes that we have seen, but also exoticism's self-awareness. This is apparent in the Romantic irony that imbues so much orientalism in France from the 1830s onwards, as well as in the role exoticism plays in deliberate challenges to naïve conceptions of 'the real' and the 'natural' towards the end of the century. This self-aware exoticism could be called a 'critical orientalism', since it mocks its own derivative or hackneyed nature; Said's own polemical thesis is part of this lineage, though in a non-ironic mode. Primary exoticism often co-exists with this critical exoticism, which accompanies it like its own cynical shadow. Their relationship is best grasped as a dynamic, dialectical movement: for the exotic dream does not disappear when mocked, and in the tradition of Romantic irony it is possible to deprecate a stance even as one takes it.

The *turquerie* and *chinoiserie* of the seventeenth and eighteenth centuries were not experienced in terms of kitsch, as worn-out or hackneyed modes fit for parody. It is with the Romantic foregrounding of originality that lack of originality itself became a thematic focus. By the 1830s, Romantic exoticism was frequently approached in an ironic, self-deprecating mode. Alfred de Musset parodied Hugo's *Orientales* in 'Namouna: conte oriental' ['Namouna: An Oriental Tale'] (1832), in which the hero converts to Islam following his reading of the *Mille et une nuits* and which emphasizes the well-worn nature of the orientalist pose. And while the Romantic emphasis on *couleur locale* might suggest a naïve faith in the power of observation and description of details to give the viewer or reader a 'typical' image of a foreign land, this is already mocked in Balzac's novella 'Un début dans la vie' ['A Start in Life'] (1842) when a character claiming to have travelled in the Orient sums up his impressions: 'Egypt – it's nothing but sand.'[26] This ironic awareness of the hackneyed nature of the exotic tradition intensified from the 1850s onwards, notably with Flaubert.

Exoticism since the Romantic period can thus be understood in terms of a dialectical movement between attraction to the foreign and ironic deprecation of this impulse. Romantic irony also focuses on the gap between real and imagined life, showing the experience of the exotic to be partly imagined and derived from pre-existing tradition. Balzac's pseudo-travel-narrative 'Voyage de Paris à Java' (1832) undermines the implicit contract of the travel narrative – that the author has been to the country described – by slipping unannounced from a narrator who recounts his exotic experience at first hand to the narrator of a frame story who never leaves France. In Segalen's novel René Leys the epistemological status of the exotic subject – here the Forbidden Palace of Beijing just before the fall of the empire – remains undecidable: is the narrative of an exotic adventure real, or is it invented? This dialectics of the real and the imaginary was given theoretical development by Segalen himself, following the theories of the philosopher Jules de Gaultier. Gaultier's 1902 law of 'Bovarysm' states that the defining characteristic of humanity is the ability to imagine that one is something that one is not, a capacity on which the exotic impulse depends.[27] The eighteenth century had already seen pseudo-travel narratives, notably Xavier de Maistre's Voyage autour de ma chambre [A Journey around My Room] (1795), but the ironic exploration of the self-sufficiency of the imagination reaches a peak a century later: in a chapter of his novel À rebours [Against Nature] (1884), Joris-Karl Huysmans' protagonist sets out on a voyage to London but gets no further than an English pub on the rue de Rivoli. And yet Segalen, while acknowledging the role of the imagination in the exotic encounter, does not avoid confrontation with the real. His Essai sur l'exotisme sought to make exoticism nothing short of an epistemological project, the struggle to conceive of an encounter with cultural difference that would not be imperialistic, Eurocentric and dehumanizing.

It is no surprise, then, that in the nineteenth century exoticism came to be associated with an anti-mimetic stance. The Islamic Orient, in particular, was adopted for the purposes of avant-garde poetic experimentalism, perhaps because of its links with the fantastic (via the Mille et une nuits) or, it has been suggested, because of the Islamic interdiction of figurative art.[28] The Eastern origins of opium also played a part in linking exoticism with the supremacy of the imagined over the real. But clearly the self-consciously derivative nature of exoticism, its knowing basis in a textual tradition rather than in direct experience of the real, helped fit it for polemical usage in challenging the mimetic and didactic functions of art. Since exoticism had a late impact in France it was marked by forms imported from British or German Romanticism and was thus experienced as 'belated' from the outset. Hugo's poetic collection *Les Orientales* (1829) is a late manifestation of European philhellenism, appearing when the Greco-Turkish conflict was all but resolved, and his preface proudly announces it to be 'a useless book of pure poetry'. Already orientalist motifs signalled a rejection of utilitarianism. Gautier, the champion of art for art's sake, took up this self-consciously anti-realist and anti-utilitarian exoticism: his Orient, like that of the symbolists after him, was a deliberately self-sufficient textual construct (*Émaux et camées* [*Enamels and Cameos and Other Poems*], 1852). And in the hands of Mallarmé the influence of Far Eastern aesthetics encouraged an elliptical style that incorporated empty spaces and absence. It is largely because of French exoticism's critical awareness of its own hackneyed and derivative nature that it comes to stand for the constructed nature of artistic and literary expression, and for a weakening of the mimetic illusion.

As we have seen, approaches to literary exoticism have too often neglected the role played by irony. This irony takes various forms, from the eighteenth-century use of Socratic irony in the naïve questions asked by a foreigner about France to the late Romantic irony that underlines an awareness of exoticism's own textually derived nature. An understanding of the role of irony can help us see French exoticism not as a simple binary opposition between 'the West' and 'the Rest' but as a dialectical movement between the real and the imagined, between confrontation with diversity and the reiteration of stereotypes.

NOTES

1. Tzvetan Todorov, *On Human Diversity: Nationalism, Racism and Exoticism in French Thought* (Cambridge, MA: Harvard University Press, 1993), p. 265. (First published as *Nous et les autres*, 1989.)
2. For example, Robert Irwin, *For Lust of Knowing: The Orientalists and Their Enemies* (London: Allen Lane, 2006). A (selective) overview of recent critical responses to Said is given by Graham Huggan in '(Not)Reading *Orientalism*', *Research in African Literatures*, 36.3 (2005), 124–36.
3. See Dennis Porter in '*Orientalism* and Its Problems', in *The Politics of Theory*, ed. Francis Barker (Colchester: University of Essex Press, 1983), pp. 179–93; Jennifer Yee, *Exotic Subversions in Nineteenth-Century French Fiction* (Oxford: Legenda, 2008).
4. Perry Anderson, 'Persian Letters (Montesquieu, 1721)', in *The Novel*, vol. 2: *Forms and Themes*, ed. Franco Moretti (Princeton, NJ: Princeton University Press, 2006), pp. 161–72 (p. 164).
5. Srinivas Aravamudan, *Enlightenment Orientalism: Resisting the Rise of the Novel* (Chicago, IL: University of Chicago Press, 2011), p. 77; see also his 'Response: Exoticism beyond Cosmopolitanism?', *Eighteenth-Century Fiction*, 25.1 (2012), 227–42 (p. 231).

6. See Suzanne Rodin Pucci, 'The Discrete Charms of the Exotic: Fictions of the Harem in Eighteenth-Century France', in *Exoticism in the Enlightenment*, ed. Roy Porter and George S. Rousseau (Manchester: Manchester University Press, 1990), pp. 145–75 (pp. 149–50).

7. Anderson, 'Persian Letters', pp. 163–5.

8. The connections between sexual fantasy and political comment in Montesquieu's fictive harem have been discussed, among many others, by Alain Grosrichard, *The Sultan's Court: European Fantasies of Asiatic Despotism*, trans. Liz Heron (London: Verso, 1998). (First published as *Structures du sérail*, 1979.)

9. Hayden White, 'The Noble Savage Theme as Fetish', in *First Images of America: The Impact of the New World on the Old*, ed. Fredi Chiappelli, vol. 1 (Berkeley, CA: University of California Press, 1976), pp. 121–35 (p. 129).

10. See Roy Porter and George S. Rousseau, 'Introduction', *Exoticism in the Enlightenment*, ed. Porter and Rousseau (Manchester: Manchester University Press, 1990), pp. 1–22 (p. 12); Christa Knellwolf, 'The Exotic Frontier of the Imperial Imagination', *Eighteenth-Century Life*, 26.3 (2002), 10–30 (p. 22).

11. Christa Knellwolf and Iain McCalman, 'Exoticism and the Culture of Exploration', *Eighteenth-Century Life*, 26.3 (2002), 1–9 (p. 3).

12. Eugenia Zuroski Jenkins, 'Introduction: Exoticism, Cosmopolitanism, and Fiction's Aesthetics of Diversity', *Eighteenth-Century Fiction*, 25.1 (2012), 1–7 (p. 5).

13. See Aravamudan, 'Response'; and Jenkins, 'Introduction', p. 3.

14. See Aravamudan, *Enlightenment Orientalism*; and Porter and Rousseau, 'Introduction', p. 7.

15. See C. W. Thompson, *French Romantic Travel Writing: Chateaubriand to Nerval* (Oxford: Oxford University Press, 2012).

16. For a discussion of the concept see Vladimir Kapor, 'Local Colour Revisited – an Essay in Conceptual Genealogy', *Postcolonial Studies*, 11:1 (2008), 39–61 (p. 50).

17. Johannes Fabian, *Time and the Other: How Anthropology Makes Its Object* (New York: Columbia University Press: 2002), pp. 25, 28. See also Thierry Hentsch, *L'Orient imaginaire: La vision politique occidentale de l'Est méditerranéen* (Paris: Minuit, 1988).

18. This point is convincingly argued for British Romanticism by Saree Makdisi, in *Romantic Imperialism: Universal Empire and the Culture of Modernity* (Cambridge: Cambridge University Press, 1998).

19. 'La même magie bourgeoise à tous les points où la malle nous déposera!' ('Soir historique'); 'Ce sont les conquérants du monde ... Ils emmènent l'éducation // Des races, des classes et des bêtes, sur ce Vaisseau.' ('Mouvement'); Arthur Rimbaud, *Poésies: Une saison en enfer. Illuminations* (Paris: Gallimard, 1999), pp. 239, 241. My translation. On Rimbaud's mockery of bourgeois exoticism see Patrick Née, *L'Ailleurs en question* (Paris: Hermann, 2009), pp. 81–2.

20. On this feeling of 'belated' exoticism at the turn of the nineteenth and twentieth centuries, see Chris Bongie, *Exotic Memories: Literature, Colonialism and the Fin de siècle* (Stanford, CA: Stanford University Press, 1991).

21. See Fabian, *Time and the Other*, pp. 11–16.

22. Aravamudan, 'Response', p. 240.

23. See Christopher L. Miller, *Blank Darkness: Africanist Discourse in French* (Chicago, IL: University of Chicago Press, 1985), pp. 140–58.

24. Aravamudan, *Enlightenment Orientalism*, pp. 6–7.

25. See Jean Bruneau, *Le 'Conte oriental' de Gustave Flaubert* (Paris: Lettres nouvelles, 1973) and Pierre Citron, 'Le rêve asiatique de Balzac', *L'Année balzacienne* (1968), 303–36.

26. 'L'Égypte, c'est tout sables'; Balzac, *La Comédie humaine*, ed. Pierre-Georges Castex, 12 vols (Paris: Gallimard, 1976–81), vol. 1, p. 779. My translation.

27. See Deborah Jenson, 'Bovarysm and Exoticism', in *The Columbia History of Twentieth-Century French Thought*, ed. Lawrence D. Kritzman (Columbia University Press, 2006), pp. 167–70.

28. See Emily A. Haddad, *Orientalist Poetics: The Islamic Middle East in Nineteenth-Century English and French Poetry* (London: Ashgate, 2002).

II

CARRIE NOLAND

Poetic experimentation

A man, silhouetted against the black background of an empty stage, stands beside a microphone, his hands gripping a sheaf of papers from which he reads in a firm yet urgent voice. Simultaneously, we hear another pre-recorded voice (and sometimes several) superimposed upon his. It is February 1986 at the Centre Pompidou; over the course of two evenings the sound poet Bernard Heidsieck will perform a marathon reading of *Derviche/Le Robert*, a 'poème sonore' composed of twenty-six sections accompanied by a taped sound track, one section for each of the twenty-six letters of the alphabet. This marathon performance has been a long time in the making: Heidsieck began the first section, 'A', eight years earlier, in 1978. Like all the other sections, 'A' takes as its primary building block the first ten words purportedly found in the dictionary *Le Grand Robert* beginning with the letter featured in the title – in this case 'Abaca', 'Abajoue', 'Abaque', 'Abatée', 'Abat-voix', 'Abducteur', 'Abée', 'Abhoc-abhac', 'Abiétinées', 'Ableret'. Here, amid this cacophony, Heidsieck confronts one of contemporary poetry's greatest challenges: how to follow language off the page into the world of technologized sound.

Of course, the ten words Heidsieck recites are not the first ten words in the dictionary but rather the first ten words that Heidsieck *does not know* ('dont le sens m'était entièrement inconnu').[1] He skips familiar words such as 'abaisser' and 'abandon' to highlight the most opaque signifiers in the French language. *Derviche/Le Robert* forms a poetic tissue composed of common expressions such as 'à coup sûr' and 'eh bien' and banal formulas taken from business and institutional settings such as 'veuillez agréer, monsieur, l'expression de mes sentiments les plus distingués', and intertwines them with unfamiliar words such as 'Badelaire' (in the 'B' section) and 'Pacqung' (in the 'P' section, 10). Heidsieck's purpose, he explains in 'Notes à posteriori', is to bring the unknown and opaque words into a public space, an ordinary verbal context, and to perform them, thus rendering them 'fleshy' ('charnelle'). Here, the obvious and empty ('eh bien') mingles with the inscrutable and empty ('Uliginaire'), leaving behind little language that can be considered meaningful or expressive with respect to the human being who is standing before us, reciting and gesticulating on stage.

Similar to many of Heidsieck's sound poems, *Derviche/Le Robert* takes advantage of the labial attack of repeated phoneme combinations to produce a rhythmic tattoo: for instance, the /a/ /b/ combination in '*Ab*aca, '*Ab*ajoue', or, in the 'S' section, '*Sab*ayon', '*Sab*ine'. As semantically empty as they might seem, the words highlighted in Heidsieck's 'abécédaire' nonetheless strike the ear as full of sonic content: they bristle with percussive consonants and sonorous vowels. The pre-recorded plosives create polyrhythms that, when repeated and echoed on multiple sound tracks, seem to turn round and round like the 'derviche' of the title. Into this 'tourbillon' of sonic matter Heidsieck then inserts a tape recording of a Paris metro entering a station. One of the first poets to include ambient sound (the Simultanéiste and Futurist poets did so earlier), Heidsieck suggests that poetry can capture within its net phenomena far beyond the page and the voice.[2] Daring and playful, his sound poems – from the 1960s on – redefine poetry as a multimedia, cross-modal enterprise. Written explicitly for the 'magnétophone' (tape recorder), his works exemplify a number of dominant tendencies animating poetry today: an interest in non-lyric and paraliterary discourses; the use of other media; and an approach to poetic language as a graphemic and sonic material independent of any expressive or communicative function.

The same year that Heidsieck first began *Derviche/Le Robert*, a young poet named Denis Roche also initiated a new type of poetic project, this one involving the visible aspects of poetic language. In 1978, Roche published the first example of what would become his signature contribution to twentieth-century poetry, the 'photo-autobiographie', in a volume titled *Notre antéfixe*. If Heidsieck was interested in exploring the life of poetry off the page, its existence as vocalized sound, Roche in contrast focuses on the page as a resource for further investigation of what constitutes poetry as a form of inscription. Without abandoning either the traditional subject matter of the French lyric poem – the 'intimate self' – or the most apparent traditional distinction between prose and poetry – versification – Roche sets about changing the way in which poetry mobilizes them both. A quick comparison of Roche with Heidsieck can give us a good sense of the vastly diverse directions poetry has taken in recent years.

Roche's *Notre antéfixe* contains nine poems, each of which covers one page with precisely twenty-seven lines. The lines are all numbered from 1 to 243 (nine pages times twenty-seven lines), and each number corresponds to a 'note' found in the following section entitled 'Notes & commentaires'. The first page, for instance, begins:

Ah!... non morrai!... in quegli accenti,... Nè ciel, nè terra...   1
La voici en effet, fracassant les arbres, foudroyant les murs   2
ans succès des mangosteens & on achète 1 pte maison en arge   3

Ah!... non morrai!... in quegli accenti,... Nè ciel, nè terra...   1
There it is actually, shattering the trees, striking the walls   2
years success of mangosteens & they buy 1 tiny house in sil   3[3]

The notes keyed to the number at the end of each line indicate that line number 1 is a citation drawn from Bellini's *Béatrice de Tende*; line number 2 is a sentence from Marguerite Duras's 1969 novel *Détruire dit-elle*; and line number 3 is drawn from the travel diary of Françoise, the woman featured with Roche in the thirty-nine black and white photographs that make up the final section of *Notre antéfixe*, Roche explains in his preface that every line of the 'antéfixe' is drawn (or 'découpée') from the books, letters, manuals, bills, brochures, postcards, even drug prescriptions, and official documents that played a role in his life – the life of a couple – during the period in which he undertook to write the volume. Roche's method displaces the locus of the personal from the words a poet has supposedly uttered to words he has found in ambient texts. That is, instead of expressing the emotions of the 'I' (in typical lyric fashion), the author crops and re-frames the many texts found in his home in such a way that these seem to express something the 'I' would be feeling. Each clipping from these texts is then submitted to a framing governed by a quantitative rule typical of the poetic genre. If, in a volume of sonnets, every page contains fourteen lines (one sonnet per page), here every page contains exactly twenty-seven lines. Further, every line is exactly the same length, as in a metered poem; only here, that length is measured not by the number of syllables (as in an alexandrine), nor by the number of beats (as in iambic pentameter), but rather by the quantity of space taken up by the characters, all of which, although drawn from handwritten letters or industrial fonts, are reduced to the same type face, visually blended into a seamless, yet utterly disjunctive, whole.

The displacements Roche effects may at first seem bizarre, but they are in fact typical of those practiced by many of the most exciting experimental poets of today. Not only have poetry's traditional means of counting been replaced by other means of counting (and by other countable things), so too the site of poetry has shifted – from the printed page to a variety of surfaces, both virtual and material. There are now poems found uniquely on the internet, on the columns of metro stations, or on DVDs. To be sure, poetry has not entirely left the page behind, but it has increased the number of physical supports it can use and networks of distribution it can engage. Poetry's movement towards formats that are hybrid and multimedia may well have been presaged by Guillaume Apollinaire's famous call for poets to 'mechanize poetry as they've mechanized the world'.[4] Apollinaire set the tone in 1913 when he privileged 'research' and 'investigation' over lyric effusion, admitting into his own verse a plethora of discourses and predicting – in 'Esprit nouveau et les Poètes' ['The New Spirit and the Poets'] – that one day poets would write for 'the phonograph and the cinema'.[5]

One might well ask, though, whether it still makes sense to call sound poems such as *Derviche/Le Robert* 'poetry' (instead of, say, 'word music'), or whether an 'antéfixe' should be considered an example of conceptual art. These experimental works certainly have their nay-sayers, poets and critics invested in the 'geste lyrique' as it has traditionally been practised, or those who believe in the fundamentally verbal-inscriptive essence of poetry. Such reservations, however, have not prevented generations of talented poets from inventing new poetic forms. Witness Pierre Alféri's 'cinépoems', Julian Blaine's installations, or Doc (k)s 'digital poems' created by means of software programs such as Flash. Given this cornucopia of multimedia practices, we might ask, along with Jean-Michel Espitallier, 'How do we recognize a poem today?'[6] Perhaps the single most defining characteristic of twentieth- and twenty-first century poetry is, paradoxically, its tendency to place the definition of poetry in question. As Jean-Marie Gleize has stated with characteristic lucidity: 'Only those who "really don't know what poetry is" are making poetry.'[7] Still – we might want to ask – are there minimal requirements for a poem to be a poem? Does a poem have to have a discernible meter? Does it have to use figurative language? Does it have to take place on the page? Are the 'chercheurs' (researchers) of today radically distinct from the poets of yesteryear? Or can we discern profound continuities between poets as distinctive as Heidsieck and Rimbaud, Roche and Mallarmé?

Surrealism and the experimental mode

To some extent French poets have always worked in the experimental mode, testing out new forms and introducing new varieties of rhetoric. However, the Surrealists were the first to declare openly that they would approach the poem as an experiment, an unfinished and provisional interrogation. They redefined the poet as a 'researcher' invested in inducing and recording experiences never treated before. At least in their public statements, the Surrealists claimed to subordinate the aesthetic to epistemological goals; they would seek to illuminate realms of (un)consciousness that traditional aesthetic constraints had inhibited them from exploring. When the movement first coalesced around 1922, the object was to invent compositional practices that could register the dream state; 'automatic writing' was supposed to release the author from the demands of craft so that he could become a 'recording device', attentive to what André Breton termed a 'higher reality', 'irrespective of any aesthetic or moral preoccupations'.[8]

The Surrealist poem was intended to produce a shock – an 'étincelle' – by juxtaposing conventionally 'distant' pieces of reality, as in a dream. Breton announced in the *Manifeste du surréalisme* [*Manifesto of Surrealism*] (1924) that the goal of the Surrealist would be to create unintentional 'rapprochements', implicit comparisons such as René Char's exquisite 'le tourbillon vint aux genoux' ['whirlwind brought to its knees'] from *Le Poème pulverisé* [*The Pulverized Poem*].[9] Citing Pierre Reverdy's definition of the image as the 'rapprochement of two realities more or less distant from each other', Breton insisted that the further apart these two realities (and the less consciously they were produced), the brighter the 'light of the image' would be.[10] Ostensibly, such 'rapprochements' would give onto an alternative world, a surreality in which, as Paul Éluard magically put it, 'La terre est bleue comme une orange' ['The earth is blue like an orange']. Paradoxically, however, the Surrealist poets, while extending the figurative ground of the lyric, were not equally revolutionary with regard to either the traditional medium of the poem (printed words on a page) or its traditional aesthetic goals (subjective expression and the creation of compelling images). In contrast, the works of Henri Michaux stand out as more daringly experimental. His collection of mescaline poems, *Misérable miracle* of 1956, recasts the poet as clinician: the poet registers the results of his experiments as they are occurring. Immediately blurring the boundaries between the verbal and the visual, the poetic and the scientific, Michaux begins *Misérable miracle* with a diagram of the chemical formula for mescaline (Trimethoxybenzeneethanamine) and ends with ink drawings supposedly completed under altered states of mind.

Nevertheless, the Surrealists (who also experimented with altered states of mind) can be credited with taking another, perhaps even more crucial step, that of recognizing the importance of new voices coming from a real 'ailleurs' (elsewhere)–such as Martinique, Haiti, and other territories within the former French Empire. Surrealists were instrumental in bringing attention to the poetry of Negritude, a movement founded in interwar Paris by a group of students from Africa and the Caribbean. Aimé Césaire (Martinique), Léon-Gontran Damas (French Guiana), and Léopold Sédar Senghor (Sénégal) found readers not only among French Surrealists but also African American and South American writers, and thus were responsible for introducing France (and French poetry) into new frameworks of analysis, such as the Black Atlantic, or the larger world of those who speak French, *francophonie*. Césaire's work in particular, most notably his *Cahier d'un retour au pays natal* [*Notebook of a Return to the Native Land*] (1939), placed intensely figurative language in the service of a clearly enunciated anti-imperialist politics.

If poetry during the first half of the twentieth century ventured forth into new areas (the exploration of altered states, the experience of colonization), it clearly did not realize the full promise of Apollinaire's predictions. Not only did poetry fail to expand significantly into other media (for example, 'the phonograph and the cinema'), it also persisted in maintaining two traditional features of lyric poetry: a central interest in the affective life of a single subject; and a fundamental preference for figurative language (the 'rapprochement' or image). However, there is a general consensus among scholars that sometime after the Second World War an important sea change took place. During the course of the 1940s, members of the Surrealist movement had been chastened by the rise of Stalinist Russia as well as experience of the Resistance and the concentration camps. During what has been called the 'era of suspicion', the poetics of the 'rapprochement' and the 'light of the image' began to give way to a searing critique of transcendence as a goal (the *sur*real) and metaphor as a vehicle. Poets who came of age during the Second World War found Surrealism's confidence in the revelatory function of figurative language to be both epistemologically ungrounded and politically evasive. Of course, poetry by Surrealist writers involved a much larger range of practices and investments than the poets of the next generation would acknowledge. Still, it was clear by the close of the war that the highly aestheticized approach to life that Surrealism often promoted could not answer the burning questions of the day. Jean-Paul Sartre's *Qu'est-ce que la littérature?* [*What Is Literature?*] of 1945–6 and Georges Bataille's *La Haine de la poésie* [*Hatred of Poetry*] of 1947, though different in orientation, both signalled an exhaustion with the preciousness of certain forms of Surrealist poetry. Bataille's text launched a critique of the traditional notion of the unified lyric subject, a critique that would soon become politicized in the works of Julia Kristeva, Denis Roche, and other authors associated with the radical Maoist journal, *Tel Quel*. Linking poetry to the figure of the individual championed by capitalist relations of production, Roche published in a 1967 issue of *Tel Quel* a poem significantly titled 'La poésie est inadmissible, d'ailleurs elle n'existe pas' [Poetry is inadmissible, and besides, it doesn't exist]. Roche alerted his readers that from now on, poetry would suffer the same fate as the conventional subject, whose identity – like the truncated and incoherently sequenced lines of 'La poésie est inadmissible' – would be 'clivé', internally divided and non-self-identical.[11]

Francis Ponge

Significantly, *Tel Quel* inaugurated its first issue in 1960 by publishing 'La figue (sèche)' ['The Fig (Dried)'], a poem by none other than Francis Ponge, a poet of the Surrealist generation who arguably ushered in a new way of looking at poetry's relation to the world. This was an important moment for poetry of the twentieth century, for it directed attention to work that until then had been marginal in relation to the two dominant tendencies of the era – Surrealism and engaged Resistance poetry – and thus rebooted the genre, sending the postwar generation in a new direction. Ponge dismissed the 'je–tu' love relation that had organized so many Surrealist poems, establishing instead an intimate exchange between words and the things to which they refer. It is worth pausing for a moment to study in greater depth Ponge's poem, for it marks the rupture between poetries of the prewar and the postwar era even as it extends some of the more radical tendencies of poetry by Mallarmé and Rimbaud.

What did 'La figue (sèche)' accomplish and why was it chosen by a group of thinkers engaged in both politics (Maoism) and philosophy (deconstruction)? What might a (dried) fig have to do with the future of poetry in French?

'La figue (sèche)'

> Pour ne savoir pas trop ce qu'est la poésie (nos rapports
> avec elle sont indirects),
> De ces figues sèches, en revanche (tout le monde voit
> cela), qu'on
> nous sert, depuis notre enfance, ordinairement aplaties
> et tassées parmi d'autres hors de quelque boîte,
> Comme je remodèle chacune entre le pouce et l'index
> un instant avant de la croquer,
> Une idée me souvient, ou survient, toute bonne à vous être
> aussitôt quittée.[12]

> While not really knowing what poetry is (our relations with it are
> never direct),
> Of these dried figs, however (you all see), those we've
> been served, since childhood, usually flattened, piled
> among others, out of some box,
> Remodeling each one between thumb and finger an instant
> before I take a bite,
> I retain an idea, or an idea retains me, ripe to leave with
> you here and now.

Ponge begins his six-section poem with a hypothesis, an 'idea', that will tell us something about what poetry 'is'. This 'idea' is related to the act of eating a dried fig, the purple mass of which will eventually remind him of something 'irréductible' – in short, a poem. As opposed to the 'indirect' relations we have with poetry, our relation to a piece of fruit, Ponge suggests, is direct and immediate; to eat a fig involves our hands, mouth, throat, and eyes. One can handle and manipulate a fig ('je remodèle chacune') before crunching it between the teeth ('avant de la croquer'). Yet this sensuously material object – which Ponge will call a few stanzas later 'Une petite bombe, dans notre sensibilité' [A little bomb, in our sensibility] (p. 886) – offers a type of 'resistance' that is satisfying in the way that both a sexual object and a thing made of 'paroles' (words) (p. 887) is satisfying. Poem, fig, sexual object – they all give pleasure (to the mouth): as Ponge will state a few lines later, a fig is an 'ensemble concourant à notre délectation' [package conspiring to give us pleasure], possessing the shape of a 'tétine' [teat] that we not only squeeze but swallow. Everyone can have the experience of snacking on figs ('tout le monde voit cela'), whereas a satisfying experience of a poem might be harder to obtain. Yet Ponge makes the same claim for his 'idea' that he makes for the ordinary fig, namely, that it can be quickly communicated, immediately appreciated in the manner of a piece of fruit: 'Une idée me souvient, ou survient, toute bonne à vous être aussitôt quittée.' Ultimately, that 'idea' is the poem itself. The poem is (like) a fig insofar as it, too, is 'ordinairement aplaties et tassées', flattened as a page and stacked among other pages in a book ('quelque boîte'). Further, a poem, too, may be 'remodelled' by the author – through the process of countless rewritings that characterize Ponge's process – or, alternatively, 'remodelled' by a reader, who performs the poem each time it is vocalized (or subvocalized). Ponge tightens the association between fig and poem, the thing described and the thing doing the describing, when he titles his poem, simply, 'La figue (sèche)'. Does this title refer to the dried fig that is the poem's subject or to the poem called 'The Fig (Dried)', which might *also* be the poem's subject? Is the poem talking about a fig or about itself?

Through what appears at first to be a clear-cut description of a simple object in the world, something common that everyone can see ('tout le monde voit cela'), Ponge arrives at a description of poetry – 'cela' – that thing (what thing?) that we do not 'know', except indirectly. Moreover, he eroticizes that thing, poetry, comparing it to a fig, then to a chapel ('Quelque église ou chapelle romane' [Some church or Roman chapel], p. 886), then to a breast ('tétine'), and finally to something resembling a vagina:

> Jouir de l'autel scintillant en son intérieur qui la remplit toute
> D'une pulpe de pourpre gratifiée de pépins.
>
> To climax from the altar shining inside it which fills it entirely
> With a purple pulp crowned with seeds.   (p. 887)

In 'La figue (sèche)', Ponge is merely extending a practice he perfected in his first volume of poetry, *Le Parti pris des choses* [*Taking the Side of Things*] of 1942. Here, he typically leads his reader via the description of an object (a lump of moss, an oyster, a sponge) to a mise-en-abyme narrative of the poem's making. Brilliantly exploiting the multiple connotations of words (as well as the complexities of their etymologies), he manages to evoke simultaneously the material attributes of the eponymous object, the attributes of poetry as a form of inscription, and the sexual act. His work is both self-reflexive and materialist, bringing attention to the everyday, the playful workings of language, and the carnal register they seem to evoke through double entendre. As opposed to the Surrealist poem, a poem by Ponge does not present us with thrilling metaphors; nor does it appear to express the speaker's 'état d'âme'. And yet there is always a sense that something has been revealed; we have been offered the occasion to see anew, to see 'cela' in a way we have never seen it before.

Ponge's practice would come to exert a major influence on poetry written during the latter part of the century. After Ponge, poetry began to turn towards more humdrum realities (such as city life in the work of Jacques Réda) while his ludic impulse is manifested in poets as diverse as Olivier Cadiot and Jacques Jouet. Moreover, his preference for describing the minute details of matter ushered in a poetics of what Gleize has called 'la littéralité' [literality], a poetics that refuses figuration.[13] In the wake of Ponge, a host of late twentieth-century poets would choose to explore this domain of the literal, the rhetorically unadorned, as a way of understanding better how language works and what it allows us to say. Ponge draws attention not only to the 'literal' but also the *letteral*, the alphabetic characters, or atomic particles, that language employs – like so many things – to build words, statements, lyric expressions. Ponge can even be held responsible for inspiring the alphabetic procedure employed by Heidsieck in *Derviche/Le Robert*, for Ponge was the first modern poet to acknowledge overtly his use of the Littré Dictionary to write poems. Finally, it was Ponge who introduced the genre of the poem-as-work-in-progress, a genre that Philippe Jaccottet would evolve into haunting meditative works such as *Paysages avec figures absentes* [*Landscape with Absent Figures*] (1970). In the early 1940s, Ponge began to produce multiple versions of a single poem, generating permutations of a kernel idea or set of statements. The first pages of the long poem *Le Savon* were composed in 1942 during Ponge's work in the Resistance; the pages then morphed into a radio play performed on Radio Cologne in 1965; finally, the radio play plus multiple rewritings appeared as a single text in 1967. Similarly, 'La figue (sèche)' was begun in 1951; new versions were created over the course of the next decade; and the full collection of versions was published in 1977 as *Comment une figue de paroles et pourquoi* [*How a Fig of Words and Why*]. Complicating the project of representation, Ponge and the generation indebted to him foreground the process by which words suggest their own sequencing and re-sequencing: 'language reacts, proposes its own solutions', he writes in *Le Grand Recueil*.[14]

Arguably, however, the most significant intervention Ponge made into poetry of the twentieth century was to abandon the conceit of a lyric 'I' committed to a mission of self-revelation. His 'I' is implicated instead in a verbal game. This game involves exploiting the phonemic, graphemic, and etymological potentials of words to generate sequences. Such an understanding of writing – as guided by the play of the signifier – resonated with theories advanced during the 1960s in other domains, such as linguistics and philosophy.[15] Jacques Derrida, another member of *Tel Quel*, provided a reading of Ferdinand de Saussure's *Cours de linguistique générale* [*Course in General Linguistics*] that supported an investigation of words as things. But Ponge's reaction against the traditional subject matter of French poetry was only one among many such reactions. During the immediate postwar period, two other major movements emerged: one associated with the journal *L'Éphémère* (published from 1967 to 1972) and the other known as the collective OuLiPo (L'Ouvroir de littérature potentielle [Workshop of Potential Literature]), founded in 1960 by Raymond Queneau and François Le Lionnais. The first was composed of the poets Yves Bonnefoy, Louis-René Des Forêts, Jacques Dupin, and André Du Bouchet, who advocated a return to the 'real'. The second mingled poets and mathematicians who recast writing as a kind of game, a process of working within tight, self-imposed constraints. Some of the most unforgettable volumes of twentieth-century poetry would come out of OuLiPo's laboratory: Raymond Queneau's *Cent mille milliards de poèmes* [*A Hundred Thousand Billion Poems*] (a stack of ten sonnets sliced up line by line so as to allow the reader to mix and match the lines in any order); Jacques Roubaud's *Autobiographie: chapitre X* (a recombinant recycling of Surrealist texts); and Jacques Jouet's *Poèmes de métro* (a volume of poems written on the metro, the number of lines of each poem determined by the number of stations traversed in a single 'trajet').

Although none of these authors took the step of removing poetry from the page, the definition of a poem was undergoing radical transformation during the postwar era. The 'cut-up' method associated with William S. Burroughs (first suggested by Pierre Schaeffer's 'musique concrète') took hold in the late 1950s when Burroughs, Brion Gysin, Allen Ginsberg, and Gregory Corso all sojourned in Paris. Burroughs, like Schaeffer, worked with a tape recorder, approaching language as a sonic substance that could be cut up and re-ordered. Meanwhile, Ginsberg's mode of delivery suggested that the poem could be a genre of performance, reaching a different audience by stepping on to the stage. It would be difficult to exaggerate the impact of Burrough's cut-up method on the evolution of French poetry from the mid twentieth century to today. French Sound Poetry, the movement to which Bernard Heidsieck belongs, is greatly indebted to Burroughs' cut-up method as well as Ginsberg's performance techniques.

The impact of Rimbaud and Mallarmé

The multimedia poetries of the 1950s and 1960s might seem to announce a rupture with the past; yet one could argue that they were actually *extending* that past, returning to ponder the most significant challenges posed by nineteenth-century predecessors such as Arthur Rimbaud and Stéphane Mallarmé. To begin with Rimbaud – he had already anticipated his successors in at least four ways. He ironized the lyric project of self-expression, parodying what he called 'la poésie subjective'; he exhibited a fascination with paraliterary genres and figured himself as a virtual subaltern; he took what I will call (anachronistically) a 'cut-up' approach to the dominant discourses of his period (literary discourses but also the 'bourgeois' discourses of economics, scientific progress, and Christianity); and he substituted for the traditional rules of prosody and versification a set of rules of his own invention. Of course, there is no straight line leading back from Roche, Heidsieck, or Ponge to Rimbaud (or to Mallarmé, for that matter): many other influences intervened in the development of twentieth-century poetry in French. Yet reading Rimbaud and Mallarmé through these later poets can shed a new light on their works, allowing us to tease out highly generative and proto-avant-garde aspects of nineteenth-century poetic writing that we might not otherwise notice.

The first and most significant move Rimbaud made was to undermine the lyric voice itself. He does so early on in his career in a letter to his teacher, Georges Izambard, dated 13 May 1871. It is worth taking a moment to look at this letter (known as the 'Lettre du Voyant' ['Letter of the Seer']); the turn it takes – from 'subjective' to 'objective' – would be crucial to the fate of French poetry in the twentieth century. Rimbaud opens his letter by citing, with no little scorn, his teacher's own words: 'There you go again professor. We are indebted to Society'.[16] Rimbaud then proceeds to twist Izambard's meaning. Instead of interpreting his 'debt to Society' as an obligation to serve, Rimbaud states that, literally, he *owes money*: 'je me fais cyniquement entretenir' ['I cynically find a way to be kept']. Rimbaud admits that he owes a debt to 'Society', but the way in which he repays that debt has nothing to do with what Izambard intended: 'everything I can invent that is stupid, dirty, bad, in action as in words, *I give it back to them*'.[17]

Rimbaud establishes somewhat sardonically what will become his *poetic* relation to society: he will pay his debt in perverse kind, returning something he has been taught (such as the poetry of Victor Hugo) but in a cut-up and remixed form that we, as readers, are invited to decipher. In Rimbaud's eyes, Izambard's sense of being indebted to Society causes him to write a poetry that is nothing more than a poetry of a subject *constructed* by that Society. Rimbaud thus anticipates Judith Butler's work on performativity by over a hundred years, suggesting that it is only by reiterating, parodying, and remixing these social discourses that we create something new. As opposed to his teacher, then, Rimbaud will write an 'objective poetry' in order to avoid the subjectivism of the lyric: 'One day', he writes to Izambard, 'I hope I will find in your principle an objective poetry ... I dirty myself as much as possible [je m'encrapule le plus possible] ... I want to be a poet, and I work to make myself *see* [Je veux être poète, et je travaille à me rendre *voyant*] ... I is an other [JE est un autre]' (p. 268).

This sequence of statements holds the key to a better understanding of both Rimbaud's poetry and the poetry he inspires in later writers. For Rimbaud, as for many poets (including the Surrealists), the 'real world' as we have been taught to see it is *not* the real world, certainly not the real world of an individual subject. Rather, what we think we see with our own eyes is actually what we are trained to see. Similarly, when we think we are expressing ourselves, we are actually expressing what the dominant discourses allow us to express. It is for this reason that Rimbaud understands his task to be that of transforming what he is given to see, say, and think, to deliver to Society a new way to see.

In characteristic manner Rimbaud depicts such transformative work as sullying and contaminating: to see in a new way requires a process of 'encrapulement'. Derived from the word 'crapule', a slang term referring to the mob (or 'peuple' in the mind of Rimbaud, inspired by the Commune of May 1871), 's'encrapuler' means both to get dirty and to frequent a lower class of society (not 'Society'). Throughout his verse, Rimbaud inverts the meanings of 'dirty' and 'clean', noble and base, figuring actions such as vomiting or covering oneself with mud as rites of purification and cleansing. Rimbaud's logic is clear: if 'Society' has abrogated to itself the lexicons of hygiene (for example, Christian purity, bourgeois cleanliness, and order), then Rimbaud will make use of the lexicons of debasement. As he writes in 'Les poètes de sept ans' ['Seven-Year-Old Poets'], one must hide in the latrines to find anything 'fresh' (p. 77); 'des vomissures / Me lava' [the vomiting / Cleansed me], he recounts in 'Le bateau ivre' ['Drunken Boat'] (p. 100). Rimbaud's affection for paraliterary genres has to do with a preference for that which is raw and untutored, less tainted by 'Société' with a capital S ('Une saison en enfer', p. 232). But whatever materials he uses, Rimbaud is aiming to depict (and enact) a process by which the lenses through which we view and experience the world – discoloured by layers of imposed beliefs – might be cleansed. The renewal of vision is a leitmotif of his entire oeuvre, as it is of many other poets who come after him, including Ponge.

To find a new subject position Rimbaud replaces the 'je' of the socialized individual (the product of a discursive regime) with a 'JE' (all upper case letters). Typographically, Rimbaud is marking out a new territory, a space for an alternative to Society's overdetermined 'je' (p. 268). But from what materials does Rimbaud propose to create this new subjectivity in discourse? One answer would be: from the fragments of earlier works. He recycles lines from Victor Hugo and borrows images from Baudelaire to produce his *Illuminations*, or 'Painted Plates'. However, his 'cut-up' approach is not designed to create a coherent whole but rather, as Gleize has noted, to prevent totalization, to keep the fragments of the 'JE' in perpetual motion.[18] Rimbaud's approach to earlier texts as a treasure to be plundered resurfaces in Tristan Tzara's *Dada Manifestos* of 1919, where statements follow one another guided by no discernible logic. Similarly, Blaise Cendrars's *Documentaires* of 1924 recasts the poet as a photographic apparatus (the first title of the volume was 'Kodak'), snapping and cropping pictures of a found text (*Mystérieux docteur Cornélius*, by Gustave Lerouge) and rearranging them into a new form.[19] Rimbaud's influence can also be found in twentieth-century poets much less openly indebted to his work, such as Emmanuel Hocquard, whose embrace of a 'modernité négative'[20] recalls Rimbaud's search for a 'poésie objective'. For Rimbaud, as for Hocquard, it is necessary to develop a system of *dérèglement* (disarticulation, fragmentation, transgression). But how to prevent the congealment of fragments into statements, statements into scenarios, and scenarios into a normative 'je' is a problem that would preoccupy Hocquard for many years.

In 1993, Hocquard published with Juliette Valéry a multimedia work, *Le Commanditaire: poème*, that many consider pivotal in the evolution of late twentieth-century poetry. Similar to Rimbaud's *Illuminations* (both prose and poem), *Le Commanditaire* is also generically unstable; however, it reaches beyond Rimbaud's scribal experiment by assimilating elements of signage and photography.[21] Like a detective novel, the work is concerned with a quest: the poet seeks to discover 'une autre fiction', something not seen before in the very fabric of the visible. For Hocquard, it is not a matter of revealing some ultimate truth – for anything that happens in language is partially artifice – but rather of fabricating 'something new in the world, something hidden, latent, . . . waiting to develop'.[22] Sounding a note we have heard in Ponge and Rimbaud, Hocquard states that work with language should lead to its purification, a cleansing of the lens through which we see.

The poet's task is to detach the visible (the image) or the sayable (the 'énoncé') from its habitual place in a continuum in order to see what it *is* as a unit of meaning.

In order to disturb 'our reading habits', Hocquard develops a method of poetry writing that constitutes a variant of Burroughs' cut-up method. In 'Un malaise grammatical' ['A Grammatical Discomfort'], a critical essay that concludes his 1992 volume, *Théories des tables*, he describes this method in greater detail, indicating his connection to earlier poets such as Rimbaud and Cendrars while exemplifying the dominant impulse of late twentieth-century experimentalism.[23] Inspired by the figure of the archaeologist who, in order to reconstruct a shattered fresco, places the coloured fragments onto a flat surface, Hocquard rearranges words 'on a table': 'I throw onto the table a random collection of "memory objects" which still have to achieve some formulation'. Hocquard's 'method' consists in discerning new relations among 'objects' (words) by treating them, precisely, *as* objects. Of course, all poets, in one form or another, construct a method, a set of rules involving the rearrangement of discursive units. Some poets begin the composition of a poem by choosing end-rhymes before filling in the rest of the line with the non-rhyming words. Mallarmé himself used this compositional procedure. (Manuscript drafts provide evidence that he began work on a strophe of *Hérodiade* by identifying the end-rhymes – 'étincela/celle-là/pubère/libère' – before determining the rest of the content.[24]) What is significantly different in the case of Rimbaud and Hocquard, however, is that they are not following the rules of an already established prosodic convention, such as that which prescribes that the final word of a line should rhyme with the final word of another line, or that the number of syllables in each line should add up to twelve (to make an alexandrine verse). Instead, like the poets of OuLiPo, these poets make up their own constraints.

Shifting the fundamentally mathematical and structural constraints of poetry from one location to another – from something conventional, like the counting of syllables, to something unconventional, like the counting of metro stations (Jouet) or spaces on a page (Roche) – is arguably *the* defining feature of today's experimental poetry. However, another, equality significant feature of experimental poetry is its intermediality: as Christophe Hanna has observed, experimental poetry systematically imports 'a process of representation proper to one domain into another'.[25] Yet intermediality is by no means the exclusive domain of late twentieth-century poets. Mallarmé is famous for having blurred the lines between the sonic and the scribal, the iconic and the letteral, long before the sound poets or the concrete poets ventured into non-verbal realms.[26]

In fact, it was Mallarmé who first rendered explicit the two procedures outlined above: the methodical transfer of a prosodic measure onto another element to be measured; and the borrowing of that measure from another medium. The prime example is, of course, *Un Coup de dés jamais n'abolira le hasard* [*A Throw of the Dice Will Never Abolish Chance*]; few experiments in poetry have had as great an impact as this groundbreaking work of 1897. Rimbaud's modest analogy between a poem and a 'painted plate' (*'illumination'*) is overshadowed by Mallarmé's daring attempt to rethink the poetic volume as a musical score. It is this type of 'transfer' (poem as score) that underlies the logic of Heidsieck's approach to words as a sonic stream, or Roche's approach to photography as a model for the framing and cropping of language, or Hocquard's approach to archaeological reconstruction as a model for the re-sorting of utterances. All these poets have generated highly calculated processes of composition by referring to other media, but, as Mallarmé wrote in *Un Coup de dés*, these processes are 'hors d'anciens calculs' – based on a calculus hitherto unknown.[27]

Mallarmé's logic

To conclude, let us take a brief look at Mallarmé's famous poem and the logic that brought him from the sonnet to the mixed media work. Even before composing *Un Coup de dés* Mallarmé had been pondering the problem brought about by his generation's abandonment of 'measure', their preference for the 'vers libre' over the 'vers strict'. Much like the poets of the post-Second World War generation who rejected the supposed 'spontaneity' of Surrealism's 'écriture automatique', Mallarmé was determined to find a *new* measure, an alternative constraint, that would nonetheless free poetry to entertain new futures. His 'Crise de vers' ['Crisis of Verse'] of 1886 acknowledges the challenge to traditional rules of versification that had been mounted by poets such as Gustave Kahn, Émile Verhaeren, Francis Vielé-Griffin, Marie Krysinska, and Rimbaud himself over the course of the 1880s. Mallarmé, who had always been something of a traditionalist, nonetheless precipitated one of the greatest revolutions in poetry when he offered a response to this challenge, this 'exquise crise, fondamentale',[28] by inventing 'a form in which all the generic elements are recast'.[29] 'The "white spaces", in fact, take on importance, strike one first of all', he wrote in his preface; 'verse requires white, like silence around it, ordinarily, to the point where the piece, lyrical or of a few feet, occupies, in its middle, about a third of the page: I do not transgress this measure [cette mesure], merely disperse it.'[30] In brief, Mallarmé respects the proportion: one-third of the page is filled with type; the other two-thirds are left blank. He simply disperses that one-third of type

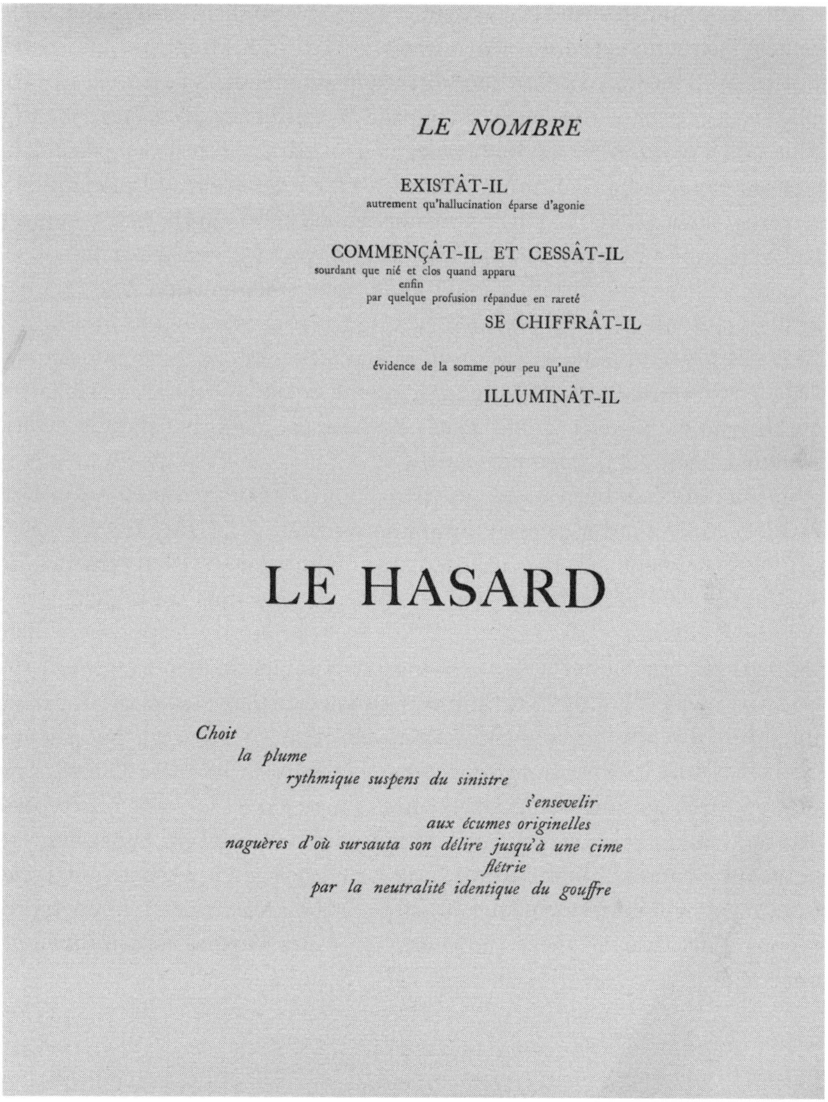

LE NOMBRE

EXISTÂT-IL

autrement qu'hallucination éparse d'agonie

COMMENÇÂT-IL ET CESSÂT-IL

sourdant que nié et clos quand apparu
enfin
par quelque profusion répandue en rareté

SE CHIFFRÂT-IL

évidence de la somme pour peu qu'une

ILLUMINÂT-IL

LE HASARD

Choit
la plume
rythmique suspens du sinistre
s'ensevelir
aux écumes originelles
naguères d'où sursauta son délire jusqu'à une cime
flétrie
par la neutralité identique du gouffre

Figure 11.1 Page from Stéphane Mallarmé, *Un Coup de dés jamais n'abolira le hasard* (Paris: Nouvelle Revue française, 1914). FC8.M2957.914c, Houghton Library, Harvard University.

across the gutter, reconceiving the surface of the open book as a single space, a canvas. It is no accident that Mallarmé sought to publish the first version of *Un Coup de dés* with an art dealer, Ambroise Vollard: he was borrowing his 'process of representation' from the visual arts. Mallarmé employed the specifics of typography to new ends, choosing different fonts, points, and weights to suggest differences in affective intensity (see Figure 11.1).

Although Mallarmé did not live to see his poem published according to his explicit instructions, he did leave notes behind indicating that his spatial choices were meant to contribute directly to the reader's experience of the text. He approached the space of the page as a meaningful surface, one that could add a new dimension to the vocal performance of the poem. Again, he did not abandon the traditional tools of poetry – counting and calculation – he merely shifted their field of application. Paul Valéry was the first to remark that Mallarmé's practice in *Un Coup de dés* would have far-reaching consequences for poetry as both a sonic and graphic phenomenon. 'He enriched the literary domain', Valéry wrote, 'with a second dimension'; he produced a 'spectacle idéographique'.[31] Born of a deep reflection on the poetic genre – 'deduced from analyses of language, of the book, of music' – Mallarmé revealed how the page could reach beyond the page by, paradoxically, remaining itself: 'la *page*, unité visuelle'.[32]

My method has been to identify an impulse for experimentation that traverses more than a century of poetic writing – arguably from Hugo's first displacement of the caesura and Rimbaud's visual rhymes to Hocquard's replacement of words with photographs and Heidsieck's recordings of the Paris metro. While contemporary experimentalism could be held accountable for driving poetry outside of poetry – off the page and away from the lyric subject – it is clear that poems of an earlier generation already pointed the way. Some readers may feel that today's poetry has lost its direction; that it has brought on its own demise. Too close an investigation into poetry's means may have atomized poetry into illegibility and irrelevance instead of promoting it – as I believe it has – to the status of an exciting multimedia form. But whatever one decides, the experiment will continue. True to its initial impulse, poetry interrogates the page, discovering there the energy to move beyond inscription into other realms.

NOTES

1. Bernard Heidsieck, *Derviche/Le Robert* (Roumainville: Al Dante, 2004), p. 10.
2. Heidsieck, *Derviche/Le Robert*, p. 11.
3. All translations are my own unless otherwise noted.
4. Guillaume Apollinaire, 'L'esprit nouveau et les poètes', *Œuvres en prose complètes*, vol. 2, ed. Pierre Caizergues and Michel Décaudin (Paris: Gallimard, 1991), p. 945.
5. Apollinaire, 'L'esprit nouveau', pp. 945, 954.
6. Jean-Michel Espitallier, *Caisse à outils: un panorama de la poésie française aujourd'hui* (Paris: Pocket, 2006), p. 23.
7. Jean-Marie Gleize, *Poésie et figuration* (Paris: Seuil, 1983), p. 299.

8. André Breton, *Manifeste du surréalisme* (1924), in *Œuvres complètes*, vol. 1, ed. Marguerite Bonnet, with the collaboration of Philippe Bernier, Étienne-Alain Hubert, and José Pierre (Paris: Gallimard, 1988), pp. 330, 328.

9. 'Le tourbillon vint aux genoux'; René Char, 'Les trois sœurs', *Le Poème pulverisé* *1945–1947*, *Œuvres complètes*, intro. Jean Roudaut (Paris: Gallimard, 1983), p. 250.

10. Breton, *Manifeste*, pp. 324, 337.

11. See Julia Kristeva, *La Révolution du langage poétique* (Paris: Seuil, 1974).

12. Francis Ponge, *Œuvres complètes*, ed. Bernard Beugnot (Paris: Gallimard, 2002), vol. 1, p. 885.

13. Jean-Marie Gleize, *Poésie et figuration*, and *À noir: poésie et littéralité. Essai* (Paris: Seuil, 1992).

14. Francis Ponge, 'My Creative Method', in *Le Grand Recueil*, 'Méthodes', *Œuvres complètes*, vol. 1, p. 531.

15. Raymond Roussel already tested out this premise with *Impressions d'Afrique* in 1910.

16. 'Vous revoilà professeur. On se doit à la Société'; Rimbaud, *Œuvres complètes* (Paris: Gallimard, 1972), p. 267. Further Rimbaud references will be to page numbers of this edition.

17. '[T]out ce que je puis inventer de bête, de sale, de mauvais, en action et en paroles, *je le leur livre*'. My emphasis.

18. Gleize, *Poésie et figuration*: '[il s'agit de] ce qui ne parvient jamais à faire discours' (p. 91); c'est le travail du négatif comme positivité: le sujet du poème tend à n'être plus le sujet, mais ce qui, dans le sujet, fait le vide, et le recommencement sans fin, à partir de la dispersion des éléments' (p. 102).

19. Cendrars called the poems in *Documentaires* 'photographies verbales'; they were 'photographs', however, not of scenes but of pages of Lerouge's book. See 'Document' in Blaise Cendrars, *Du monde entier: Poésies complètes* *1912–1924* (Paris: Gallimard, 1967), p. 133.

20. Emmanuel Hocquard, *ma haie: un privé à Tanger 2* (Paris: P.O.L., 2001), p. 25.

21. Between the covers, we find photographs (of buildings, a highway, faces, a stream), lists of numbered sentences, and short prose fragments. Are the photographs the 'silent partner' (one meaning of 'commanditaire') of the verbal enterprise? Or is the 'silent partner' the reader who invests in discovering the meaning?

22. Emmanuel Hocquard and Juliette Valéry, *Le Commanditaire: poème*, 'Fiction B.' (Paris: P.O.L., 1993), n.p.

23. Emmanuel Hocquard, 'Un malaise grammatical', in *Théorie des tables* (Paris: P.O.L., 1992), n.p.

24. See Michel Murat, *Le Coup de dés de Mallarmé: Un recommencement de la poésie* (Paris: Belin, 2005), p. 48, n. 13. This is how Mallarmé begins a 'brouillon' of Finale I.

25. Christophe Hanna, *Nos dispositifs poétiques* (Paris: Questions théoriques, 2010), p. 132.

26. In the words of Antoine Raybaud: 'the transfer of one form of expression onto another' is at the very core of the avant-garde: Verlaine borrowed phonic effects from music; Rimbaud thought in visual terms; and Mallarmé 'work[ed] on the materiality of the book'; *Fabrique d'Illuminations* (Paris: Seuil, 1989), p. 119.

27. Stéphane Mallarmé, *Un Coup de dés jamais n'abolira le hasard*, in *Œuvres complètes*, vol. 1, ed. Bertrand Marchal (Paris: Gallimard, 1998), p. 373.

28. Mallarmé, 'Crise de vers', in *Œuvres complètes*, vol. 2, ed. Bertrand Marchal (Paris: Gallimard, 1945), p. 204.

29. '[U]ne forme où tous les éléments du genre sont refondus'; Murat, *Le Coup de dés de Mallarmé*, p. 38.

30. Mallarmé, 'Édition préoriginale, "Cosmopolis", 1897, Observation relative au poème', in *Œuvres complètes*, vol. 1, p. 391. My emphasis.

31. Paul Valéry, '*Un Coup de dés*; Lettre au directeur des *Marges*', *Œuvres complètes*, vol. 1, ed. Jean Hytier (Paris: Gallimard, 1957), p. 627.

32. Valéry, '*Un Coup de dés*', p. 626. Emphasis in the original.

12

EDWARD J. HUGHES

The renewal of narrative
in the wake of Proust

In 1922, the year of Marcel Proust's death, Gustave Lanson's history of French literature, *Histoire de la littérature française*, a work first published in 1894, went into its seventeenth edition. It carried a reworked final section on the late nineteenth and early twentieth centuries, which expressed the hope that the twentieth century, in bringing 'masterpieces of which we have no conception and which will overturn all our beliefs', will thereby succeed in extending a literary tradition and so preserve 'the face of eternal France'.[1] If the mood in France after the First World War helps explain the tone of patriotic exhortation, Lanson's wish to defend and illustrate French culture is significantly based on the optimistic view that art will assume previously unimagined directions.

Proust's *À la recherche du temps perdu* [*In Search of Lost Time*], the last volume of which appeared posthumously in 1927, may have come too late for Lanson but his novel was to provide a striking example of one such new, unimagined direction. Proust experienced difficulty establishing his reputation. Already in 1912, he was struggling to find a publisher for the first instalment of what was to become a multi-volume novel. And when the publishing house Fasquelle commissioned a report from the poet Jacques Madeleine on the manuscript for the first volume, *Du côté de chez Swann* [*The Way by Swann's*], the feedback was unremittingly negative: the volume intended by Proust as an introduction was longer than a Zola novel; the reader had the feeling of being in the dark; and Madeleine expressed his distaste for the psychological portrait of the boy protagonist: 'it is the monograph of a sickly young boy ... who exhibits a sensitivity, an impressionability and a meditative subtlety that are excessive'.[2]

Clearly, Proust risked alienating readers brought up on a diet of nineteenth-century realism. The opening pages of *Du côté de chez Swann*, with their focus on a protagonist hovering between sleep and consciousness, signalled a radical turning away from what had come to be established, most recently by Naturalism, as the primary terrain of the novel genre: namely social representation. By choosing to begin the novel with an evocation of the world of dream, it was as though Proust were providing proof of the view independently formulated by his contemporary Freud working in the field of psychology. Proust's sense of the experimental quality of his writing is captured in a 1908 notebook containing early plans for the writing of what was to grow into *À la recherche du temps perdu*. He wonders about the course his work is taking: 'Laziness or doubt or powerlessness taking refuge in doubts about the form of art. Am I to write a novel, a philosophical study, am I a novelist?'[3]

In a letter of 1912, Proust observed that he was working on 'a book which in truth does not at all resemble the classical novel'.[4] By November 1913, when *Du côté de chez Swann* appeared, published by Grasset at the author's expense, Proust was more assertive. In an interview to help launch the volume, he dismissed the suggestion that his novel had been shaped by the work of his contemporary, the influential philosopher Henri Bergson, whose *Matière et mémoire* [*Matter and Memory*] (1896) was, as the work's subtitle suggests, an 'Essay on the relation of the body to the mind'. Proust affirmed that the purpose of his novel was to make visible the invisible substance of time, a substance that is nevertheless, he insisted, felt and lived. It was also to deliver 'a psychology in time', with individual characters' lives grasped in their pluridimensionality, across multiple encounters and sightings; and to the accusation made by Jacques Madeleine that his work merely peddled 'subtleties', Proust countered that these in fact constituted 'realities'.

He confirmed the psychological character of his novel by placing centre-stage the workings of memory. Through the functioning of involuntary memory, as he termed it, sections of the narrator's past are spontaneously re-experienced via sensory triggers, most famously in the form of the madeleine cake, the tasting of which draws the adult hero miraculously back to his boyhood.[5] Proust concludes his November 1913 interview by asserting that the elements that make up his work were provided not by reason but by his sensitivity: 'I first perceived them obscurely in my inner depths and had as much difficulty converting them into something intelligible as if they were as alien to the world of the intelligence as ... a musical motif, let's say.'[6] The exploratory character which Proust thus claims for his novel, its rejection of rationalism, and the stress it lays on subjectivity and interiority help explain in substantial measure the central place of *À la recherche du temps perdu* in the twentieth-century French novel. Likewise, the reference to transpositions being made across media (as evidenced by the life-as-musical-motif analogy here) points to the novel as an experimental space. In Proust's novel, music, painting, and drama are all associated with the protagonist Marcel's quest for self-knowledge.[7]

In foregrounding the emotions and focusing on the terrain in which they are experienced and understood, Proust establishes a key plank in his understanding of selfhood.[8] He had originally planned to give his novel the overall title 'Les Intermittences du cœur' [Intermittences of the Heart], a formulation that allowed Proust to apply the idea of cardiac malfunction to the emotional world, but he was to shy away from this title.[9] Nevertheless, the gravitational pull of emotional disruption and unpredictability was to persist. He placed the 'Intermittences of the Heart' title in that part of the volume *Sodome et Gomorrhe* [*Sodom and Gomorrah*] where he explores a powerful instance of emotional upheaval. The adolescent hero, returning to the Norman seaside town of Balbec some time after the death of his grandmother, feels, for the first time, an intense sense of loss at her passing. At the time of her death, he had been incapable of such emotion. This experience of delayed mourning allows the narrator to grasp that the emotional life, crucially, works intermittently: 'to the disturbances of memory are linked the intermittences of the heart'.[10]

Commenting on the episode, Samuel Beckett translates the momentous line in *Sodom and Gomorrah* in which Proust's first-person narrator is confronted with 'this dolorous synthesis of survival and annihilation'.[11] The grandmother lives on in her grandson's memory and yet is dead. Beckett also renders into English the sequel, in which the narrator solemnly records 'an impression ... whose double and mysterious furrow had been carved, as by a thunderbolt, within me, by the inhuman and supernatural blade of Death, or the revelation of Death'.[12] Reflecting on the force of intermittence in the sphere of the emotional life and its independence from chronological time, Beckett proposes a Proust shorthand in which time works along cardiac and not solar lines.[13] In the same way, the unpredictable surge of memory for Proust's protagonist reminds us of what Freud independently observed, namely that 'the ego ... is not even master in its own house, but must content itself with scanty information of what is going on unconsciously in its mind'.[14] The relegation of rationality which Proust had signalled in his earlier work on the nineteenth-century literary critic Charles Augustin Sainte-Beuve (the Sainte-Beuve essay opens with the line: 'Daily, I attach less value to the intellect'[15]) provides a bold formulation of authorial self-positioning.

The Proustian method of characterization, by extension, lays stress on the concept of myriad subjectivities and we find the prototype for this in the early pages of *Du côté de chez Swann*. There, the first-person narrator reflects on how his great-aunt had conceived of the life lived by a frequent visitor to the family home, Charles Swann: 'she injected and invigorated with all that she knew about the Swann family the dark and uncertain figure who emerged ... from a background of shadows'.[16] This evocation from the narrator's boyhood paves the way for what is presented as a general law of social identity: 'none of us constitutes a material whole, identical for everyone ... our social personality is a creation of the minds of others'.[17] Proust's narrator thus opens up the multiple subjectivities at work in the world of recognition and social interaction. In the same textual development, he reflects that his parents' ignorance of the prestige enjoyed by Swann in high Parisian society does not prevent them from, to use Proust's metaphor, stuffing the 'corporeal envelope' that is Swann with their own perceptions of him: 'They had ... been able to garner in this face disaffected of its prestige, vacant and spacious ..., the vague, sweet residue – halfmemory, half-forgetfulness – of the idle hours spent together after our weekly dinners.'[18] The compact formulation, 'half-memory, half-forgetfulness' (the French reads 'mi-mémoire, mi-oubli'), captures the co-presence of recollection and oblivion and allows Proust to stress the place of subjectivity and fallibility in the workings of memory.

If Proust's narrative interrogates the notion of stable identity, his enthusiastic reader Beckett develops a fictional world that explores deep anxiety about selfhood. Born in Ireland, Beckett was to become a highly successful writer both in English and in French and indeed in the same way that much of his adult life was lived in France, so his literary output is today seen as belonging as much to twentieth-century French literature as to the Anglophone literary tradition. Part I of Beckett's *Molloy* (1951) describes a disoriented first-person narrating subject unable to say how he got to the room where he initially finds himself and he goes on to describe the forgetfulness that makes up his being. This fragile constitution of subjecthood extends to much of the novel. In a form of contagion, the attitude of disorientation afflicting Molloy comes to be progressively inherited by Moran, the protagonist in Part II of the novel who is tasked with tracking down Molloy and who appears drawn into an ever more labyrinthine and ultimately fruitless quest.

Evoking 'the long confused emotion which was my life',[19] Molloy articulates a pessimistic vision of the world. He refers to 'the long sonata of the dead' and attributes his apparent aimlessness to 'the buckled wheel that carried me, in unforeseeable jerks, from fatigue to rest, and inversely' (pp. 23, 66). Puzzling over what being and identity might constitute, he describes himself as having endured a disorienting exile from words. And as if to echo the seventeenth-century dramatist Pedro Calderón de la Barca's *Life Is a Dream*, Molloy reveals that for a time in his life, 'my waking was a kind of sleeping' (p. 53).

This blind groping provides a key narrative driver for much of the novel. Molloy is a writer as the opening page of the work obliquely indicates, the weekly visit of someone who collect sheets of paper in exchange for money providing a transactional dimension about which Molloy protests: 'Yet I don't work for money. For what then? I don't know' (p. 7). The sombre reflection on the act of written composition may be linked to Beckett's *Proust* essay in which he dismisses both 'the literature that "describes"' and 'the realists and the naturalists worshipping the offal of experience' (p. 78). Molloy stresses the problematic character of verbal articulation, explaining to his reader that, had he been capable of it, his utterance might have taken the verbal formulation it comes to acquire in his text: 'I heard a murmur, something gone wrong with the silence, and I pricked up my ears like an animal I imagine, which gives a start and pretends to be dead' (p. 88). The recording of a primitive awareness recalls the pre-verbal sentience evoked by Proust's narrator in the opening pages of *À la recherche du temps perdu*, where the hero waking from sleep experiences life 'as it may quiver in the depths of an animal'.[20]

That dimension of Proust's novel which explores the subterranean dimension of human interaction is returned to in the work of Nathalie Sarraute. If the young priest in Georges Bernanos's *Journal d'un curé de campagne* [*The Diary of a Country Priest*] (1936) complains that humankind is obliged to channel what is most precious via 'things so unstable and ever changing, alas, as words', Sarraute seeks to give prominence to psychological states not easily or customarily given verbal articulation.[21] In this regard, she stresses the workings of the tropism, that is to say the process whereby an organism turns in a particular direction under the influence of an external stimulus. *Tropismes* [*Tropisms*] (1939) draws specifically on botany, Sarraute applying to human interaction the concept of tropistic or micro-psychological movement that conveys pulses of cognitive and emotional life that literature has traditionally struggled to identify and formulate.[22]

If the tropism is to be found throughout Sarraute's fiction, an instructive example is provided by the novel *Portrait d'un inconnu* [*Portrait of a Man Unknown*] (1948). In his introduction to the work, Jean-Paul Sartre evokes the category of the 'anti-roman' or anti-novel to reflect this new development in French prose fiction that was set to gain ground in the 1950s and 1960s. Observing that as a genre, the novel was in the process of reflecting on itself, Sartre saw the resulting 'anti-roman' as turning away from the conventional novel's concern with notions of plot, characterization and sequential chronology. *Portrait d'un inconnu* works on the tensions existing between socially formed attitudes, most notably in the shape of the 'lieu commun' or commonplace, and forms of human behaviour that exist outside the clichés through which social consensus is channelled. The visit to a Dutch museum to see a painting also entitled *Portrait of a Man Unknown* provides an emblem of this process. The canvas – the work of an unknown artist – underscores the notion of anonymity and unknowability that is central to Sarraute's novel. For the third-person narrator who is viewing the painting, making out the contours of the figure depicted is likened to the hesitant groping of someone who is blind. This image of a tentative apprehension of reality captures Sarraute's project more generally. In a related way, she writes of the concept of the 'sous-conversation' or sub-conversation, that which lies under the surface of everyday communication. Sarraute's aim, significantly therefore, is not to be anti-mimetic, a characteristic that became quickly associated with the *nouveau roman* or French 'new novel' school to which she belonged. Rather she works to retrieve an area of experience that is customarily overlooked. Writing in 1962, Sarraute distinguishes between two realities, the one journalistic and the other, that which is sought by the novelist, 'that which is not yet known, which ... demands the creation of new modes of expression, new forms'.[23] Citing the artist Paul Klee – 'Art does not restore the visible, rather it renders visible'[24] – Sarraute sees the function of the novel as being to excavate those precious deposits that are formed by the 'sub-conversation', deposits that have become lost in 'the gangue' or worthless earth and stones 'of the visible, of the already known, of the already expressed'.[25] In this way, Sarraute rejects the commonplace and the commonsensical, the narrator in *Portrait d'un inconnu* making a plea for those who wander fearfully in what is evoked as a form of penumbra.[26]

Jacques Madeleine's assertion that Proust's work dealt in 'subtleties' rather than engaging with 'realities' comes to anticipate, then, the antagonism that is central to the storyline of *Portrait d'un inconnu* and to Sarraute's prose fiction more generally. Sarraute sees in the evolving genre of the novel a continuing engagement with psychological material and she asserts that 'for me this subject matter is the sole basis of the novel'.[27] As one critic observes, by proposing a new psychological subject matter, Sarraute retains an element of realist traction which sets her work apart from the formalism for which the French new novel was renowned.[28]

In her essay 'L'ère du soupçon' ['The Age of Suspicion'], first published in *Les Temps modernes* in February 1950, Sarraute contrasts Balzac's character Eugénie Grandet (seen as a figure replete with an identity that is conveyed in terms of dress, social situation, and psychology) with twentieth-century avatars of the novelistic protagonist. Superficially, the evocation of the miser and his daughter in *Portrait d'un inconnu* recalls the narrative of *Eugénie Grandet* and yet the scope of the later work signals a rejection of Balzacian realism. Sarraute celebrates the impact of James Joyce, Proust and Freud who succeed in mapping the flow of interior monologue and 'the vast, as yet almost unexplored regions of the unconscious'.[29]

Sarraute's 'era of suspicion' title reflects a broader cultural mood. Prose fictions of the mid-twentieth century in France such as Sartre's *La Nausée* [*Nausea*] (1938), Camus's *La Chute* [*The Fall*] (1956), and Marguerite Duras's *Moderato Cantabile* (1958) all generate for the texts' readers an atmosphere of intense introspection and psychological complexity. Or as Bernanos observed in striking terms in his first novel *Sous le soleil de Satan* [The Star of Satan] (1926),[30] the human soul functions as an 'impenetrable night', with the simplest of feelings meeting and colliding according to 'secret affinities, like electrical clouds'.[31]

Looking at other art forms, Sarraute asserts that from Impressionism onwards, the field of painting functions, as it were, 'in the first person', by which she means that it has increasingly followed the way of interrogation through its radical departure from conventional forms of pictorial representation. Mid-twentieth-century cinema, she further suggests, similarly gravitates towards 'le soupçon'. Suspicion, in the form of the particularity of an individual perspective often marked by a knowledge that is lacunary, thus undermines the notion of the character as secure embodiment of social identity and reality.[32]

It was the critic Émile Henriot who, in a 1957 review of Sarraute's *Tropisms*, coined the label 'nouveau roman'.[33] In the same review, Henriot explores *La Jalousie* [*Jealousy*] (1957), one of Alain Robbe-Grillet's best-known novels.[34] The stress on formalist technique and a much-publicized turning away from psychological intrigue were part of the self-positioning associated with the French 'new novel' grouping and Robbe-Grillet was a prominent exponent of this experimental work. In a series of short texts that form a literary manifesto, *Pour un nouveau roman* [*Towards a New Novel*] (1963), he champions, among other things, the steering away from sequential, early-to-late chronology and the discarding of conventional techniques of characterization and of the traditional sense of an ending.[35] *La Jalousie* exemplifies this orientation, although one senses that the wish to withhold the stuff of traditional novelistic intrigue acquires a ludic character in a work whose title exploits the ambiguity in the French term 'jalousie' (which can mean both jealousy and a slatted window blind). Conventional reader expectations of amorous intrigue are reflected in the depiction of sexual infidelity in the nineteenth-century novel, a tradition no less present in Proust's novel, where the protagonist Marcel obsessively polices the movements of his lover Albertine. Robbe-Grillet simultaneously awakens and frustrates such expectations. Thus, while the components of the adultery plot are present in potential form in *La Jalousie* (the temporary absence of a partner, an atmosphere of surveillance, signs of male aggression), the assembling of textual blocks in the work pointedly delivers a narrative sequence that eschews any explicit concession to the novel of adultery, to psychologiz-ing and to the sense of a *telos* or ending. By confronting his reader with a forthright negation of novelistic conventions, Robbe-Grillet seeks to under-score the claims to difference of the new novel.

By contrast (and this helps demonstrate differences of writing practice among the so-called 'new novelists' and, by extension, to highlight the limitations of the 'new novel' label itself), Michel Butor's *La Modification* [*Second Thoughts*] (1957) energetically promotes the invasion of interiority, to re-apply the concept which Jean-Yves Tadié uses in relation to *À la recherche du temps perdu*.[36] While not having the extensiveness of Proust's work, Butor's novel analyses consciousness in the intensive manner charac-teristic of his predecessor. *La Modification* explores the significant life-change being envisaged by its bourgeois protagonist, Léon Delmont, who, in a strikingly innovative move by Butor, is designated in the novel as 'vous' (the formal second-person pronoun 'you'). Delmont's intention is to leave his wife Henriette and the family home in Paris and start a new life in the French capital with his Roman mistress Cécile. Through its account of a train journey to Rome undertaken by the protagonist in pursuit of this objective, the novel offers protracted reflection on his emotional relationships. Crucially, these are mapped onto the railway itinerary, in addition to being linked to previous and projected journeys along the same route. The experi-ences thus plotted across time include memories of travel to the Rome of the Fascist era with Delmont's then young wife Henriette, the present moment of travel in the company of unknown fellow passengers, and projections regard-ing the future direction of the relationship with Cécile. In a manner that recalls Proust's Albertine cycle, the experience is one of intense upheaval, the narrator identifying 'that sort of inward dizziness which persists, which possesses you again'.[37]

Reflecting on Marcel's attachment to Albertine, Proust's narrator con-cludes that 'love is space and time made apprehensible to the heart' and one could argue that a similar conjunction of the affective, the spatial, and the temporal marks the intensity of emotion conveyed in *La Modification*.[38] But this same conjunction also allows the novel's second-person protagonist to realize that the attachment to Cécile only functions 'in so far as Rome speaks and beckons to you through her'[39]; this realization helps prepare the denouement. As Pierre-Louis Rey remarks of Butor's novel, the claims to modernity made by the French 'new novel' notwithstanding, the configura-tion of Rome, Paris, and the search for love reworks would-be eternal themes of romance.[40]

Tradition is further served, up to a point, by the sense of an ending in Butor's novel. Thus in spite of regular disruptions to chronology, the narrative closes as the second-person narrator arrives at Rome's Stazione Termini; and what had been planned as a surprise visit to propose a new life to his mistress has now mutated into the protagonist's decision to recommit to his marriage. A less traditional feature of the denouement is that it appeals self-reflexively to literature with the protagonist committing to a project of writing, work that will displace any planned amorous sequel. The denouements in Proust and Butor thus overlap, to the extent that a central feature of Proust's novel is the manner in which it foregrounds the linkage between selfhood and the act of writing. The protagonist Marcel will write the experience of his life, the narrator noting that the work that he will produce will be the book that the reader has read; and, in the case of *La Modification*, the book that the protagonist hurriedly bought in the station in Paris and that remains unread during the journey to Italy, serving merely to mark his place on the train, now stands as an emblem for the protagonist's newfound project: to write a book, 'to try and bring to life in the form of literature this crucial episode in your experience'.[41] Moreover, just as Proust's narrator invites his readers to be the readers of themselves, in the way that the optician's shop in Combray can provide spectacles to meet all needs, so the use in Butor of the 'you' form of narrative voice establishes a form of complicity between the protagonist and the reader.[42]

In a brief essay entitled 'Le roman comme recherche' [The Novel as Search] (1955), Butor argues that new novelistic forms have the capacity to enhance our understanding of the real. He adds that formalist invention in the novel (of the kind that we see in *La Modification* with its imbrication of train timetable and the route of a sentimental education) paves the way for a more developed realism. This perspective helps modify the assumption that the French 'new novel' primarily involved experimentation at the level of form. Whereas Robbe-Grillet energetically announces a turning away from mimesis in *Pour un nouveau roman*, Butor, like Sarraute, may be read as part of a continuum that reaches back to Proust. Butor advocates 'attentive reading' and argues that 'not only the creation of a novel but also the reading of a novel is a form of waking dream'.[43] His character Delmont is similarly described as being 'transfixed like a sleepwalker interrupted in his wanderings'.[44]

This dimension of dream may be extended to other French prose-writing of the century. In André Breton's experimental work *Nadja* (1928), with its splicing of prose and photography, the first-person narrator insists that the way of 'the outer world' is 'a matter of sleep-walking'.[45] Dismissing the 'empiricists of the novel' who provide characters with their physical and moral characteristics, Breton rails against the genre more generally and insists that 'psychological literature, with all its fictitious plots' is doomed

(*Nadja*, pp. 17–18). Breton's broadly factual narrative begins with the question 'Who am I?' and he goes on to ask Nadja, a woman living on the margins of society, dismissive of social falsehood and convention and prone to mental illness: 'Who are you?' (*Nadja*, pp. 11, 71). Privileging interrogation, Breton, a prominent exponent of Surrealism, condemns the practices of psychiatry. As if to trump Proust's reflection (in his November 1913 interview designed to promote the *Swann* volume) that his work 'was in no way based on reasoning', Breton exhorts the reader in *Nadja* to 'thrus[t] one's head … out of the jail … of logic, that is out of the most hateful of prisons'.[46] *Nadja* celebrates incommunicability as pleasure, sees life as a cryptogram and discards 'any notion of teleological justification' (*Nadja*, pp. 23, 112, 115).

The notion of a waking dream is similarly pertinent to the work of Claude Simon. Here again, as we have seen with Sarraute and Butor, Proust provides an instructive lead-in. While the social history of Proust's day is an essential feature of *À la recherche du temps perdu*, its incorporation is often brought about obliquely. In the closing volume, *Finding Time Again*, the narrator protests against calls from nationalist writers in the First World War for literature to depict the struggles of the nation at war. The narrator's argument is that the writer best enhances national prestige by focusing on his art. If Proust's work provides a complex example, then, of how the referent, that is to say the world of social reality around us, is worked into literature, Claude Simon is also significant in this regard. As a member of the 'nouveau roman' grouping, he was forthright in asserting that the norms of literary realism were no longer tenable. Thus in *Le Jardin des Plantes* (1997), he quotes approvingly Flaubert's observation in his correspondence that the reader who comes to a book in the expectation of knowing whether or not the baroness will marry the count is set to be confounded.[47] Reading for the plot is thus devalorized. In the same text, Simon reproduces discussion from a literary colloquium in which are contrasted the idea of a referential illusion (specifically the retrieval of a battle scene from the Second World War which forms a leitmotif in Simon's work) and 'the pure materiality of an ordered set of letters' (272). Although labelled a 'roman' or novel, *The Jardin des Plantes* contains significant autobiographical elements. Thus, the character identified as S. conveys to the journalist questioning him about his experience of conflict in war the sense that it involved a 'sort … of semi-sleep-walking' (215).

This blurring of reality as it assumes an oneiric character marks one of Simon's most celebrated novels, *La Route des Flandres* (1960) [*The Flanders Road*]. With minimal narrative signposting provided, the confusing early pages of the work juxtapose two scenes in a dislocation that is both temporal and spatial: the traumatic episode from the Second World War when a

French cavalry brigade of which Claude Simon was a member is heavily defeated in an early engagement with the German army; and, alongside this, the spectacle at a racecourse, with its horses, jockeys in their silks and elegant spectators. The drawing together of pomp and putrefaction, nimble-footed thoroughbreds and the corpses of dead horses being absorbed into the soil of the battlefield, is part of a confusing collocation. The overlaying of memories provokes an experience of disorientation not only for the reader but also for the narrator, whose perspective is clouded by the scene of carnage. As the teller who has survived the war protests: 'But there was no grandstand, no elegant public to look at us: I could still see them silhouetted ahead of us (Quixotic shapes diminished by the light that gnawed, corroded the outlines)'.[48] Significantly, the trauma of war drives the character Georges to abandon 'once and for all that posture of the mind which consists of seeking a cause or a logical explanation for what you see or for what happens to you' (24). Numerous links back to Proust are to be found in the work of Simon, perhaps most notably in the latter's *The Jardin des Plantes*. In the closing lines of *The Flanders Road*, Simon evokes the image of the world crumbling 'like an abandoned building, unusable, left to the incoherent, casual, impersonal and destructive work of time' (231). The fullness of scale recalls the ending of *Du côté de chez Swann* in which the narrator reflects: 'and houses, roads, avenues are as fleeting, alas, as the years' (430). The parallel may be extended if we return to Proust's principle of intermittence as applied to the emotional life. Indeed a precise textual echo from Proust's novel is to be found in one of the numerous reflections in *The Flanders Road* on the spectacle of mortal remains on the battlefield. Laying stress on death lived not as an abstract concept but as a force that is brutal and violent, as something 'that ha[s] no need of reasons to strike', Simon uses the same formulation – 'la brusque révélation de la mort' [the sudden revelation of death] – that is to be found in the 'Intermittences of the Heart' section of Proust's *Sodom and Gomorrah*.[49]

Yet in tracing the Proust/Simon link, it is important to note significant divergences. As Françoise van Rossum-Guyon observes, the triumph of subjectivity is central in Proust's novel. Thus a life previously seen as lacking in purpose comes to be valorized if we accept the narrator's claims about the realization of his vocation as writer in *Finding Time Again*. This contrasts with the much less clearly defined 'I' in *The Flanders Road* for whom there is no celebratory turn to writing as is the case with Proust's resounding telos.[50]

Simon characterizes his own novelistic production as having an essentially compositional dimension, as a working with words which 'always reminds me of the title of one chapter in a mathematical textbook: "Arrangements, Permutations, Combinations"'. 'Bricolage' (working or tinkering with material), he suggests, succeeds in bringing out 'the completely craftsmanlike and empirical character of this labour which consists of assembling and organising'.[51] In a 1984 interview, he writes of composing 'in an arduous way, like a worker, or rather like an artisan'.[52] This angle of vision in which he promotes the principle of textual permutation will help assuage the doubts of readers whose instinct, always to be frustrated in the encounter with Simon's work, may be to attempt to establish coherence at the level of plot and characterization.

In stressing the practice of word composition, Simon implicitly questions the ability of narrative to convey the meaning of experience. This contrasts markedly with what we find not just in Proust but also in Butor, both of whom seek to give form to what nevertheless risks being, for the protagonists Marcel and Delmont, the disjointed experience of living. For Simon, by contrast, there can be no move towards summation and synthesis of the kind that we find at the close both of *Finding Time Again* and *Second Thoughts*. Simon underscores the fragmented character of experience, finding an endorsement of this position in the work of Montaigne, whose reflections on selfhood lie at the heart of the *Essais*. The epigraph to *The Jardin des Plantes* is drawn from this source: 'We are entirely made up of bits and pieces, woven together so diversely and so shapelessly that each one of them pulls its own way at every moment.'[53]

The experience of life as lived in the body (a question that is also explored incidentally in Montaigne's work) is another salient feature in Proust and in the twentieth-century French novel more generally. In *À la recherche du temps perdu*, the linkage between selfhood and writing acquires a corporeal inflection. The narrator insists in *Le Temps retrouvé* [*Finding Time Again*] on how his pursuit of a literary vocation is given urgency by his consciousness precisely of life's transience. Marcel reflects that, with his mind housed in a mortal body, the writing-of-a-life which he is attempting is rendered precarious.[54] The narrating subjects in Beckett's prose fiction (and his theatre too) are heirs to this sense of precariousness, as we see in the case of Molloy confronted by 'all that inner space one never sees, the brain and heart and other caverns where thought and feeling dance their sabbath'.[55] If the individual's corporeality and perception are here bound up inextricably, the link between embodiment and perception assumes other directions in the modern French novel. In Marguerite Duras's work *L'Amant* [*The Lover*] (1984), the autobiographical project of the first-person narrator is grounded in a self-perception that is essentially bodily. Recording how her face changed between the ages of eighteen and twenty-five, the narrator likens this physiological evolution to an encounter with textuality: 'I watched this process [of ageing] with the same sort of interest I might have taken in the reading of a book'.[56] Duras extends this effect of strangeness to include the figure of the mother, who is now remembered, the narrator insists, defectively: 'In my head I no longer have the scent of her skin, nor in my eyes the colour of her eyes. I can't remember her voice, except sometimes when it grew soft with the weariness of evening . . . It's over . . . That's why I can write about her so easily now, so long, so fully. She's become . . . cursive writing.'[57] This representation of the mother in *L'Amant* echoes the fallible memory of the loved one's body and voice that marks the narrator's hymn to the lost grandmother in Proust's novel. With both novelists, an awareness of the senses as fallible in the search for the deceased translates into textual copiousness.

Mindful of Marthe Robert's argument that novelists draw archaic elements of the family romance into their fictions, we can consider other twentieth-century French novelistic representations of progenitors.[58] Less expansively than is the case with Proust and Duras, Camus's *L'Étranger* [*The Outsider*] (1942) opens with a bemused Meursault relating the news of his mother's death, this in a narrative which comes to pivot around not only a story of homicide with a racial dimension but also an alleged indifference to the mother that assumes matricidal proportions; the opening of Beckett's *Molloy* describes the eponymous protagonist as finding himself mysteriously in his mother's bedroom; Annie Ernaux's autobiographical texts, *La Place* [*Positions*] (1983) and *Une Femme* [*A Woman's Story*] (1987) are centred around a guilt-laden grieving for deceased parents[59]; and in Sarraute's *Enfance* [*Childhood*] (1983), the narrator, in conversation with her alter ego, revisits the scene in which the child implicitly relegates her mother to a position of inferiority by finding the hairdresser's doll beautiful. The mother's aggression derives from her sense that the daughter, by implying a comparison, has performed an act of what one critic has termed 'difference and dissension'.[60]

In *L'Amant*, the failure to recognize the mother provides indirectly a reformulation of those foundational moments in Proust where the figures of the mother and grandmother are integral to Marcel's sense of selfhood. The concession wrung in *Du côté de chez Swann* from the mother who is coerced into reading George Sand to her fretting son comes to be interpreted by the latter as his inflicting harm on her, a harm that is metaphorically scored on her face.[61] The traces of matricidal guilt that are woven into Camus's tale about Meursault and in a more diffuse way into Duras's *L'Amant* are thus already forthrightly expressed in Proust's novel.

Pursuing further how these progenitors help shape narratives of selfhood in Proust and beyond, we see the artefacts of modernity providing key triggers for reflection on Self/Other relations. The protagonist Marcel dismisses as an act of vanity his elderly grandmother's wish to be photographed and fails to appreciate that this was her way of facilitating his future memory of her;[62] and hearing her disembodied voice on the telephone prompts misrecognition on Marcel's part.[63] In *L'Amant*, photography serves a similarly memorial function, with the mother here too being photographed in her old age. Duras's narrator describes a particular evening in Saigon: 'I looked at my mother, I could hardly recognize her'.[64] The brutal failure to recognize that is present in the scenes from both Duras and Proust brings its own revelatory power. The suggestion in *L'Amant* is that writing is as much a form of matricide as an act of filial devotion, hence perhaps the use of the metaphor of spatial vastness to describe what writing might deliver: 'The story of my life doesn't exist ... There are great spaces where you pretend there used to be someone.'[65]

A reviewer of Proust, writing in 1920, commended him as an author 'who enables the novel to take another step forward in the study of human kind'.[66] With its tone of cognitive optimism, it recalls the exuberance of Gustave Lanson that we considered earlier: the nation's beliefs, Lanson predicted, would be gloriously overturned by the masterpieces that French literature would go on to produce. The contrast with the hesitant tone of Proust in 1908 when faced with the seemingly disparate elements he was assembling could not be more marked. His achievement in the *Recherche* was to orchestrate these elements: anxiety about selfhood; the limits of intellect; the ramifications of embodied consciousness; the historical and social referent; love, sexuality and loss; the place and status of textual composition. As Walter Benjamin observed, with Proust in mind, 'all great works of literature establish a genre or dissolve one'.[67] Proust's *Recherche* was already embracing and shaping 'an age of suspicion', one in which the challenge was to clear away, to use again another of Sarraute's formulations, 'the gangue ... of the already known, of the already expressed'.[68]

NOTES

1. Gustave Lanson, *Histoire de la littérature française* (Paris: Hachette, 1922), p. 1182. Unless otherwise stated, the translations in this chapter are my own.
2. Jacques Madeleine, 'Rapport de lecture', in Marcel Proust, *Du côté de chez Swann*, ed. Antoine Compagnon (Paris: Gallimard, 1988), pp. 446–50 (p. 450).
3. Marcel Proust, *Le Carnet de 1908*, ed. Philip Kolb (Paris: Gallimard, 1976), p. 61.
4. Marcel Proust, *Correspondance de Marcel Proust*, ed. Philip Kolb, 21 vols (Paris: Plon, 1970–93), vol. 11, p. 252; cited in Christine M. Cano, *Proust's Deadline* (Urbana, IL: University of Illinois Press, 2007), p. 34.
5. Marcel Proust, *The Way by Swann's*, trans. Lydia Davis (London: Penguin, 2002), pp. 46–50.

6. Élie-Joseph Bois, 'À la recherche du temps perdu', *Le Temps*, 13 November 1913, p. 4, reproduced in *Du côté de chez Swann*, ed. Compagnon, pp. 451–3.
7. See Richard Bales, 'Proust and the Fine Arts', in *The Cambridge Companion to Proust*, ed. Richard Bales (Cambridge: Cambridge University Press, 2001), pp. 183–99.
8. See Inge Crosman Wimmers, *Proust and Emotion: The Importance of Affect in 'A la recherche du temps perdu'* (Toronto: University of Toronto Press, 2004).
9. Proust changed the title, fearing overlap with a contemporaneous publication, Gustave Binet-Valmer's *Le Cœur en désordre* [*Disorder of the Heart*].
10. Marcel Proust, *Sodom and Gomorrah*, trans. John Sturrock (London: Penguin, 2002), p. 159.
11. Samuel Beckett, *Proust/Three Dialogues with Georges Duthuit* (London: John Calder, 1965), pp. 42–3.
12. Beckett, *Proust*, p. 43.
13. Beckett, *Proust*, p. 60.
14. Sigmund Freud, *Introductory Lectures on Psychoanalysis*, trans. James Strachey (Harmondsworth: Penguin, 1974), p. 326. There is no specific mention of Freud in Proust's work. For an exploration of links between the two writers, see Malcolm Bowie, *Freud, Proust and Lacan: Theory as Fiction* (Cambridge: Cambridge University Press, 1987), especially Chapter 3, 'Freud and Proust', pp. 68–97.
15. Proust, *Against Sainte-Beuve and Other Essays*, trans. John Sturrock (Harmondworth: Penguin, 1994), p. 3.
16. Proust, *The Way by Swann's*, p. 22.
17. Proust, *The Way by Swann's*, p. 22.
18. Proust, *The Way by Swann's*, p. 23.
19. Samuel Beckett, *Molloy/Malone Dies/The Unnameable* (London: John Calder, 1959), p. 25; subsequently abbreviated to *Molloy* and referred to by page number in the text.
20. Proust, *The Way by Swann's*, p. 9.
21. Georges Bernanos, *The Diary of a Country Priest*, trans. Pamela Morris (London: Bodley Head, 1975), p. 50.
22. Nathalie Sarraute, *Tropisms* and *The Age of Suspicion*, trans. Maria Jolas (London: John Calder, 1963).
23. Nathalie Sarraute, 'Les deux réalités', *Esprit*, 329 (July 1964), pp. 72–5 (p. 72).
24. Paul Klee, 'Schöpferische Konfession', in *Tribune der Kunst und der Zeit* (Berlin: Erich Reiss, 1920), vol. 13, pp. 28–40 (p. 28).
25. Sarraute, 'Les deux réalités', p. 72.
26. Nathalie Sarraute, *Portrait of a Man Unknown*, trans. Maria Jolas (London: John Calder, 1959), p. 27.
27. Nathalie Sarraute, 'Tolstoï', *Les Lettres françaises*, 842 (22–8 September 1960), pp. 1, 5 (p. 1).
28. Roger McLure, *Sarraute, 'Le Planétarium'* (London: Grant and Cutler, 1987), p. 9.
29. Sarraute, *Tropisms* and *The Age of Suspicion*, p. 88.
30. Georges Bernanos, *The Star of Satan*, trans. Pamela Morris (London: John Lane, 1940).
31. Georges Bernanos, *Œuvres romanesques complètes* (Paris: Gallimard, 1961), p. 83; referred to in Jean-Yves Tadié, *Le Roman au XXᵉ siècle* (Paris: Belfond, 1990), p. 193.

32. Sarraute, *Tropisms* and *The Age of Suspicion*, p. 95.
33. Émile Henriot, 'Un nouveau roman', *Le Monde* (22 May 1957), pp. 8–9.
34. Alain Robbe-Grillet, *Jealousy*, trans. Richard Howard (New York: Grove, 1959).
35. Alain Robbe-Grillet, *Snapshots* and *Towards a New Novel*, trans. Barbara Wright (London: Calder and Boyars, 1965).
36. Tadié, *Le Roman au XXᵉ siècle*, p. 40.
37. Michel Butor, *Second Thoughts*, trans. Jean Stewart (London: Faber and Faber, 1958), p. 180.
38. Marcel Proust, *The Prisoner/The Fugitive*, trans. Carol Clark and Peter Collier (London: Penguin, 2002), p. 356.
39. Butor, *Second Thoughts*, p. 220.
40. Pierre-Louis Rey, 'Le roman au xxᵉ siècle', in *Histoire de la France littéraire: Modernités XIXᵉ–XXᵉ siècle*, ed. Patrick Berthier and Michel Jarrety (Paris: Presses Universitaires de France, 2006), pp. 43–90 (p. 78).
41. Butor, *Second Thoughts*, p. 64. Similarly, Proust's narrator writes: 'all these raw materials for a literary work were actually my past life'; Marcel Proust, *Finding Time Again*, trans. Ian Patterson (London: Penguin, 2002), p. 208.
42. As Martha Nussbaum reflects, 'Proust's novel addresses itself to a reader who is eager for understanding of her own loves'; *Upheavals of Thought: The Intelligence of Emotions* (Cambridge: Cambridge University Press, 2001), p. 514.
43. Michel Butor, 'Le roman comme recherche', in *Essais sur le roman* (Paris: Gallimard, 1992), pp. 7–14 (p. 11).
44. Butor, *Second Thoughts*, pp. 181–2.
45. André Breton, *Nadja*, trans. Richard Howard, intro. Mark Polizzotti (London: Penguin, 1999), p. 154.
46. Proust, *Du côté de chez Swann*, p. 453; Breton, *Nadja*, p. 143.
47. Claude Simon, *The Jardin des Plantes*, trans. Jordan Stump (Evanston, IL: Northwestern University Press, 2001), p. 40.
48. Claude Simon, *The Flanders Road*, trans. Richard Howard (London: John Calder, 1985), p. 22.
49. Claude Simon, *La Route des Flandres* (Paris: Minuit, 1960), p. 83; *The Flanders Road*, p. 69; Proust, *Sodom and Gomorrah*, p. 162. See above note 12.
50. Françoise van Rossum-Guyon, '"Ut pictura poesis"': A Reading of *La Bataille de Pharsale*' in (ed.) C. Britton, *Claude Simon* (London and New York: Longman, 1993), pp. 82–95 (p. 94).
51. Claude Simon, 'Fiction Word by Word' in (ed.) Britton, *Claude Simon*, pp. 41–5 (p. 44).
52. Interview with Claire Paulhan, *Les Nouvelles* (15–21 March 1984), 42–5 (p. 45).
53. Montaigne, 'On the Inconstancy of Our Actions', *The Complete Essays*, trans. M. A. Screech (London: Penguin, 1991), Book II, Essay 1, pp. 373–80 (p. 380).
54. Proust, *Finding Time Again*, p. 345.
55. Beckett, *Molloy*, p. 10.
56. Marguerite Duras, *The Lover*, trans. Barbara Bray (London: Collins, 1985), p. 8.
57. Duras, *The Lover*, p. 32.
58. Marthe Robert, *Origins of the Novel*, trans. Sacha Rabinovitch (Brighton: Harvester, 1980), p. 42.

59. Annie Ernaux, *A Woman's Story*, trans. Tanya Leslie (London: Quartet, 1990); Annie Ernaux, *Positions*, trans. Tanya Leslie (London: Quartet, 1991).
60. Nathalie Sarraute, *Childhood*, trans. Barbara Wright (London: John Calder, 1984), pp. 83–4. See Chapter 1 of Ann Jefferson, *Nathalie Sarraute, Fiction and Theory* (Cambridge: Cambridge University Press, 2000), pp. 17–38.
61. Proust, *The Way by Swann's*, p. 41.
62. Marcel Proust, *In the Shadow of the Young Girls in Flower*, trans. James Grieve (London: Penguin, 2002), pp. 367–8.
63. Marcel Proust, *The Guermantes Way*, trans. Mark Treharne (London: Penguin, 2002), pp. 131–3.
64. Duras, *The Lover*, p. 90.
65. Duras, *The Lover*, p. 11.
66. Georges Le Cardonnel, Review in *La Minerve française*, 15 January 1920 (4), pp. 219–23. See *Correspondance de Marcel Proust*, vol. 19, p. 73.
67. Qtd in David Ellison, *A Reader's Guide to Proust's 'In Search of Lost Time'* (Cambridge: Cambridge University Press, 2010), p. 3.
68. Sarraute, 'Les deux réalités', p. 72.

13

CHARLES FORSDICK

French literature as world literature

The entangled and problematic relationships between 'nation', 'language', and 'literature' are long-standing ones. The interconnections between these terms (as well as between the social and cultural phenomena they describe) have attracted considerable critical attention in the context of recent discussions of French (and more generally French-language) literature. This is not surprising, for it is scrutiny of this highly significant matrix of terms and phenomena that allows us to understand the processes of exclusion and inclusion whereby French literature as a national literature has evolved and been progressively reconstructed. At the same time, it permits analysis of the cultural practices and products according to which the limits of such a literature are identified, tested, and often creatively transgressed. The principal challenge in addressing such elastic concepts – each of which constitutes a significant keyword in its own right – remains that of recognizing the multiplicity of phenomena they may be seen to encompass and the range of understandings they may be thought to generate.

In the French case, it is the privileging of language which has often served to bind them together. Linda Hutcheon notes that, in general, 'European notions of the cultural identity of a people revolved around ideas not only of ethnic purity but of singular language',[1] and this is particularly true in France, where the monolingualizing tendencies of the post-Revolutionary state deployed French – as a language of administration, instruction, and social control – as a tool of centralization. The monolingual paradigm evident in this context asserts a clear coincidence of language, community, and place. Social coherence is defined linguistically, with literature in a national language serving as a key means of ensuring continuity. The postcolonial emergence of 'Francophone' voices has, however, firmly destabilized any sense of geographical fixity, linguistic singularity or hexagonal boundedness with which French literature may have been traditionally associated. This is an observation that is evident in a variety of critical attempts to uncouple the 'French' in 'French literature' from any overtly national associations: Peter France, for instance, proposed a firmly post-national and deterritorialized 'literature in French'; Roger Little, with the term 'Francographic', outlined a form of writing defined not by geography but by language alone; and Christie McDonald and Susan Suleiman have explored more recently what they dub 'French global', an expansive approach to literary production that resonates with the equally recent notion of a *littérature-monde en français* [world literature in French].[2]

Such alternative labels reveal the extent to which the role played by national literature in the creation and maintenance of a territorialized national identity, as well as in nurturing the sense of shared belonging and self-imagining on which this depends, has – since the aftermath of the Second World War and the wars of colonial independence – been placed under increasing pressure in France. This shift has occurred not least in a context in which the feasibility of any singularized model of national identity has been challenged by growing evidence of the transnational and translingual mobility, of the multilingualism, and of the cultural diversity of a globalized and increasingly digital world. At the same time, it is important to recognize that – in the wider French-speaking world – it is not only in multilingual locations outside France (most notably in Belgium, Quebec, Switzerland, and a number of other countries in North and Sub-Saharan African, the Caribbean, and the Indian Ocean) that language choice is a political act. France itself also has other (sub-)national languages, most notably Basque, Breton, and Provençal, the long-standing use of which is often an active rejection of the hegemony of French; it is also increasingly home to other languages that have accompanied more recent waves of migration and are now evident in the country's linguistic landscape, such as Arabic and Chinese.

The new approaches to literary history inherent in postcolonialism and in a project such as 'French global' have, moreover, encouraged a historicization of such shifts. Earlier manifestations of multilingual configurations – stretching back to the beginnings of a recognizably French literature in the medieval period – reveal the extent to which insistence on any neat coincidence of nation, language, and identity in a single body of texts is either mythological or ideological (and at times both). Such observations – relating in particular to questions of national identity and the politics of literature – were raised in a series of discussions held at the 'Étonnants Voyageurs' ['Astonishing Travellers'] festival in Saint-Malo in May 2013.[3] These were part of the Edinburgh World Writers' Conference, a peripatetic series of fifteen gatherings marking the fiftieth anniversary of the Edinburgh International Writers' Conference of August 1962.[4] The subjects of these Saint-Malo debates echoed those of sessions at the original event in Scotland, during which participants challenged the limitations of national literatures and posited the need for development of transnational connections for their reinvigoration. The tenor of these earlier exchanges was picked up in Saint-Malo in 2013 by the translingual author of Bosnian origin Velibor Čolić in a reflection entitled 'Le chant des guerriers – la littérature nationaliste' ['The Song of the Warriors – Nationalist Literature'] that served as prelude to a discussion on the question 'Is there a national literature?'[5] Drawing on his personal experience in the former Yugoslavia, he stated on the subject of his paper: 'The following text is not a questionnaire on national literature, still less a scientific enquiry; it is a bitter realization: the boundary between a national literature and a nationalist literature is very slight.'[6] His thesis was that some of the worst crimes of the late twentieth century are to be seen as extreme by-products of national literatures at the point at which they tip into becoming nationalist. This claim has, not surprisingly, been challenged, especially by Sub-Saharan African authors, from whom the frame of the national continued to provide a means of resistance to external, global forces. The choice of Čolić, who since 1998 has been writing his novels directly into French, was, however, a deliberately strategic one, an illustration of the contemporary challenges to, and current transformations of, French national literature with which writers of non-French origin are actively associated. Responding to the question 'Should literature be political?', the author of Afghan origin Atiq Rahimi (whose *Syngué sabour* [*The Patience Stone*] was awarded the Prix Goncourt in 2008) summed up the potentially leavening effect of the writer from elsewhere who comes to the French language as an outsider: 'By changing our place in the world, we will finish some day by changing the world.'[7]

This chapter seeks to explore the recent emergence within French literature of a substantial group of authors known increasingly as 'translingual', in other words those whose relationship to France, French, and Frenchness is not based primarily on colonialism and its afterlives, but is linked instead to a choice to migrate culturally, linguistically and usually also geographically into a sphere of French influence. The phenomenon is not a new one and has firm historical precedents. Though customarily personal, this choice is not necessarily a free one, and the active francophilia of some translingual writers is to be counterbalanced with the enforced displacement of others. In one of the most helpful studies of this phenomenon in French, Robert Jouanny links the circumstances that lead to an author migrating translingually to the French language to a series of 'Francophone singularities', suggesting a variety of motivations – often elided in accounts of these authors that seek to present them collectively – for those who elected and were not obliged to work in French.[8] The writings of such authors therefore often lack evidence of the clear patterns seen in the work of postcolonial authors, for whom the relationship to the French language and to France itself is regularly marked by inequalities in the distribution of power and by traces of domination. Although at times the product of semi-colonial situations, the translingual writer relates more often to his or her adopted medium of expression in terms of active affiliation or affinity, which is to say '"coming to French" rather than being born into it'.[9] Anne-Rosine Delbert identifies two principal camps of translingual writers: the 'sedentary ones' (such as Julien Green and Patrick Besson), who acquire French in a domestic environment; and the 'nomads' (such as Jorge Semprún), for whom the encounter with the language occurs as a result of the disruption of departure and resettlement.[10] Choice of French may, moreover, be political or aesthetic, and linguistic selection may contain an additional degree of arbitrariness: as Stephen Kellman notes, had Vladimir Nabokov not been forced to flee Paris for the United States in 1940 he might subsequently have become a great French writer.[11]

Identifying translingualism: historical precedent and contemporary practice

It is also important to recognize the history of the modern and contemporary phenomenon, linked in particular to the ways in which France and the French language served throughout the eighteenth and nineteenth centuries for writers and intellectuals throughout Europe. The emergence of the phenomenon known as 'world literature' (*littérature-monde*) has suggested, however, that the early twenty-first century may be seen as a quintessentially 'translingual' moment, although it is important to recognize twentieth-century precedents, triggered not least by the political upheavals of revolution and war. Samuel Beckett, Romain Gary, Joseph Kessel, and Nathalie Sarraute belong to an earlier generation of such authors. Included in this group is also the Russian-born author Irène Némirovsky, recognized posthumously in 2004 when her novel *Suite française* was awarded the Prix Renaudot, but prominent also in the interwar period when she was associated with the search for a writer who might be dubbed the 'French Conrad'. This term was used in the results of a survey published in *Les Nouvelles littéraires* between March and May 1940.[12] The *enquête* was conducted by the Anglo-French journalist Georges Higgins, and was triggered in part by the award of the Prix Goncourt to Henri Troyat for *L'Araigne* [*The Spider*] in 1938. Its context was, however, firmly that of the *drôle de guerre* [phoney war], and publication of *Les Nouvelles littéraires* would indeed be discontinued shortly after the series of articles had appeared as a result of the Nazi occupation. This early enquiry into what would subsequently be known as translingual writing in French was consequently related to one of the most acute crises of national identity in the twentieth century, reflecting the place of literary production in such questions.

The terms of the questionnaire on which the survey was based merit attention, not least because they reveal a further stage in ongoing debates around Anglo-French cultural rivalry. Three decades earlier, an inferiority complex relating to French colonial literature had been articulated in terms of the search for 'le Kipling français' (a quest triggered by Kipling's receipt of the Nobel Prize for Literature in 1907).[13] The identification of a potentially reinvigorating external – translingual – input into French interwar literary culture was presented instead as the activity of a group 'French Conrads', an ambivalent designation that again constructs an English-language benchmark, while suggesting that it might be met or even surpassed by an author who instead elected to migrate to French. Ten authors responded to the 1940 survey, including Némirovsky and Troyat, as well as Jean Malaquais, Joseph Kessel, and Julien Green. The responses suggest an eclecticism in these authors' various relationships to France and the French language that is similar to the variety of allegiances and motivations characterizing contemporary translingual writing. Kessel brushes off any comparison with Conrad, underlining the place that France and French had played in his life since childhood, suggesting he saw himself as bi- rather than translingual. Némirovsky describes a similarly sustained association with France. However, of the respondents to the survey, it is she who reflects most clearly on the implications of biculturalism, expressing a wish to be seen as 'more a French writer than a Russian', but presenting her translingual identity and practice in terms of a continuum and as an amalgamation of perceived origin and adopted home: 'it is impossible for me to distinguish where one ends and the other starts'. The provenance of the authors is presented in national terms, although the inclusion of the author of German origin Ernst Erich Noch and Némirovsky herself (who would subsequently die in Auschwitz in 1942) suggests in the context of 1940 an inclusivity and openness that would rapidly be suppressed in the Vichy years.

The identification of this group of authors suggests an awareness that the diversification of French literature through the external input of the translingual writer does not so much constitute a threat as a source of potential literary reinvigoration; what remains unclear is whether this manoeuvre represents (to adopt a colonial metaphor) an 'associationist' one, disrupting the boundaries of national literary production, or is rather 'assimilationist', reflecting the capacity of French literature to renew itself through the recuperation, absorption, and normalization of contributions perceived to be external. These poles remain highly relevant for analysis of contemporary translingual literature in French. The *Nouvelles littéraires* survey also makes it clear that translingual authors – like postcolonial authors – do not write according to a formula, and that their work is inevitably shaped by the individual circumstances that motivated their linguistic migration. At the same time, the degree to which such writers acknowledge their translingualism is variable, although it is evident that the sources and lived implications of the phenomenon have a thematic as well as linguistic impact. For translingual writers share, to varying degrees, a relationship to the French language and to France itself that may be characterized as one of 'strangerhood', meaning that it is legitimate to ask whether – in Susan Suleiman's terms – their writing reveals a 'preoccupation with language, identity and foreignness that distinguishes it from the works of monolingual French writers'.[14] Such a question fails, of course, to acknowledge that such a distinction is evident in the work of several sub-national and diasporic groups within France whose mother tongue is not the country's dominant language, and whose relationship to French is accordingly problematized; it also does not reflect the observation in the work of key Francophone thinkers such as Jacques Derrida, Édouard Glissant, and Abdelkebir Khatibi that monolingualism does not necessarily betoken a proprietorial relationship to a single language and indeed tends to disguise connections even within a national literature to a multiplicity of different languages. This is an observation that is pertinent for the writing practice of many translingual authors.

In an important essay in 2002 cited above, Linda Hutcheon explores the importance of 'rethinking the national model' – and in particular the dominance of the national model, with its reliance on 'ethnic and often linguistic singularity, not to say purity' – in literary studies.[15] Writing dubbed 'postcolonial', produced in or beyond France, challenges any ethnic or geographical criterion whereby French literature may previously have been defined. Translingual writing signals in addition the need for rethinking notions of linguistic boundaries. To the 'French Kipling' and the 'French Conrad' we might now add the 'French Rushdie', an imagined figure who emerged in the 1990s, most notably in relation to discussions about the future of French national literature generated in the periodical *Gulliver* and the 'Étonnants Voyageurs' festival in Saint-Malo, both of which rose to prominence in the early 1990s. Linked by the Pour une littérature voyageuse [for a travelling literature] movement, *Gulliver* and 'Étonnants Voyageurs' were part of an anti-structuralist, neo-realist return to narrative that sought to promote 'a literature which articulates the real' ('une littérature qui dise le réel'). Inspired by the cross-Channel model of *Granta*, the authors associated with this group sensed a deficit and even a crisis in French literature where they found no openness either to travel writers similar to Bruce Chatwin or to

postcolonial writers similar to Salman Rushdie. The 1992 manifesto of the
Pour une littérature voyageuse group already appears to reflect its preten-
tions to foster a form of world writing.[16]

Translingual writing and *littérature-monde*

The 1990s witnessed further shifts in the French literary landscape, primarily
as a result of the award of numerous major prizes to key 'Francophone'
authors such as Tahar Ben Jelloun and Patrick Chamoiseau. Frustration at
the continued assertion of national frames in which French-language literature was seen to be produced and consumed, at the persistent division
between 'French' and 'Francophone' writers, as well as at the perceived
hierarchy between their works, led a group of authors previously associated
with the Saint-Malo festival to launch, in March 2007, a manifesto 'Pour une
littérature-monde en français' ('For a world literature in French').[17] This
publication – as well as the controversies it generated – has attracted considerable critical attention, not least because of the apparent oxymoronic
aspiration it articulates for a literature that is at once global and monolingual. The manifesto also fails to acknowledge the importance of the sociol-
ogy of literature and of recognition of the ways in which phenomena such as
prizes (presented by the signatories as a positive means of affirmation) tend to
shore up the inequalities that the manifesto seeks to denounce.[18] What
nevertheless remains positive about the intervention is the extent to which
the manifesto rendered public long-standing disquiet over the role of
'Francophone literature' as a cultural ghetto. It also – in describing 'language
freed from its exclusive pact with the nation, free henceforth from any
powers other than those of poetry and imagination, whose only boundaries
will be those of the mind' – challenges the continued pertinence of the
national as a category for understanding twenty-first-century literary production. Translingual writing plays a key role in these debates, and at least
four of the manifesto's forty-four signatories (the Canadian Nancy Huston;
the German-born Esther Orner, of Polish origin and now resident in Israel;
the Chinese-born author Dai Sijie; and the Slovenian Brina Svit) may be seen
to belong to that category. The context of the intervention – outlined in the
opening sentence of the manifesto – was the award the previous autumn of
five of France's major literary prizes to 'writers from beyond-France' ('des
écrivains d'outre-France'): the Prix Goncourt and the Grand Prix du roman
de l'Académie française to Jonathan Littel for *Les Bienveillantes* [*The Kindly
Ones*]; the Renaudot to Alain Mabanckou for *Mémoires de porc-épic*
[*Memoirs of a Porcupine*]; the Femina to Nancy Huston for *Lignes de faille*
[*Fault Lines*]; and the Goncourt des lycéens to Léonora Miano for *Contours*

du jour qui vient [*Contours of the Coming Day*]. The designation 'des écrivains d'outre-France' is an elastic one, for it includes Francophone post-colonial authors Mabankou (from the Congo) and Miano (from Cameroon) as well as Littel and Huston, both translingual authors of North American origin with differing relationships to the French language. This conflation disguises the erasure of different histories at the centre of the manifesto, and the convergence of often very different modes of writing in French that the document assumes. The central target of the signatories remains a narrowly defined French national literature, reminiscent in its description more of a nineteenth-century nation-based model than the eclectic postcolonial, post-modern assemblage that has characterized literary production in French since the 1980s. Central to the manifesto was nevertheless a sense that a very different, post-national frame was required to understand the production of contemporary literature in French.

This emergent *littérature-monde en français* would appear thus to be not only deterritorialized, but also dehistoricized, the product not of a series of French-speaking nation spaces, but of a more hazily defined Francosphere. Responses to the manifesto focused on its polemical assault on Francophonia as a literary category: in the text itself, the signatories presented their work as the 'death certificate of Francophonie', a move denounced by advocates of the postcolonial political apparatus that the term often designates, but welcomed by those who had long sought a transcendence of the French/Francophone binary divide. Often lost in these debates, however, was the distinctiveness of translingual writing, and the fact that the 2006 prize laureates listed above were part of a clear pattern of cultural recognition evident around such literary production since the final two decades of the twentieth century: in 1995, the Goncourt and the Goncourt des lycéens were awarded to what may be seen as the archetypal contemporary translingual text, *Le Testament français* [*The French Testament*] by Andreï Makine, a work that was also recognized by the Prix Médicis (also awarded, exceptionally, that year to *La Langue maternelle* [*Mother Tongue*] by Vassilis Alexakis); François Cheng and Dai Sijie had won the Femina in 1998 and 2003 for *Le Dit de Tianyi* [*The Tale of Tianyi*] and *Le Complexe de Di* [*Mr Muo's Traveling Couch*] respectively; and Némirovsky had, as has been noted, been awarded a posthumous Renaudot for *Suite française* in 2004. Factoring the distinctiveness of translingual writing back into contemporary debates around *littérature-monde* underlines the importance of discerning new ways of approaching literary history while allowing recognition that disruption of the category of the 'national' in debates regarding French literature has a longer history than the *littérature-monde* manifesto implies.

Expanding translingualism: rethinking the national frame

A recent proliferation of studies on translingual writing has underlined the contemporary visibility of the phenomenon in a variety of contexts, while excavating its historical precedents and their cross-cultural reach. Kellman has provided one of the most useful overviews, presenting translingualism as the defiance of linguistic boundaries and as the mockery of any attempt to create hierarchies between them. By identifying Samuel Beckett and Eugène Ionesco as two early (French) practitioners, he highlights the ways in which the theatre of the absurd, with its foregrounding of a language stretched to breaking point, may be seen as the archetypal stage for translingual concerns. Kellman is keenly aware, however, of the instability of the label 'translingual' and the variety of linguistic engagements it betokens. He outlines a 'taxonomy of literary translingualism', distinguishing, for instance, between 'ambilinguals', who would have written important literary works in more than one language (such as Beckett and Alexakis, equally at home in English and French, and Greek and French respectively), and 'monolingual translinguals', who have elected to work only in their adopted language.[19] Translingualism suggests, however, a linguistic dislocation and an associated adoption of another language in a process that is customarily more personal than collective. Translingual writing is often also associated with self-translation. This process is either a systematic means of creating two texts in parallel (as is the case with Alexakis), or becomes a subterfuge (adopted for example by Makine who, to attract publishers, was initially forced to present his texts as pseudotranslations). Such works are not to be conflated with translation, however, and provide a very different model of literary production, circulation, and reception. It is increasingly apparent that the contemporary phenomena of globalization and post-monolingualism have clear implications for the ways in which texts are generated, produced, and consumed.

Translingual literature has emerged in different forms in different linguistic traditions. Translingual writing in English has, for instance, a dynamic of its own, associated with the dominant role (as well as with the sheer scale and diversity) of the Anglosphere. There are as a result clear tensions between Anglophone translingualism and that in other languages, meaning that there cannot be a universal understanding of translingualism. The French case remains, as a result, very different, not least because the linguistic strangeness generated by authors who migrate from other languages into French is more often generated not by disruption, but by a knowing intimacy with, proximity to, and often deep respect for French literary language. This is one of the reasons why translingual writing in French may be seen in part as a work of continuity and confirmation rather than the signal of radical new direction in French literature.

Works belonging to this category tend to be absorbed into existing publishing processes and other circuits of validation such as literary prizes. While welcomed into a French canon, translingual writers nevertheless have the potential actively to diversify and on occasion even disrupt these processes of literary production. There is no single translingual paradigm, and Francophilia certainly does not serve as the default position of the writer who migrates translingually to French. While many translingual texts serve to explore subject matter related to the geographical, cultural, and often linguistic origins of their authors, this material is also regularly approached in terms of intercultural contact or of the progressive hybridization of the literary gaze.

Between languages and cultures: Makine, Alexakis, Dai

Many translingual writers adopt the myth of French as a language of liberty, a tendency exemplified by the Polish-born writer Marek Halter, for whom French is 'the only language in which I have experienced no oppression'.[20] At the same time, translingual writers often appear to be tasked with defending French culture against perceived decadence and decline. This tendency is evident in the openness of institutions such as the Académie française to authors who have adopted French as their language of expression (translingual authors to join the *immortels* include Eugène Ionesco (in 1970), and more recently François Cheng (2002) and Michael Edwards (2013)). Such inclusiveness reflects what may be seen as an openness of French literature to outside contributions, but also indicates the extent to which acceptance into French literature is filtered and seen to be associated with responsibilities and even indebtedness. This is a position with which Andreï Makine is associated, not least when he evokes 'that ineffable French essence that interested me above all'.[21]

Makine is an author of Soviet origin whose acquisition of French was the result of early exposure to the language. Without access to contemporary French literature, he read classic texts (notably Proust, who serves as a clear intertext for *Le Testament français*), and discovered in them a counterpoint to the Soviet propaganda of his schooling. The French language becomes associated as a result with visions of freedom, but of a freedom to which he was not granted full or equal access. For having moved to France, Makine was obliged to present his early works as self-translations or pseudo-translations in order to attract the interest of publishers – and was even obliged on one occasion to translate his French manuscript into Russian for a publisher wishing to see its 'original' version. These anecdotes – included in *Le Testament français* – eloquently reveal the expectation that the work of writers from elsewhere, even if permitted to be written and published in French, is associated with a sense of residual exoticism. The reception of the writings of translingual authors often reflects this appetite for socio-ethnographic 'authenticity' about authors' cultural origins, but, although *Le Testament français* may be seen to cater for a French imagination of Russia (as well as of French cultural superiority), the text is in fact a much more subtle reflection on cross-cultural representation and on the narrator's negotiation at various stages of his life of bilingualism, biculturalism, and the shifting and ambiguous Franco-Russian identity.

Le Testament français is primarily a *Bildungsroman*, an account of the evolution of its narrator's attitude to, and relationship with France and French, and a reflection as a result on language, culture, and identity. The evolution in the narrator's relationship with the language is mapped onto geographical movement as an initially vicarious association through family ties is replaced by an actual move to France in later life. Nevertheless, the French language is associated from the outset with conversations with the narrator's grandmother and with the narratives and memorabilia that link her to her French past – and is as a result seen as a 'fabulous grafting in our hearts', a 'family dialect' or 'intimate argot' that functions as a naturalized language.[22] As he grows up, however, and becomes at a particular moment conscious of making a linguistic error (in fact, of hesitating between two possible terms in French), he reaches a realization that the French he speaks is a foreign language – an 'instrument-language used, refined, perfected'[23] – whose potential is to allow literary transcription and even re-enchantment of the everyday. French becomes a 'language of astonishment', providing escape not so much from a Soviet reality as from what Gabriella Safran calls the 'banality of an ordinary, monolingual life'.[24] Even when he appears to write in a single language – French – Makine does not therefore locate himself monolingually, but sees his interstitial location, 'between two languages', as a site of intense experience and perception, and also of enhanced creativity.[25] As a translingual writer, he aspires to produce an 'intermediary language' that encapsulates the state of being in a 'between-two-languages'.[26] Translation, as a shuttling between languages, is as a result central to the text, but not in the reductively inter-linguistic sense that posits a binary relationship between an imagined Russian 'original' and a French text passed off as a pseudo-translation. Translation is seen instead as a form of translingual re-creation.

In the novel's concluding twist, the reader is returned to the Russian gulag to discover an unexpected truth about the woman the narrator had thought was his biological mother. Not only does this revelation imply that the liberation with which the acquisition of French is associated is only partial; but it also suggests that the narrator's links to France and the French language were learnt or acquired, and not genetically inherited. In Makine's account, allegiance to a national culture and its linguistic manifestations has few links to biology, and is associated more with the power of the imagination. Like many translingual authors, Makine ultimately defies those who seek to categorize his work or reduce it to a single linguistic tradition. As Agata Sylwestrzak-Wszelaki notes, it is unclear whether he is a 'Russian writer in the French language' or a 'French novelist of Russian origin',[27] not least because his work, though written in French, aspires to maintenance of a balance between the author's two languages. Makine defies such a binary choice between allegiances, but Le Testament français ends with a silence: 'I only lacked the words that could say it.'[28] Moving beyond the monolingualism of a national literary tradition towards a genuinely translingual form of expression remains an aspiration, only partially realized in the text itself, but Makine's achievement is nevertheless to open literature in French to the possibilities of such a manoeuvre.

The self-conscious exploration of language acquisition and of the interstitial experience of personal identity to which this leads motivates in different ways the work of Vassilis Alexakis, whose Langue maternelle shared with Le Testament français the Prix Médicis in 1995. Marianne Bessy has described Alexakis's work as 'a twin text',[29] often written simultaneously in French and Greek, and dependent otherwise on a discipline of self-translation. Like Makine, Alexakis expresses uncertainty over his own literary classification: 'My publisher himself admitted to me that he was puzzled: should he put me in his French literature series or his foreign literature series?'[30] Having written his first three novels in French in the 1970s, Alexakis returned to Greek in the 1980s to publish Talgo, but then began to work again in French, writing La Langue maternelle in Greek (but allowing it to appear first in its French version) and Les Mots étrangers [Foreign Words] in French. This process of alternation is modulated by the process of self-translation, and the majority of works written by Alexakis in Greek have been published in French first, raising questions common to translingual writing of what constitutes the 'copy' and what the 'original'.

Much of Alexakis's work focuses on the experience of living between French and Greek, between France and Greece, a theme whose geographical reality is central to his work Paris–Athènes (1997). This text is an account of shuttling between languages and places. A narrative motivated by the fear of losing his Greek, it constitutes a search to understand not so much the meaning of being bilingual (which, as a condition, is not rare), but rather the challenges of being a translingual author. Alexakis has noted: 'Languages are difficult to learn but easy to forget',[31] and it is the fear of forgetting Greek that motivates *La Langue maternelle*, a novel of linguistic loss triggered by the death of the narrator Pavlos's mother and by a comment made by a former partner Vaguélio who says that, after twenty-four years in Paris, the narrator speaks his mother tongue as a foreigner would. The work describes a return to Greece and the accompanying experience of double linguistic alienation as the language loss associated with exile is supplemented by changes to the Greek language in the post-dictatorship period. The return to the 'mother tongue' of the title is pursued via the narrator's search to understand the enigmatic epsilon in the inscription at the temple at Delphi. In a notebook whose writing is in parallel to that of the text, Pavlos ascribes to this character various explanations that chime with his own concerns described in the text: *ekpatrisménos* [expatriated], *épistrophi* [the return], *ta ellènika* [my mother tongue]. His conclusion, however, is that it represents *ellipsi* [lack].[32] The Delphic epsilon indicates the possibility of knowledge, but at the same time betokens an absence – of voice, of language, of familial ties. In focusing on a sense of lack, Alexakis concludes the quest for return with a sense of self-estrangement, with what Bessy describes as 'a need for foreignness, for distance, and for non-conformity in relation to the place they are from and in relation to their own subjectivity'.[33] *La Langue maternelle* ends – as does *Le Testament français* – with a sense of lack and a threat of silence.

For Alexakis, the relationship to French remains nevertheless an ambiguous one. *Les Mots étrangers* (2002) is an autofictional work, recounting language acquisition, in which – following the death of his father – the narrator at the age of fifty-two decides to learn Sango, the language of the Central African Republic (of which there are around 400,000 speakers). The acquisition of this third language, seemingly unrelated to French and Greek, allows him to 'fall back into a world of linguistic strangeness',[34] to distance himself from his languages of literary expression and to see both more objectively. As such, it narrates the discovery of a linguistic third space, the identification of which permits a reconfiguration of the relationship between his two customary languages of expression. By extracting himself, via his engagement with Sango, from the languages he customarily deploys for literary expression, Alexakis proposes a degree of self-reflexivity that is not unusual in translingual writing, and outlines, on a metacritical level, the linguistic challenges faced by the author who comes to French from outside the language.

Whereas Alexakis and Makine situate themselves in relation to French literature through a reflection on communication and on their rapport with the French language, other translingual authors allude explicitly in their work to the corpus of texts in relation to which, by adopting French, they will be located. A key example of such an approach is Dai Sijie's *Balzac et la petite tailleuse chinoise* [*Balzac and the Little Chinese Seamstress*] (2000), a novel that reflects explicitly on the mobility of texts between national traditions – and on the transformed meanings that such movement implies. Dai is a representative of what Yinde Zhang dubs a substantial tradition of 'francophonie chinoise' [Chinese francophonia], a group of authors first evident in the work of early twentieth-century authors such as Tcheng Ki-tung and Cheng Tcheng, and represented more recently by the novels, poetry, memoirs, and theatre of key figures such as the *académicien* François Cheng and the Nobel laureate Gao Xingjian.[35] *Balzac et la petite tailleuse chinoise* is set during the Cultural Revolution in Mao's China, and describes the ways in which the rural re-education of its bourgeois protagonists is supplemented by the discovery of a suitcase of Chinese translations of clandestine Western novels (including, as the title suggests, works by Balzac). French literature awakens a talent for storytelling in the narrator, and becomes a source of resistance and self-discovery in what is in many ways another *Bildungsroman*. The novel was a commercial success, both in its first French edition and in its numerous translations. The reception of the work – similar to that of *Le Testament français* – often presented the novel, however, as an exotic text, describing a radically different cultural milieu, which nevertheless posited the superior, subversive, and even civilizing potential of French culture.

While it is true that the French literary texts in the novel provide the protagonists with an escape from their forced labour, Dai presents them in a distorted form, translated, reinterpreted, re-inscribed, and re-narrated by the boys as they seek to use the works in a parallel re-education of the seamstress of the title. As such, the novel presents what Zhang dubs a 'Balzac exported and reimported',[36] a cross-cultural and translingual rewriting of French classics. The work's true impact on the French reader is not one of comforting confirmation of the superiority of a French literary tradition, but is instead one of profound defamiliarization. These transformations are particularly marked in the case of the little seamstress, whom the protagonists see as a rustic Madame Bovary figure in need of instruction, but who – in escaping their attentions and leaving her environment for the city – effects a radical rewriting of a French classic by defying the narrative that the protagonists had suggested for her. As Karen L. Thornber notes, the dynamics of such a translingual refiguring of canonical works are complex, 'problematizing French discourse in Chinese (translation) in Chinese discourse in French (translation)'.[37] Like Makine and Alexakis, Dai has been subjected to various forms of taxonomic recuperation. The absorption of his work into French national literary culture has been supplemented most notably by inclusion in the category of 'Overseas Chinese Literature'.[38] A close reading of the text reveals, however, its author's resistance to any such classification, and the challenge it constitutes – through its subject matter as well as through its poetics of representation – to a singularized literary categorization, whether this be national or diasporic.

Conclusion: beyond monolingualism

Translingual literature in French constitutes a variegated corpus in terms of subject matter, of style, of the origin of the writer, and of the author's investment in French literature. Many of the texts in that corpus have never-theless in recent years been recognized by French prize culture and drawn actively into the French literary field. Notwithstanding such institutional recuperation, translingual writing in French leads increasingly to recognition of the need for a transcultural approach to literary history. Such an under-standing acknowledges, on the one hand, that literature in French is itself always already culturally diverse, regulated according to national frames but persistently spilling beyond them; and it makes necessary, on the other, an awareness of the frames of cultural diversity and multilingualism in which literary works – even within a single language tradition – emerge and evolve. As such, translingualism is in the vanguard of a disruptive but increasingly pervasive paradigm of post-monolingualism, a reminder that the monolin-gual orientation of literary expression is under increasing pressure – exposed as the legacy of a set of assumptions that solidified in Western Europe in the eighteenth century, and led to the singularization and equation of language, nation, community, identity, and place.

Translingual literature betokens a loosening of monolingualizing pressure, and constitutes a particular form of the multilingual practices available in literature, the extreme of which is the radical linguistic mixing in texts evident, for instance, in the contemporary poetry of a writer such as Caroline Bergvall. It is evident that French literary culture has the mechanisms to recuperate and assimilate difference – many of the texts mentioned above are, for instance, gathered in the Folio collection – and perhaps it is the ambilingual author such as Alexakis who maintains maximum freedom, since he draws on each of the linguistic systems with which he is associated without creating a firm alle-giance to either. The presence of translingual writers serves a dual purpose, simultaneously radical and conservative, disrupting a national tradition, but maintaining the distinctiveness of French as a world language that seeks to punch above its weight. National literatures have a tendency to retain their coherence despite pressures to the contrary, and the absorption of translingual writing reflects in part their ability to reinvent themselves.

What is nevertheless clear is that the traditional 'linguistic family romance' of which literature is an essential vehicle is under increasing strain as we see the potential for national literatures to be de-colonized, de-ethnicized, and de-territorialized. Translingual literature in French is often, however, more about the demonstration of potential or the indication of cultural complexity than the actual performance of new literary possibilities. As such, it can be associated with the recurrent 'passionate search for new forms' that Makine associates with 'francité' [Frenchness],[39] a form of continuous self-renewal that, in this case, draws on resources from without. It is clear that such writing permits an openness to linguistic and cultural diversity and even to multi-lingualism, but within a space that is (pace Glissant and others) ostensibly still monolingual. At the same time, however, translingual authors encourage us to read literature in French – and to understand the genesis of that literature – in ways that adopt what Robert Stam has called a 'relational, contrapuntal, polycommunal multiperspectival history'.[40] In the light of this idea, translingual writing in French would appear to allow us a glimpse of French as a language detached from its close ties to a single nation, of French literature as a body of texts whose transnational dimensions are fully apparent. It remains to be seen whether our capacities and expectations as readers are prepared for such a shift, and whether the institutions of the French literary establishment are willing to accommodate the full implications of such a change.

NOTES

This chapter was completed while Charles Forsdick was Arts and Humanities Research Council Theme Leadership Fellow for 'Translating Cultures' (AH/K503381/1); he records his thanks to the AHRC for its support.
1. Linda Hutcheon, 'Rethinking the National Model', in *Rethinking Literary History*, ed. Linda Hutcheon and Mario J. Valdés (New York: Oxford University Press, 2002), pp. 3–49 (p. 17).
2. Peter France, ed., *The New Oxford Companion to Literature in French* (Oxford: Oxford University Press, 1995); Roger Little, 'World Literature in French; or Is Francophonie Frankly Phoney?', *European Review*, 9 (2001), 421–36; and Christie McDonald and Susan Rubin Suleiman, ed., *French Global: A New Approach to Literary History* (New York: Columbia University Press, 2010).
3. For information on the festival, see http://www.etonnants-voyageurs.com (accessed 7 July 2015).
4. On the Edinburgh event in 1962, see Angela Bartie and Eleanor Bell, ed., *The International Writers' Conference Revisited: Edinburgh. 1962* (Glasgow: Cargo Publishing, 2012).
5. For the text of Čolić's intervention, see http://www.etonnants-voyageurs.com/spip.php?article11359 (accessed 7 July 2015). An edited version appears as

'Words of War', in *The Twenty-First-Century Novel: Notes from the Edinburgh World Writers' Conference*, ed. Jonathan Bastable and Hannah McGill (Edinburgh: Edinburgh University Press, 2014), pp. 238–41.

6. All translations in this chapter are my own unless otherwise stated.

7. Atiq Rahimi, 'Words as Pledge', in *The Twenty-First-Century Novel: Notes from the Edinburgh World Writers' Conference*, ed. Jonathan Bastable and Hannah McGill (Edinburgh: Edinburgh University Press, 2014), pp. 139–43 (p. 143).

8. Robert Jouanny, *Singularités francophones, ou Choisir d'écrire en français* (Paris: Presses universitaires de France, 2000).

9. Susan Rubin Suleiman, 'Choosing French: Language, Foreignness, and the Canon (Beckett/Némirovsky)', in *French Global: A New Approach to Literary History*, ed. Christie McDonald and Susan Rubin Suleiman (New York: Columbia University Press, 2010), pp. 471–87 (p. 472).

10. Anne-Rosine Delbert, *Les Exilés du langage: Un siècle d'écrivains français venus d'ailleurs (1919–2000)* (Paris: Pulim, 2005).

11. Stephen Kellman, *The Translingual Imagination* (Lincoln, NE: University of Nebraska Press, 2000), p. 64.

12. Three articles appeared in *Les Nouvelles littéraires* on 30 March 1940 (with responses from Henri Troyat, Ernst Erich Noth, André Beucler), 6 April (with responses from Irène Némirovsky, A. Roubé-Jansky, and Jean Malaquais), and 4 May (with responses from Joseph Kessel, Julien Green, Elian J. Finbert, Farjallah Haik, and Ventura García Calderón).

13. On 'le Kipling français', see Yaël Schlick, 'The "French Kipling": Pierre Mille's Popular Colonial Fiction', *Comparative Literature Studies*, 34.3 (1997), 226–41.

14. Suleiman, 'Choosing French', p. 473.

15. Hutcheon, 'Rethinking the National Model', p. 3.

16. Alain Borer, Nicolas Bouvier, Michel Chaillou, et al., *Pour une littérature voyageuse* (Brussels: Complexe, 1992).

17. For the text of the manifesto, see http://www.lemonde.fr/livres/article/2007/03/15/des-ecrivains-plaident-pour-un-roman-en-francais-ouvert-sur-le-monde_883572_3260.html (accessed 7 July 2015).

18. On the manifesto, see Jacqueline Dutton, '*Littérature-monde* or Francophonie? From the manifesto to the great debate', *Essays in French Literature and Culture*, 45 (2008), 43–68; and Alec Hargreaves, Charles Forsdick, and David Murphy, ed., *Transnational French Studies: Postcolonialism and Littérature-monde* (Liverpool: Liverpool University Press, 2010).

19. Kellman, *The Translingual Imagination*, p. 12.

20. Qtd in Delbart, *Les Exilés du langage*, pp. 130, 131.

21. Andreï Makine, *Cette France qu'on oublie d'aimer* (Paris: Flammarion, 2006), p. 23.

22. Andreï Makine, *Le Testament français* (Paris: Mercure de France, 1995), pp. 56, 41.

23. Makine, *Le Testament français*, p. 271.

24. Makine, *Le Testament français*, p. 271; Gabriella Safran, 'Andreï Makine's Literary Bilingualism and the Critics', *Comparative Literature*, 55.3 (2003), 246–65 (p. 256).

25. Makine, *Le Testament français*, p. 272.

26. Makine, *Le Testament français*, p. 279.

27. Agata Sylwestrzak-Wszelaki, *Andreï Makine: L'identité problématique* (Paris: L'Harmattan, 2010), p. 22.
28. Makine, *Le Testament français*, p. 343.
29. Marianne Bessy, *Vassilis Alexakis: Exorciser l'exil* (Amsterdam: Rodopi, 2011), p. 88.
30. Vassilis Alexakis, *Paris–Athènes* (Paris: Fayard, 1997), p. 18.
31. Vassilis Alexakis, in *La Langue française vue de la Méditerranée*, ed. Patrice Martin and Christophe Drevet (Léchelle: Zellige, 2009), pp. 15–18 (p. 15).
32. Vassilis Alexakis, *La Langue maternelle* (Paris: Gallimard, 1995), p. 412.
33. Bessy, *Vassilis Alexakis: Exorciser l'exil*, p. 98.
34. Bessy, *Vassilis Alexakis: Exorciser l'exil*, p. 122.
35. Yinde Zhang, *Littérature comparée et perspectives chinoises* (Paris: L'Harmattan, 2008).
36. Zhang, *Littérature comparée et perspectives chinoises*, p. 136.
37. Karen L. Thornber, 'French Discourse in Chinese, in Chinese Discourse in French: Paradoxes of Chinese Francophone Émigré Writing', *Contemporary French and Francophone Studies*, 13.2 (2009), 223–32 (p. 230).
38. Laifong Leung, 'Overseas Chinese Literature: A Proposal for Clarification', in *Reading Chinese Transnationalisms: Society, Literature, Film*, ed. Maria Ng and Philip Holden (Hong Kong: Hong Kong University Press, 2006), pp. 117–27.
39. Makine, *Cette France qu'on oublie d'aimer*, p. 39.
40. Robert Stam, 'Multiculturalism and the Neo-Conservatives', in *Dangerous Liaisons: Gender, Nation, and Postcolonial Perspectives*, ed. Anne McClintock, Aamir Mufti, and Ella Shohat (Minneapolis, MN: University of Minnesota Press, 1997), pp. 188–203 (p. 197).

14

ELISABETH LADENSON

Literature and sex

French literature has for a very long time been known, and alternately celebrated and deplored, for its emphasis on sex. When Joyce's *Ulysses* was first published in unexpurgated form in 1922, to cite one notable example, many commentators expressed their reactions to the novel's objectionable aspects through allusions to French authors. For Edmund Gosse, Joyce was 'a sort of Marquis de Sade', his novel 'as obscene as Rabelais'; Shane Leslie felt that it touched 'the lower depths of Rabelaisian realism'; the demagogic editorialist James Douglas went so far as to opine that 'The obscenity of Rabelais is innocent compared with its leprous and scabrous horrors.'[1] Throughout the censorship debates of the twentieth century in the Anglophone world, French literature as a general category was regularly evoked as representing the *ne plus ultra* of obscenity, with Rabelais, Zola, and above all Sade cited as exemplary figures of literary unacceptability.

The evocation of French literary works as vehicles of moral corruption began in the Middle Ages, with chivalric romance literature. Doubtless the first such reference is the famous episode in Canto V of Dante's *Inferno* (early fourteenth century) in which Francesca da Rimini recounts, from the Second Circle of Hell, her narrative of adulterous relations with her brother-in-law inspired by their reading of the thirteenth-century romance of Lancelot of the Lake. Some four centuries later, though with somewhat less dire results, the main character of Charlotte Lennox's 1752 novel *The Female Quixote* is led by her readings of the seventeenth-century works of Madeleine de Scudéry to believe she is living in a romance novel (since she is a young woman, her unfortunate adventures, unlike those of her eponymous Spanish forebear, chiefly involve mistaking all the men she encounters for pining suitors).[2] The idea of French literature per se as a vehicle of moral corruption, however, did not become a literary commonplace until the mid nineteenth century. Victorian literature is particularly rich in allusions to the corrupting force of French novels, especially – though not exclusively – on young women.

The dangerous French novel of the Victorians

The pernicious influence of French works held sway with great force as a leitmotif in English literature throughout much of the nineteenth century, starting in the 1840s, heyday of Balzacian realism. Characters in Victorian novels regularly compromise their moral integrity or reputation by reading, or (worse) being seen reading, French works. A number of female characters in Thackeray's novels acquire dangerous political and social ideas by reading Voltaire and Rousseau, or fall into moral laxity under the influence of Lamartine, Balzac, George Sand, or Eugène Sue. In most cases, however, the allusion is not to any specific work or author, but rather to nameless representatives of the generic category of 'French novel', often qualified by alarming adjectives. The envious monk who narrates Browning's poem 'Soliloquy of the Spanish Cloister' (first published in 1842), for instance, plans to slip a 'scrofulous French novel' into the reading-matter of another monk, with the expectation that the mere sight of its 'grey paper with blunt type' will send his enemy straight to perdition.[3] A character in Mary Elizabeth Braddon's bestselling 1862 sensation novel *Lady Audley's Secret* announces: 'I feel like the hero of a French novel: I am falling in love with my aunt.'[4] Trollope's *Eustace Diamonds* (1871) features a scene in which the conniving adventuress Lizzie Eustace hastily prepares to greet a visitor by concealing her French novel and taking up a Bible.[5] In Oscar Wilde's 1890 *Picture of Dorian Gray*, it is under the influence of a French novel (unnamed, but manifestly based on Huysman's 1884 decadent work *À rebours* [*Against Nature*]) with its 'metaphors as monstrous as orchids' that the protagonist explores various vices in his spiralling downward trajectory.[6] One final example, among many: a French novel described as 'abject, horrid, unredeemed vileness from beginning to end' plays a key role in Henry James's 1899 novel *The Awkward Age*, in which a young girl's admission of having read it is enough to compromise her marriageability.[7]

Several questions are raised by this fictional epidemic of literary corruption. To what extent was this trope of the generic French novel endowed with the power to corrupt the young people of England as well as Browning's Spanish monks by its mere presence justified by actual French novels of the time? And why are the works at issue almost never identified? The answer to the latter would seem to lie in the more or less satirical nature of these allusions, as well as the hyperbolic efficacy of a generic reference. It is also possible that in some cases the naming of dangerous French novels might have been seen to serve as a recommendation, however negative, and thus itself been taken as an incitement to corruption. Even when specific authors are mentioned, individual titles almost never appear; the dangers would seem to lie in French Romanticism as a general category, followed by French realism. However irredeemably vile the novel young Nanda admits to reading in *The Awkward Age* may seem to her mother and potential suitor, the work in question cannot be construed to be a book containing explicit sex. Zola, the publication of whose works in expurgated translation had caused an uproar, and a court case, ten years before James's novel appeared, would have been the author most readily brought to mind for contemporary readers. Nanda's novel cannot possibly, in any case, be one of Sade's works, which did not circulate freely in any language until more than fifty years after *The Awkward Age* was published. Instead, it would presumably have been construed as one of the Flaubertian realist or Zolian naturalist works which provoked varying degrees of controversy in France throughout the century, and which greatly contributed to the particular reputation of nineteenth-century French literature elsewhere. *Madame Bovary* (1857), perhaps the most notorious of those works, features another female Quixote, also the best-known victim of literary poisoning. Ironically, Emma is led to her demise by the corrupting force of Romantic literature: by their very lack of realism, her readings creating unrealistic expectations, which encourage her toxic dissatisfaction with her tedious provincial existence.

French literature of the nineteenth century did, certainly, concern itself with sex, and, what's more, illicit sex, to a degree unthinkable in Victorian Britain – or rather, thinkable but unnameable, except with recourse to French novels. While 'the marriage plot' was central to English novels from Austen through James, adultery tended to be the focus in French literature during the same period, *Madame Bovary* being again the most famous example. In addition, incest (brother–sister) was introduced as a Romantic theme in Chateaubriand's 1802 *René*; and Braddon might well have had Stendhal's *Chartreuse de Parme* (1839) in mind for the 'falling in love with my aunt' reference in *Lady Audley's Secret*. Even more problematically, prostitution remained a major preoccupation of French literature from Mérimée's *Carmen* (1847) and Dumas *fils*'s hugely successful *Dame aux camélias* [*Lady of the Camellias*] (1848; itself inspired by l'Abbé Prévost's 1731 *Manon Lescaut*), on through the early twentieth century with the works of Proust and Colette, among others.

So great was the fear of moral contamination by French literature in England during the nineteenth century that Lord Chief Justice Campbell brandished a copy of *La Dame aux camélias* for emphasis in the House of Lords when making his argument for the Obscene Publications Act of 1857. In the late 1880s the elderly bookseller Henry Vizetelly was repeatedly prosecuted for publishing bowdlerized translations of a number of works of French realism, including novels by Flaubert – notably *Madame Bovary*, in its first English translation, by Eleanor Marx (daughter of Karl) – and Zola. Vizetelly was eventually convicted and sent to prison for several months, largely on the strength of Zola's *La Terre*. (The latter had attracted particular opprobrium for a scene in which a young girl witnesses the farmyard fecundation of a cow by a bull; this passage was read as a *mise-en-abyme* of the novel's potential for corruption of impressionable readers.) Any of these realist or naturalist works might have done duty for young Nanda's illicit reading in *The Awkward Age*. Yet despite the emphasis on adultery and sexual deviance in particular and sexuality in general, which led it to be seen as the gold standard of indecency, French literature during this period was still relatively decorous in its depictions of sexual activity, as compared to that of earlier centuries as well as what followed.

Historical overview

The history of sex as a major theme in French literature begins in the Middle Ages, and varies greatly in tone and content according to genre. The *fabliaux*, a popular and often highly obscene genre that flourished in the twelfth and thirteenth centuries, were an important precursor for much of what followed. Remarkable in themselves, the *fabliaux* also exerted durable influence on such authors as Chaucer and Boccaccio, as well as profoundly marking the French tradition. For many centuries, following Greek and Roman example, representations of sexual passion in French literature were largely divided along generic lines. Passionate love, divorced from the basely corporeal, was the subject of high genres, especially tragedy, whereas sexuality per se, reduced to the quest for satisfaction of bodily urges, was relegated to the low forms of comedy. Adultery provided material for a variety of literary forms, furnishing plotlines for courtly love narratives in chivalric romance, as well as the cuckoldry scenarios central to the *fabliaux* with their randy priests cavorting with the bored wives of dim-witted peasants (to name one popular scenario). This basic divide, along with similar plotlines, persists throughout the Renaissance, where it can be seen in the ribald grotesqueries of Gargantua and Pantagruel, as opposed to the more decorous love lyrics of the Pléiade poets. It then resurfaces in seventeenth-century theatre, with the high-genre passion tragedies of Corneille and Racine on the one hand and the comedies of Molière, with their emphasis on sexual duplicity, on the other. The late seventeenth and eighteenth centuries saw an efflorescence of what eventually came to be called pornography. (The word itself, from the Greek for 'prostitute-writing', began to enter the popular vocabulary in the late eighteenth century, following Restif de La Bretonne, who wrote about the lives of prostitutes under the by-line 'Le Pornographe'; the term did not take on its current valence until the mid nineteenth century.) During this period there appeared a number of works predicated on the detailed depiction of sexual acts and manifestly destined to be read 'with one hand', as Jean-Jacques Rousseau would memorably characterize the genre. These pornographic novels, which were quickly translated into a number of languages and became clandestine bestsellers in a variety of countries, followed the *fabliaux* line in that they often centrally featured lubricious clerics duping clueless girls into sex under the guise of religious communion. Over the course of the eighteenth century, this pornographic strain combined with the philosophical tales then in vogue in France, along with the vogue of novels inspired by Richardson's hugely popular *Pamela* and *Clarissa*, to yield the libertine novel, which took such hybrid, often parodic forms as the 1748 *Thérèse philosophe*.

In short, although the classical division of genres continued to obtain to some degree, the relatively frank depiction of sexuality remained an integral part of much of French literature throughout the entire period from the Middle Ages to the eighteenth century, in large part because of the libertine tradition. By the end of the eighteenth century, the years immediately preceding the Revolution saw this genre reach its apogee in Laclos's *Liaisons dangereuses*. Finally, during the Revolutionary period itself and its aftermath, the Marquis de Sade, repeatedly imprisoned under successive regimes, sat in his cell pushing the libertine tradition to a point of no return. Sade's contribution to this history is key, not just because his version of the libertine novel went far beyond anything that had previously been seen in terms of the graphic depiction, discussion, and recommendation of a great variety of sexual acts, including but not limited to sexual violence, but also because of its considerable entailments for posterity. The extravagantly depraved tableaux on display in his works are not simply the product of a *sui generis* imagination given full reign, but were evidently inspired as well by his readings in the pornographic libertine, Richardsonian, and gothic precedents of the eighteenth century. In particular, he melded the gothic aesthetic with conventions of the pornographic libertine novel, which he divorced from the comic elements of the *fabliaux* tradition that continued to mark the genre, to form the sort of high-minded philosophically inflected pornographic ethos which has been a key influence on the representation of sex in French literature ever since.

Middle Ages and Renaissance

Despite its effect on Francesca da Rimini and her equally unfortunate brother-in-law, the story of Lancelot and Guinevere has a relatively low sex quotient in the grand scheme of medieval French literature. As noted, much of chivalric romance is predicated on adultery, and yet this aspect tends to get lost in courtly love narrative. Apart from the *fabliaux* themselves, French literature of the Middle Ages contains one squarely canonical work almost entirely predicated on the allegorical depiction and theoretical discussion of various forms of sexual activity: the thirteenth century *Roman de la rose*. The first part of this famous poem was written by Guillaume de Lorris, and chronicles the attempts of a courtier to woo his beloved, the eponymous symbolic rose, with the aim of entering her walled garden. In the much longer second part, added by Jean de Meun towards the end of the thirteenth century, various allegorical figures hold forth on love, including a lengthy and relatively detailed polemic against sodomy pronounced by Genius. The work concludes with the Lover's eventual penetration of the Beloved's garden by means of his battering ram, aided by Venus with her flaming torch. In the early fifteenth century the *Roman de la rose* went on to occasion France's first major literary controversy, with Christine de Pizan objecting to it on the grounds of vulgarity, incitements to debauchery, and misogyny.

The *fabliaux*, despite their exponentially greater raunchiness, elicited no such public debate, nor did they traffic in allegory or high-minded argument (as the medieval rhetorician Geoffroy of Vinsauf observed, 'a comic subject rejects artfully laboured diction'[8]). The word itself would seem to be a diminutive of *fable*, and designates relatively short, comical tales written in octosyllabic, rhymed verse (the standard form of lyric poetry during the same period). Scholars have never managed to agree on where they came from or who their audience was, but this genre, often but not always anonymous (Rutebeuf and Jean Bodel are among the best-known authors), was popular in France during the twelfth and thirteenth centuries. Stories from the *fabliaux* inspired authors from Chaucer and Boccaccio until the eighteenth century – among others, Diderot's ribald novel *Les Bijoux indiscrets* [*The Indiscreet Jewels*], with its talking vaginas, was inspired by a *fabliau* predicated on the same idea ('Le Chevalier qui fist parler les Cons' ['The Knight Who Made Cunts Talk'], attributed to Garin (early thirteenth century)). The cast of characters and general plotlines of this corpus is familiar from such works as Boccaccio's mid-fourteenth-century *Decameron* and Marguerite de Navarre's *Heptaméron* two centuries later, both of which borrowed freely from this tradition, which centrally features lubricious clerics, frustrated wives, clueless husbands, and stupid peasants.

What sets the *fabliaux* apart from later avatars of the same sorts of stories in later canonical works such as those of the authors mentioned is the poems' greater emphasis on anatomical specificity, as well as their liberal use of vulgar terms to designate the relevant body parts. One *fabliau*, for instance, recounts a couple each of whom wishes for the other to be better endowed with genitals, upon which the husband sprouts phalluses over his entire body, while the wife is covered with vaginas, all of which is described in great specificity. By the end both parties have thought better of their wishes and both are restored to their original forms, having learned their lesson. Unlike the works of later authors inspired by this tradition, the *fabliaux* often dwell on the relevant body parts in detail, a tendency later on confined to pornographic literature – that is, works the major aim of which is to excite the reader by detailed depiction of sexual acts. Despite their insistence on anatomical description of lower body parts, however, the *fabliaux* are not pornographic (according to the above definition of the term, at least), because their chief aim would seem manifestly to be comical rather than aphrodisiac.

The same may be said of the much of the sexually explicit literature of the French Renaissance. Writers of the sixteenth century produced a great deal of highly erotic love poetry (for example, Louise Labé's 'Baise m'encor, rebaise moi et baise' ['Kiss Me Again, and Again, and Once More']), as well as explicitly sexual verse, some of it a subcategory of the *blason* genre, which enumerated the beloved's physical attributes. Poetic *blasons*, often highly erotic, were very popular during the Renaissance, most often taking the form of apostrophes to the body parts in question. Clément Marot's 1535 'Blason du beau tétin' ['Blazon of the Beautiful Tit'], with its celebration of a young virgin's breast (concluding with an envious reference to the man who will make it into a young matron's breast), to which he added a *contre-blason* or negative version, in the form of his 'Blason du laid tétin' ['Blazon of the Ugly Tit'], which catalogues unpleasant breast characteristics (culminating in some truly revolting descriptions), are exemplary early specimens of this genre. Ronsard's 1553 *Folasteries* concludes with a sonnet beginning 'Je te salue, ô merveillette fente' ('I salute you, oh marvelous little slit'), dedicated to the charms of that 'petit trou, trou mignard, trou velu / D'un poil follet mollement crespelu' ('small hole, cute little hole, hole velveted / With wild softly curly fur'). In preference to this hymn to the vagina, however, the anthologies of posterity have retained his 'Ode à Cassandre' ('Mignonne, allons voir si la rose' ['Darling Let Us See If the Rose']), which, while it is couched as a seduction poem, foregrounds the *tempus fugit ergo carpe diem* theme rather than dwelling on the desired act itself.

The early sixteenth-century works of Rabelais, in sharp contrast, are exceptional in that they remained canonical as philosophically representative of the Renaissance humanist tradition and rejection of medieval scholasticism, even as they paid homage to the raunchiest excesses of the *fabliaux*, with which Rabelais was entirely familiar. In *Pantagruel* (1532), for instance,

Panurge proposes replacing the ramparts of Paris with a wall made out of female genitals, on the basis that they are cheaper than stone, even if such a structure would, he concedes, attract flies; this exchange leads to a lengthy digression in the form of a parodic fable involving a lion and fox who come upon a peasant woman and stuff her vagina with moss in an effort to heal what they take to be a purulent wound. Panurge then takes his revenge on a noble lady who rejects his advances by strewing pieces of the uterus of a bitch in heat on the train of her dress, in church, so that she is assailed by the attentions of all the male dogs of Paris. It is clear, then, why the name of Rabelais became not only an adjective indicating robust excess in terms of eating and drinking, both of which are foregrounded in his work, but also a byword for obscenity in nineteenth- and twentieth-century England. What is less evident is how his writing managed to remain a central part of the literary canon in France during the following centuries, which saw a considerable tightening of the parameters of acceptable public discourse.

Seventeenth and eighteenth centuries

The poetic tradition of the *fabliaux* was carried on in the seventeenth century by Jean de La Fontaine, who published several volumes of libertine *Contes et nouvelles en vers* [*Tales and Stories in Verse*] starting in the 1660s, alongside his Aesop-inspired *Fables*, which have edified French children ever since. Many of La Fontaine's *Contes* are verse adaptations of stories from Boccaccio's *Decameron*, and feature a familiar cast of cuckolded husbands and clueless virgins seduced by wily priests (Colette took the title of one of these poems, 'Comment l'esprit vient aux filles' ['How Girls Get Their Wits'], as the subtitle of her 1919 novella *Mitsou*).

Following its models in fifth-century BCE Athens, the neo-classical theatre of seventeenth-century France relied on adultery and various accessory sexual deviations for its major plot devices, but, once again, the treatment differed widely according to genre. Thus Racine's *Phèdre* (first performed in 1677) approached its subjects – adultery, symbolic incest, with bestiality in the background – in terms of tragic passion derived from Greek mythology, while Molière's *École des femmes* (*School for Wives*, 1662), for instance, took on similar themes (minus bestiality) in a strictly comical vein, that is to say, among other differences, with an emphasis on the absurdity of sexual jealousy. Both works feature doomed inter-generational sexual obsessions, but they play out in highly divergent ways, according to genre. And just as the comedies of Aristophanes directly took on topical current events in a manner unthinkable in the tragedies of the day (for example, *Lysistrata*, with its Peloponnesian War setting), Molière's *Tartuffe* (1664) was able to address the hypocrisy of the clergy through broad sexual satire. In any case, with the exception of Racine's plays commissioned for the young ladies of Saint-Cyr, the vast majority of both tragic and comic plays of this period concern themselves more or less decorously, according to genre, with similar themes of sexual passion and betrayal. Like that of fifth-century Athens, the officially sanctioned literature of the reign of Louis XIV approached its subjects with caution, but with more or less caution according to genre.

At the same time, a vigorous underground literary pornography industry began to develop, following the example set by Italian writers of the Renaissance, especially Pietro Aretino, best known for his *Sonneti lussoriosi* [*Lusty Sonnets*], written to accompany a series of engravings illustrating sexual positions. Aretino's *Ragionamenti* [*Dialogues*] (1534–6), a series of erotic prose dialogues between two women, one more mature and experienced, the other young and innocent, set the tone for the European pornographic prose tradition. In France, Brantôme's *Vie des dames galantes* [*Lives of Fair and Gallant Ladies*], published posthumously in 1666, fifty years after the author's death, considered among other topics the varieties of cuckoldry and whether it was possible to be cuckolded by a woman. (This question would resurface in various forms during the nineteenth and early twentieth centuries, when lesbianism became a favourite topic of both popular and more 'serious' literature; Brantôme's answer is a provisional no, but the husband must be vigilant lest his wife acquire a taste for illicit pleasures and move on to more dangerous pastimes.) Shortly before *La Vie des dames galantes* appeared, the Aretinian tradition took hold in France with the anonymous appearance of *L'Eschole des filles* [*School for Wenches*], published in 1655 (seven years, it might be noted, before the first production of Molière's *École des femmes*). *L'Eschole des filles* explicitly announces itself as an instruction manual for *demoiselles*, and takes the form of two dialogues between the relatively experienced Suzanne and her naïve cousin Fanchon. Samuel Pepys, who bought the volume in 1668 in plain covers with the intention of burning it so that it would not be found among his effects, confided to his diary that it was 'the most bawdy, lewd book that I ever saw'.[9] In 1687 the governess of the *demoiselles d'honneur* of the French *dauphine*, Louis XIV's daughter-in-law, was appalled to find her charges reading the same work.

L'Eschole des filles was the first of a long series of *Ragionamenti*-inflected French works, all of which were quickly translated into English and other languages and circulated in clandestine form throughout Europe. The most famous of these novels was *L'Académie des dames*, also known variously as *Satire sotadique; Des secrets de l'Amour et de Vénus;* and *Dialogues de Luisa Sigea*. First published in Latin in 1660 as *Aloisiae Sigeae Toletanae Satyrica*

Sotadica de Arcanis Amoris et Veneris, this work, announced as having been written in Spanish by Luisa Sigea (a royal maid-of-honour in Spain who had died in 1560) and translated into Latin by Jean Meursius (a humanist from Leyden who had died in 1653), seems to have been written by a French jurist named Nicolas Chorier in both Latin and French versions, the latter appearing in 1680. It consists of seven dialogues between Tullia and Ottavia, the second of which ('Tribadicon') takes on the subject of sex between women. *L'Académie des dames* achieved lasting notoriety, with Chorier heralded as the French answer to Aretino; the work continued to be referred to in the nineteenth century as having established the classical pornographic tradition in France.

That tradition, characterized by male-authored dialogues between women, often philosophically inflected (however parodically so) – *L'Eschole des filles* was already subtitled *La Philosophie des dames* – continued apace throughout the eighteenth century, with an increasing quotient of anticlerical philosophical musing during the Enlightenment. The preponderance of hypocritical, randy priests and monks in these narratives, which started in the twelfth century with the *fabliaux* – the Gregorian Reforms in the late eleventh century having decreed a celibate clergy – proved a durable theme in pornographic French literature. (Georges Bataille's 1928 *Histoire de l'œil* [*The Story of the Eye*] provides a noteworthy late example.) Stories involving the sexual exploits of supposedly celibate Catholic religious figures were tremendously successful in the seventeenth and eighteenth centuries, not only in France and other Catholic countries, where their transgressive appeal was obvious, but also in Protestant countries where they did double duty as both pornography and anti-papist propaganda. In 1683, notably, a novel entitled *Vénus dans le cloître, ou, La religieuse en chemise*, by the pseudonymous 'Abbé Du Prat', and consisting, once again, of dialogues between two women, one more experienced than the other – this time two nuns – was published, anonymously, later to be republished in various forms in various languages, the dialogues in this cases taking on masturbation, lesbianism, flagellation, and other topics. In the guise of *Venus in the Cloister, or the Nun in Her Smock*, this work enjoyed a long and much-censored career in the United Kingdom as well as in France and other countries.

The clandestine traffic in books during the eighteenth century extended to both Enlightenment philosophy and what later came to be known as pornography, and indeed the two categories were often not easily distinguishable, both subsumed under the rubric *philosophie*. Philosophical narratives often contained ribald elements (for example, the 'lesson in experimental physics' that young Cunégonde finds Dr Pangloss giving her mother's chambermaid in the bushes in an early passage of *Candide*, published anonymously by

Voltaire in 1759). One of the most notorious of the many *fabliaux* and *Ragionamenti*-inflected works of the French Enlightenment was *Thérèse philosophe*, anonymously published in 1748 (the same year John Cleland's *Memoirs of a Woman of Pleasure*, popularly known as *Fanny Hill*, was published in England, eventually to become the most often-censored English novel; in France it also proved a perennial favourite, translated under the title *La Fille de joie*). *Thérèse philosophe* is an exemplary case of Enlightenment pornography. Loosely based on a convent scandal that had occurred several decades earlier, this anonymous novel, which has been attributed to various authors including Boyer d'Argens, combines parodic philosophical discourse with highly pornographic scenes including material taken straight from the *fabliaux* tradition. Thérèse recounts in detail scenes involving a randy priest who deflowers her under the guise of purifying her soul by the introduction of a holy instrument. Such passages, interspersed with philosophical dialogues, exemplify both the tradition itself and the various forms it was to take subsequently, because they at once take up familiar themes from the Chaucer–Boccaccio–Rabelais *fabliau*-inspired lineage and treat them in a manner characteristic of modern pornography. Such narratives most often took the form of male-authored works in which girls and women recount the stories of their sexual experiences, often to other women, without entirely understanding what they are recounting. In Thérèse's detailed description of her encounter with the priest, for instance, her cluelessness adds to the salacious interest of the text while also prolonging the discussion through her lack of understanding.

Also in 1748, the philosopher Denis Diderot brought out, anonymously, his first novel, *Les Bijoux indiscrets*. As noted above, it was directly inspired by a *fabliau*, although it is written in the orientalist fashion inspired by Galland's early eighteenth century translation of *The Thousand and One Nights*, of which other examples are Montesquieu's 1721 *Lettres persanes* and Crébillon *fils*'s 1742 libertine novel *Le Sopha*. With its main character's magic ring which incites women's genitals to tell their stories, Diderot's tale may be seen as something of an allegory for the many works which were to follow over the next two centuries, in which male authors ventriloquized depictions of female sexuality. Such works include, especially, various novels by Sade. Much of the nineteenth-century French realist tradition, with its doomed heroines who try fruitlessly to follow the path of virtue but inevitably slide into vice and penury (often followed by death), also derives in large part from the more lugubrious forms of this eighteenth-century model.

The Marquis de Sade is a crucial figure, even *the* crucial figure, in the history of modern representations of sexuality in French literature. He wrote three increasingly explicit versions of his best-known work, *Justine. Les*

Infortunes de la vertu [*The Misfortunes of Virtue*] (1787), and its successor, *Justine, ou, Les malheurs de la vertu* (1791), are both first-person accounts of the stubbornly ingenuous heroine's mistreatments at the hands of everyone she encounters. The third version, *La Nouvelle Justine*, was published at the turn of the century in a huge ten-volume illustrated edition which also included the complementary, victorious story of Justine's libertine sister, Juliette. The influence of Richardson's novels – especially his immensely popular and much-parodied *Pamela, or Virtue Rewarded* (1741) – is evident from the titles and subtitles, as is the equally perverse nod to Rousseau's 1761 bestseller *La Nouvelle Héloïse* in the title of the third version. Sade's writing also bears the evident marks of the late eighteenth-century gothic trend, with its lurid events taking place in obscure castles. Sade paid explicit homage to the English gothic novelists Ann Radcliffe and, especially, Matthew Lewis – whose 1796 *The Monk* is almost as sadistic as the works of Sade himself – in his 1799 essay 'Idées sur le roman'. In addition to Richardson, Rousseau, and the gothic novel – as well as his lengthy incarcerations and the bloody Revolutionary events taking place outside his various cells – Sade's writing is also heavily indebted to the pornographic tradition already alluded to (like her philosophical predecessor, Justine goes by the name Thérèse). Some of his works are written in dialogue form, for instance *La Philosophie dans le boudoir* (1795), which, like most of his novels as well as those which preceded him in this tradition, centrally concerns the sexual education of a young girl. Here, however, the pupil's encyclopaedic instruction at the hands of a group of libertines, emphasizing lessons on sodomy and other unnatural or rather counter-natural vices, reaches its climax in her enthusiastic participation in the sewing-up of her own mother's vagina.

Sade's seemingly aberrant works represent the point at which a number of literary subgenres come together in an extravagant form fuelled by both individual and collective history. His relation to the *fabliau*-inspired comic sexual tradition detailed above is a complicated one. On the one hand, his writing recycles many of the elements which dominate sexually explicit narrative from the *fabliaux* themselves through Boccaccio, Rabelais, Aretino, the various anonymous authors of pornographic novels in the seventeenth and eighteenth centuries, as well as, among others, Crébillon *fils* and Diderot. On the other hand, despite their fundamental absurdities (for example, the philosophical disquisitions pronounced by the characters in *La Philosophie dans le boudoir* during the throes of sexual passion and regularly interrupted by orgasmic exclamations), his works are at the same time unrelenting in their high-minded dogmatic seriousness. Whatever grotesque orgiastic extravagances his characters may be engaging in, Sade never loses track of the need to drive home his basic point about the inherently sadistic nature of both human nature and Nature itself, and the concomitant need to explore rather than attempt to repress this essential truth.

As a result, even though he paid explicit homage to the *fabliaux* in the form of a collection of fables to which he gave that title, Sade's writings do something unprecedented with the tradition inspired by them. His works preserve many of its trappings, while doing away with what had previously been at the heart of sexually explicit narrative since the twelfth century: humour. The most famous contemporary counterexample, Laclos's 1782 *Liaisons dangereuses*, perhaps the best-known libertine novel, is by no means broadly comical, and yet its tale of libertines intent on corrupting their ingenuous prey recycles a number of recognizable gestures from the comical-ribald tradition. One thinks, for instance, of the letter in which the Vicomte de Valmont writes to the virtuous Présidente de Tourvel, using a courtesan's buttocks as writing desk, and consisting entirely of double-entendres about how he feels his heart swell as he writes (etc.). Sade's writing contains no such ludic touches; he is unswerving in his serious-minded philosophical insistence on the misfortunes of virtue and benefits of vice.

Nineteenth and twentieth centuries

While it was during this period in particular that French literature became globally notorious for its depictions of sex, the nineteenth century was at once characterized by a preoccupation with deviant sexuality and, because of changing social mores and censorship regimes, relatively decorous in its approach to the subject. Sex between characters in mainstream novels during the Restoration in particular (for example, Stendhal) is implied, but never depicted; it is often represented by an opportune chapter break, sometimes accompanied by a line of dots of ellipsis. In other works, illicit erotic desire is representable because never fulfilled. Characters like Chateaubriand's incestuously inclined siblings in his *René* may pine away romantically, contemplate suicide, immure themselves in convents, and eventually die of phthisis or inanition, but they never act on their desires, and indeed their desires are never explicitly named. Unlawful desires may be portrayed as having been acted upon, but such acts are never actually depicted, nor are they directly evoked at all.

The nineteenth and twentieth centuries saw a steadily increasing emphasis on a number of forms of sexual behaviour: adultery, notably, which had already provided important material for French literature from Chrétien de Troyes through Madame de Lafayette's *Princesse de Clèves* (1678) and beyond, became an obsessive focus of realist novels in particular during the nineteenth century. This period also saw a proliferation of plots involving prostitution, as well as same-sex themes, mainly in the form of lesbianism during the nineteenth century, with both male and female homosexuality the focus of a great deal of attention throughout the twentieth. One of the major erotic commonplaces in nineteenth-century French literature is the passion of a young man for an older, generally married woman; starting with Benjamin Constant's *Adolphe* in 1816, the topic is treated in countless novels, both Romantic and realist, including notably Stendhal's *Le Rouge et le noir* (1830), a number of Balzac's works, and Flaubert's *Éducation sentimentale* (1862). This theme continued into the twentieth century with Colette's *Chéri* (1920) and *Le Blé en herbe* [*The Green Wheat*] (1923) and Raymond Radiguet's *Le Diable au corps* [*The Devil in the Body*] (1923). Balzac's encyclopaedic *Comédie humaine* series set the standard for depiction of sexuality in modern French literature, and his earlier works also include a few remarkably unexpected plotlines. The 1830 story 'Une passion dans le désert' deserves mention for its unlikely romance between a Napoleonic soldier and a panther, and 'Sarrazine' (also 1830), later the focus of Roland Barthes's 1970 structuralist analysis *S/Z*, depicts an ostensibly heterosexual man's obsession with a transvestite castrato. In the decadent literature of the late nineteenth century, writers such as Barbey d'Aurevilly (for example, *Les Diaboliques*, 1874) and Rachilde (for example, *Monsieur Vénus*, 1884; *La Marquise de Sade*, 1887) went on to explore a vertiginous panoply of perverse, often gender-bending erotic scenarios.

Balzac's master-criminal Vautrin is the nineteenth century's most prominent literary homosexual. His taste for pretty young men is entirely clear, and yet he is never overtly depicted as a homosexual, nor are his sexual exploits ever alluded to. His virility is consistently foregrounded, moreover, in terms of both his muscular physique, with details such as the vigorous tufts of hair on his hands doing duty for phallic robustness according to the laws of Balzacian physiognomy, and by the same token his criminal omnipotence. The figure of the effeminate homosexual does not come into play until the early twentieth century, before which effeminate men in French novels and stories are invariably heterosexual dandies; their masculine female counterparts tend to be alluring dominatrices (or, beyond a certain age, conniving harpies).

Lesbianism and prostitution are major topics in nineteenth-century literature, both with roots in the eighteenth century. The ordeals of Diderot's ingenuous nun in *La Religieuse* [*The Nun*] (written *c.* 1780; posthumously published 1796) had included – among mistreatment at the hands of sadistic clerics of various sorts – the amorous attentions of a lubricious mother superior, which episode inaugurated more than a century's worth of Sapphic goings-on in mainstream novels and poetry. In 1835, Balzac's *La*

Fille aux yeux d'or [*Girl with the Golden Eyes*] provided a sensational model for later approaches to the subject. Its story combines erotically charged Spanish exoticism (popular at the time: see, for example, Mérimée's *Carmen*) with incestuously tinged heterosexual jealousy of a lesbian relationship, as well as sexual violence. That same year, Théophile Gautier's *Mademoiselle de Maupin*, chiefly famous for its preface arguing against censorship, also caused a stir, with its story of a woman who dresses as a man to learn what men are like, in the process attracting the romantic attentions of both men and women. The majority of (male-authored) lesbian plots in nineteenth-century French literature involve male jealousy of amorous relations between women, often including as well the theme of lesbian fears of heterosexual betrayal, as in Baudelaire's poem 'Femmes damnées: Delphine et Hippolyte', one of two lesbian-themed poems among the six removed from his *Fleurs du mal* following his censorship trial in 1857.

Treatments of prostitution in nineteenth-century fiction can be roughly divided between whores with a heart of gold – basically virtuous women trapped in a life of prostitution despite their better natures, whose stories are recounted through the men who fall in love with them and try to save them – and truly whorish whores motivated by a combined love of sex and money. The former (Romantic) strain found its inspiration in Prévost's *Manon Lescaut* (1731), and reached its apogee in Dumas *fils*'s bestselling 1848 novel *La Dame aux camélias*, which had enduring success as a stage play as well as inspiring Verdi's 1853 opera *La Traviata*. Zola's *Nana* (1880), whose heroine is at once devoted to the pleasures of the flesh and essentially venal, exemplifies the realist (or naturalist) apogee of the essential whore, whose depraved climb to sexual and social power and subsequent grotesque downfall is depicted in the novel as embodying the decline and fall of the Second Empire. The figure of the prostitute held immense appeal for Flaubert and Baudelaire, both of whom celebrated prostitution as at once the truth of women's nature and a metaphor for literary publication, in the sense that popular success as a writer during the 'bourgeois century' inevitably entailed putting the tastes of the public before artistic integrity. The metaphor of authorial prostitution was an insistent theme in nineteenth-century French literature starting with Balzac's *Illusions perdues* [*Lost Illusions*].

Many of the erotic subjects treated in more or less discreet form during the nineteenth century were taken up in twentieth-century French literature, in direct proportion to their relative previous unrepresentability. When divorce became legal in France in 1884, adultery ceased to be quite as central to fictional plots as before. Male homosexuality gained both prominence and increasingly graphic representation, beginning with *L'Immoraliste*, André Gide's coming-out story disguised as a philosophical *récit*, in 1902. Gide was to revisit the subject in various forms throughout the following decades, including *Corydon*, a Socratic dialogue, and the autobiography *Si le grain ne meurt* [*If It Die*] (both published in 1924). Male homosexuality had also been treated by other writers, for instance by Francis Carco in *Jésus-la-Caille* (1914) with its treatment of male homosexuality and prostitution in the working-class underside of Parisian society, and most prominently in Proust's *À la recherche du temps perdu* (1913–27). Proust's huge novel, which also deals with prostitution, is insistent in its emphasis on both male and female homosexuality, especially starting with the fifth volume, *Sodome et Gomorrhe*. Gide and Proust both took their ideas about same-sex love (among men) from late-nineteenth-century German sexology, but they represent divergent approaches to the subject. The former, committed to an ideal vision of Greek-inspired virile pederasty, was repelled by the latter's depiction of male inversion, with its assumption that men who desire men are themselves inherently feminine. The stakes of this debate involved not only the essential misogyny that haunts Gide's depiction, but also the idea foregrounded in Proust's novel that homosexuals are doomed to be attracted to those very men who will never desire them. These opposing takes on male homosexuality have persisted ever since, even as they have been to some extent reconciled in later approaches to the subject, including the works of Jean Genet, and, later on, the AIDS memoirs of Hervé Guibert, among other gay writers of the late twentieth century.

Lesbianism too continued to preoccupy French writers in the twentieth century, starting with Colette's *Claudine à l'école* (1900). This novel bears a somewhat perverse relation to the tradition of male-authored depictions of female sexuality, since it was initially published under the name of her husband Willy (Henri Gauthier-Villars). Claudine's sexuality, in this and the rest of the novels, which take her name, is entirely polymorphous: the entire world is eroticized in Claudine's view, contributing to the immense popular success of the series. Colette's long career was largely devoted to the exploration of female sexuality in its various forms, most famously chronicling the world of courtesans in *Chéri* (1920) and *Gigi* (1944). Starting in the 1940s, a number of startlingly candid accounts of same-sex desire and experience were published, including Violette Leduc's memoir-novels, starting with *L'Asphyxie* [*In the Prison of Her Skin*] (1946) and including *La Bâtarde* (1962). Along with Genet's highly graphic prison novels (for example, *Notre-Dame-des-fleurs* (1944)) these works opened French literature up to an unprecedented diversity of experiences in terms of both sexuality and social class, the consequences of which are visible, for instance, in the autofiction trend of the late twentieth and early twenty-first centuries.

In the meantime, despite the fact that most of Sade's works were largely unavailable until well into the twentieth century, his importance has been enduring, profound, and widespread. France in the nineteenth century pro-duced a markedly less robust literary pornography industry than Victorian England, at least in part because the works of Sade were in such demand among purveyors of clandestine literature. *Gamiani* (1831), attributed to Alfred de Musset and featuring a central character who bears a close resem-blance to George Sand, is the most prominent work of nineteenth-century French literary pornography. Flaubert pays extravagant homage to the Marquis in his letters, in which he refers to Sade simply as 'l'Homme', 'le Grand Homme', 'le Maître', 'le Vieux' (etc.). Because his works were both infamous and censored, therefore difficult to obtain, Sade's name became a seemingly permanent byword for both sexual and literary freedom following his death in 1814.

Once censorship had loosened up somewhat in the early twentieth century, Sade's works began to be published or republished in anthologies and limited editions, and his influence is manifest in most of twentieth-century French literature's explicitly sexual works. Authors such as Apollinaire brought out Sade-inspired pornographic novels (*Les Onze mille verges* [*The Eleven Thousand Pricks*] (1907)), and the Surrealists, who venerated the Marquis as a precursor of their movement, seeing in him a Surrealist *avant la lettre*, paid tribute to their idol in various forms. Such homages continued punctu-ally throughout the twentieth century, including a number of novels by Bataille, including *Histoire de l'œil*, as well as the particularly notorious *Histoire d'O*, brought out in 1954 by Jean-Jacques Pauvert, who had just published the complete works of Sade. This highly explicit novel, with its preface by the prominent writer and editor Jean Paulhan, elicited a great deal of controversy, not least because of its mysterious authorship. Its pseudon-ymous by-line, Pauline Réage, was suspected to be a cover for Paulhan himself, or else any number of male writers. *Histoire d'O* recounts the experiences of a woman who willingly gives herself up to extravagantly sadistic mistreatment at the hands of a group of libertines in a castle, to please her lover. Her narrative thus combines the viewpoints of the hapless victim Justine and her vice-embracing sister Juliette; it is, in any case, highly Sadean. In 1996 Dominique Aury, then in her eighties, revealed that she had written the novel, for Paulhan, her lover at the time.

In addition to many Sade-inspired fictional works, the twentieth century saw a great number of essays devoted to reconsidering the Sade legacy, by, among others, Bataille, Pierre Klossowski, Simone de Beauvoir, and Jacques Lacan, starting in the 1920s and reaching an apogee in the mid 1960s. Pauvert's postwar project of publishing Sade's complete works for the first time occasioned a much-publicized 1950s court case resulting in mitigated suppression of several of his works, which nonetheless became easily available, as they have been ever since. The representation of sex in French literature has been haunted by Sade ever since, not only in terms of his manifest influence on major authors and important works, but also in the sense that, unlike the literature of other countries, French literature has over the past century in particular been marked by a signal absence of light-heartedness and humour in its approach to sex. One of the very few exceptions to this rule is the novels of Raymond Queneau, many of which fit squarely into the pre-Sadean ribald comic tradition.

French literature of the late twentieth and early twenty-first century has tended to be highly explicit in its depictions of sexuality, with novels such as Michel Houellebecq's *Les Particules élémentaires* [*Atomised*] (1998), which, along with his other works, focuses on the idea of a nefariously free-market modern sexuality based on an oppressive economic model of eroticism exacerbated by feminism among other by-products of the 'sexual revolution'. The same author's *Plateforme*, which caused a stir in 2001, provides a graphic apologia for third-world sexual tourism. In recent years French literature has seen a number of women writers graphically recounting their sexual experiences. Such works often causing controversy, for instance Christine Angot's *L'Inceste* (1999), which tells the story of the author's adolescent affair with her estranged father, and *La Vie sexuelle de Catherine M.* (2001), which catalogues the copious sexual experiences of its author, Catherine Millet, a prominent art critic. Virginie Despentes's 1994 *Baise-moi* [*Fuck Me*] made into a film by the author in 2000, is perhaps the most daring and violent, as well as thoughtful, of recent novels in this vein; she has also written an autobiographically inflected essay about the more sordid social aspects of female sexual experience, *King Kong théorie* (2006). Despentes is one of the few contemporary French writers to use humour (however dark) in writing about sex. In *Baise-moi*, two women, sex workers who have nothing to lose, go on a killing spree throughout France. On their way they encounter an architect whose bookshelves contain the complete works of the Marquis de Sade. The meeting does not end well, for anyone.

NOTES

1. Edmund Gosse, letter to Louis Gillet, 7 June 1924, reprinted in *James Joyce: The Critical Heritage*, ed. Robert H. Deming (New York: Barnes and Noble, 1970), p. 313; Shane Leslie, *Quarterly Review*, 238 (October 1922), reprinted in *James Joyce: The Critical Heritage*, p. 5. See also *Prudes on the Prowl: Fiction and Obscenity in England, 1850 to the Present Day*, ed. David Bradshaw and Rachel Potter (Oxford: Oxford University Press, 2013).

2. Charlotte Lennox, *The Female Quixote* (London: A. Millar, 1752), for example, vol. 1, p. 93.

3. Robert Browning, *Dramatic Lyrics*, ed. Charlotte Porter and Helen A. Clarke (New York: Thomas Y. Crowell, 1898), p. 18.

4. Mary Elizabeth Braddon, *Lady Audley's Secret* (Leipzig: Tauchnitz, 1862), p. 81.

5. Anthony Trollope, *The Eustace Diamonds* (New York: Dodd, Mead, and Company, 1923), vol. 1, p. 109.

6. Oscar Wilde, *The Picture of Dorian Gray* (New York: Brentano's, 1913), p. 185.

7. Henry James, *The Awkward Age* (London: Heinemann, 1899), p. 61.

8. Trans. by Howard Bloch in Denis Hollier, *New History of French Literature* (Cambridge, MA: Harvard University Press, 1994), p. 71.

9. Donald Thomas, *A Long Time Burning* (London: Praeger, 1969), p. 27.

15

IAN JAMES

The literary-philosophical essay

From the sixteenth century onwards the literary-philosophical essay in France emerges as a form that tells the story of the modern philosophical subject. Early modern French philosophy sought to found the thinking subject as a self-positing and autonomous entity which would form the bedrock for knowledge of the natural world. When René Descartes, in the seventeenth century, based his philosophical method on the famous Cogito, 'I think therefore I am', he sought this bedrock in a simple self-enunciating act of thought. Yet, in his *Discours de la méthode* [*Discourse on Method*], Descartes called upon literary narrative in order to present that method to the uncertain judgment of others. Montaigne, before Descartes, and Jean-Jacques Rousseau after him opted for an even more uncertain mode. They portray a philosophical subject whose ground cannot be fully secured. In Montaigne's 'scribbling' of his life's experience in his *Essais* and in Rousseau's 'shapeless account' of the successive modifications of his soul in the *Rêveries du promeneur solitaire* [*Reveries of a Solitary Walker*], the philosophical subject appears as a foundation for knowledge while its lived experience seems fluid and uncertain, its boundaries insecure. In the twentieth century, the French literary-philosophical essay pursues this legacy of ambivalence. The essays of key contemporary French thinkers bear witness to the fluidity, the permeable limits and the groundlessness of the philosophical subject.

The French essay and philosophical modernity

Michel de Montaigne inaugurated the French essay. Three of the principal concerns in his *Essais* recur in much subsequent literary-philosophical thought. First, he relates philosophical reflection directly to the thinker's experience of existence. Second, he is preoccupied with the nature of the subject itself, its status, its identity, and its stability over time. And third, he tries to find a discursive form that can adequately convey the first two concerns. Montaigne even gave this kind of writing its name, 'essay' (meaning 'attempt' or 'trial'). It developed in response to the distinct philosophical issues of the early modern period: experience and the philosophical subject of experience. With Montaigne, the essay form became 'literary-philosophical' rather than simply and purely 'philosophical', because literary form, narrative description and aspects of style seem to be the most adequate techniques to convey the nature of experience, of existence, and of the subject who experiences and exists.

In his essay 'De l'expérience' ['On Experience'] Montaigne places a strong emphasis on the diversity and multiplicity of the objects of experience. In a formulation strikingly similar to key ideas developed in late twentieth-century French philosophy, he affirms: 'Resemblance does not make things as much alike as difference makes them dissimilar.'[1] Noting that the Greeks and Romans used eggs as a perfect example or measure of similarity, Montaigne recalls the existence of one ancient who was supposedly able to be so good at distinguishing between them that he would never mistake one for the other. The emphasis on dissimilarity and difference appears to be in direct opposition to the Platonic doctrine of ideal forms which hold that there is an ideal, unique, and eternal form of 'eggness' from which all earthly eggs derive their shared identity as eggs. For Montaigne the diversity of existing things is more fundamental, and more real, than any ideal concept we may have of any one thing or set of things. Thus the: 'conclusions that we seek to draw from the likeness of events are unreliable, because events are always unlike' and therefore diversity is the quality 'most universal in the appearance of things' (Essais, p. 275; Essays, p. 344). Montaigne extends this emphasis on heterogeneity to the sphere of human events, acts and judgments. He unequivocally affirms 'the infinite diversity of human actions' and that this diversity cannot be subsumed into the logic of 'fixed immutable laws'. With this he affirms the irreducible multiplicity of human judgments and opinions (Essais, pp. 276, 277; Essays, pp. 345, 347). He decisively extends this affirmation of heterogeneity to the sphere of the self and to the experience the subject has of itself. Referring to the Socratic injunction to 'know thyself' Montaigne states uncompromisingly: 'nobody knows anything about himself'. In his own lengthy self-study he finds 'in myself an infinite depth and variety' that appears inexhaustible, leaving him only with the sense of 'how much I have still to learn' (Essais, pp. 285–6; Essays, p. 356).

Montaigne's arguments relating to the irreducibly diverse nature of the objects of experience (things, events, actions) and of the self or subject who experiences (opinions, judgments, inner identity) stand in stark contrast not only to the Platonic doctrine of ideal forms but also to Plato's arguments concerning the quarrel between art and philosophy in Book x of *The Republic*. Montaigne's essays develop as a literary-philosophical form on the basis of a general *philosophical* opposition to Platonic thought.

The 'quarrel' between literature and philosophy is, if we believe Plato, as old as philosophy itself. In his discussion of artistic representation and truth in *The Republic*, he is able to refer to 'a long-standing quarrel between poetry and philosophy' (x.606). In Book x the Platonic denigration of dramatic poetry, whose greatest exemplar is Homeric verse, forms part of a wider attack on poetry, art, and 'literary' representation in general. The artist or poet 'is an image maker whose images are phantasms far removed from reality' (x.604). That which is most real, the eternal essence, the unique and ideal form, *is* Truth itself and lies in the domain of the supra-sensible beyond worldly experience. The world of sensible experience lies at one inferior remove from the ideal realm of forms, and the dimension of artistic representation at yet one further remove: 'The art of representation, then, is a long way from reality ... it grasps only a small part of any object, and that only an image' (x.598). Thus the images of art and literary or poetic representation are 'poor things by the standard of truth' (x.604): they appeal only to our inferior apprehensions of the senses, to the uncertain and unreliable domain of appearance and therefore also to base bodily passions, thus leading the philosopher to conclude 'we could not but banish such an influence from our commonwealth' (x.606).

If, however, there is no supra-sensible realm of unique and ideal forms which give an eternal and universal identity to the multiplicity of things, then artistic representation cannot be denigrated as a third-degree remove from truth, as phantasm and falsity. If, as Montaigne affirms, there is *only* the infinite multiplicity of things existing without the underpinning of the essential sameness or identity guaranteed by the realm of ideal forms, then the multiplicity, equivocation, and ambiguity of artistic representation is, in fact, likely to bring us closer to reality rather than further away from it. In this context we see Montaigne being critical of the discourse of philosophy insofar as philosophers, referring us to laws of nature, 'falsify them and present nature's face painted in over-bright colours and too sophisticated' (*Essais*, p. 284; *Essays*, p. 354). Conversely, he praises the discourse of Apollo, the god of, among other things, poetry and music, who 'always spoke to us in a double, obscure and oblique sense' in a form characterized by 'irregular and perpetual motion, without model and without goal' (*Essais*, p. 279; *Essays*, p. 348).

There is a necessary link between Montaigne's affirmation of multiplicity and of the infinite variety of subjective experience and the literary form and fluid structure of the essay itself. For only a provisional, experimental discourse, one that is able to articulate equivocation, obscurity, and oblique-ness, can hope to be adequate to the heterogeneity of experience. Montaigne's characterization of the 'generous spirit' is instructive: 'No generous spirit stays within itself; it constantly aspires and rises above its own strength. It leaps beyond its attainments . . . Its pursuits have no bounds or rules; its food is wonder, search ambiguity' (*Essais*, pp. 278–9; *Essays*, p. 348). Generosity, in this sixteenth-century context, would connote a certain elevation or nobility and perhaps also therefore singularity of spirit. This characterization of a generous spirit is entirely different from a philo-sophical subjectivity that seeks to found itself on stable ground, to set limits to thought and thereby guide it along the prescribed pathways of reason, certainty, and logical or mathematical deduction. The essay form is a much closer approximation to an infinitely diverse experience than a more sys-tematic discourse of philosophy. Thus Montaigne's 'medley', his 'scribbling', which, he says, is nothing 'but a record of my life's experiences', can be understood as the key moment in the development of the essay as a distinct form within philosophy itself (*Essais*, p. 289; *Essays*, p. 361). In developing the essay, Montaigne highlights key tensions within philosophical moder-nity. Grounding knowledge in experience, he also confronts the question of the subject of experience: the limits of its possible knowledge, uncertainties relating to its foundations, its stability, and its identity.

The example of Montaigne allows the Platonic polemic against dramatic poetry and art to be understood as just one instance of a specific tension within the discourse of philosophy. For philosophy, and even Plato's philo-sophy of ideal forms, is composed of language just as are poetry and litera-ture. Perhaps philosophy, in order to instantiate itself *as* philosophy, needs to distance itself from literature in order to ground its own privileged relation to truth. This is a problem worked out within philosophical modernity in the wake of Montaigne.

The story Descartes tells is one of the best known in modern philosophy. It is a story of his discovery that the philosophy of his day had weak founda-tion, and of his decision to leave 'entirely the study of letters' so that he could ground knowledge solely on his own thought and not on his experience of the world.[2] It is also a story that relates, as he does in the *Meditations*, his admiration for the solid foundations of mathematics (*Discours*, p. 36; *Discourse*, p. 6). Famously the *Discours* is the story of his method of systematic doubt and his discovery of the Cogito as the foundation of all certain knowledge and the basis of the philosophical grounding of the subject as a 'thinking thing' (*res cogitans*). The *Discours* is a literary-philosophical fable about the method by which philosophy will be able to abandon all reliance on fable, story, and narrative. The *Discours* demonstrates the ambivalence of the literary-philosophical form in its Cartesian moment. Philosophy here wants to leave the terrain of the literary in order to secure a ground of indubitable self-evidence. Yet at the same time philosophy calls upon literary and narrative form because the philosophical subject nevertheless still has a history. Like the subject of Montaigne's *Essais*, Descartes's *res cogitans* is a philosophical subject necessarily existing in historical and biographical time with a story to tell rather than a simple self-positing substance. Yet it also is a subject that wishes to extricate itself from the quagmire of doubt and scepticism bequeathed by Montaigne. So despite this desire to move beyond the legacy of doubt, the Cartesian subject nevertheless remains beholden to the story of its own self-discovery. In this moment of equivocation the self-founding subject of certainty also makes a necessary appeal to an instance of narrative or fabulous telling that lies in excess of the supposedly autonomous moment of self-founding.

Rousseau's *Rêveries* also depict the philosophical subject as a consciousness endowed with a lived temporality. In this case the story of the subject must be recounted in a narrative because it is irreducible to logic, formal deduction, or systematic argument. Rousseau describes the record of his ten promenades as: 'a shapeless account of my reveries', immediately signalling at the very beginning of the work that it will not be a systematic argument.[3] He concedes that a more formal method might be desirable but that, given his preoccupations, such a form would simply not be adequate to the experience he is trying to convey; it might be necessary 'to proceed in an ordered and methodical way, but this task is beyond me, and indeed it would distract from my aim, which is to come to an understanding of the sequence of change and effect that has occurred in my soul' (*Rêveries*, p. 28; *Reveries*, pp. 8–9). Rousseau's aim, then, is to portray a philosophical subjectivity which, like Montaigne's before it, is not stable, but rather varied, fluid, and changing. In a way that recalls Montaigne's emphasis on dissimilarity and multiplicity, the world of experience that Rousseau's philosophical subjectivity encounters is also a world of constant fluidity and change: 'Everything on earth is in a state of constant flux. Nothing keeps the same fixed shape, and our affections, which are attached to external things, like them necessarily pass away and change . . . there is nothing solid in them for the heart to become attached to' (*Rêveries*, p. 99; *Reveries*, p. 55). In such a world of flux it is evident that a 'shapeless account' would be the most appropriate, even necessary, discursive form for the presentation of Rousseau's philosophical meditations and that a formal deductive presentation would convey nothing of the truth he attempts to articulate.

Yet, as with Descartes's *Discours*, there is a degree of ambivalence or equivocation here. The Rousseau who affirms the flux of self and world in the *Rêveries* is also the Rousseau who admires the work and ambition of Carl

Linnaeus, the eighteenth-century botanist who developed a classificatory system for plants. In the seventh promenade Rousseau laments the prejudice of his contemporaries to find in the world of plants only a pharmaceutical resource and cites Linnaeus as one of the key figures who has helped to retrieve 'botany from pharmacy schools in order to return it to the domain of natural history' (*Rêveries*, p. 126; *Reveries*, p. 73). The subject of experience here, placed before a world of multiplicity and flux, is also endowed with a desire for classification, for the development of taxonomies, and for the systematization of knowledge and of the objects of knowledge. This praise for systematization in knowledge brings Rousseau closer to the ambition of Diderot and D'Alembert, collaborators on the vast project of classification that was the *Encyclopédie*, than to the scepticism of Montaigne. Yet Rousseau's experience, as recounted in the *Rêveries*, is an experience of a philosophical subjectivity whose discrete boundaries and relation to the world of things is far from being stable or secure. This is evident in his description of awaking from one of his reveries in the fifth promenade:

> Emerging form a long and happy reverie and finding myself surrounded by greenery, flowers, and birds, and letting my eyes wander into the distance over the romantic shores bordering a vast stretch of clear and crystalline water, I absorbed into my fictions all these delightful objects, and, finding myself at last brought back to myself and my surroundings, I could not distinguish between fiction and reality. (*Rêveries*, p. 102; *Reveries*, p. 57)

This is a subjectivity whose boundaries are far from distinct. Entirely unlike the Cartesian *res cogitans* that can experience the certainty of its existence in the total absence of the world of things, the Rousseauian subject flows into the world just as the world flows into it.

So, from Montaigne onwards, philosophical modernity, as articulated in the French literary-philosophical tradition, appears to be ambivalently poised between two opposing inclinations. On the one hand there is the desire to ground knowledge and thought within the subject of experience. On the other there is the experience of this subject itself as without ground or secure foundation, as having insecure or permeable limits and an uncertain relation to the objects of knowledge, and, finally, as being constituted in its fluid temporality, its historicity and the formless flux of its inner life. This ambivalence is radicalized into a crisis or full-blown dissolution of philosophical subjectivity in the twentieth-century French essay.

Existence and experience

Twentieth-century French philosophical thought is reputed to be excessively difficult or obscure. It becomes more approachable, however, if it is seen as aligning itself with a literary rather than a formal logical mode of presentation. As was the case with Montaigne and Rousseau this literary style arises as a necessary means to express a complex and fluid reality. Henri Bergson was one of the most famous and influential French philosophers during the late nineteenth century and the first two decades of the twentieth. Born in 1859, already in the late 1880s Bergson was developing a theory of subjective consciousness that further radicalized the emphasis on fluidity and flux expressed in the work of French thinkers in earlier centuries. In his *Essai sur les données immédiates de la conscience* [*Essay on the Immediate Data of Consciousness*] Bergson called into question whether the flux or 'duration' of lived consciousness could be represented *at all* in language or discourse. We experience, he argued: 'an extraordinary difficulty to think of duration in its original purity'.[4] The heterogeneity of the durational flux of lived consciousness and of the sensible qualities of experience is, for Bergson, in excess of what rational thought and the symbolic codes of language can grasp. So, in order to describe lived consciousness *as such*, philosophy cannot rely on clear and distinct concepts or mathematical precision as Descartes aspired to do centuries earlier. Rather it must use language creatively, it must rely on metaphor, analogy, and even align itself with a poetic or an aesthetic approach. Later in the twentieth century Bergson's scepticism in relation to the possibility of representing consciousness develops into a full-blown rejection of the subject as a category or philosophically circumscribable instance.

For example, one of the most world famous philosophers of the mid twentieth century, Jean-Paul Sartre, insisted in his 1940 essay, *The Imaginary: A Phenomenological Psychology of the Imagination*, that human consciousness is always consciousness *of* something. This led him to describe it in terms of 'image-consciousness' and to speak of 'the imaging structure of consciousness'.[5] For Sartre, when we are conscious of a thing we are always perceiving an image of a thing, and consciousness emerges as a faculty for the presenting or representing of images. This faculty is 'spontaneous and creative' and is also, as it is in Bergson, a temporal flux or duration, a lived 'life' of image-consciousness, that 'endures, becomes organized, disintegrates' (*L'Imaginaire*, pp. 37, 22; *The Imaginary*, pp. 15, 7). As spontaneously and creatively representing, and as a flux or duration, this consciousness is not a susceptible to formal deduction or logical grounding. Indeed, for Sartre, image-consciousness is prior to the instance of the subject or of personal identity, instances that now take on the status of second-degree fictions. Consciousness, in its primordial form, is impersonal, anonymous, and bears no traits other than its 'negativity', that is to say, its status as nothingness, as not being a thing as such since it is always only *not* that of which it is conscious. Thus in Sartrean terms it is impossible to treat consciousness as a formally deducible or circumscribable 'thinking' thing. It cannot be a direct object of philosophical reflection since consciousness, in always being the image-consciousness of something that it is not, cannot objectify itself. All that Sartrean philosophical discourse can hope to do is give phenomenological *descriptions* of the structure and intentional directedness of consciousness in relation to its 'image-contents'. It is this resistance of consciousness to objectification, and the impossibility of reducing it to a substantive subject or 'thing', that necessitates a descriptive method for Sartrean existential philosophy. The method of phenomenological description gives it a literary rather than a logical or deductive character. Thus some of the most important moments of Sartre's thinking are dramatic scenes in which consciousness and its contents are described, for example, the famous description of the waiter and of *mauvaise foi* in *L'Être et le néant* [*Being and Nothingness*], or, in the same text, of the phenomenological structure of guilt or shame.[6] Similarly Simone de Beauvoir relies on phenomenological description when she details the way women experience their bodies in *Le Deuxième Sexe* [*The Second Sex*], for instance, descriptions of pregnancy and motherhood or even the daily rituals of cooking.[7] It is not surprising that both Sartre and Beauvoir wrote fictional texts alongside their philosophical works, since the descriptive form of their existential and phenomenological reflection calls into question the boundaries between the discourse of philosophy and fiction.

Georges Bataille and Maurice Blanchot radicalized even further the dissolution of philosophical subjectivity into an anonymous, impersonal, and refractory consciousness exceeding any possibility of representation or objectification. Neither Bataille nor Blanchot were philosophers by profession. Both came to prominence in the 1930s and in the decades following the Second World War. Their works are positioned at the intersection of philosophy and other areas. Bataille drew on, among other things, anthropology, economics, and literature; Blanchot worked as a literary critic and novelist as well as a literary-philosophical essayist. Sartre dismissed Bataille's 1943 essay *L'Expérience intérieure* as a rather confused, latter-day expression of mysticism.[8] However, while Bataille does align the 'inner experience' of the title with the tradition of Christian mysticism (he refers to St John of the Cross and Meister Eckhart), he also sharply distinguishes it from any religious impulse and insists that 'experience reveals nothing and cannot found belief, nor set out from it'.[9] Rather, inner experience, for Bataille, is the experience of the dissolution of the limits of the subject. It is similar to something like religious or mystical ecstasy perhaps. However, rather than the melding of the self with some kind of infinite beyond that religious or

248

mystical experience would imply, the ecstatic 'inner experience' Bataille aims to evoke is more a state of non-self of the kind that might come to us in the extremity of erotic experience or in the approach to death. Rather than as a form of mysticism, then, inner experience here must be understood in the context of Bataille's long-standing preoccupation with human finitude, with death and eroticism, with sacrificial practices and those elements of collective sacred experience that cannot be confined solely to the religious impulse. As a certain kind of encounter with existence, Bataille's inner experience relates to those moments of extremity in which the limits of individuation are exposed and dispersed in such a way as to call into question the entirety of our being. 'Experience', he writes, 'is, in fever and anguish, the putting into question (to the test) of that which a man knows of being' (*L'Expérience*, p. 16; *Inner Experience*, p. 4). Since it concerns knowledge of being, Bataille's experience necessarily has a philosophical import, yet is entirely irreducible to philosophical subjectivity and discursivity.

There is a strange paradox at the heart of Bataille's inner experience: it is an experience but not a content of a philosophical subject who experiences. It puts all that can be known of being to test but does not yield any possibility of discursive or conceptual knowledge. This paradox leads Bataille to question the status of the text he is writing: 'These statements have an obscure theoretical appearance ... They are not logically demonstrable. One must *live* experience' (*L'Expérience*, pp. 20–1, original emphasis; *Inner Experience*, p. 8). What matters here is not what can be said of inner experience but rather experience itself. Despite its fundamental existential import, Bataille's inner experience resolutely differentiates itself from the discourse of philosophy: 'The difference between inner experience and philosophy resides principally in this: that in experience what is stated is nothing if not a means and even, as much as a means, an obstacle' (*L'Expérience*, p. 25; *Inner Experience*, p. 13). Discursivity in this context is at best a means to take us towards something which would remain radically non- or extra-discursive. Taken in this light Bataille's paradoxical inner experience must be understood as the antithesis of the writing of philosophy. Where philosophy would produce knowledge and circumscribe being through the work of a philosophical subject capable of subsuming the indeterminacy of existence into the determinacy of concepts, inner experience results in a state of non-knowledge and is a *site*, not a subject: a site of the dispersal of subjectivity.

In turn, the writing of inner experience itself, when taken on its own terms, resists generic determination or categorization as a discursive form. It attempts to perform itself as a kind of discursive self-sacrifice, dramatizing a loss of subjectivity and an expenditure of conceptual meaning, while at the same time affirming that the experience of loss and dispersal evoked always lies elsewhere, in excess of the power or possibility of symbolic representation. Towards the end of *L'Expérience intérieure* Bataille does align certain kinds of poetry with a sacrifice or loss of discursive meaning and he does engage in affirmative terms with the Marcel Proust's narrative treatment of temporality and subjectivity (*L'Expérience*, pp. 156–75; *Inner Experience*, pp. 135–52). Yet the extremity of inner experience would appear to place Bataille's paradoxical writing of experience beyond the categories of 'poetry' or 'literature' just as much as it is beyond the discourse of philosophy. While Bataille's writing leans towards poetry, or towards a literary mode of dramatization, it is also irreducible to them insofar as it gestures towards an experience that would lie beyond the limits of both.

Conversely, in Maurice Blanchot's writing it is precisely literature, or more specifically 'literary experience', that emerges as the privileged site of the dissolution of the philosophical subject. In *L'Espace littéraire* [*The Space of Literature*] (1955) Blanchot develops his thinking of literary experience as 'impersonal'. When authors write, Blanchot argues, their sense of personal identity, the 'I' of everyday activity and engagement, gives way to something altogether more anonymous and impersonal. In the act of writing, one enters a space of language which is shared, which exceeds personal intention and meaning, and which will continue to exist long after the death of the self who writes. Literary writing, for Blanchot, is an experience in which the subject is exposed to a loss of self or identity. He discusses at great length the literary experience and works of a range of iconic modern writers, among others, Stéphane Mallarmé, Franz Kafka, Rainer Maria Rilke, Friedrich Hölderlin, and Fyodor Dostoyevsky, and uses these examples to draw conclusions about the nature of writing: 'To write', he suggests, 'is to break the bond that unifies the word with myself.'[10] For Blanchot the writing of literature is not a use of language which performs a work of worldly communication between discrete subjectivities. Rather the imaginary space of literature is curiously, but quite radically, detached from the world; it presents the totality of an imaginary space, or of an imaginary world, in the total negation of the actual space of the world. In this way literary writing detaches the writer from any circuit of communication understood as a relation of addresser to addressee: 'The writer belongs to a language which no one speaks, which is addressed to no one, which has no centre, and which reveals nothing' (*L'Espace*, p. 21; *Space*, p. 26). The space of literature and of literary experience is not, for Blanchot, a space where the writer can say 'I' with any groundedness in an individual identity or subjectivity, since it is a space where the 'I' of language is spoken out of an anonymous and impersonal realm. When the writer writes: 'Where he is, only being speaks – which means that language doesn't speak any more, but is. It devotes itself to the pure passivity of being', and writers themselves become: 'the empty place where impersonal affirmation emerges' (*L'Espace*, pp. 21, 61; *Space*, pp. 27, 55). This is clearly a very difficult form of thinking which draws on a number of difficult modern philosophical contexts, most notably the thought of German thinkers such as G. W. F. Hegel, Edmund Husserl, and Martin Heidegger. What is important to note is that, for Blanchot, literary experience, like Bataille's inner experience, has consequences for the discourse of philosophy. For Blanchot, literary space, as the production of an imaginary world in the absence, or negation, of the real or actual world, calls into question the entirety of existence and affirms the loss of the writer's subjectivity and identity within an impersonal and anonymous realm in which all of being is at stake.

Seen in this light Blanchot's literary experience does indeed appear to emerge as a rival to philosophy. Perhaps more precisely it can be seen to emerge as an experience that would entirely supersede the work of philosophical discourse. In one of his many slightly oblique allusions Blanchot refers to the Cartesian philosophical method when he asserts that the literary work: 'brings neither certitude nor clarity. It assures us of nothing, nor does it shed any light upon itself. It is not solid, it does not furnish us with anything indestructible or indubitable upon which to brace ourselves' (*L'Espace*, p. 295; *Space*, p. 223). Yet it is nevertheless a 'contact with being' experienced as an 'an experiment, but one that remains undetermined' (*L'Espace*, p. 105; *Space*, p. 87). As such literary experience, for Blanchot, would be a more fundamental experience than that of philosophical reflection and would displace the discourse of philosophy and its attempts to bring being or existence into the realm of conceptual determination. This becomes even more apparent in the section of *L'Espace littéraire* entitled 'Le Dehors, la nuit' [The Outside, the Night'] where Blanchot, again rather allusively, describes three moments of philosophy's relation to the indeterminacy of existence. These three moments are, respectively, that of the Greeks, of the speculative rationality of the Enlightenment (Kant), and, finally, of Hegelian dialectical thought (*L'Espace*, pp. 219–20; *Space*, pp. 167–8). In each case Blanchot suggests that the goal of philosophy is to master the limit that separates the determinate from the indeterminate. In the case of Hegel's philosophy the goal would be to follow a dialectical movement between the two, which would lead to an ever greater appropriation of the indeterminate by the determinate. Using a densely metaphorical language of the 'night' to refer to indeterminacy and of the 'day' to refer to conceptual-philosophical determination, Blanchot suggests that there is a yet more radical indeterminacy that would bear the name of the 'other night'. The 'other night' would be irreducible to any dialectic of day and night, determinacy and indeterminacy, and would therefore also be irreducible to the power or possibilities of philosophical reflection. For Blanchot, only literary experience, as the total negation of the world, can open up the space of the 'night' of indeterminacy in a manner which does not affirm a dialectical movement of conceptual appropriation. Rather literary space opens up the 'night' of indeterminacy in a limitless and abyssal movement of approach towards this more radical and irrecuperable exteriority of thought and language, this 'other night'. In its non-dialectical, interminable and always unfinished movement towards the 'other night', literary experience and literary space become, for Blanchot, the most fundamental mode of experience per se. This movement of interminable and limitless approach towards the indeterminacy and exteriority of being displaces all the claims to truth that could be made by philosophical discourse.

Blanchot consistently uses densely metaphorical language in *L'Espace littéraire* and also calls upon myth (most notably the myth of Orpheus) in the unfolding of his arguments. This suggests that his own writing is also at the same time performing itself *as* literary experience and extending itself *as* literary space. Blanchot's writing would thus enact the very affirmation of the indeterminacy and impersonality of being that its pages describe. It could therefore be understood as a becoming literary or critical or reflective discourse. Yet, as is the case with Bataille's writing of inner experience, it is arguable that the extremity of literary experience in Blanchot is such that 'literature', considered as distinct discursive genre or institution with its own limits and generic boundaries, is called into question here, since, when taken as a bounded institution rather than as an unbounded experience or space, literature cannot, any more than philosophy, capture or contain the radical indeterminacy that is at stake. In this sense it is arguable that the literary space or experience described in *L'Espace littéraire* leads as much to the displacement of the identity and limits of literature as it does those of philosophy.

In both Bataille and Blanchot, then, what might first appear as the displacement of philosophy by literature in fact emerges as the dispersal of the very identity of the 'literary' and 'philosophical'. Any possible opposition or rivalry between them cannot be sustained in the face of the extremity and exorbitance of experience itself. In this context the literary-philosophical, rather than opposing the literary to the philosophical, could be said to displace both in favour of a paradoxical and interminable movement of writing.

Writing and fragment

Later in twentieth-century France structuralism became the principal literary-philosophical challenge to philosophy. Structuralism in the French context was a very broad movement which dominated the humanities and the social sciences in the 1960s and 1970s, in particular, anthropology, sociological enquiry, literary studies, psychoanalysis, and certain strains of Marxist political theory. Borrowing from the model of language developed by the Swiss linguist Ferdinand de Saussure, structuralism sought to interrogate human, social, cultural, political and psychic phenomena in terms of their underlying symbolic structures and structural interrelations rather than as isolated, independent, or autonomous entities. In particular, structuralism viewed the conscious or thinking subject as an instance or 'effect' of an overarching symbolic order. So, for the structuralist, when we say 'I' or attribute characteristics to define ourselves, or indeed, when we articulate any conscious or unconscious thought as such, we do so with reference to, and by means of, a symbolic system which 'produces' us as subjects. In this context, the ability of theoretical discourse to circumscribe the symbolic structure of the subject itself becomes a topic of dispute. Most notably the philosopher Jacques Derrida rose to fame for his critique of structuralist thought in the late 1960s. Associated with the term 'deconstruction', Derrida's writing on structuralism in this period was also part of the post-structuralist turn within French theory. So, for example, Derrida, in the short essay 'Le facteur de la vérité', attacks the pretensions of Lacanian theory. Jacques Lacan was the leading proponent of what might be termed structuralist psychoanalytic theory. Psychoanalysis here attempted to theorize the structure of the subject within a wider symbolic field or order. Derrida's polemic against Lacan in 'Le facteur de la vérité' attacks the idea that psychoanalytic theory can offer a discourse of the 'truth' of the subject and attacks also its claims that such a discourse can, in turn, uncover the 'truth' of a literary text.[11]

Central to Derrida's reading is the argument that the theory elaborated in Lacan's *Seminar* has a 'rigorously philosophical import' ('Facteur', p. 454; *Post Card*, p. 426). This, for Derrida, is because Lacanian psychoanalytic discourse offers an account of the 'truth' of the subject and its structural positioning within a symbolic order rather than a discernment of the uncertainty and fluid nature of the subject within the movement of writing. For Derrida, something like a subject does articulate itself in the symbolic processes of language, but what he calls 'writing' is altogether too messy, too heterogeneous, and too contingent to be articulated as a structured and determinable whole amenable to theoretical determination. Like philosophy, Lacanian theory wants to account for the subject in a systematic way and rely on the category of truth: 'a certain type of statement about truth is given, multiplied, at a certain precise moment, in the form of a system' ('Facteur', p. 490; *Post Card*, p. 462). It is the desire to determine the subject in terms of a theoretically circumscribable system or movement of structuration that makes a discourse such as Lacan's eminently philosophical. In this context Derrida can be seen to be representative of a general tendency within this poststructuralist moment (which includes literary-theoretical figures such as Hélène Cixous and Roland Barthes, discussed below) to align theory per se with philosophy. Not only does Lacanian theoretical discourse, like philosophical discourse, aim to systematize questions of subjectivity and truth in a conceptual manner but both theory and philosophy, Derrida would argue, align themselves squarely with what he discerns as the 'logocentric' tradition within Western thought from the Greeks onwards. Logocentrism, for Derrida, is the attitude which poses an immediacy, proximity, or relation of unmediated presence between the thought and concept, concept and word, and between the word and the moment of speech or conscious intention to speak. A thinker such as Cixous also aligns this tradition with the dominance of the masculine and uses the term 'phallogocentrism'. In relation to Lacanian theory in 'Le facteur de la vérité' Derrida describes its mode of discourse in terms that align it squarely with Hegelian philosophy by arguing that psychoanalysis subsumes the uncertain dispersal of the subject (within the movement of writing) into the theoretical determination of a system or structure: 'The agency of the Lacanian letter is the *relève* of writing into the system of speech' ('Facteur', p. 493; *Post Card*, p. 465). Or, in rather less specialized or opaque terms, Derrida is suggesting that the Lacanian theorization of the subject takes that which is fragmented or irreducibly fragmentary (the subject dispersed in writing) and rationalizes it into a formalizable system unity (speech understood in quasi-Saussurean terms as that which is produced from the system of language).

Yet, if Derrida's attack on Lacan in 'Le facteur de la vérité' interprets psychoanalytic theory as a most classical expression of philosophy's desire for systematic truth, it does so in order to affirm literature and its 'effets de fiction' as that which both escapes and subverts the desire of theory and philosophy for systematicity. So when Lacan reads Edgar Allen Poe's short story, 'The Purloined Letter', as a fable for the symbolic structure of the unconscious subject, Derrida interprets this in terms of the philosophical desire of psychoanalysis for truth in general. In his turn Derrida himself takes Poe's fictional text as being exemplary of how the movement of literary writing, and 'writing' in general, cannot be framed or contained by theoretical discourse. According to Derrida, the subject for Lacan is divided and fragmented within the Symbolic order but then dialectically restored as the object of psychoanalytic theory which 'edifies an ideal philosophy against fragmentation' ('Facteur', p. 494; *Post Card*, p. 466). Yet any real, close, or careful reading of the actual movement of writing, or of what Derrida calls the 'scene of writing', will lead to the conclusion that: 'Measured against the squaring of this scene of writing, perhaps there is no possible enclosure here for an analytical situation' ('Facteur', p. 522; *Post Card*, pp. 493–94).

Derrida's critique of psychoanalytic theory in 'Le facteur de la vérité' affirms writing as a practice or process whose effects cannot be theoretically or philosophically circumscribed but must be read, discerned, and experienced in excess of theoretical closure. Other works published around the same time as Derrida's essay, such as Hélène Cixous's and Catherine Clément's *La Jeune Née* [*The Newly Born Woman*] (1975) or Roland Barthes's *Fragments d'un discours amoureux* [*A Lover's Discourse: Fragments*] (1977) similarly call upon writing as a resource of indeterminacy in order to counter the pretensions of philosophy and theory to systematic truth. Cixous, Clément, and Barthes were all associated with trends within both structuralism and poststructuralism, and all worked at the intersections of philosophy, psychoanalysis, and cultural or literary theory and criticism. In *La Jeune Née* both Cixous and Clément, like Derrida, align philosophy with the reproduction of a (phal)logocentric tradition which, they argue, is centred on the binary oppositions of masculine–feminine or active–passive, and which is organized according to the subordination of the feminine to the masculine, and the abasement of the former by the latter.[12] In this context writing, as 'feminine writing', is characterized as the other of the masculine-centred symbolic order that philosophy reproduces. Writing here is: 'the passageway, the entrance, the exit, the dwelling place of the other in me' and displaces or subverts the masculine subject that is violently grounded in the symbolic binaries of philosophical discourse.[13] Likewise, in Barthes's *Fragments*, writing becomes an 'amorous discourse' in which the subject, if there is one, is not the desiring subject of psychoanalysis, which is to say the subject whose structure of desire can be theoretically determined and circumscribed, but rather an amorous subject, one whose status and amorous drives lie beyond the capture of theory, a subject that is more radically dispersed, dissolved, and flowing outside of itself. The 'subject' here speaks in the figures and fragments of amorous writing but, like Bataille's experience, 'cannot be lodged' within the limits of that writing.[14]

As was the case in the earlier essays by Bataille and Blanchot, writing in these texts from the 1970s is certainly aligned with literature and against philosophy but, at the same time, its indeterminacy is not something which can be contained within the generic bounds of literature or within literary norms. One of the key literary-philosophical insights of this period is that neither philosophy nor literature can escape writing as their condition of possibility. This insight led younger French philosophers in the 1970s, such as Jean-Luc Nancy and Philippe Lacoue-Labarthe, to engage extensively with the question of the relation of philosophy to literature in their collaborations in the literary-philosophical review *Poétique* and in works such as *L'Absolu littéraire* [*The Literary Absolute: The Theory of Literature in German Romanticism*].[15] It also led other philosophers such as Alain Badiou to call for a return of philosophy to a mathematical orientation. Badiou's championing of mathematics is also accompanied by a desire to entirely bracket off questions of lived existence and consciousness, of sensible experience, and of individual subjectivity.[16] These are precisely the central issues of the French literary-philosophical essay since Montaigne. It is likely that, as long as the experience of self, consciousness, and of individual or collective subjectivity remain something of a mystery to writers, philosophers, and scientists alike, the tradition of the literary-philosophical essay will endure as a distinct form of philosophical reflection in its own right.

NOTES

1. Michel de Montaigne, *Essais*, Book III (Paris: Flammarion, 1979), p. 275; trans. J. M. Cohen, *Essays* (Harmondsworth: Penguin, 1958), p. 344.

2. René Descartes, *Discours de la méthode* (Paris: Flammarion, 2000), p. 38; *The Discourse on Method and the Meditations*, ed. David Weissman and William Theodore Bluhm (New Haven, CT: Yale University Press, 1996), p. 8.

3. Jean-Jacques Rousseau, *Les Rêveries du promeneur solitaire* (Paris: Bordas, 1977), p. 27; *Reveries of a Solitary Walker*, trans. Russell Goulbourne (Oxford: Oxford University Press, 2011), p. 8.

4. Henri Bergson, *Essai sur les données immédiates de la conscience* (Paris: Presses universitaires de France, 1927), p. 79; *Time and Free Will: An Essay on the Immediate Data of Consciousness*, trans. F. L. Pogson (New York: Cosimo, 2008), p. 106.

5. Jean-Paul Sartre, *L'Imaginaire: Phénoménologie psychologique de l'imagination* (Paris: Gallimard, 1940), p. 360; *The Imaginary: A Phenomenological Psychology of the Imagination*, trans. Jonathan Webber (London: Routledge, 2010), p. 187.

6. Jean-Paul Sartre, *L'Être et le néant* (Paris: Gallimard, 1943), pp. 94-5; pp. 259-61.

7. Simone de Beauvoir, *Le Deuxième Sexe II* (Paris: Gallimard, 1949), in particular Chapters 5 and 6 of Part II, pp. 219-386.

8. Jean-Paul Sartre, 'Un nouveau mystique', in *Situations*, vol. 1 (Paris: Gallimard, 1992), pp. 143-88.

9. Georges Bataille, *L'Expérience intérieure* (Paris: Gallimard, 1943), p. 16; *Inner Experience*, trans. Leslie Anne Boldt (New York: SUNY, 1988), p. 4.

10. Maurice Blanchot, *L'Espace littéraire* (Paris: Gallimard, 1955), p. 20; *The Space of Literature*, trans. Ann Smock (Lincoln, NE: University of Nebraska Press, 1989), p. 26.

11. Jacques Derrida, 'Le facteur de la vérité', in *La Carte postale* (Paris: Aubier-Flammarion, 1980), pp. 439–524; *The Post Card*, trans. Alan Bass (Chicago, IL: University of Chicago Press, 1987), pp. 411–96.

12. Hélène Cixous and Catherine Clément, *La Jeune Née* (Paris: Union générale d'éditions, 1975); *The Newly Born Woman*, trans. Betsy Wing (Minneapolis, MN: University of Minnesota Press, 1975), pp. 64–5.

13. Cixous and Clément, *The Newly Born Woman*, pp. 85–6.

14. Roland Barthes, *Fragments d'un discours amoureux* (Paris: Seuil, 1977), pp. 10, 114; *A Lover's Discourse: Fragments*, trans. Richard Howard (London: Vintage, 2002), pp. 6, 98.

15. Jean-Luc Nancy and Philippe Lacoue-Labarthe, *L'Absolu littéraire* (Paris: Seuil, 1978).

16. On this point see, for instance, Alain Badiou, *Logiques des mondes* (Paris: Seuil, 2006), pp. 111, 334; *Logics of Worlds*, trans. Alberto Toscano (London: Continuum, 2009), pp. 101, 317.

16

WARREN MOTTE

The novel in the new millennium

Among all literary genres, the novel has consistently pretended to be *new*, a discursive form continually in flux as it seeks to innovate, often foregrounding that process of innovation, as if the *new* itself were the privileged subject of the novel. The very word 'novel' suggests something distinct and unsuspected, something that will lead us down paths that are largely untrodden. Yet by now we are so used to the term that we can adduce it in our conversations (and in our titles) as a given, as something that is utterly axiomatic. It is useful, however, to take a step back and interrogate it from time to time, because the designation 'novel' is very mobile these days – and extremely embattled as well. In adjusting to its *new* circumstances, it has become a far more elastic notion than it used to be, far more able to accommodate different kinds of literary practices under its banner. For the novel in recent years has been assailed and called into question by a variety of hybrid forms, for instance, 'autofiction', 'biofiction', 'faction', and 'geofiction', to name just a few. As each of those names suggests, such practices meld fiction with something else, something more 'real' as it were, and less obviously imaginary. Yet the fictional dimension of such experiments persists – and indeed prospers – across the broad horizon that they sketch. Perhaps it is fiction itself (and our own need to visit fictional worlds) that is so resilient.

The novel is currently in crisis in France; that much seems clear. But it is not the only crisis that the form has survived, and not even the only one in living memory. One thinks, for example, of the 'new novel' in the 1950s, and of the way that writers such as Alain Robbe-Grillet, Michel Butor, Nathalie Sarraute, Robert Pinget, Marguerite Duras, and Claude Simon promised to rid the novel of such tiresome appendages as plot and psychology, clearing the way for a novel emphasizing *écriture*, or writing itself. That programme, pursued over the course of fifteen years or so, produced a very distinguished body of work; and the best of those texts will continue to mark the history of the genre in France for a long time to come. Nevertheless, the audience for those novels became a more specialized one as the novels themselves became more arduous. When yet another generation of writers took up the programme of its elders and pursued it more radically still (I'm speaking here about the so-called 'new new novelists', figures like Pierre Guyotat, Jean Ricardou, Jean-Pierre Faye, Maurice Roche, and the young Philippe Sollers), the consequences for the novel and its readership were even more troubling.

In short, to all appearances, the French novel by the late 1970s had written itself into a crisis. Gazing back still further into the past, one can discern many other crises. Raymond Queneau, perhaps the most eminent 'writer's writer' of the French twentieth century, complains in 1937 that the novel is largely undefined and unregulated. Write what one may, he contends, the result will always be a novel.[1] André Gide, one of the undisputed literary arbiters of his generation, argues in 1925 that the genre is a fundamentally lawless one.[2] Paul Valéry swears to André Breton that he will never write the kind of novel that begins, 'The Marquise went out at five o'clock.'[3] And so forth. I do not intend to catalogue all of the crises that the novel has survived during its history as a cultural form, but I shall suggest that crisis is the novel's most characteristic mode, that in some sense the novel has always been in crisis, that it has always asked itself about its own conditions of possibility and about how it ought to be.

In that very light, the crisis of the novel in the 1970s may seem a bit less dire, if no less real. Patently enough, nevertheless, the genre in those years was in need of new direction and new vigour. A group of young writers took up that challenge and faced it directly, proposing a rehabilitation of the idea of the story as a means of bringing the French novel back into the mainstream. Jean Echenoz published Le Méridien de Greenwich in 1979,[4] and his example was quickly followed by other novelists such as Jean-Philippe Toussaint, Marie Redonnet, Marie NDiaye, Christian Gailly, François Bon, Éric Chevillard, and Christian Oster. A decade later, still other writers weighed in, for example, Hélène Lenoir, Iegor Gran, Emmanuel Carrère, Marie Darrieussecq, Patrick Deville, Éric Laurent, and Marie Cosnay, all of whom helped to set the stage for the French novel's entrance into the new millennium – and of course for the crises that would necessarily attend it there.

For my part, I prefer to consider the idea of crisis as something that fuels the novel, rather than as something that paralyses it. Moreover, I view that notion as a helpful one which allows us to see the novel in clear profile as we survey it across time. I should mention that I'm referring to the 'serious' novel here, rather than to the 'popular' novel. (I am not particularly happy with those labels, but I can find no better for the moment. Furthermore, I fear that my readerly prejudices are showing – but who among us can claim to be without them?) More precisely still, I am interested in what I shall call the 'critical novel'. I shall describe it as a novel that is cognizant of the crisis in which it takes its place, and which it serves in some measure to provoke; a novel that takes a critical position with regard to its own traditions and protocols; a novel that encourages its readers to engage with it in a manner that is actively critical, seeking in that manner to establish a significantly articulative and reciprocal interplay between the process of production and that of reception. Whatever other stories critical novels may tell, they also (and inevitably) tell fables of the novel, tales involving the genre's past, its present, and its future. The critical novel takes a great many shapes, but each of them testifies directly and materially to the genre's endurance and its agility. I am moreover persuaded that it is the very site wherein the novel as a cultural form renews itself and launches out upon new horizons. In what follows, I would like briefly to sketch a few of those different shapes. Each of the novels that I shall discuss appeared in the new millennium, and each of them seems to me exemplary of the broad variety of possibility that the critical novel puts on offer.

Let me begin with Christian Gailly's *Un soir au club* [*An Evening at the Club*] (2001).[5] Its protagonist, Simon Nardis, is a jazz piano player. More precisely, he *had been* a jazz piano player until a decade previously, when the multiple temptations of that milieu – alcohol, drugs, casual sex – finally got the better of him and he was forced to abandon his music and the lifestyle associated with it. The narrator assures us that Simon had been a figure to contend with in the jazz world, one whose playing caused the vernacular of the jazz piano to evolve in important ways. To the people who knew him, it was unthinkable that Simon should turn away from that world so utterly, even to the point of never touching a piano again. It is proper and fitting, then, that the crisis of this novel should come when Simon turns back to the piano. Wandering into a jazz club during a business trip in the provinces, Simon embraces 'night', 'jazz', 'alcohol', and 'woman' (in the first cases figuratively, in the final case literally) yet again. The results of his decision will prove to be either catastrophic or serendipitous, depending upon the lens through which they are viewed. Music echoes throughout this novel. Most of it is jazz music, some of it explicitly labelled as the music of Thelonious Monk, Charlie Parker, Miles Davis, Sonny Rollins, John Coltrane – or indeed Simon Nardis. But jazz is in competition here with another sort of music – classical music – which is the only kind Simon has listened to in the last ten years. The giants of that tradition – Bach, Bartók, Haydn, Schubert, Ravel, Beethoven, Mozart, Schumann, Debussy – stride through these pages too. Yet in the final analysis that competition is unbalanced, skewed in advance in favour of jazz. For while classical music offers Simon order, peace of mind, and a sleek, architectonic beauty, jazz tempts and finally seduces him with its promise of freedom from constraint, its boundless possibility of expression, and a besotted, erotic anarchy. Through all of this, Gailly puts the question of art and its demands squarely on the table, and the question of vocation as well. How can one recognize a vocation when it comes calling? What is the sense of a lifework in a life that is so dramatically undefined? In a similar manner, the question of style is very broadly at issue. What does it mean to have a style of one's own? How much borrowing and imitation does it take to develop such a style? What happens when one begins to mimic one's own style? Those questions, and many others like them, are played out and tested in this novel in the context of music and its aesthetics. It is abundantly clear, however, that Gailly is calling upon us to consider them with regard to literature, in a novel that insistently reminds us that writing is a precarious undertaking, too.

Writing is likewise very much on Gérard Gavarry's mind in *Hop là! un deux trois* [*Hoppla! 1 2 3*] (2001),[6] a novel that pleases and astonishes not only because it tells a very fine story, but also by virtue of the fact that its form suggests dramatically new possibilities for the genre itself. Set in the underprivileged suburbs of Paris, a site largely neglected in French fiction, the novel puts on display characters rarely seen in the books we read: supermarket employees, fatigued commuters, long-distance truck drivers, and unemployed, irretrievably disenfranchised youths. At first glance, the tale that Gavarry tells is a fairly simple one, focusing upon an adolescent named Ti-Jus Deux-Rivières who rapes and murders his mother's supervisor, Madame Fenerolo; and the narrative archetype that Gavarry appeals to is the biblical account of Judith's seduction and decapitation of Holofernes. Like the Book of Judith, Gavarry's novel investigates the nature of violence. What complicates the story, however, is the fact that Gavarry tells it three times over, in three separate parts of his novel. The first part relies on tropical images, as if the suburbs themselves had suddenly been transplanted to a vastly more exotic shore. Gavarry's characters speak to each other using words borrowed from the lexicon of the coconut industry, in a jargon that, in the first instance at least, appears to be impenetrable. The second part transforms the suburbs into a seascape; here, the characters' discourse is awash in arcane nautical terms. The final part invokes the mythology surrounding centaurs, and, like those figures, its lexicon is a hybrid creation, where modern French and ancient Greek rub elbows with each other in intriguing ways. The leaps from one discursive mode to another are vertiginous ones, and they may leave the reader dizzy. One of the points that Gavarry is seeking to make, however, is that the novel itself is a privileged site of transformation. At the same time, he is suggesting that there are many ways of looking at quotidian life, and that in certain cases the apparently limpid surface of ordinary things conceals depths that prove, upon examination, far more exotic than we might have expected.

Jean-Philippe Toussaint began his career with a series of novels peopled by pleasantly quirky protagonists who slouch through life as best they can, awkwardly grappling with small dilemmas largely of their own creation. *Faire l'amour* [*Making Love*] (2002),[7] his seventh book, is far darker than any of its predecessors, however. The absurdist qualities that Toussaint has always put on display in his writing are present here, but they are considerably leavened by the grimness of the problem with which the anonymous narrator and his companion Marie grapple. The story is set in Tokyo, where Marie, a fashion designer, has been invited to exhibit her latest collection. For good or for ill, the narrator has come along for the ride. It is a Tokyo beset by cold, by snow, and by darkness, both literal and spiritual. Jetlagged and ill, abstracted from the banality of their everyday life in Paris and the anaesthetic habits of the quotidian, living for once face-to-face, these two people are forced to come to terms with the fact that neither loves the other in the way that they once did. The earthquakes that recur with regularity during their stay in Tokyo serve only to remind this couple of the seismic nature of their own relationship. Disaster comes in many different shapes, of course, and Toussaint speculates incisively on how people react to disaster, whether that disaster be vast or local, natural or personal. The ground beneath their feet is extremely shaky, both literally and figuratively; and as these two people attempt to figure out where they will go from here, one begins to understand that Toussaint is talking not only about them, but about the novel as well.

Marie NDiaye's *Autoportrait en vert* [*Self-Portrait in Green*] (2005)[8] is elliptical, sibylline, and dense; it is also her richest piece of fiction to date. The title belies the work's content, since there is very little here that is easily identifiable as autobiography; yet NDiaye is clearly playing on her reader's desire to locate an autobiographical dimension in the text. Instead, what she offers her readers is a dreamlike fable about a woman dressed in green. She lives near Bordeaux on the banks of the Garonne, itself green and in flood. The narrator sees her standing in front of her house every time she passes by, without fail, and she wonders if the woman in green remains standing there, even when she herself is not there to perceive her. More than a physical presence in this tale, the woman in green is an archetype, a site where certain ominous traits converge and take form. We meet other women too, and the narrator offers us bits and pieces of their stories, always suggesting that the essential remains untold and untellable. Dazzling narrative leaps await the reader of this book, as the narrator shifts her focus without warning from the evocation of the woman in green to the story of Jenny, a woman whose former husband has remarried, having fallen in love with a woman in green. Further along, the narrator visits her own father, who has moved from Paris to Burkina Faso. He has divorced her mother and married one of the narrator's childhood friends, a woman whom the narrator can now barely recognize, so dramatically has she changed, having morphed into a woman in green. She also introduces her mother, living now in Marseille with two young daughters and a lover named Rocco. The narrator's relations with her mother are strained, and in pondering them she comes to a staggering truth: 'My mother is a woman in green, untouchable, disappointing, infinitely mutable, very cold and knowing how to become, by force of will, extremely beautiful, yet also knowing how not to do so' (p. 72; my translation). Seen in another light, that passage serves as an apposite description of *Autoportrait en vert* itself. For, rather than a self-portrait, what NDiaye puts on stage here is the dream of a self-portrait, in a text that plays cannily with narrative meaning, refusing conventional strategies of coherence, and proclaiming again and again its own 'greenness'.

In all of Marie Redonnet's novels, from the mid 1980s until now, she has put marginal figures on stage, protagonists who perch precariously on the edges of mainstream society. Their situations progress ineluctably from bad to worse, yet they somehow remain hopeful in the face of adversity. They are true naïfs, in the noblest sense of the term: pure of spirit, innocent of guile, and consequently very largely unequipped to negotiate the harsh labyrinth of the real. Their narrations are likewise naïve: they tell their stories in a straightforward, unembellished, simple manner, apparently unaware of their own status as storytellers. They cannot easily be situated in time or space (at least with regard to the phenomenal world that we like to think we know); social commentary in those stories is typically deferred to the level of metaphor; and political discourse is largely absent. In *Diego* (2005)[9] however, Redonnet broadened her writerly palette in significant ways. It is the tale of Diego Aki, a clandestine immigrant to France. Like Redonnet's other heroes, he is clearly a person of the margins; he is naïve; his narration is candid and almost childlike in its transparency. Yet the world in which he lives is immediately recognizable as our own, and the lessons that he learns serve to put our own worldview on trial in ways that are both pungent and inevitable. Diego arrives in France from a place in Africa called 'Tamza', where he had been imprisoned for many years – and tortured – for revolutionary activity. Making his way to Paris, ever fearful of the police because of his illegal status, he falls in with a group of African militants in the *banlieue*, working as a night watchman in a warehouse and then a brothel. The hospitality towards refugees that the French have long prided themselves upon has clearly been strained, in a post-9/11 context where new arrivals are regarded with deep suspicion; and part of Redonnet's purpose in this novel is to call our attention to that fact, as Diego attempts to make a place for himself in society. He dreams of making a movie, a largely autobiographical statement cast in the form of fiction. And indeed he will succeed in making that film, a work where the fiction he invents affords meaning and coherence to the reality he has lived, both for him and for others. Unlike Redonnet's other novels, *Diego* draws to a close on a note of cautious, measured optimism. Among the many considerations that are at issue in this text, Redonnet provides a sustained meditation on fiction and its uses. Diego recognizes that stories – whatever other purposes they may have – can be used as survival tactics. Moreover, the way that Diego comes to terms with his status as an outsider comments wryly upon the way the status of the novel itself has evolved in recent years, in a cultural landscape where it no longer enjoys the pre-eminence that it once did.

Among all of the writers I have mentioned, Marie Cosnay is undoubtedly the least known. She inaugurated her career in 2003 with *Que s'est-il passé?* [*What Happened*],[10] and to date she has a dozen titles to her credit. I find *Villa Chagrin* [*Villa Sorrow*] (2006)[11] especially intriguing, in part because it is such a refreshingly peculiar text, and cannot be described accurately by appealing to the categories that we habitually use. The notion of character is put on trial here; indeed, one might claim that it is a river, the Adour, that occupies centre stage in this book, rather than a person. Just like the Adour, *Villa Chagrin* is very fluid, very dynamic, and constantly changing. A great variety of narrative currents run through it. There is the story of the painter Bram van Velde and his companion, Marthe Arnaud-Kuntz, who grapple with catastrophe both personal and political. There is the story of Pierre M., a man who struggles to come to terms with life, finally renouncing those efforts. The narrator, an anonymous woman, gives us occasional glimpses of the man she loves, a figure who is seemingly always on the move from city to city, working on this, then that. Through all of this, Cosnay meditates (much as Redonnet does in *Diego*) on the way that society treats the stranger. She carefully reconstructs the circumstances that led to Bram van Velde's incarceration in 1938 in the prison that gives its name to the text. Fleeing wartime Spain and seeking refuge in France, Van Velde had run afoul of the law by virtue of the fact that his identity papers were not acceptable to the French authorities. For her part, Cosnay wonders if things have changed so very much since that time. She invites her reader to think closely about current immigration policy in France and, more generally, about hospitality as a social ideal. The different tales that Cosnay tells comment upon and illuminate each other throughout *Villa Chagrin*, in a process that serves to channel their mobility while at the same time impelling them, together, towards a newly identified place. Such a dynamic can be imagined, I think, as something much like a river – or something much like a novel.

Éric Chevillard typically organizes his novels around a theme or idea that he pursues relentlessly and obsessively, well past the limits of the imaginable and into the realm of the absurd. Such is the case of *Sans l'orang-outan* [*Without the Orangutan*] (2007),[12] his fifteenth novel, except that here, the theme Chevillard has chosen – the disappearance of a species – is (alas) not utterly unimaginable. The tale begins just as the last two orangutans have expired. They are mourned by Albert Moindre, the narrator of the novel, who had been their keeper in an animal reserve. Initially at least, he is alone in foreseeing the consequences of their extinction. He understands that our ecosystem has been fatally wounded in its most vital point. Catastrophe ensues, and in the second part of his novel Chevillard paints a picture of a post-apocalyptic site wherein humans struggle to survive in a world deva-stated by in turn sandstorms, by ice and snow, by rising floodwaters, where ill-equipped hunters are locked in unequal combat with giant walruses. One of the first casualties is the notion of beauty and the pleasure we may take in it. Art has become impoverished because people have no time for it in their new circumstances. Language is reduced to the merely declarative. Clearly enough, one of the chief notions that Chevillard seeks to put forward is the idea that literature itself has become an endangered species in our cultural ecology. Chevillard chooses to address that problem through play, in the broadest sense of the word, playing words against each other in search of new meaning, playing ideas against each other in order to see where they might lead. His game in *Sans l'orang-outan* is far darker than in his previous novels, however, and it has never been more serious in its purpose.

Jean Rolin's *L'Explosion de la durite* (2007)[13] presents itself as a minor epic. Its narrator conveys a used Audi from Paris to the Congo, where it will be put to use as a taxi; a small disaster marks this saga, when the Audi's radiator hose explodes en route. Along the way, Rolin offers a variety of perspectives on daily life in Paris, on cargo ships, and in postcolonial Africa, flirting with autofiction as he does so. His narrator is himself named 'Jean Rolin', and he encourages us to imagine that the events he recounts *might* have occurred, in a world somewhat less fictional than we assumed it to be. One trait which that world shares with the one we recognize as our own is its unpredictability. The best-laid plans must necessarily bow to circumstances, and circumstances, on a trip like this one, change vertiginously. In narrative as in travel, when one encounters an obstacle, one must change tack. Thus, Rolin's account of the journey is full of excurses, meditations on the life of Congolese refugees in France, for instance, or on the impossibly vexed political history of the Congo itself. Imposing figures such as Patrice Lumumba and Che Guevara wander through these pages, and the examples of writers such as Joseph Conrad and W. G. Sebald serve as signposts along an otherwise unmarked road. Rolin's prose style recalls that of Sebald in many ways. Like Sebald, Rolin is a master of sentence structure, honing his syntax with considerable elegance, allowing his sentences to reach beyond normative bounds in an effort to bring forth meaning more fully. He is not afraid to loiter here and there, taking his time to develop ideas he finds upon his way, as it were. Although the radiator hose explodes, there is no explosion of truth. Instead, through a deftly ironical and dispassionate gaze, Rolin focuses most closely upon small things, the very ones which in the aggregate compose the fabric of existence in the first world, in the third world, or indeed in a fictional world.

As if it were not hard enough keeping track of all the multiple guises the novel has assumed in recent years, in the spring of 2008 Antoine Volodine revealed that for many years he had been practicing literature under a variety of different names, in addition to his own. He is responsible, notably, for more than a dozen titles at the École des Loisirs, a publishing house specializing in works for a young audience. 'Elli Kronauer' made a name for himself there between 1999 and 2001, with five books for young adults; and 'Manuela Draeger' launched the 'Bobby Potemkine' series there in 2002, a series currently listing eight titles. More recently still, 'Lutz Bassmann' penned two books for the Éditions Verdier. In the light of this tidal wave of pseudonyms, one may wonder what other guises Volodine has assumed. 'Michel Houellebecq'? 'Christine Angot'? 'Jean d'Ormesson'? Or does *all* of contemporary French literature flow from his fertile pen? *Songes de Mevlido* [*Mevlido's Dreams*] (2007)[14] strikes me as his most accomplished novel to date, and he actually signed it with his own name – or rather with the pseudonym that he adopted when he began publishing his work at the Éditions Denoël in the mid 1980s. Its landscape is classic Volodine: a post-Revolutionary world in a time some 300 years after our own, verging upon the end of history, when all but the most quixotic hopes for the future of humankind have revealed their emptiness, and the future (such as it is) undoubtedly belongs to spiders. Gigantic, mutant birds abound in this world: ravens, owls, seagulls, buzzards, guinea-fowl, turkeys, chickens, and talking crows. Their cacklings assault the ear, and their droppings pollute the streets. The human fauna, by and large, is less attractive still. Comatose junkies line the kerbs; former child-soldiers still kill for a nod or a wink; feral commissars and bent cops belabour a population of madmen and moral cripples. Mevlido himself has been reborn in this world as a long-term deep-penetration agent, sent by obscure powers in a final effort to save a foundering humanity. He is beset by dreams, nightmares, and reveries of various sorts, states that he cannot differentiate from his waking quotidian. They are his only means of communicating with the people who sent him to this foul place – and his only reality. As we watch him struggle, a character named Mingrelian watches him, too. He is a novelist by trade, but his works have failed to elicit much interest, granted their eccentricity: 'Mingrelian's art, influenced by post-exoticism, plays with uncertainty, failure, the conflation of contraries, and nothingness' (p. 419; my translation). Clearly enough, we are squarely in the domain of the specular here, and the multiple ironies in which Volodine wraps Mingrelian's project comment in intriguing, canny ways upon Volodine's own work. Mingrelian is doubled by an anonymous narrator who is one of the few to read and appreciate his work. That narrator follows Mevlido step by step – and indeed his voice is often confused with Mevlido's own, suggesting thus a fragile identity of author, narrator, and character in a fictional world where nothing can be taken for granted.

Families and their small dramas provide the material for much of Hélène Lenoir's work, and in *La Folie Silaz* [*The Silaz Madness*] (2008)[15] she sketches a clan so shattered that one wonders if the can be called a family at all. As the novel opens, Odette, the matriarch, has just died. For years, she had tried to hold her younger folk together, as they strained against each other in mutual dislike and misunderstanding; and now they must ponder a very uncertain future. The burden of that pondering falls, as if naturally, upon the women in the family. For the men are strangely absent, either figuratively or literally. Georges Silaz, in particular, has spent his whole adult life wandering the world from one burning political cause to another, largely out of touch with the others – if not out of mind. As those others gather for Odette's funeral, Georges's absence looms ever larger. No one can imagine where he might be, and his truancy means something very different for each of them. The gaze that Lenoir casts upon her characters is a stern one wherein understanding is untempered by pity. When she catalogues the fragile tropisms that play themselves out as individuals long estranged from each other meet again, her touch is as deft as it is delicate. Clearly, the madness invoked in the novel's title is a full-blown syndrome, afflicting all of the characters here – if each in a different way. Narrative technique bears the traces of that madness, too: as this tale becomes darker and grimmer, staggering towards disaster, narrative tone becomes more obsessive, more repetitive. It dins the Silaz madness into our ears, projecting it upon us as if it were contagious. Small wonder if one begins to envy the absent Georges, because at least he has sense enough not to run headlong into the kind of craziness that has been his family's hallmark, undoubtedly preferring the calmer, safer, more predictable conditions of armed revolution.

Since Pierre Michon made his entry into the literary world with *Vies minuscules* [*Tiny Lives*] in 1984,[16] he has acquired a reputation for close scrutiny of phenomena that play themselves out within a very limited arena. *Les Onze* [*The Eleven*] (2009)[17] is no exception, for it is devoted to a close analysis of the painting which bears that title, François-Élie Corentin's depiction of the Comité de Salut Public during the French Revolution, one of the most recognizable works in the Louvre. Upon first reading this novel, I confess that I was chagrined not to recognize either Corentin or his painting – until I realized that Michon had simply invented both. Yet, even then, the hyperrealism that characterizes his narration is enough to shake one's faith in easy distinctions between fact and fiction. The idea that Michon pursues is that under certain conditions, figments can be made to seem more real to us than objects in the material world. That imagined reality fuels, in turn, a text where a baldly constative tone coaxes the reader into a labyrinth of doubt. *Ut pictura poesis* indeed. Michon is a very canny and subtle writer, and it is thus reasonable to assume that the multiple ironies that circulate in this novel are not merely otiose, but are intended to signify broadly. Quite apart from his reading of Corentin's masterpiece (which is in itself welcome, of course), Michon is trying to get at another kind of reading here, I think. Rubbing history against fiction vigorously, hoping to make sparks fly, he asks us to reflect upon narrative and its uses. More particularly still, *Les Onze* invites us to savour a story so well told and convincing that it deserves to be true, despite the constraints of the real.

Between more traditional novels like *Au piano* [*Piano*] (2003) and *14* [*1914*] (2012), Jean Echenoz made three successive forays into biofiction: *Ravel* (2006), *Courir* [*Running*] (2008), and *Des éclairs* [*Lightning*] (2010).[18] Centred, respectively, on the composer Maurice Ravel, the long-distance runner Emil Zátopek, and the inventor Nikola Tesla, these texts interweave biography and fiction in such a way that it is impossible to disintricate those two discursive modes. Echenoz takes possession of his subjects and turns them to his own uses. He conceives them as artists, each one in his own way, whether the particular canvas they adopt be music or sport or technology. In all three cases, what interests Echenoz most of all is the notion of creation, and the performance through which that creation is made public. The same concerns animate *Au piano* very broadly, as Echenoz tells the story of a concert pianist who is more and more crippled by stage fright. It is legitimate to view the three biofictions that follow *Au piano* as different experiments in which Jean Echenoz sets out to test the artistic vocation, and the problems that attend it, in a variety of contexts. I do not mean to suggest that nothing else is going on in these three texts, because ich is abundantly furnished with other interests. Nevertheless, the concern with art and its vexations is paramount in each of them, and that concern clearly reflects upon narrative prose itself. More simply put, just as each of these texts prompts the committed reader of Echenoz to wonder where he will go next as a writer, so too do they encourage us to ask the same sort of question – but in broader perspective this time – about the novel as a cultural form.

Christine Montalbetti is one of the most intriguing writers to appear in the new millennium. She began her career with subtle, finely crafted novels such as *Sa fable achevée, Simon sort dans la bruine* [*His Story Told, Simon Goes out into the Mist*] (2001), *L'Origine de l'homme* [*The Origin of Man*] (2002), *Expérience de la campagne* [*Experience of the Countryside*] (2005), and *Western* (2005).[19] I would like to say a few words about a more recent text, *L'Évaporation de l'oncle* [*The Uncle's Evaporation*] (2011).[20] Set in a rural and pleasantly timeless Japan, it is the tale of an uncle who disappears from his brother's home, and of the nephew who sets out in search of him, many years later. Montalbetti tells that story in an unhurried manner, paying attention to small things, such as silverfish, centipedes, grasshoppers, and mosquitoes, not to mention earwigs, bedbugs, and slugs. Each person we meet along the way has a story to tell, and that storytelling leads us into intriguing worlds whose existence we did not suspect. From time to time, fantastic happenings assail us. Given certain conditions, late at night when everyone is asleep, ordinary household objects can come to life and express themselves. A teapot bemoans the fact that it is constantly placed on the fire; a paper lantern becomes a raging face; a dishrag mutates suddenly into a demon. More conventional kinds of adventure can be found here, as well. There is even a duel between two samurai, bloody enough for the most sanguinary of readers; but we cannot know for certain if the nephew witnessed it, or only imagined it – nor perhaps does it matter very much. Montalbetti is keenly attentive to surfaces, most notably smooth, reflective surfaces like the ones presented by a lacquered table, by silk cushions, by a tea caddy, or by the skin of a lover's shoulder. The narrative surface that she constructs in *L'Évaporation de l'oncle* is likewise smooth and reflective, polished, subtle, and full of nuance. Yet beneath that surface, Montalbetti suggests, secrets lurk, some of them isolated and apparently unconnected, some to the contrary deeply embedded in other secrets. She sketches those secrets with the lightest of touches, playing suavely as she does so upon notions of novelistic teleology and readerly anticipation. In that fashion, Montalbetti encourages us to think about storytelling and its uses, and more particularly about the set of attitudes, norms, and expectations that we assemble when we sit down to read a novel. In other words, *L'Évaporation de l'oncle* is a particularly evolved example of the species that I have called the critical novel; and, as such, it contributes significantly to the reshaping of the genre in our time.

Patrick Deville's *Kampuchéa* (2011) takes its place as the third volume in a trilogy that includes *Pura Vida: Vie & mort de William Walker* [*Pura Vida: Life and Death of William Walker*] (2004) and *Equatoria* (2009),[21] and which circles the globe at the equator – touching down in Central America, in the Congo, and in Cambodia – as it examines the notion of place. For it is place, much more than person, that interests Deville in these texts. Or, more precisely, place as a construct that organizes a variety of other things. In *Kampuchéa*, for instance, Deville tells the story of Cambodia, roughly from Henri Mouhot's 'discovery' of the temples of Angkor Wat in 1860 to the present time, putting on offer a meditation on history, on geography, on politics, on culture, and on the way those categories necessarily overlap in a place that has always found itself precariously situated 'between the anvil and the hammer' (p. 187; my translation). One of the central – and most difficult – questions that Deville asks is how one may come to terms with the reality of systematic human atrocity such as that perpetrated by the Khmer Rouge, how one may begin to comprehend a phenomenon that, by virtue of its gravity and its sheer dimensions, benumbs us. His own approach is multiple and constantly mobile. In order to see how a utopian ideal produces a murderous state, he gazes at his different subjects through different lenses, from various vantage points. He considers the way that Cambodia has always had to fend off its envious neighbours. He reflects upon the European colonization of the region known as 'Indochina', and on the rich literary tradition that it inspired, from Pierre Loti and Joseph Conrad to André Malraux and Graham Greene. Moving up the Mekong river in a sampan, he thinks about the relation of geography and history, and about the way that individual people take their place in a far broader panorama of event. Reading the Khmer writer Soth Polin, he wonders about the uses of literature. In Deville's view, his own project demands a new kind of narrative form. If he calls this book a novel, he does so at a time when that genre is constantly in question. The interrogation that he pursues in *Kampuchéa* is intended to restructure and reinvigorate the way we understand literature, but what is also at issue is the way we understand our world; and for Deville those two enquiries are deeply and necessarily interrelated.

I would like to bring my discussion of the contemporary critical novel to a close by invoking, very briefly, a narrative form a bit different from the ones I have mentioned, but no less intriguing, a form I am tempted to call 'novelistic criticism'. Pierre Bayard's recent writing exemplifies that form nicely, and most especially the dimension of his work that he calls 'detective criticism', and which includes three volumes to date: *Qui a tué*

Roger Ackroyd? [Who Killed Roger Ackroyd? The Mystery behind the Agatha Christie Mystery] (1998), *Enquête sur Hamlet: le dialogue de sourds [Inquest into Hamlet: A Dialogue of the Deaf]* (2002), and *L'Affaire du chien des Baskerville [Sherlock Holmes Was Wrong: Reopening the Case of 'The Hound of the Baskervilles']* (2008).[22] In each of these books, Bayard addresses himself to a miscarriage of justice, placing some of the most renowned and cherished detectives in our fictional culture dramatically on trial. And indeed these books play out much like a trial – or, rather, like a detective novel, complete with an explosion of truth at the end. They are fun and fireworks; yet their principal interest resides, I think, in the vision of the mutual permeability of real and fictional worlds. Bayard contends that those worlds necessarily communicate with one another in largely unfettered conversation, and that such a conversation has consequences in both worlds. He nourishes that contention with care, fully aware that it is one that may amuse, provoke, intrigue, and delight us by turn, in function of our constantly shifting allegiances. I shall say no more about Bayard here, except to remark that his work provides a particularly convincing example of the novel's protean character and of its continued vitality in our culture. For clearly enough, and however dire the 'crises' that afflict it may appear to be, the novel remains an astonishingly supple and resilient form. It still speaks directly to us in a variety of voices; it responds to our readerly needs in different ways; it shifts its terms as we ourselves rethink ours; and in some sense it helps us to find our way – a feature that is particularly welcome in this perplexing and uncertain new millennium.

NOTES

1. Raymond Queneau, 'Technique du roman', in *Bâtons, chiffres et lettres* (1950; rev. edn, Paris: Gallimard, 1965), pp. 27–33.
2. André Gide, *Les Faux-monnayeurs* (Paris: Gallimard, 1925), p. 183.
3. See André Breton, *Manifestes du surréalisme* (Paris: Gallimard, 1975), p. 15.
4. Jean Echenoz, *Le Méridien de Greenwich* (Paris: Minuit, 1979).
5. Christian Gailly, *Un soir au club* (Paris: Minuit, 2001).
6. Gérard Gavarry, *Hop là! un deux trois* (Paris: P.O.L, 2001).
7. Jean-Philippe Toussaint, *Faire l'amour* (Paris: Minuit, 2002).
8. Marie NDiaye, *Autoportrait en vert* (Paris: Mercure de France, 2005).
9. Marie Redonnet, *Diego* (Paris: Minuit, 2005).
10. Marie Cosnay, *Que s'est-il passé?* (Le Chambon-sur-Lignon: Cheyne, 2003).
11. Marie Cosnay, *Villa Chagrin* (Lagrasse: Verdier, 2006).
12. Éric Chevillard, *Sans l'orang-outan* (Paris: Minuit, 2007).
13. Jean Rolin, *L'Explosion de la durite* (Paris: P.O.L, 2007).
14. Antoine Volodine, *Songes de Mevlido* (Paris: Seuil, 2007).

15. Hélène Lenoir, *La Folie Silaz* (Paris: Minuit, 2008).

16. Pierre Michon, *Vies minuscules* (Paris: Gallimard, 1984).

17. Pierre Michon, *Les Onze* (Lagrasse: Verdier, 2009).

18. Jean Echenoz, *Au piano* (Paris: Minuit, 2003); *14* (Paris: Minuit, 2012); *Ravel* (Paris: Minuit, 2006); *Courir* (Paris: Minuit, 2008); *Des éclairs* (Paris: Minuit, 2010).

19. Christine Montalbetti, *Sa fable achevée, Simon sort dans la bruine* (Paris: P.O.L, 2001); *L'Origine de l'homme* (Paris: P.O.L, 2002); *Expérience de la campagne* (Paris: P.O.L, 2005); *Western* (Paris: P.O.L, 2005).

20. Christine Montalbetti, *L'Évaporation de l'oncle* (Paris: P.O.L, 2011).

21. Patrick Deville, *Kampuchéa* (Paris: Seuil, 2011); *Pura Vida: Vie & mort de William Walker* (Paris: Seuil, 2004); *Equatoria* (Paris: Seuil, 2009).

22. Pierre Bayard, *Qui a tué Roger Ackroyd?* (Paris: Minuit, 1998); *Enquête sur Hamlet: le dialogue de sourds* (Paris: Minuit, 2002); *L'Affaire du chien des Baskerville* (Paris: Minuit, 2008).

GUIDE TO FURTHER READING

1. Romance, *roman*, and novel

Brownlee, Kevin, and Marina Scordilis Brownlee, ed. *Romance: Generic Transformations from Chrétien de Troyes to Cervantes*. Hanover, NH: University Press of New England, 1985.

Bruckner, Matilda Tomaryn. *Chrétien Continued: A Study of the 'Conte du Graal' and Its Verse Continuations*. Oxford: Oxford University Press, 2009.

Burns, E. Jane. *Arthurian Fictions: Re-reading the Vulgate Cycle*. Columbus, OH: Ohio State University Press, 1985.

Haidu, Peter. 'Romance: Idealistic Genre or Historical Text?' In *The Craft of Fiction: Essays in Medieval Poetics*. Ed. Leigh A. Arrathoon. Rochester, MI: Solaris, 1984, pp. 1–46.

Huot, Sylvia. *The 'Romance of the Rose' and Its Medieval Readers: Interpretation, Reception, Manuscript Transmission*. Cambridge: Cambridge University Press, 1993.

Jackson, W. T. H. 'The Nature of Romance', *Yale French Studies*, 51 (1974), 12–25.

Jameson, Fredric. 'Magical Narratives: Romance as a Genre', *New Literary History*, 7 (1975), 135–63.

Kelly, Douglas. *The Art of Medieval French Romance*. Madison, WI: University of Wisconsin Press, 1992.

Kern, Edith. 'The Romance of Novel/Novella'. In *The Disciplines of Criticism: Essays in Literary Theory, Interpretation, and History*. Ed. Peter Demetz, Thomas Greene, and Lowry Nelson, Jr. New Haven, CT: Yale University Press, 1968, pp. 511–30.

Showalter, Jr., English. *The Evolution of the French Novel, 1641–1782*. Princeton, NJ: Princeton University Press, 1972.

2. Joan of Arc and the literary imagination

Fraoli, Deborah A. *Joan of Arc: The Early Debate*. Woodbridge: Boydell, 2000.

Hobbins, Daniel. *The Trial of Joan of Arc*. Cambridge, MA: Harvard University Press, 2005.

Kelly, Henry Ansgar. 'The Right to Remain Silent: Before and After Joan of Arc', *Speculum* 68.4 (1993), 992–1026.

Meltzer, Françoise. *For Fear of the Fire: Joan of Arc and the Limits of Subjectivity.* Chicago, IL: University of Chicago Press, 2001.

Pernoud, Régine, and Marie-Véronique Clin. *Joan of Arc: Her Story.* Trans. and rev. Jeremy duQuesnay Adams. New York: Palgrave Macmillan, 1998.

Sullivan, Karen. *The Interrogation of Joan of Arc.* Minneapolis, MN: Minnesota University Press, 1999.

Warner, Marina. *Joan of Arc: The Image of Female Heroism.* New York: Knopf, 1981.

Wheeler, Bonnie, and Charles T. Wood, ed. *Fresh Verdicts on Joan of Arc.* New York: Garland, 1996.

Winock, Michel. 'Joan of Arc'. In *Realms of Memory: The Construction of the French Past.* Ed. Pierre Nora, trans. Arthur Goldhammer. New York: Columbia University Press, 1998, pp. 433–82.

3. Poetry and modernity

Bizer, Marc. 'Letters from Home: The Epistolary Aspects of Joachim Du Bellay's *Les Regrets*'. *Renaissance Quarterly*, 52.1 (1999): 140–79.

Bizer, Marc. 'Ronsard the Poet, Belleau the Translator: The Difficulties of Writing in the Laureate's Shadow'. In *Translation and the Transmission of Culture between 1300 and 1600.* Ed. Jeanette Beer and Kenneth Lloyd-Jones. Kalamazoo, MI: Medieval Institute Publications, Western Michigan University, 1995, pp. 176–226.

Castor, Grahame. *Pléiade Poetics: A Study in Sixteenth-Century Thought and Terminology.* Cambridge: Cambridge University Press, 1964.

Grafton, Anthony, and Lisa Jardine. *From Humanism to the Humanities: Education and the Liberal Arts in Fifteenth- and Sixteenth-Century Europe.* London: Duckworth, 1986.

Greene, Thomas. *The Light in Troy: Imitation and Discovery in Renaissance Poetry.* New Haven, CT: Yale University Press, 1982.

Hollier, Denis, ed. *A New History of French Literature.* Cambridge, MA: Harvard University Press, 1989.

Jones, Ann Rosalind. *The Currency of Eros: Women's Love Lyric in Europe, 1540–1620.* Bloomington, IN: Indiana University Press, 1990.

Knecht, R. J. *The French Renaissance Court, 1483–1589.* New Haven, CT: Yale University Press, 2008.

Moss, Ann. 'Being in Two Minds: The Bilingual Factor in Renaissance Writing'. In *Acta Conventus Neo-Latini Hafniensis.* Binghamton, NY: Medieval and Renaissance Texts and Studies, 1994, pp. 61–74.

Quint, David. *Origin and Originality in Renaissance Literature: Versions of the Source.* New Haven, CT: Yale University Press, 1983.

Shapiro, Norman R., and Hope H. Glidden, ed. *Lyrics of the French Renaissance: Marot, Du Bellay, Ronsard.* New Haven, CT: Yale University Press, 2002.

4. The graphic imagination and the printed page

Chartier, Roger. *The Author's Hand and the Printer's Mind*. Trans. Lydia G. Cochrane. Cambridge: Polity, 2014.

Conley, Tom. *The Graphic Unconscious: The Early Modern French Writing*. Cambridge: Cambridge University Press, 1992.

Conley, Tom. *The Self-Made Map: Cartographic Writing in Early Modern France*. Minneapolis, MN: University of Minnesota Press, 1996.

Jameson, Fredric. *The Geopolitical Aesthetic: Cinema and Space in the World System*. London: Indiana University Press, 1992.

Kritzman, Lawrence. *The Fabulous Imagination*. New York: Columbia University Press, 2009.

O'Brien, John, ed. *The Cambridge Companion to Rabelais*. Cambridge: Cambridge University Press, 2011.

Pettegree, Andrew. *The French Book and the European Book World*. Leiden: Brill, 2007.

Suarez, Michael F., and H. R. Woudhuysen. *The Book: A Global History*. Oxford: Oxford University Press, 2013.

Van Orden, Kate. *Music, Authorship, and the Book in the First Century of Print*. Berkeley, CA: University of California Press, 2013.

5. Tragedy and fear

Campbell, John. *Questioning Racinian Tragedy*. Chapel Hill, NC: University of North Carolina Press, 2005.

Eagleton, Terry. *Sweet Violence: The Idea of the Tragic*. Oxford: Blackwell, 2003.

Felski, Rita, ed. *Rethinking Tragedy*. Baltimore, MD: Johns Hopkins University Press, 2008.

Goodkin, Richard. *Birth Marks: The Tragedy of Primogeniture in Pierre Corneille, Thomas Corneille, and Jean Racine*. Philadelphia, PA: University of Pennsylvania Press, 2000.

Ibbett, Katherine. *The Style of the State in French Theater, 1630–1660: Neoclassicism and Government*. Farnham: Ashgate, 2009.

Lyons, John. *Kingdom of Disorder: The Theory of Tragedy in Classical France*. West Lafayette, IN: Purdue University Press, 1999.

6. *Galant* culture

Beasley, Faith. *Salons, History, and the Creation of Seventeenth-Century France: Mastering Memory*. Aldershot: Ashgate, 2006.

DeJean, Joan. *Tender Geographies: Women and the Origins of the Novel in France*. New York: Columbia University Press, 1998.

Goldsmith, Elizabeth C. *Exclusive Conversations: The Art of Interaction in Seventeenth-Century France*. Philadelphia, PA: University of Pennsylvania Press, 1988.

Lougee, Carolyn. *Le Paradis des femmes: Women, Salons, and Social Stratification in Seventeenth-Century France*. Princeton, NJ: Princeton University Press, 1976.

Newman, Karen. *Cultural Capitals: Early Modern London and Paris*. Princeton, NJ: Princeton University Press, 2007.

Russo, Elena. *Styles of Enlightenment: Taste, Politics, and Authorship in Eighteenth-Century France*. Baltimore, MD: Johns Hopkins University Press, 2008.

Seifert, Lewis C. *Fairy Tales, Sexuality, and Gender in France, 1690–1715: Nostalgic Utopias*. Cambridge: Cambridge University Press, 1996.

Welch, Ellen R. *A Taste for the Foreign: Worldly Knowledge and Literary Pleasure in Early Modern French Fiction*. Newark, DE: University of Delaware Press, 2011.

7. Varieties of doubt in early modern writing

Cave, Terence, *How to Read Montaigne*. London: Granta, 2007.

Cottingham, John, ed. *The Cambridge Companion to Descartes*. Cambridge: Cambridge University Press, 1992.

Curley, E. M., *Descartes against the Skeptics*. Oxford: Blackwell, 1978.

Hammond, Nicholas, ed. *The Cambridge Companion to Pascal*. Cambridge: Cambridge University Press, 2003.

Hunter, Graeme. *Pascal the Philosopher: An Introduction*. Toronto: University of Toronto Press, 2013.

Langer, Ullrich, ed. *The Cambridge Companion to Montaigne*. Cambridge: Cambridge University Press, 2005.

Moriarty, Michael. *Disguised Vices: Theories of Virtue in Early Modern French Thought*. Oxford: Oxford University Press, 2011.

Moriarty, Michael. *Early Modern French Thought: The Age of Suspicion*. Oxford: Oxford University Press, 2003.

Popkin, Richard H. *The History of Scepticism from Savonarola to Bayle*, rev. edn. New York: Oxford University Press, 2003.

8. Nature and Enlightenment

Anderson, Wilda. *Diderot's Dream*. Baltimore, MD: John Hopkins University Press, 1990.

Ballaster, Rosalind. *Fables of the East: Selected Tales 1662–1785*. Oxford: Oxford University Press, 2005.

Connors, Logan. *Dramatic Battles in Eighteenth-Century France: 'philosophes', 'anti-philosophes' and Polemical Theatre*. SVEC, 2012:07. Oxford: Voltaire Foundation, 2012.

Cryle, Peter. *Geometry in the Boudoir: Configurations of French Erotic Narrative*. Ithaca, NY: Cornell University Press, 1994.

Darnton, Robert. *The Forbidden Bestsellers of Pre-Revolutionary France*. New York: Norton, 1995.

Delon, Michel, ed. *Encyclopedia of the Enlightenment*, trans. Gwen Wells, 2 vols. Chicago, IL: Fitzroy Dearborn, 2001.

Delon, Michel, ed. *The Libertine: The Art of Love in Eighteenth-Century France*, trans. John Goodman. New York: Abbeville, 2013.

Douthwaite, Julia. *The Wild Girl, Natural Man and the Monster: Dangerous Experiments in the Age of Enlightenment*. Chicago, IL: University of University of Chicago Press, 2002.

Goodman, Dena. *The Republic of Letters: A Cultural History of the French Enlightenment*. Ithaca, NY: Cornell University Press, 1996.

Hobson, Marian. *Diderot and Rousseau: Networks of Enlightenment*. Ed. and trans. Kate E. Tunstall and Caroline Warman. *SVEC*, 2011: 04. Oxford: Voltaire Foundation, 2011.

Jones, Colin. *The Great Nation: France from Louis XV to Napoleon*. London: Penguin, 2002.

Leigh, John. *The Search for Enlightenment: An Introduction to Eighteenth-Century French Writing*. London: Duckworth, 1999.

Lough, John. *The 'Encyclopédie'*. London: Longman, 1971.

Outram, Dorinda. *Panorama of the Enlightenment*. London: Thames and Hudson, 2006.

Riskin, Jessica. *Science in the Age of Sensibility: The Sentimental Empiricists of the French Enlightenment*. Chicago, IL: University of Chicago Press, 2002.

Russo, Elena. *Styles of Enlightenment: Taste, Politics and Authorship in Eighteenth-Century France*. Baltimore, MD: Johns Hopkins University Press, 2007.

Schmidt, James, ed. *What Is Enlightenment? Eighteenth-Century Answers and Twentieth-Century Questions*. Berkeley, CA: University of California Press, 1996.

Starobinski, Jean. *The Emblems of Reason*. Trans. Barbara Bray. Cambridge, MA: MIT Press, 1988.

9. Nostalgia and the creation of the past

Bann, Stephen. *The Clothing of Clio: A Study of the Representation of History in Nineteenth-Century Britain and France*. Cambridge: Cambridge University Press, 1984.

Crossley, Ceri. *French Historians and Romanticism: Thierry, Guizot, the Saint-Simonians, Quinet, Michelet*. London: Routledge, 1993.

Glencross, Michael. 'The Cradle and the Crucible: Envisioning the Middle Ages in French Romanticism', *Studies in Medievalism*, 8 (1996), 100–24.

Glencross, Michael. *Reconstructing Camelot: French Romantic Medievalism and the Arthurian Tradition*. Cambridge: Boydell and Brewer, 1995.

Gossman, Lionel. *Between History and Literature*. Cambridge, MA: Harvard University Press, 1990.

Lough, John, and Muriel Lough. *Introduction to Nineteenth-Century France*. London: Longman, 1978.

Lukács, György. *The Historical Novel*. Trans. Hannah Mitchell and Stanley Mitchell. New York: Humanities Press, 1965.

Pao, Angela C. *The Orient of the Boulevards: Exoticism, Empire and Nineteenth-Century French Theatre*. Philadelphia, PA: University of Pennsylvania Press, 1998.

Samuels, Maurice. *The Spectacular Past*. Ithaca, NY: Cornell University Press, 2004.

Ward, Patricia A. *The Medievalism of Victor Hugo*. University Park, PA: Pennsylvania State University Press, 1975.

10. Exoticism and colonialism

Aravamudan, Srinivas. *Enlightenment Orientalism: Resisting the Rise of the Novel*. Chicago, IL: University of Chicago Press, 2011.

Forsdick, Charles. *Victor Segalen and the Aesthetics of Diversity: Journeys between Cultures*. Oxford: Oxford University Press, 2000.

Lowe, Lisa. *Critical Terrains: French and British Orientalisms*. Ithaca, NY: Cornell University Press, 1991.

Miller, Christopher L. *Blank Darkness: Africanist Discourse in French*. Chicago, IL: University of Chicago Press, 1985.

Miller, Christopher L. *The French Atlantic Triangle: Literature and Culture of the Slave Trade*. Durham, NC: Duke University Press, 2008.

Said, Edward. *Orientalism: Western Conceptions of the Orient*. London: Penguin, 2003.

Segalen, Victor. *Essay on Exoticism: An Aesthetics of Diversity*. Trans. Yaël Schlick. Durham, NC: Duke University Press, 2002.

Todorov, Tzvetan. *On Human Diversity: Nationalism, Racism and Exoticism in French Thought*. Trans. Catherine Porter. Cambridge, MA: Harvard University Press, 1993.

Yee, Jennifer. *Exotic Subversions in Nineteenth-Century French Fiction*. Oxford: Legenda, 2008.

11. Poetic experimentation

Acquisto, Joseph, ed. *Thinking Poetry: Philosophical Approaches to Nineteenth-Century French Poetry*. New York: Palgrave Macmillan, 2013.

Arnar, Anna Sigridur. *The Book as Instrument: Stéphane Mallarmé, the Artist's Book, and the Transformation of Print Culture*. Chicago, IL: University of Chicago Press, 2011.

Krueger, Cheryl. *The Art of Procrastination: Baudelaire's Poetry in Prose*. Newark, DE: University of Delaware Press, 2007.

Lyu, Claire. *A Sun within a Sun: The Power and Elegance of Poetry*. Pittsburgh, PA: University of Pittsburgh Press, 2006.

Noland, Carrie. *Poetry at Stake: Lyric Aesthetics and the Challenge of Technology*. Princeton, NJ: Princeton University Press, 1999.

12. The renewal of narrative in the wake of Proust

Bales, Richard, ed. *The Cambridge Companion to Proust*. Cambridge: Cambridge University Press, 2001.

Bowie, Malcolm. *Proust among the Stars*. London: HarperCollins, 1998.

Brewer, Mária Minich. *Claude Simon: Narrativities without Narrative*. Lincoln, NE: University of Nebraska Press, 1995.

Britton, Celia. *The Nouveau Roman: Fiction, Theory and Politics*. London: Macmillan, 1992.

Crosman Wimmers, Inge. *Proust and Emotion: The Importance of Affect in 'À la recherche du temps perdu'*. Toronto: University of Toronto Press, 2004.

Ellison, David R. *Of Words and the World: Referential Anxiety in Contemporary French Fiction*. Princeton, NJ: Princeton University Press, 1993.

Ellison, David R. *A Reader's Guide to Proust's 'In Search of Lost Time'*. Cambridge: Cambridge University Press, 2010.

Goldthorpe, Rhiannon. *Sartre: Literature and Theory*. Cambridge: Cambridge University Press, 1984.

Hodson, Leighton, ed. *Marcel Proust: The Critical Heritage*. London: Routledge, 1989.

Jefferson, Ann. *The Nouveau Roman and the Poetics of Fiction*. Cambridge: Cambridge University Press, 1980.

O'Beirne, Emer. *Reading Nathalie Sarraute: Dialogue and Distance*. Oxford: Clarendon Press, 1999.

Prendergast, Christopher. *Mirages and Mad Beliefs: Proust the Skeptic*. Princeton, NJ: Princeton University Press, 2013.

Sheringham, Michael. *Beckett: 'Molloy'*. London: Grant & Cutler, 1985.

Watt, Adam, ed. *Marcel Proust in Context*. Cambridge: Cambridge University Press, 2013.

13. French literature as world literature

Brincourt, André. *Langue française, terre d'accueil*. Monaco: Éditions du Rocher, 1997.

Delbart, Anne-Rosine, *Les Exilés du langage: un siècle d'écrivains français venus d'ailleurs (1919–2000)*. Paris: Pulim, 2005.

Jouanny, Robert. *Singularités francophones, ou Choisir d'écrire en français*. Paris: Presses Universitaires de France, 2000.

Kellman, Steven G., ed. *Switching Languages: Translingual Writers Reflect on their Craft*. Lincoln, NE: University of Nebraska Press, 2003.

Kellman, Steven G. *The Translingual Imagination*. Lincoln, NE: University of Nebraska Press, 2000.

Porra, Véronique. *Langue française, langue d'adoption: une littérature 'invitée' entre création, stratégies et contraintes (1946–2000)*. Hildesheim: Olms, 2011.

Suleiman, Susan Rubin. 'Choosing French: Language, Foreignness, and the Canon (Beckett/Némirovsky)'. In *French Global: A New Approach to Literary History*, ed. Christie McDonald and Susan Rubin Suleiman. New York: Columbia University Press, 2010, pp. 471–87.

14. Literature and sex

Best, Victoria, and Martin Crowley. *The New Pornographies: Explicit Sex in Recent French Fiction and Film*. Manchester: Manchester University Press, 2007.

Bloch, Howard. *The Scandal of the Fabliaux*. Chicago, IL: University of Chicago Press, 1994.
Cryle, Peter. *Geometry in the Boudoir: Configurations of French Erotic Narrative*. Ithaca, NY: Cornell University Press, 1994.
DeJean, Joan E. *The Reinvention of Obscenity: Sex, Lies, and Tabloids in Early Modern France*. Chicago, IL: University of Chicago Press, 2002.
Gaunt, Simon. *Gender and Genre in Medieval French Literature*. Cambridge: Cambridge University Press, 1995.
Ladenson, Elisabeth. *Dirt for Art's Sake: Books on Trial from Madame Bovary to Lolita*. Ithaca, NY: Cornell University Press, 2007.
Ladenson, Elisabeth. *Proust's Lesbianism*. Ithaca, NY: Cornell University Press, 1999.
Lucey, Michael. *Gide's Bent: Sexuality, Politics, Writing*. New York: Oxford University Press, 1995.
McAlpin, Mary. *Female Sexuality and Cultural Degradation in Enlightenment France*. Farnham: Ashgate, 2012.
Seifert, Lewis C. *Fairy Tales, Sexuality, and Gender in France, 1690–1715: Nostalgic Utopias*. Cambridge: Cambridge University Press, 1996.

15. The literary-philosophical essay

Bensmaïa, Réda. *The Barthes Effect: The Essay as Reflective Text*. Minneapolis, MN: University of Minnesota Press, 1987.
Forsdick, Charles, and Andrew Stafford, ed. *The Modern Essay in French*. Oxford: Peter Lang, 2005.
Fraser, Theodore P. *The French Essay*. Boston, MA: Twayne, 1986.
Hill, Leslie, Brian Nelson, and Dimitris Vardoulakis. *After Blanchot. Literature, Criticism, Philosophy*. Newark: University of Delaware Press, 2005.
James, Ian. *The New French Philosophy*. Cambridge: Polity, 2012.
Korhonen, Kuisma. *Textual Friendship: The Essay as Impossible Encounter, from Plato and Montaigne to Levinas and Derrida*. Amherst, NY: Humanity Books, 2006.
Schrift, Alan D., ed. *A History of Continental Philosophy*. London: Routledge, 2010.

16. The novel in the new millennium

Blatt, Ari J. *Pictures into Words: Images in Contemporary French Fiction*. Lincoln, NE: University of Nebraska Press, 2012.
Hippolyte, Jean-Louis. *Fuzzy Fiction*. Lincoln, NE: University of Nebraska Press, 2006.
Kemp, Simon. *French Fiction into the Twenty-First Century: The Return to the Story*. Cardiff: University of Wales Press, 2010.
Koop, Marie-Christine, and Rosalie Vermette, ed. *France in the Twenty-First Century: New Perspectives*. Birmingham, AL: Summa, 2009.
Motte, Warren. *Fables of the Novel: French Fiction since 1990*. Normal, IL: Dalkey Archive Press, 2003.
Motte, Warren. *Fiction Now: The French Novel in the Twenty-First Century*. Normal, IL: Dalkey Archive Press, 2008.

INDEX

Anouilh, Jean, 19, 21, 29, 30, 31, 33
Apollinaire, Guillaume, xii, 171, 173, 184, 238
Aquinas, Thomas, 102, 109, 116
Aretino, Pietro, 230, 231, 233
Aristotle, 1, 78–9
Arnauld, Antoine, 109, 110, 116
Arthurian romance, 5, 6, 7, 8, 273, 277

Badiou, Alain, 256, 257
Balzac, Honoré de, 146–9, 161, 162, 217, 235–6
Barrès, Maurice, 19, 20
Barthes, Roland, xiii, 53, 235, 254, 255, 257, 280
Bataille, Georges, 173, 231, 238, 248–50, 255
Baudelaire, Charles, 48–50, 135, 148–9, 236
Beauvoir, Simone de, xiii, 248, 256
Beckett, Samuel, 189–91, 212
Bede, 8, 16, 22
Ben Jelloun, Tahar, 210
Benoît de Sainte-Maure, 6, 16
Bergson, Henri, xii, 188, 247, 256
Bernanos, Georges, xii, 27, 191, 193, 201
Bernard of Clairvaux, 5, 15
Bernardin de Saint-Pierre, Jacques Henri, 129, 134, 155, 157
Bertrand, Aloysius, 139, 140, 150, 186
Blanchot, Maurice, xiii, 248, 250, 251, 252, 255, 256, 280
Bodel, Jean, 227
Boileau, Nicolas Despréaux, 89
Braddon, Mary Elizabeth, 223, 224, 240
Brantôme, Pierre de, 230
Breton, André, xii, 147, 172, 185, 195, 202, 205, 259, 271
Browning, Robert, 223, 240
Buffon, Georges-Louis de, 130, 132, 134

Burroughs, William S., 177, 181
Butor, Michel, 194, 195, 196, 198, 202, 258

Cadiot, Olivier, 176
Camus, Albert, ix, xii, 193, 199
Carco, Francis, 237
Cendrars, Blaise, 180, 181, 185
Cervantes, Miguel de, 15, 273
Césaire, Aimé, xii, 172
Chamoiseau, Patrick, 210
Chapelain, Jean, 88
Char, René, 172, 185
Charrière, Isabelle de, x, 119, 121, 132, 133
Chateaubriand, François-René de, xii, 121, 133, 138, 142, 150, 156, 157, 158, 159, 166, 224, 234
Cheng, François, 211, 213, 217
Chrétien de Troyes, xi, 5, 7, 8, 16, 234, 273
Cicero, 37, 42, 116
Cixous, Hélène, xiii, 254, 255, 257
Clément, Catherine, 255
colonialism and postcolonialism, 151–65, 205–7, 209–11, 265
Corneille, Pierre, 74–8, 90, 225
Corso, Gregory, 177
Cosnay, Marie, 264, 271

Damas, Léon-Gontran, 172
Deleuze, Gilles, 28, 53, 68
Derrida, Jacques, xiii, 53, 177, 209, 253, 254, 255, 257, 280
Descartes, René, xi, 107, 108, 109, 110, 113, 116, 120, 124, 241, 276
Deville, Patrick, 259, 270, 272
Diderot, Denis, 83, 112, 118, 120, 128, 131–3
Dolet, Étienne, 69
doubt, in the seventeenth-century, 102–16

Du Bellay, Joachim, 42–7, 71
Du Guillet, Pernette, 38, 39
Dumas, Alexandre, 19, 144
Dumas, Alexandre, *fils*, 224
Duras, Marguerite, xiii, 170, 193, 198, 199, 200, 202, 203, 258

Echenoz, Jean, 259, 268, 271, 272
Éluard, Paul, 172
Enlightenment, the, 118–33
Ernaux, Annie, 199, 203
Espitallier, Jean-Michel, 171, 184
essay, 63–8, 241–56
exoticism, 123, 151–65

fabliaux, 225, 226
fairy tale, 98–100
Faye, Jean-Pierre, 259
Flaubert, Gustave, ix, xii, 145, 146, 158, 161, 162, 164, 167, 196, 224, 235, 236, 238
Francophone literature, *see* world literature
Freud, Sigmund, 64, 69, 188, 189, 192, 201
Fromentin, Eugène, 162

Gailly, Christian, 259, 260, 271
Galland, Antoine, 127, 128, 129, 153, 160, 161, 232
Gary, Romain, 207
Gassendi, Pierre, 109, 117, 119
Gautier, Théophile, 139, 140, 145, 146, 148, 150, 158, 162, 165, 236
Gavarry, Gérard, 261, 271
Geoffrey of Monmouth, 5, 7, 16
Gerson, Jean, 5, 16, 20, 21, 25
Gide, André, xii, 161, 236, 259, 271, 280
Gillet, Louis, 239
Gilli, Patrick, 32
Gleize, Jean-Marie, 171, 176, 180, 184, 185
Glissant, Édouard, 209, 219
gothic:
    architecture, 136, 138, 139, 140, 141
    novel, 4, 161, 226, 233
    script, 56–9, 67
Green, Julien, 207, 208, 220, 235
Gregory the Great, 4, 15
Guattari, Félix, 68
Guyotat, Pierre, 259

Hardy, Alexandre, 77
Heidsieck, Bernard, 168–71
Henry of Huntingdon, 8, 16
Higgins, Georges, 207
history, 5–10, 136–7

Hobbes, Thomas, 99
Hugo, Victor, xii, 137, 139, 141, 142, 143, 147, 148, 150, 161, 163, 165, 179, 180, 184, 278
Huston, Nancy, 210
Huysmans, Joris-Karl, 139, 164

Isidore of Seville, 6, 15

Joan of Arc, 18
John of Salisbury, 6, 7, 8, 16
Jouet, Jacques, 176, 177, 181
Joyce, James, 192, 222, 239

Kant, Immanuel, 118, 251
Kessel, Joseph, 207, 208, 220
Khatibi, Abdelkebir, 209
Kristeva, Julia, 173, 185

Labé, Louise, 39, 228
La Bruyère, Jean de, 84
Lacan, Jacques, 201, 238, 253, 254
Lacoue-Labarthe, Philippe, 255, 257
La Fontaine, Jean de, 93, 229
Laforgue, Jules, 162
Lamartine, Alphonse de, 19, 136, 158, 223
La Mothe Le Vayer, François de, 133
language, 52–4, 71, 73, 74, 99, 125, 147, 153, 157, 163, 246, 250–4
    French and *francophonie*, 204–19
    poetic, 168–9, 175–8
Lanson, Gustave, 187, 200
La Rochefoucauld, François de, 88, 93, 114, 115, 116, 117
Le Cardonnel, Georges, 203
Lennox, Charlotte, 222, 240
Lenoir, Hélène, 259, 267, 272
Littel, Jonathan, 210
Locke, John, 123, 126, 134
Lorris, Guillaume de, xi, 10–15, 16, 227
Loti, Pierre, viii, 157, 159, 161, 162, 270

Mabanckou, Alain, 210
Maintenon, Françoise de, 91, 98, 100
Mairet, Jean de, 79
Maistre, Xavier de, 164
Malebranche, Nicolas, 109, 117
Marot, Clément, 36–7, 42–4, 61, 228
Mercier, Louis-Sébastien, 133, 134
Mérimée, Prosper, 139, 140, 141, 148, 224, 236
Meun, Jean de, xi, 10–15, 16, 227
Miano, Léonora, 210

Michelet, Jules, 20, 27, 136, 137, 146, 149
Michon, Pierre, 268, 272
Middle Ages, 138, 139, 140
   Romance of the Rose, 225
   Romanticism and, 136–7, 138, 140–3
   see also fabliaux, gothic, Joan of Arc
modernity, 47, 158, 194, 199, 244, 246
Molière, xi, 89, 91, 92, 100, 225, 229, 230
Montaigne, Michel de, 63–8, 79, 103–15,
   155, 198, 241–7
Montalbetti, Christine, 269, 272
Montesquieu, Charles de Secondat de, xii,
   118, 121, 123, 126, 133, 152, 153, 154,
   155, 165, 166, 232
Morelly, Étienne-Gabriel, 129, 130, 134
Murat, Michel, 98, 99, 101, 185, 186
Musset, Alfred de, 19, 145, 163, 238

Nancy, Jean-Luc, ix, 255, 257
nature, 155
   and the Enlightenment, 118–33
NDiaye, Marie, 259, 262, 271
Némirovsky, Irène, 207, 208, 211,
   220, 279
Nerval, Gérard de, 149, 158, 166
Nicole, Pierre, 109–10, 115–16
Nolly, Émile, 162
nostalgia, Romantic, 135–49
novel
   seventeenth-century, 85–90, 93–6
   eighteenth-century, 231–4
   nineteenth-century, 234–6
   twentieth-century, 187–200, 213–16,
      236–9
   twenty-first-century, 271
   nouveau roman, 191–5
   sex and the, 223–5, 231–4

Pascal, Blaise, 107–13, 125
Paulhan, Jean, 202, 238
Péguy, Charles, 19–21, 27–9
Petrarca, Francesco, 50
Pinget, Robert, 258
Pizan, Christine de, 19–22, 227
Plato, 78, 84, 107, 242, 243, 244, 280
Pléiade poets, *see* poetry, Renaissance
poetry
   Renaissance, 34–50
   romance, 10–15
   Romantic and modern, 168–83
Préchac, Jean de, 100
Prévost, Antoine-François, 236

printing, 182–4
   Renaissance, 52–68
Proust, Marcel, 116, 187–200, 224, 237

Queneau, Raymond, 177, 239, 259, 271

Rachilde, 235
Racine, Jean, 70–2, 77–8, 79–80, 113, 137,
   225, 229
Radiguet, Raymond, 235
Raynal, Guillaume Thomas François, 131,
   134, 155
Réage, Pauline, 238
Redonnet, Marie, 259, 263, 264, 271
religion, 95, 98, 102–3, 105–7, 110–16,
   123, 138
   nature and, 118
   see also Wars of Religion
Reverdy, Pierre, 172
Revolution, 136
Rimbaud, Arthur, 159, 161, 171–84
Robbe-Grillet, Alain, xiii, 193, 195, 202, 258
Roche, Denis, 169–70
Rolin, Jean, 265, 266, 271
romance, 3–15
Romanticism, 135–49, 156–9
   see also Middle Ages
Ronsard, Pierre de, 40–50, 59–63, 228
Roubaud, Jacques, 177
Rousseau, Jean-Jacques, 91, 120–1, 126,
   129–30, 131–2, 155, 226, 245–6
Roussel, Raymond, 185

Sacy, Isaac Le Maistre de, 117
Sade, Donatien Alphonse de, 129, 222,
   232–4, 238–9
Said, Edward, 152, 158, 160, 163, 165, 278
Saint-Simon, Louis de Rouvroy de, 90, 100
Sand, George, 199, 223, 238
Sarraute, Nathalie, 191–3, 207
Sartre, Jean-Paul, xii, 53, 173, 191, 193, 247,
   248, 256, 279
Saussure, Ferdinand de, 177, 253
scepticism, *see* doubt
Scève, Maurice, 38, 39, 40, 50
Scudéry, Madeleine de, 73, 87–93, 98–9, 139
Segalen, Victor, viii, 151, 152, 162, 163,
   164, 278
Senghor, Léopold Sédar, 172
Sévigné, Marie Chantal de, 86, 88, 96, 97, 100
sex, literature and, 222–39
Shakespeare, William, 34, 72, 73, 137, 150

Sijie, Dai, 210, 211, 217
Smith, Adam, 117
Sophocles, 71, 84
Soulié, Frédéric, 144, 150
Stendhal, 137, 144, 147, 150, 224, 234, 235
Sue, Eugène, 144, 150, 223
Surrealism, 171–3, 179, 195–6

Thierry, Augustin, 136, 149, 166
Toussaint, Jean-Philippe, 259, 262, 271
tragedy, 70–84
travel writing, 145, 146, 153–64, 209–10
Trollope, Anthony, 223, 240
Troyat, Henri, 207, 208, 220

Urfé, Honoré d', 85–7

Valéry, Paul, 180, 184, 186, 259
Verlaine, Paul, 185
Ventadorn de, Bernart, 11, 16, 17
Vigny, Alfred de, 142–4
Villedieu, Marie-Catherine Desjardins de, 92, 93, 99, 100
Volodine, Antoine, 266, 271
Voltaire, 19, 112, 118, 121–6, 154, 223, 232

Wace, 5, 7, 16
Wars of Religion, 35, 36, 42, 52, 63, 73, 85, 94, 105, 113, 123
Wilde, Oscar, 223, 240
world literature, 204–19

Xingjian, Gao, 217

Cambridge Companions to ...

AUTHORS

Edward Albee edited by Stephen J. Bottoms

Margaret Atwood edited by Coral Ann Howells

W. H. Auden edited by Stan Smith

Jane Austen edited by Edward Copeland and Juliet McMaster (second edition)

Beckett edited by John Pilling

Bede edited by Scott DeGregorio

Aphra Behn edited by Derek Hughes and Janet Todd

Walter Benjamin edited by David S. Ferris

William Blake edited by Morris Eaves

Boccaccio edited by Guyda Armstrong, Rhiannon Daniels, and Stephen J. Milner

Jorge Luis Borges edited by Edwin Williamson

Brecht edited by Peter Thomson and Glendyr Sacks (second edition)

The Brontës edited by Heather Glen

Bunyan edited by Anne Dunan-Page

Frances Burney edited by Peter Sabor

Byron edited by Drummond Bone

Albert Camus edited by Edward J. Hughes

Willa Cather edited by Marilee Lindemann

Cervantes edited by Anthony J. Cascardi

Chaucer edited by Piero Boitani and Jill Mann (second edition)

Chekhov edited by Vera Gottlieb and Paul Allain

Kate Chopin edited by Janet Beer

Caryl Churchill edited by Elaine Aston and Elin Diamond

Cicero edited by Catherine Steel

Coleridge edited by Lucy Newlyn

Wilkie Collins edited by Jenny Bourne Taylor

Joseph Conrad edited by J. H. Stape

H. D. edited by Nephie J. Christodoulides and Polina Mackay

Dante edited by Rachel Jacoff (second edition)

Daniel Defoe edited by John Richetti

Don DeLillo edited by John N. Duvall

Charles Dickens edited by John O. Jordan

Emily Dickinson edited by Wendy Martin

John Donne edited by Achsah Guibbory

Dostoevskii edited by W. J. Leatherbarrow

Theodore Dreiser edited by Leonard Cassuto and Claire Virginia Eby

John Dryden edited by Steven N. Zwicker

W. E. B. Du Bois edited by Shamoon Zamir

George Eliot edited by George Levine

T. S. Eliot edited by A. David Moody

Ralph Ellison edited by Ross Posnock

Ralph Waldo Emerson edited by Joel Porte and Saundra Morris

William Faulkner edited by Philip M. Weinstein

Henry Fielding edited by Claude Rawson

F. Scott Fitzgerald edited by Ruth Prigozy

Flaubert edited by Timothy Unwin

E. M. Forster edited by David Bradshaw

Benjamin Franklin edited by Carla Mulford

Brian Friel edited by Anthony Roche

Robert Frost edited by Robert Faggen

Gabriel García Márquez edited by Philip Swanson

Elizabeth Gaskell edited by Jill L. Matus

Goethe edited by Lesley Sharpe

Günter Grass edited by Stuart Taberner

Thomas Hardy edited by Dale Kramer

David Hare edited by Richard Boon

Nathaniel Hawthorne edited by Richard Millington

Seamus Heaney edited by Bernard O'Donoghue

Ernest Hemingway edited by Scott Donaldson

Homer edited by Robert Fowler

Horace edited by Stephen Harrison

Ted Hughes edited by Terry Gifford

Ibsen edited by James McFarlane

Henry James edited by Jonathan Freedman

Samuel Johnson edited by Greg Clingham

Ben Jonson edited by Richard Harp and Stanley Stewart

James Joyce edited by Derek Attridge (second edition)

Kafka edited by Julian Preece

Keats edited by Susan J. Wolfson

Rudyard Kipling edited by Howard J. Booth

Lacan edited by Jean-Michel Rabaté

D. H. Lawrence edited by Anne Fernihough

Primo Levi edited by Robert Gordon

Lucretius edited by Stuart Gillespie and Philip Hardie

Machiavelli edited by John M. Najemy

David Mamet edited by Christopher Bigsby

Thomas Mann edited by Ritchie Robertson

Christopher Marlowe edited by Patrick Cheney

Andrew Marvell edited by Derek Hirst and Steven N. Zwicker

Herman Melville edited by Robert S. Levine

Arthur Miller edited by Christopher Bigsby (second edition)

Milton edited by Dennis Danielson (second edition)

Molière edited by David Bradby and Andrew Calder

Toni Morrison edited by Justine Tally

Alice Munro edited by David Staines

Nabokov edited by Julian W. Connolly

Eugene O'Neill edited by Michael Manheim

George Orwell edited by John Rodden

Ovid edited by Philip Hardie

Petrarch edited by Albert Russell Ascoli and Unn Falkeid

Harold Pinter edited by Peter Raby (second edition)

Sylvia Plath edited by Jo Gill

Edgar Allan Poe edited by Kevin J. Hayes

Alexander Pope edited by Pat Rogers

Ezra Pound edited by Ira B. Nadel

Proust edited by Richard Bales

Pushkin edited by Andrew Kahn

Rabelais edited by John O'Brien

Rilke edited by Karen Leeder and Robert Vilain

Philip Roth edited by Timothy Parrish

Salman Rushdie edited by Abdulrazak Gurnah

Shakespeare edited by Margareta de Grazia and Stanley Wells (second edition)

Shakespearean Comedy edited by Alexander Leggatt

Shakespeare and Contemporary Dramatists edited by Ton Hoenselaars

Shakespeare and Popular Culture edited by Robert Shaughnessy

Shakespearean Tragedy edited by Claire McEachern (second edition)

Shakespeare on Film edited by Russell Jackson (second edition)

Shakespeare on Stage edited by Stanley Wells and Sarah Stanton

Shakespeare's History Plays edited by Michael Hattaway

Shakespeare's Last Plays edited by Catherine M. S. Alexander

Shakespeare's Poetry edited by Patrick Cheney

George Bernard Shaw edited by Christopher Innes

Shelley edited by Timothy Morton

Mary Shelley edited by Esther Schor

Sam Shepard edited by Matthew C. Roudané

Spenser edited by Andrew Hadfield

Laurence Sterne edited by Thomas Keymer

Wallace Stevens edited by John N. Serio

Tom Stoppard edited by Katherine E. Kelly

Harriet Beecher Stowe edited by Cindy Weinstein

August Strindberg edited by Michael Robinson

Jonathan Swift edited by Christopher Fox

J. M. Synge edited by P. J. Mathews

Tacitus edited by A. J. Woodman

Henry David Thoreau edited by Joel Myerson

Tolstoy edited by Donna Tussing Orwin

Anthony Trollope edited by Carolyn Dever and Lisa Niles

Mark Twain edited by Forrest G. Robinson

John Updike edited by Stacey Olster

Mario Vargas Llosa edited by Efrain Kristal and John King

Virgil edited by Charles Martindale

Voltaire edited by Nicholas Cronk

Edith Wharton edited by Millicent Bell

Walt Whitman edited by Ezra Greenspan

Oscar Wilde edited by Peter Raby

Tennessee Williams edited by Matthew C. Roudané

August Wilson edited by Christopher Bigsby

Mary Wollstonecraft edited by Claudia L. Johnson

Virginia Woolf edited by Susan Sellers (second edition)

Wordsworth edited by Stephen Gill

W. B. Yeats edited by Marjorie Howes and John Kelly

Zola edited by Brian Nelson

TOPICS

The Actress edited by Maggie B. Gale and John Stokes

The African American Novel edited by Maryemma Graham

The African American Slave Narrative edited by Audrey A. Fisch

Theatre History by David Wiles and Christine Dymkowski

African American Theatre by Harvey Young

Allegory edited by Rita Copeland and Peter Struck

American Crime Fiction edited by Catherine Ross Nickerson

American Modernism edited by Walter Kalaidjian

American Poetry Since 1945 edited by Jennifer Ashton

American Realism and Naturalism edited by Donald Pizer

American Travel Writing edited by Alfred Bendixen and Judith Hamera

American Women Playwrights edited by Brenda Murphy

Ancient Rhetoric edited by Erik Gunderson

Arthurian Legend edited by Elizabeth Archibald and Ad Putter

Australian Literature edited by Elizabeth Webby

British Literature of the French Revolution edited by Pamela Clemit

British Romanticism edited by Stuart Curran (second edition)

British Romantic Poetry edited by James Chandler and Maureen N. McLane

British Theatre, 1730–1830, edited by Jane Moody and Daniel O'Quinn

Canadian Literature edited by Eva-Marie Kröller

Children's Literature edited by M. O. Grenby and Andrea Immel

The Classic Russian Novel edited by Malcolm V. Jones and Robin Feuer Miller

Contemporary Irish Poetry edited by Matthew Campbell

Creative Writing edited by David Morley and Philip Neilsen

Crime Fiction edited by Martin Priestman

Early Modern Women's Writing edited by Laura Lunger Knoppers

The Eighteenth-Century Novel edited by John Richetti

Eighteenth-Century Poetry edited by John Sitter

Emma edited by Peter Sabor

English Literature, 1500–1600 edited by Arthur F. Kinney

English Literature, 1650–1740 edited by Steven N. Zwicker

English Literature, 1740–1830 edited by Thomas Keymer and Jon Mee

English Literature, 1830–1914 edited by Joanne Shattock

English Novelists edited by Adrian Poole

English Poetry, Donne to Marvell edited by Thomas N. Corns

English Poets edited by Claude Rawson

English Renaissance Drama, second edition edited by A. R. Braunmuller and Michael Hattaway

English Renaissance Tragedy edited by Emma Smith and Garrett A. Sullivan Jr.

English Restoration Theatre edited by Deborah C. Payne Fisk

The Epic edited by Catherine Bates

European Modernism edited by Pericles Lewis

European Novelists edited by Michael Bell

Fairy Tales edited by Maria Tatar

Fantasy Literature edited by Edward James and Farah Mendlesohn

Feminist Literary Theory edited by Ellen Rooney

Fiction in the Romantic Period edited by Richard Maxwell and Katie Trumpener

The Fin de Siècle edited by Gail Marshall

The French Enlightenment edited by Daniel Brewer

French Literature edited by John D. Lyons

The French Novel: from 1800 to the Present edited by Timothy Unwin

Gay and Lesbian Writing edited by Hugh Stevens

German Romanticism edited by Nicholas Saul

Gothic Fiction edited by Jerrold E. Hogle

The Greek and Roman Novel edited by Tim Whitmarsh

Greek and Roman Theatre edited by Marianne McDonald and J. Michael Walton

Greek Comedy edited by Martin Revermann

Greek Lyric edited by Felix Budelmann

Greek Mythology edited by Roger D. Woodard

Greek Tragedy edited by P. E. Easterling

The Harlem Renaissance edited by George Hutchinson

The History of the Book edited by Leslie Howsam

The Irish Novel edited by John Wilson Foster

The Italian Novel edited by Peter Bondanella and Andrea Ciccarelli

The Italian Renaissance edited by Michael Wyatt

Jewish American Literature edited by Hana Wirth-Nesher and Michael P. Kramer

The Latin American Novel edited by Efraín Kristal

The Literature of the First World War edited by Vincent Sherry

The Literature of London edited by Lawrence Manley

The Literature of Los Angeles edited by Kevin R. McNamara

The Literature of New York edited by Cyrus Patell and Bryan Waterman

The Literature of Paris edited by Anna-Louise Milne

The Literature of World War II edited by Marina MacKay

Literature on Screen edited by Deborah Cartmell and Imelda Whelehan

Medieval English Culture edited by Andrew Galloway

Medieval English Literature edited by Larry Scanlon

Medieval English Mysticism edited by Samuel Fanous and Vincent Gillespie

Medieval English Theatre edited by Richard Beadle and Alan J. Fletcher (second edition)

Medieval French Literature edited by Simon Gaunt and Sarah Kay

Medieval Romance edited by Roberta L. Krueger

Medieval Women's Writing edited by Carolyn Dinshaw and David Wallace

Medievalism edited by Louise D'Arcens

Modern American Culture edited by Christopher Bigsby

Modern British Women Playwrights edited by Elaine Aston and Janelle Reinelt

Modern French Culture edited by Nicholas Hewitt

Modern German Culture edited by Eva Kolinsky and Wilfried van der Will

The Modern German Novel edited by Graham Bartram

The Modern Gothic edited by Jerrold E. Hogle

Modern Irish Culture edited by Joe Cleary and Claire Connolly

Modern Italian Culture edited by Zygmunt G. Baranski and Rebecca J. West

Modern Latin American Culture edited by John King

Modern Russian Culture edited by Nicholas Rzhevsky

Modern Spanish Culture edited by David T. Gies

Modernism edited by Michael Levenson (second edition)

The Modernist Novel edited by Morag Shiach

Modernist Poetry edited by Alex Davis and Lee M. Jenkins

Modernist Women Writers edited by Maren Tova Linett

Narrative edited by David Herman

Native American Literature edited by Joy Porter and Kenneth M. Roemer

Nineteenth-Century American Women's Writing edited by Dale M. Bauer and Philip Gould

Old English Literature edited by Malcolm Godden and Michael Lapidge (second edition)

Performance Studies edited by Tracy C. Davis

Piers Plowman by Andrew Cole and Andrew Galloway

Popular Fiction edited by David Glover and Scott McCracken

Postcolonial Literary Studies edited by Neil Lazarus

Postmodernism edited by Steven Connor

The Pre-Raphaelites edited by Elizabeth Prettejohn

Pride and Prejudice edited by Janet Todd

Renaissance Humanism edited by Jill Kraye

The Roman Historians edited by Andrew Feldherr

Roman Satire edited by Kirk Freudenburg

Science Fiction edited by Edward James and Farah Mendlesohn

Scottish Literature edited by Gerald Carruthers and Liam McIlvanney

Sensation Fiction edited by Andrew Mangham

The Sonnet edited by A. D. Cousins and Peter Howarth

The Spanish Novel: from 1600 to the Present edited by Harriet Turner and Adelaida López de Martínez

Textual Scholarship edited by Neil Fraistat and Julia Flanders

Travel Writing edited by Peter Hulme and Tim Youngs

Twentieth-Century British and Irish Women's Poetry edited by Jane Dowson

The Twentieth-Century English Novel edited by Robert L. Caserio

Twentieth-Century English Poetry edited by Neil Corcoran

Twentieth-Century Irish Drama edited by Shaun Richards

Twentieth-Century Russian Literature edited by Marina Balina and Evgeny Dobrenko

Utopian Literature edited by Gregory Claeys

Victorian and Edwardian Theatre edited by Kerry Powell

The Victorian Novel edited by Deirdre David (second edition)

Victorian Poetry edited by Joseph Bristow

Victorian Women's Writing edited by Linda H. Peterson

War Writing edited by Kate McLoughlin

Women's Writing in Britain, 1660–1789 edited by Catherine Ingrassia

Women's Writing in the Romantic Period edited by Devoney Looser

Writing of the English Revolution edited by N. H. Keeble